R

8 3 OCT 2019

3 0 JAN 2016

0 4 OCT 2019

- 8 OCT 2019

8 3 OCT 2019

Richmond upon Thames Libraries

To renew this item please call the renewals
hotline on 0115 929 3388 or renew online at
www.richmond.gov.uk/libraries

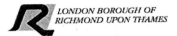
LONDON BOROUGH OF
RICHMOND UPON THAMES

D1437906

TOP COW
PRODUCTIONS, INC.

90710 000 098 119

HEROES AND VILLAINS ENTERTAINMENT PRESENTS

NETHER WORLD

WRITTEN BY:
BRYAN EDWARD HIL
AND ROB LEVIN

LINE ART BY:
TONY SHASTEEN
WITH DENNIS CALERO

COLORS BY:
DAVE MCCAIG
WITH LEE LOUGHRID

LETTERS BY:
TROY PETERI

EDITED BY:
FILIP SABLIK

London Borough of Richmond
Upon Thames

DISCARDED

R

90710 000 098 119

FROM

Askews & Holts

AF   RICHMOND UPON THAMES

£14.99

9781607064312

LIBRARY SERVICE

WANT MORE INFO? Check out
www.topcow.com
for news and exclusive Top Cow merchandise!

**To find the comic shop
nearest you call:**
1-888-COMICBOOK

For Heroes and Villains Entertainment™:
Markus Goerg, Dick Hillenbrand, & Mikhail Nayfeld
For rights inquiries contact
Heroes and Villains Entertainment: 323 850 2990
info@heroesandvillains-ent.com

For Top Cow Productions, Inc.:

Marc Silvestri - CEO
Matt Hawkins - President & COO
Filip Sablik - Publisher
Bryan Rountree - Editor
Elena Salcedo - Event & Logistics Coordinator
Jessi Reid - Social Marketing Coordinator

IMAGE COMICS, INC
Robert Kirkman - chief operating officer
Erik Larsen - chief financial officer
Todd McFarlane - president
Marc Silvestri - chief executive officer
Jim Valentino - vice-president

Eric Stephenson - publisher
Todd Martinez - sales & licensing coordina
Jennifer de Guzman - pr & marketing dire
Branwyn Bigglestone - accounts manage
Emily Miller - administrative assistant
Jamie Parreno - marketing assistant
Sarah deLaine - events coordinator
Kevin Yuen - digital rights coordinator
Tyler Shainline - production manager
Drew Gill - art director
Jonathan Chan - senior production artist
Monica Garcia - production artist
Vincent Kukua - production artist
Jana Cook - production artist
www.imagecomics.con

Netherworld, Volume 1. May 2012. **FIRST PRINTING.** ISBN: 978-1-60706-431-2, $19.99. Published by Image Cor
Inc. Office of Publication: 2134 Allston Way, Second Floor, Berkeley, CA 94704. Originally published in single magazine forma
NETHERWORLD #1-5. Netherworld © 2012 Heroes and Villains Entertainment and Top Cow Productions, Inc. All rights rese
"Netherworld," the Netherworld logos, and the likeness of all characters (human or otherwise) featured herein are trademark
Heroes and Villains Entertainment and Top Cow Productions, Inc. Image Comics and the Image Comics logo are trademarks of Ir
Comics, Inc. The characters, events, and stories in this publication are entirely fictional. Any resemblance to actual persons (l
or dead), events, institutions, or locales, without satiric intent, is coincidental. No portion of this publication may be reproduce
transmitted, in any form or by any means, without the express written permission of Top Cow Productions, Inc. Printed in KOI

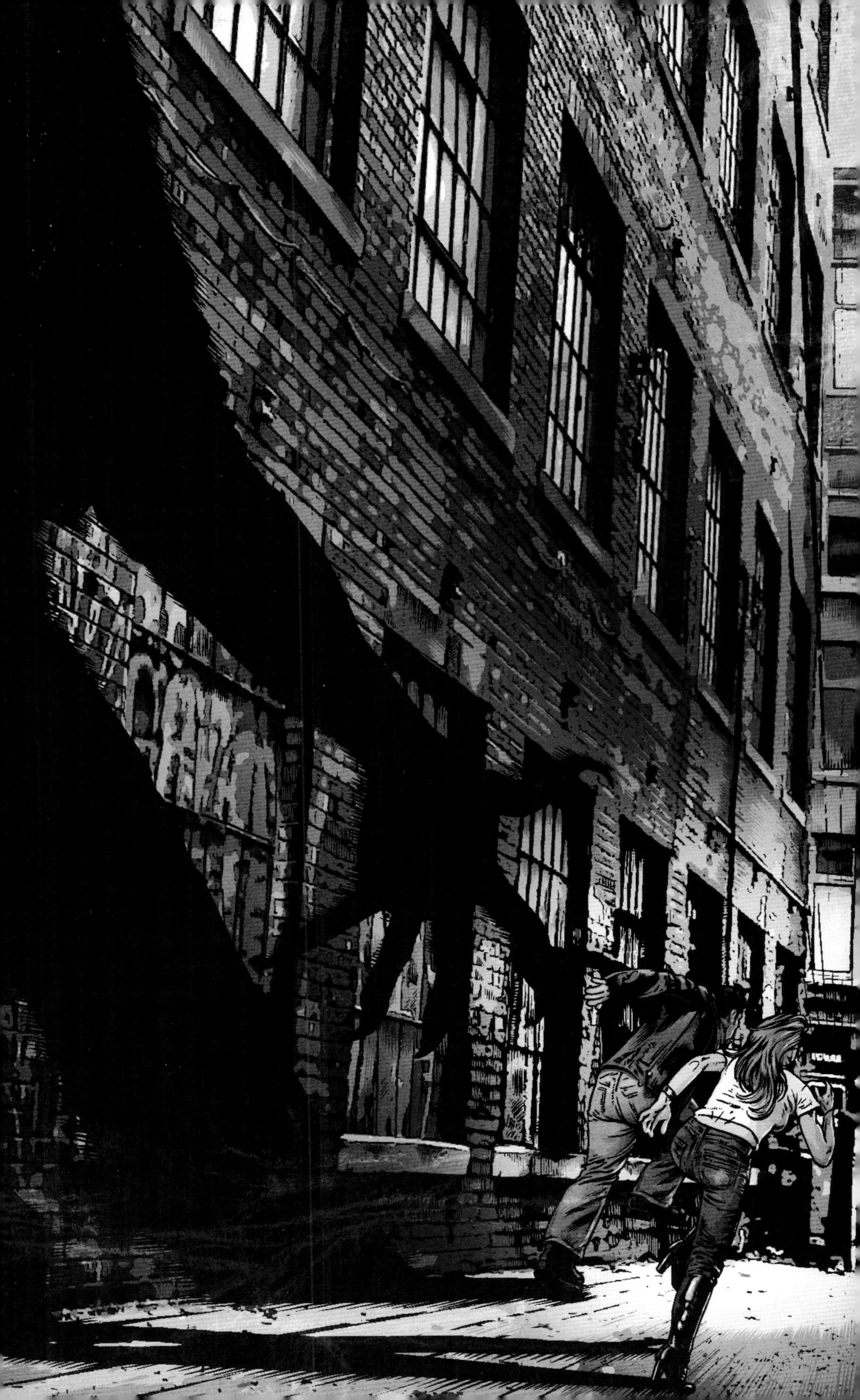

TABLE OF CONTENTS

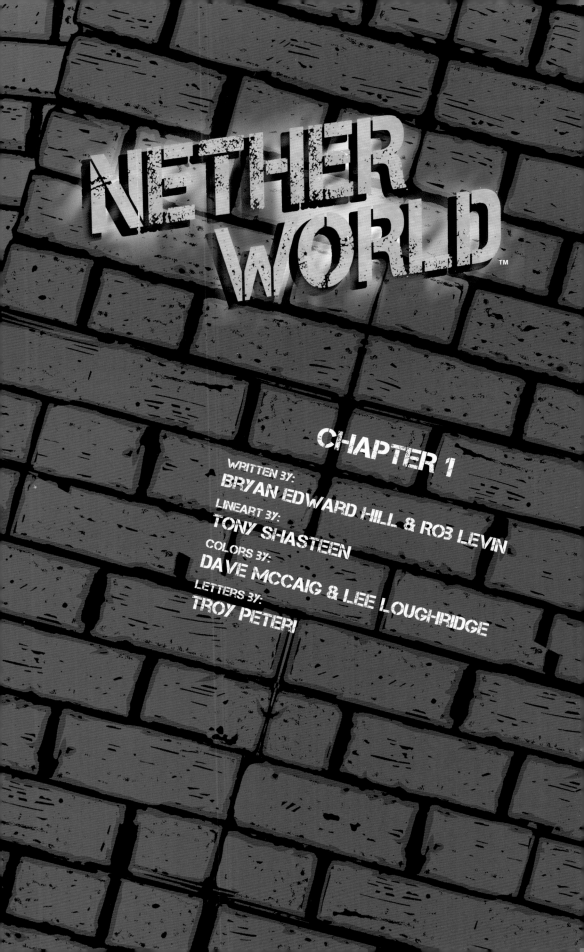

NETHER WORLD

CHAPTER 1

WRITTEN BY:
BRYAN EDWARD HILL & ROB LEVIN

LINEART BY:
TONY SHASTEEN

COLORS BY:
DAVE MCCAIG & LEE LOUGHRIDGE

LETTERS BY:
TROY PETERI

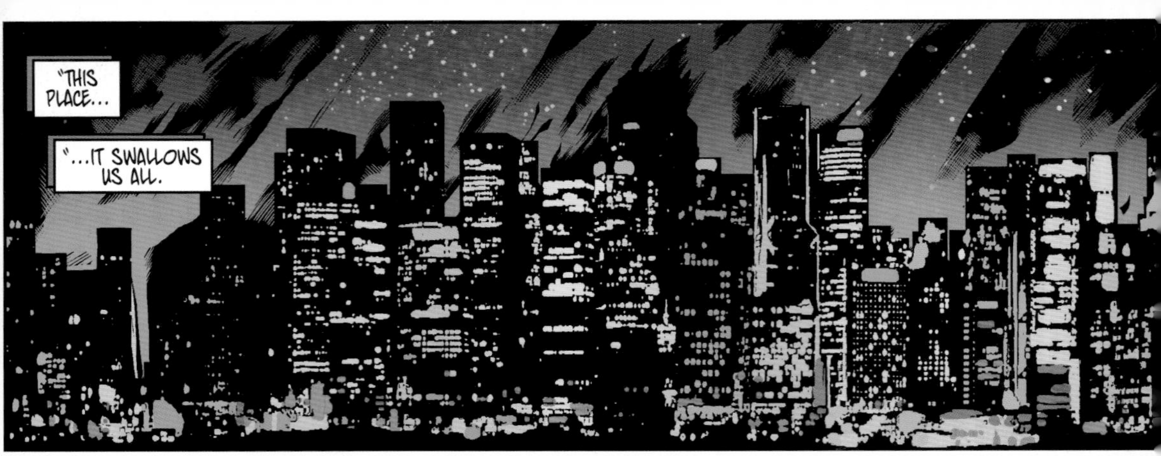
"THIS PLACE...
"...IT SWALLOWS US ALL.

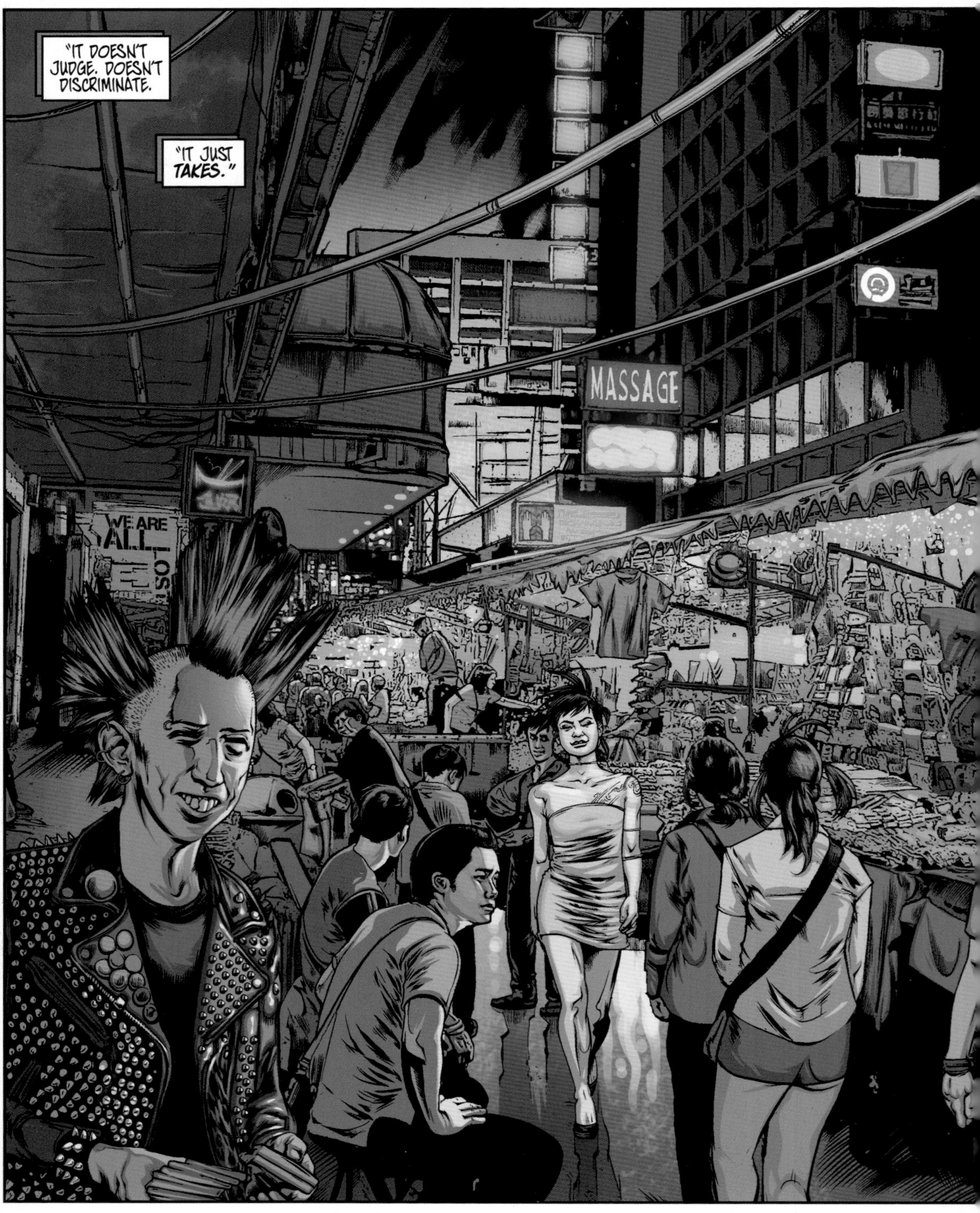
"IT DOESN'T JUDGE. DOESN'T DISCRIMINATE.
"IT JUST *TAKES.*"
MASSAGE
WE ARE ALL

REYS ON
INNOCENT.

"IT PREYS
ON THE
GUILTY.

"WRITING'S ON
THE WALLS,
FRIEND."

RE
OST.
WHAT
AN?

U GOT
CASH,
ANKET?

SORRY,
LADY.

"WORKING
HERE."

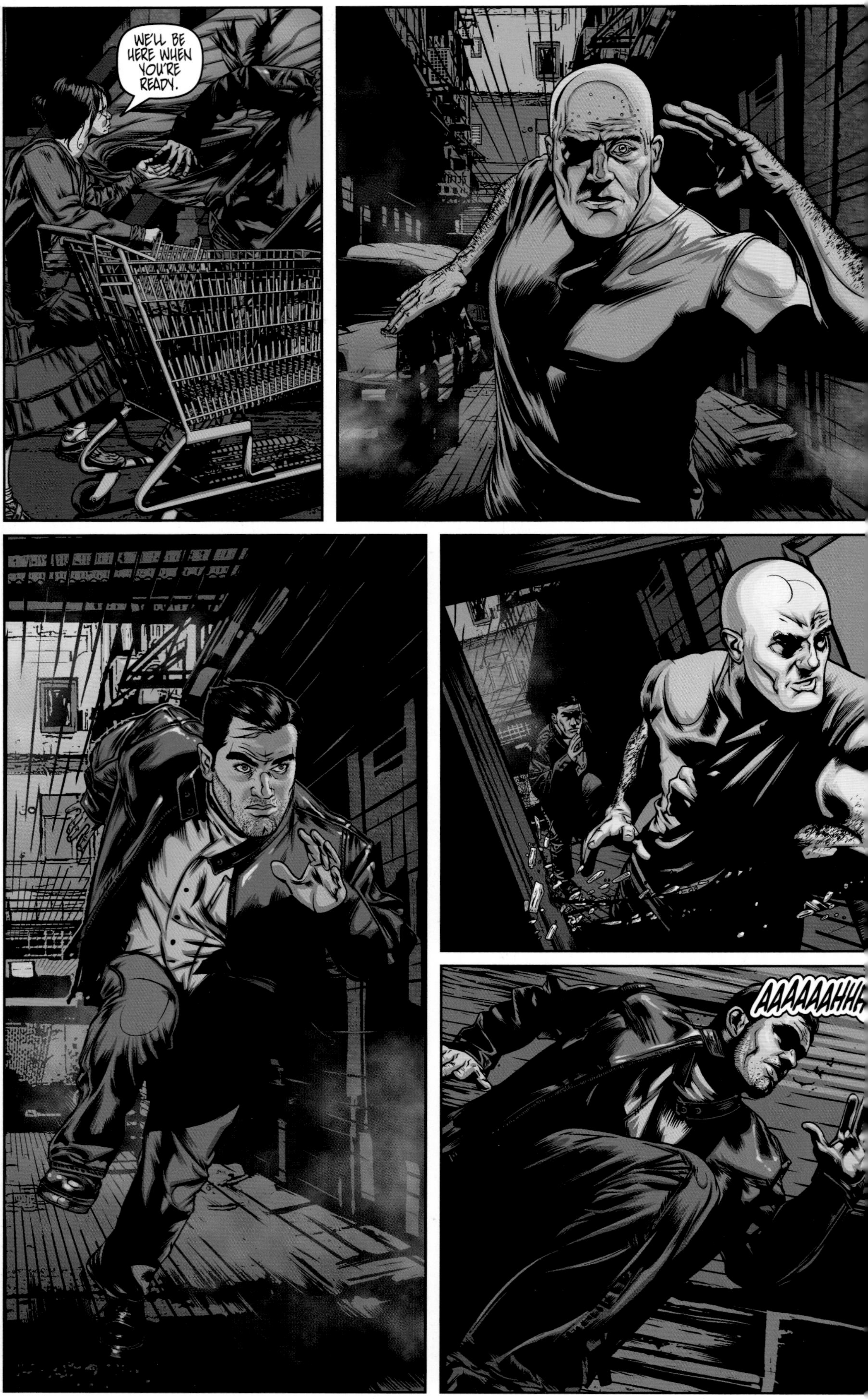
WE'LL BE HERE WHEN YOU'RE READY.
AAAAAAHH

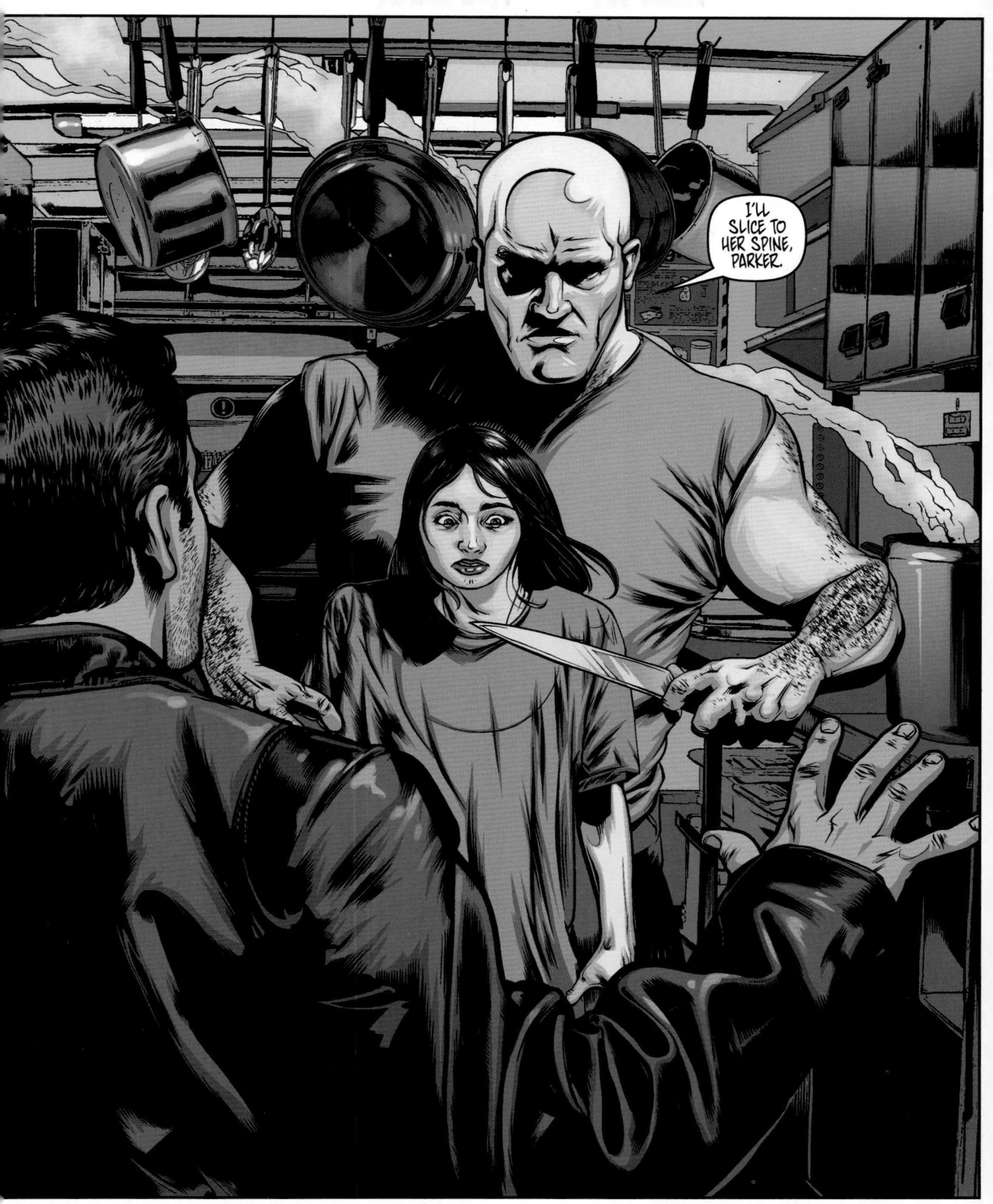
I'LL SLICE TO HER SPINE, PARKER.
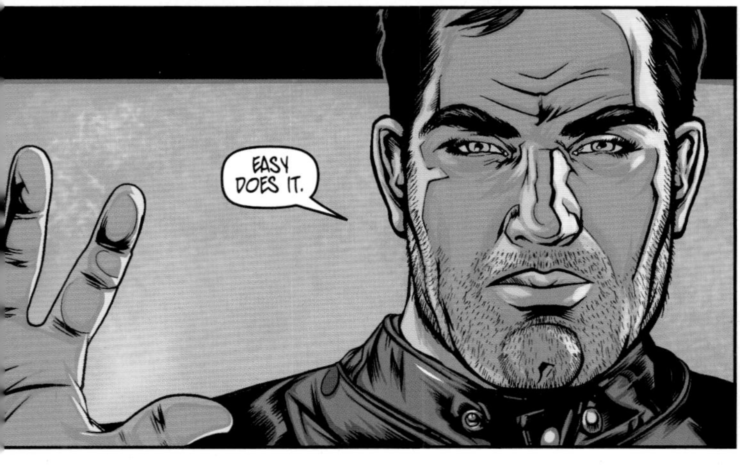
EASY DOES IT.
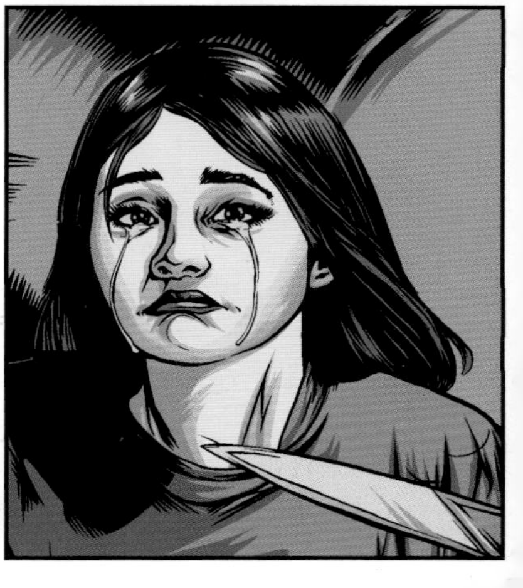

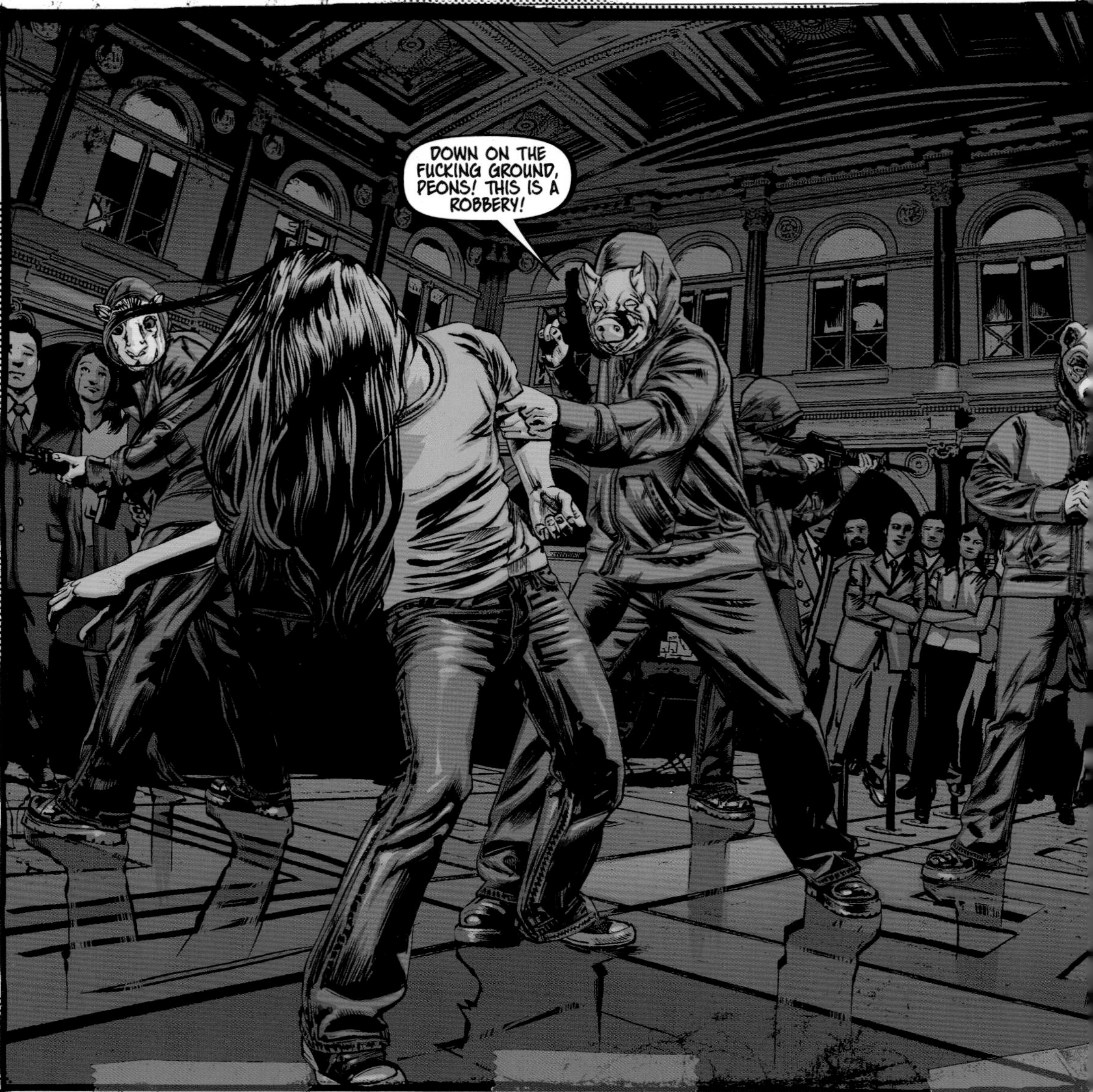
DOWN ON THE FUCKING GROUND, PEONS! THIS IS A ROBBERY!
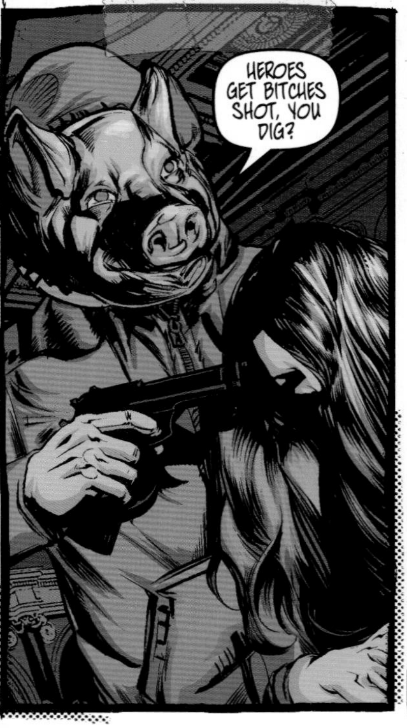
HEROES GET BITCHES SHOT, YOU DIG?
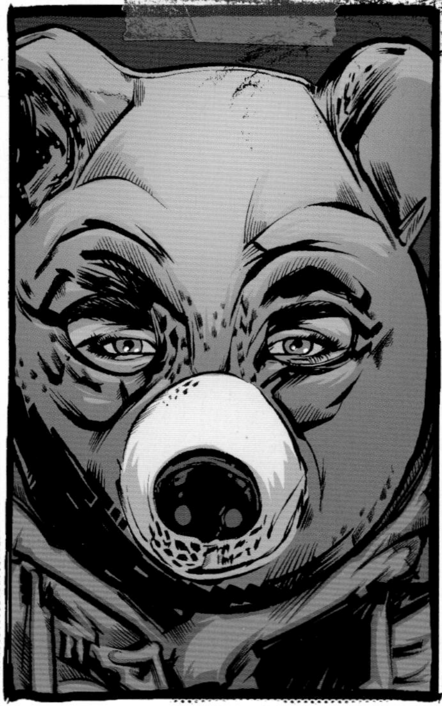
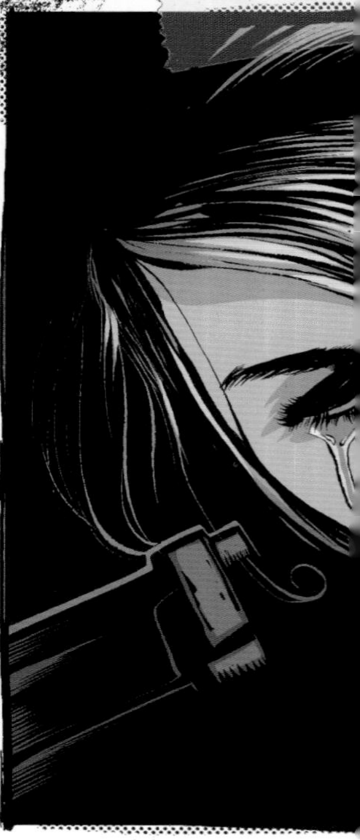

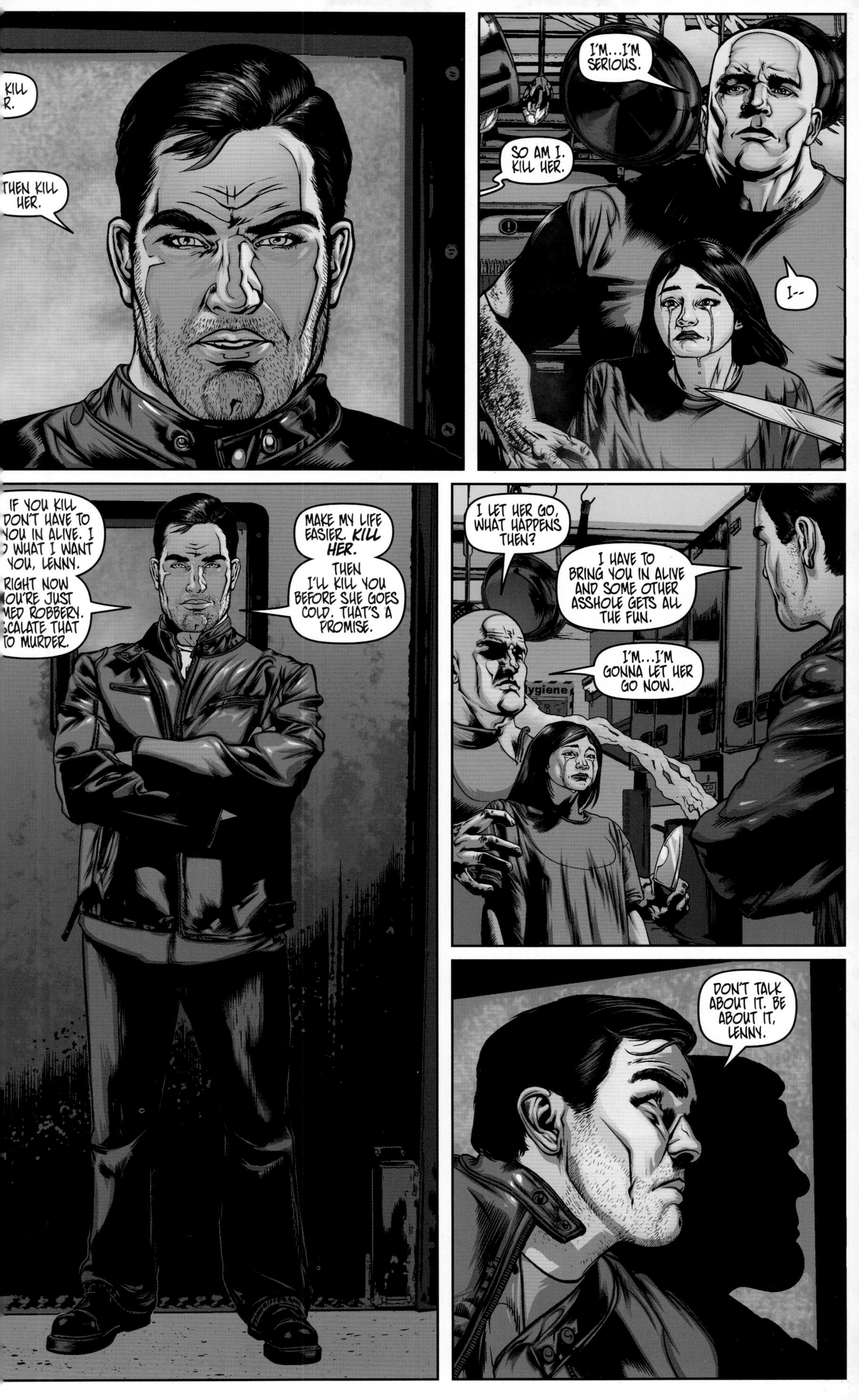
KILL
R.
THEN KILL
HER.
I'M...I'M
SERIOUS.
SO AM I.
KILL HER.
I--
IF YOU KILL
DON'T HAVE TO
YOU IN ALIVE. I
WHAT I WANT
YOU, LENNY.
RIGHT NOW
OU'RE JUST
MED ROBBERY.
SCALATE THAT
TO MURDER.
MAKE MY LIFE EASIER. KILL HER.
THEN I'LL KILL YOU BEFORE SHE GOES COLD. THAT'S A PROMISE.
I LET HER GO, WHAT HAPPENS THEN?
I HAVE TO BRING YOU IN ALIVE AND SOME OTHER ASSHOLE GETS ALL THE FUN.
I'M...I'M GONNA LET HER GO NOW.
DON'T TALK ABOUT IT. BE ABOUT IT, LENNY.

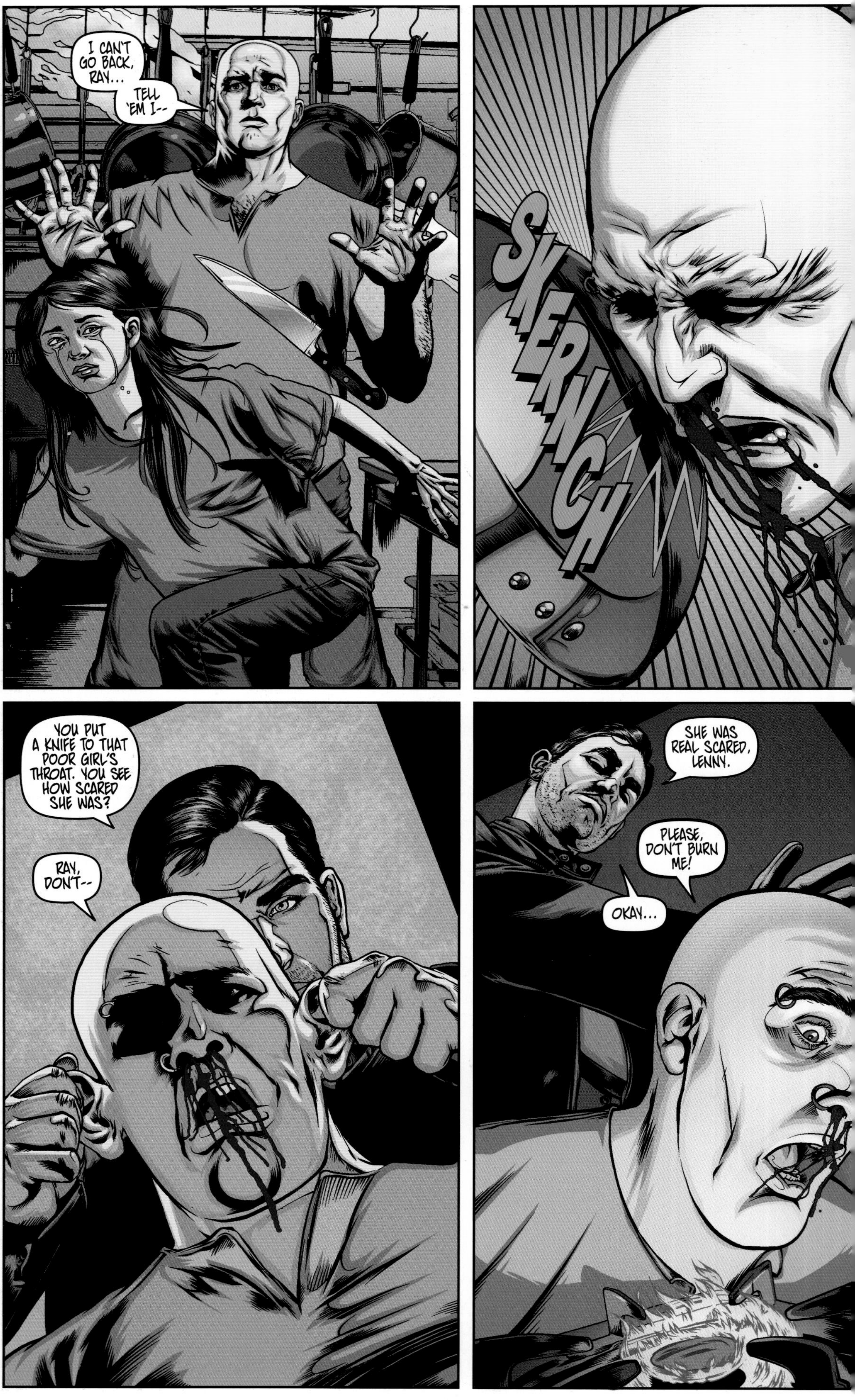
I CAN'T GO BACK, RAY...
TELL 'EM I--
SKERNCH
YOU PUT A KNIFE TO THAT POOR GIRL'S THROAT. YOU SEE HOW SCARED SHE WAS?
RAY, DON'T--
SHE WAS REAL SCARED, LENNY.
PLEASE, DON'T BURN ME!
OKAY...

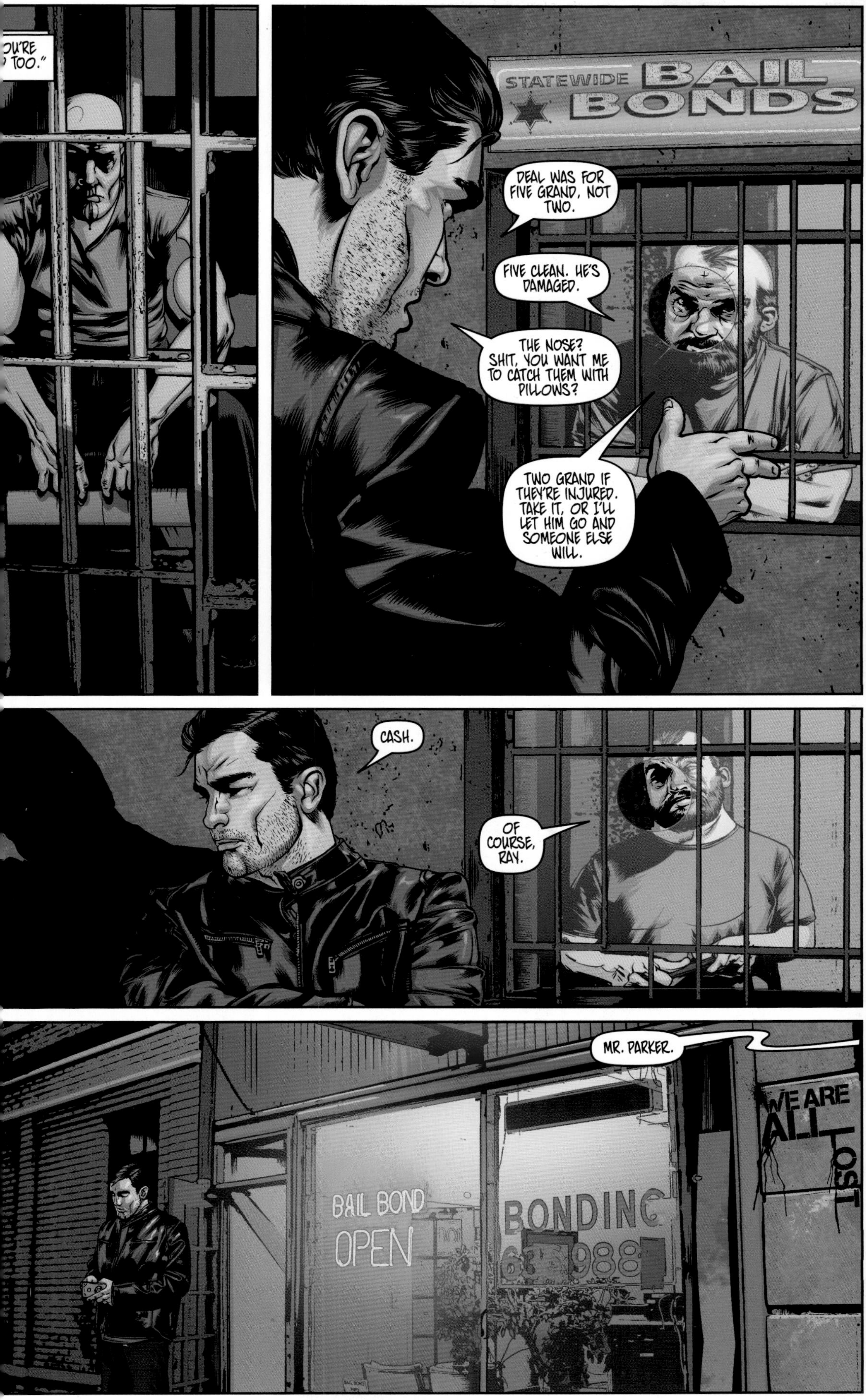
STATEWIDE BAIL BONDS
DEAL WAS FOR FIVE GRAND, NOT TWO.
FIVE CLEAN. HE'S DAMAGED.
THE NOSE? SHIT, YOU WANT ME TO CATCH THEM WITH PILLOWS?
TWO GRAND IF THEY'RE INJURED. TAKE IT, OR I'LL LET HIM GO AND SOMEONE ELSE WILL.
CASH.
OF COURSE, RAY.
MR. PARKER.
BAIL BOND
OPEN
BONDING
WE ARE ALL LOST

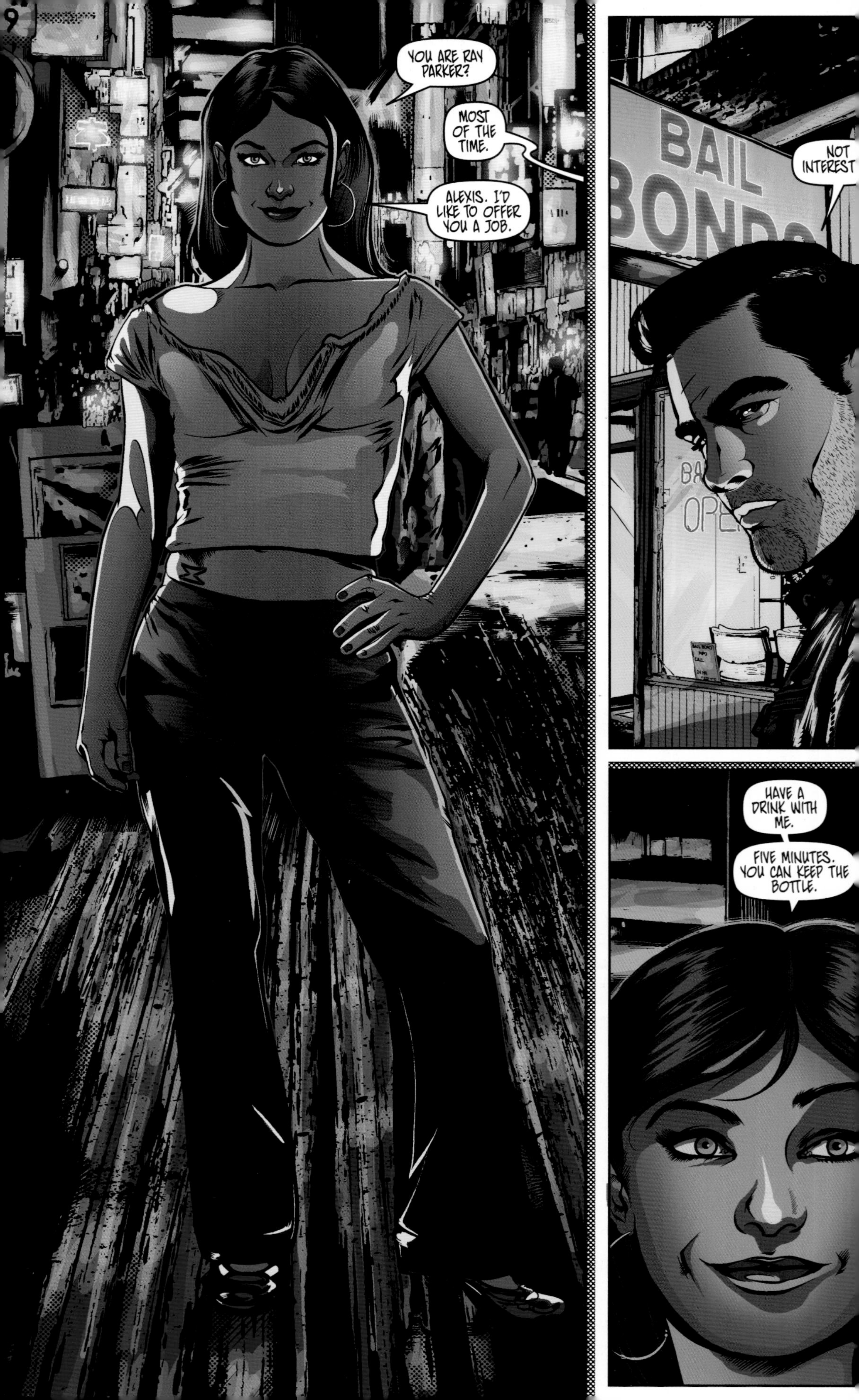
9
YOU ARE RAY PARKER?
MOST OF THE TIME.
ALEXIS. I'D LIKE TO OFFER YOU A JOB.
BAIL BONDS
NOT INTEREST
HAVE A DRINK WITH ME.
FIVE MINUTES. YOU CAN KEEP THE BOTTLE.

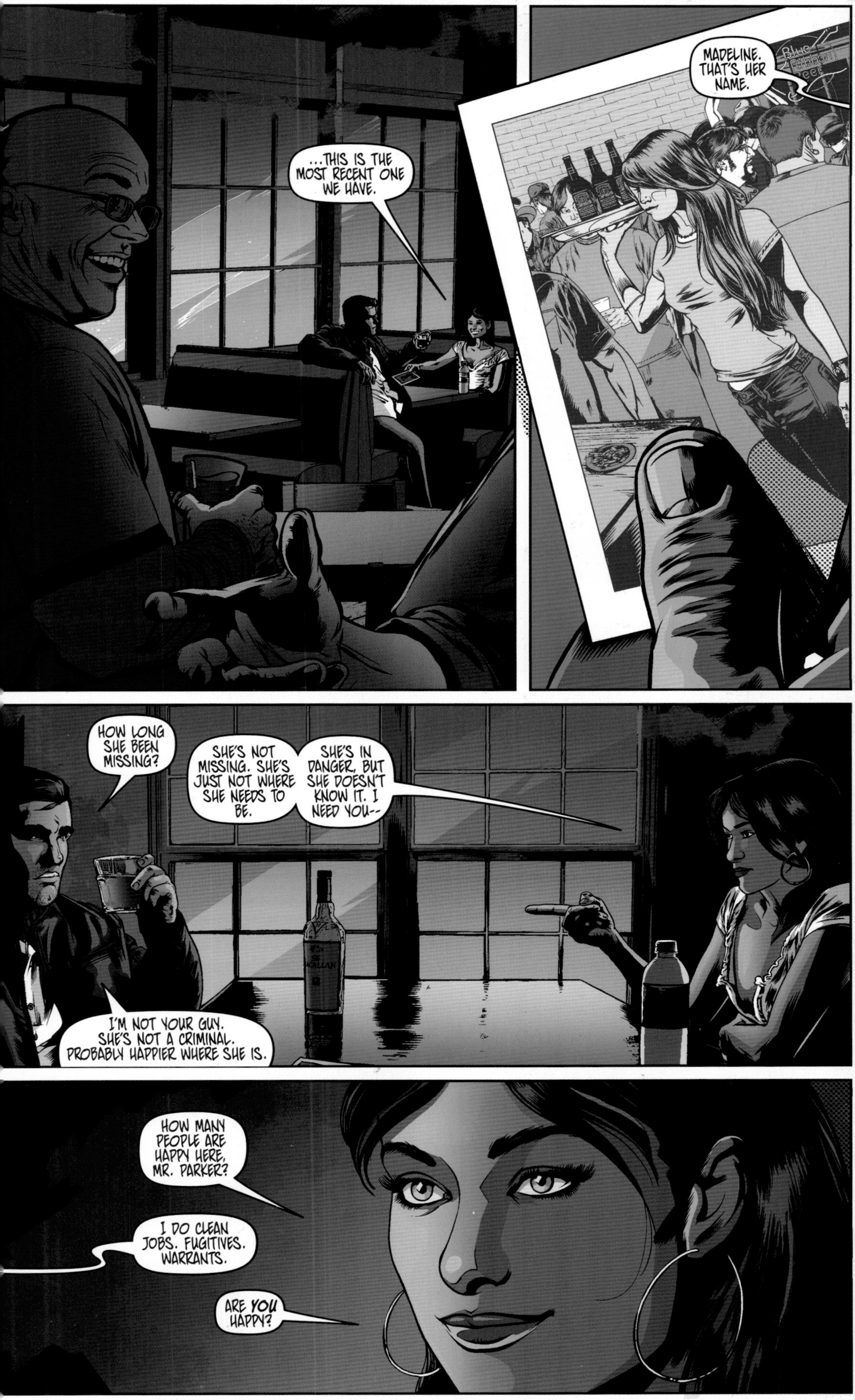
...THIS IS THE MOST RECENT ONE WE HAVE.
MADELINE. THAT'S HER NAME.
HOW LONG SHE BEEN MISSING?
SHE'S NOT MISSING. SHE'S JUST NOT WHERE SHE NEEDS TO BE.
SHE'S IN DANGER, BUT SHE DOESN'T KNOW IT. I NEED YOU--
I'M NOT YOUR GUY. SHE'S NOT A CRIMINAL. PROBABLY HAPPIER WHERE SHE IS.
HOW MANY PEOPLE ARE HAPPY HERE, MR. PARKER?
I DO CLEAN JOBS. FUGITIVES. WARRANTS.
ARE *YOU* HAPPY?

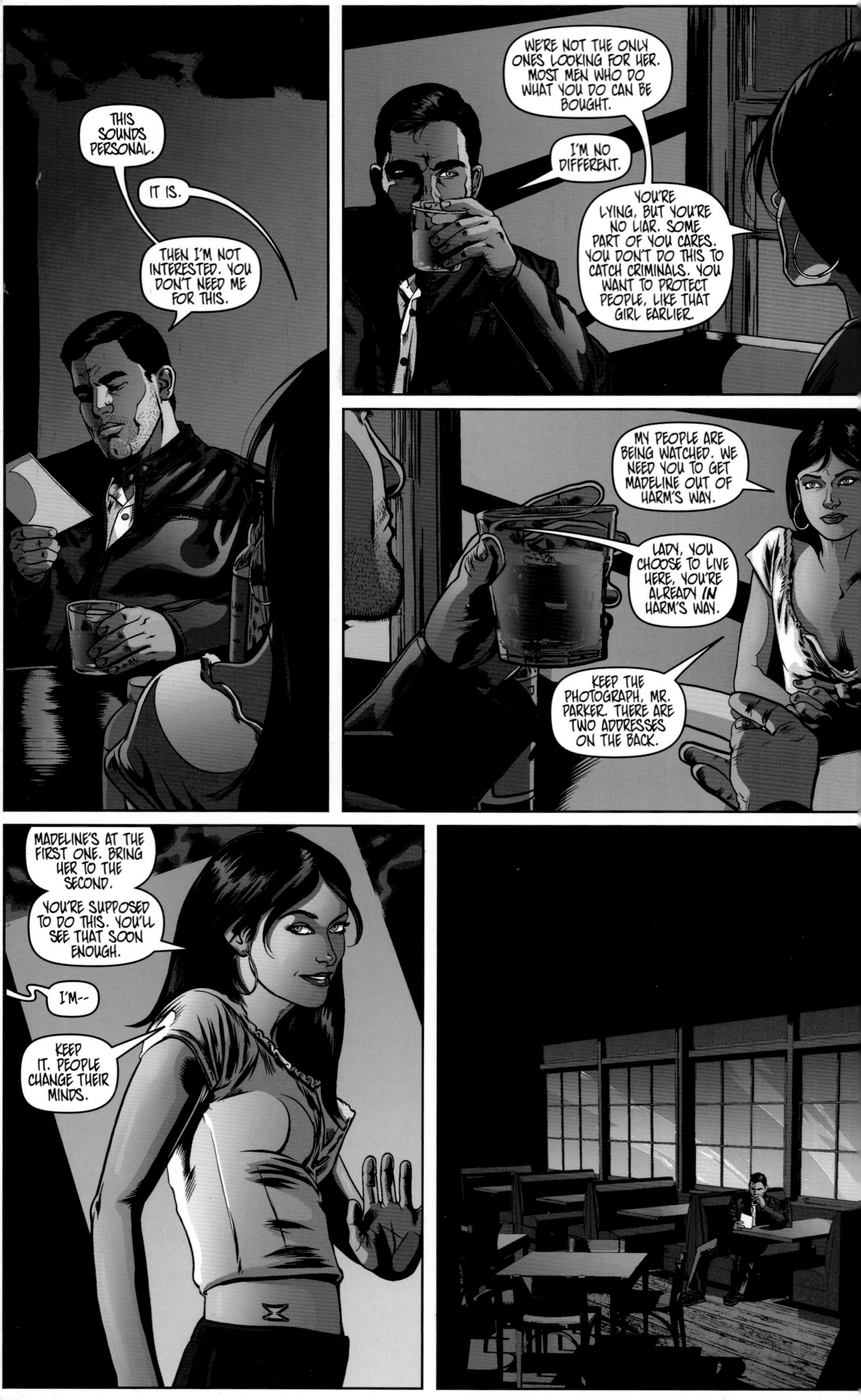

THIS SOUNDS PERSONAL.
IT IS.
THEN I'M NOT INTERESTED. YOU DON'T NEED ME FOR THIS.
WE'RE NOT THE ONLY ONES LOOKING FOR HER. MOST MEN WHO DO WHAT YOU DO CAN BE BOUGHT.
I'M NO DIFFERENT.
YOU'RE LYING, BUT YOU'RE NO LIAR. SOME PART OF YOU CARES. YOU DON'T DO THIS TO CATCH CRIMINALS. YOU WANT TO PROTECT PEOPLE, LIKE THAT GIRL EARLIER.
MY PEOPLE ARE BEING WATCHED. WE NEED YOU TO GET MADELINE OUT OF HARM'S WAY.
LADY, YOU CHOOSE TO LIVE HERE, YOU'RE ALREADY *IN* HARM'S WAY.
KEEP THE PHOTOGRAPH, MR. PARKER. THERE ARE TWO ADDRESSES ON THE BACK.
MADELINE'S AT THE FIRST ONE. BRING HER TO THE SECOND.
YOU'RE SUPPOSED TO DO THIS. YOU'LL SEE THAT SOON ENOUGH.
I'M--
KEEP IT. PEOPLE CHANGE THEIR MINDS.

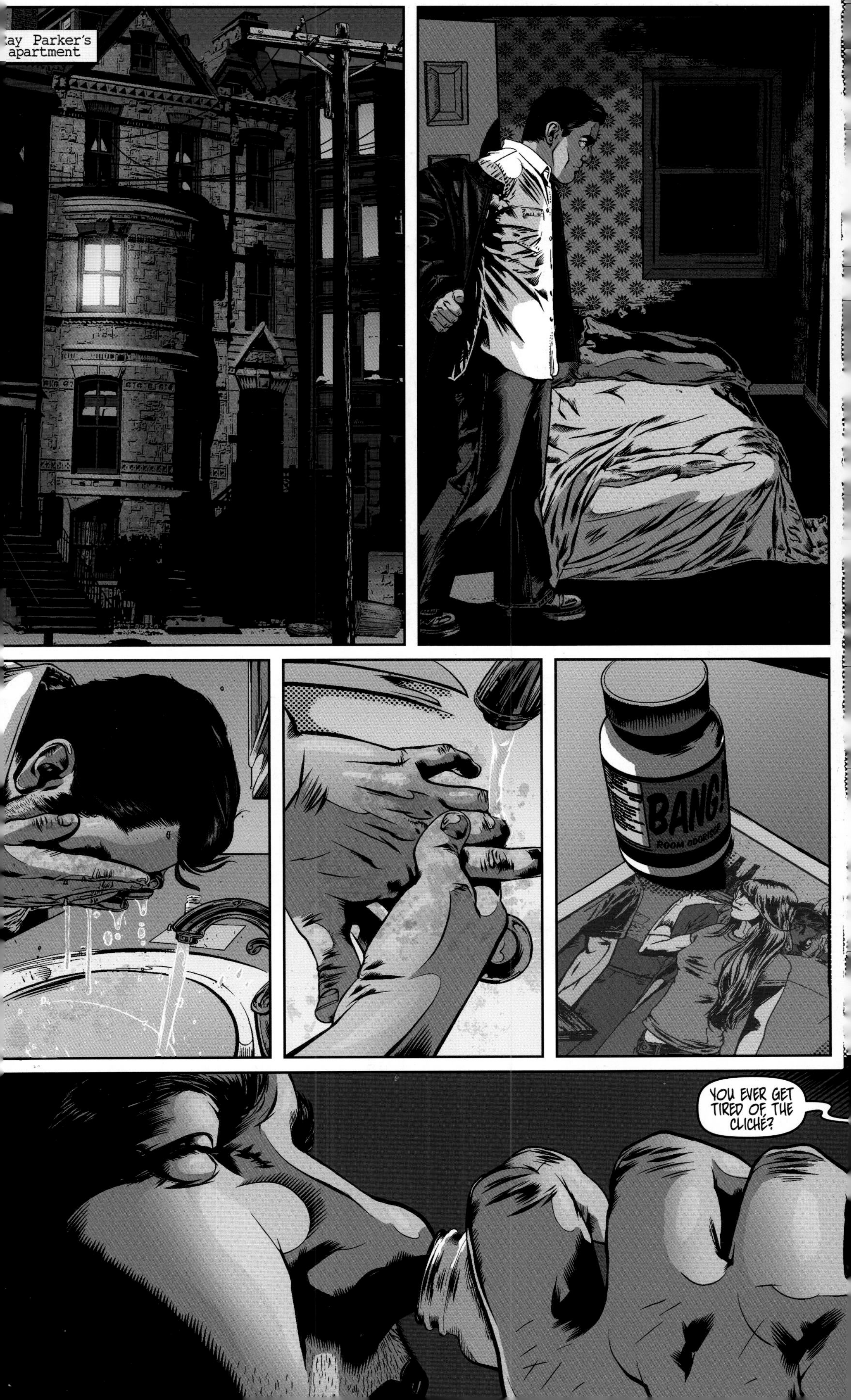
ay Parker's apartment
BANG!
ROOM ODORISOR
YOU EVER GET TIRED OF THE CLICHÉ?

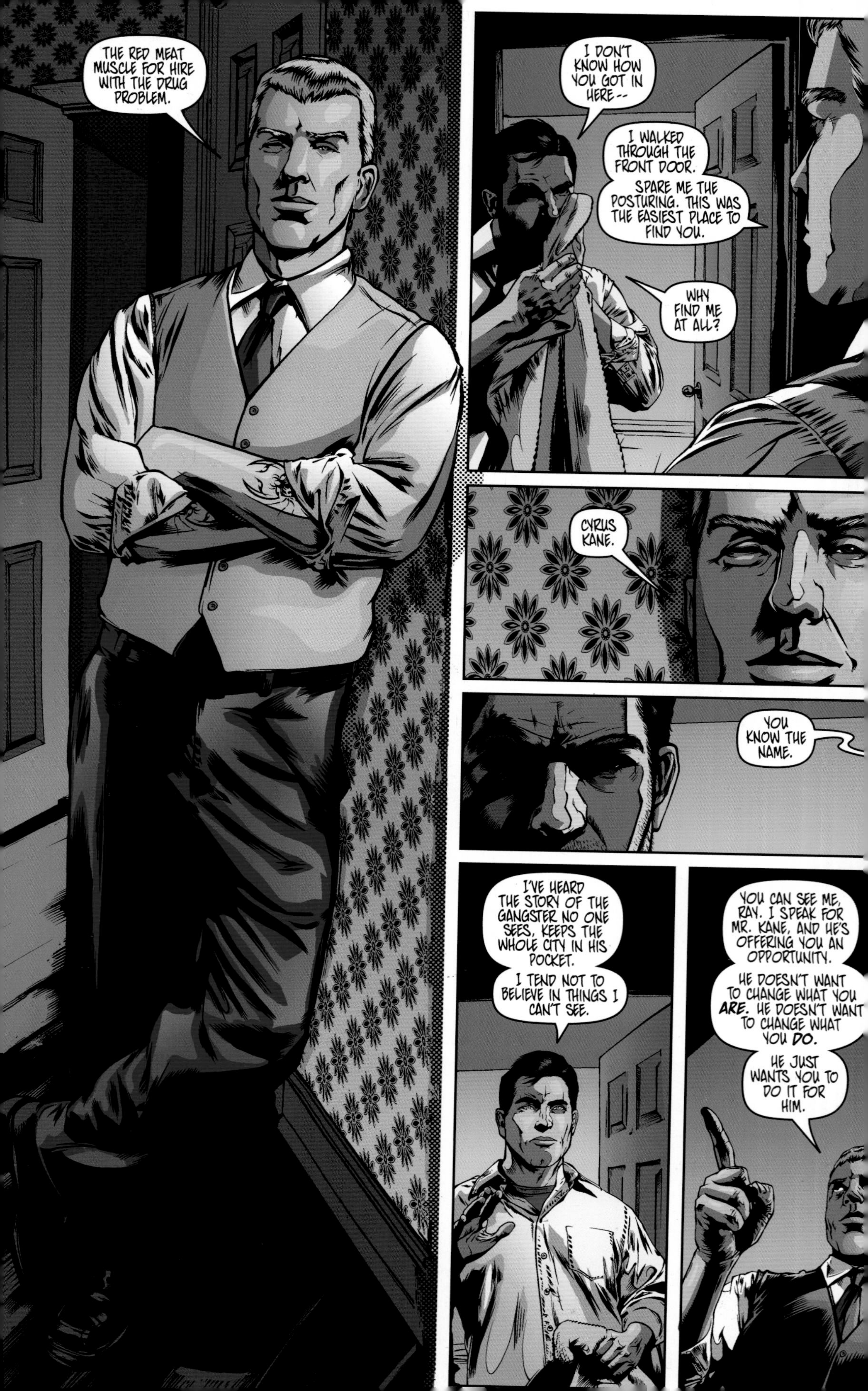
THE RED MEAT MUSCLE FOR HIRE WITH THE DRUG PROBLEM.
I DON'T KNOW HOW YOU GOT IN HERE--
I WALKED THROUGH THE FRONT DOOR.
SPARE ME THE POSTURING. THIS WAS THE EASIEST PLACE TO FIND YOU.
WHY FIND ME AT ALL?
CYRUS KANE.
YOU KNOW THE NAME.
I'VE HEARD THE STORY OF THE GANGSTER NO ONE SEES, KEEPS THE WHOLE CITY IN HIS POCKET.
I TEND NOT TO BELIEVE IN THINGS I CAN'T SEE.
YOU CAN SEE ME, RAY. I SPEAK FOR MR. KANE, AND HE'S OFFERING YOU AN OPPORTUNITY.
HE DOESN'T WANT TO CHANGE WHAT YOU **ARE.** HE DOESN'T WANT TO CHANGE WHAT YOU **DO.**
HE JUST WANTS YOU TO DO IT FOR HIM.

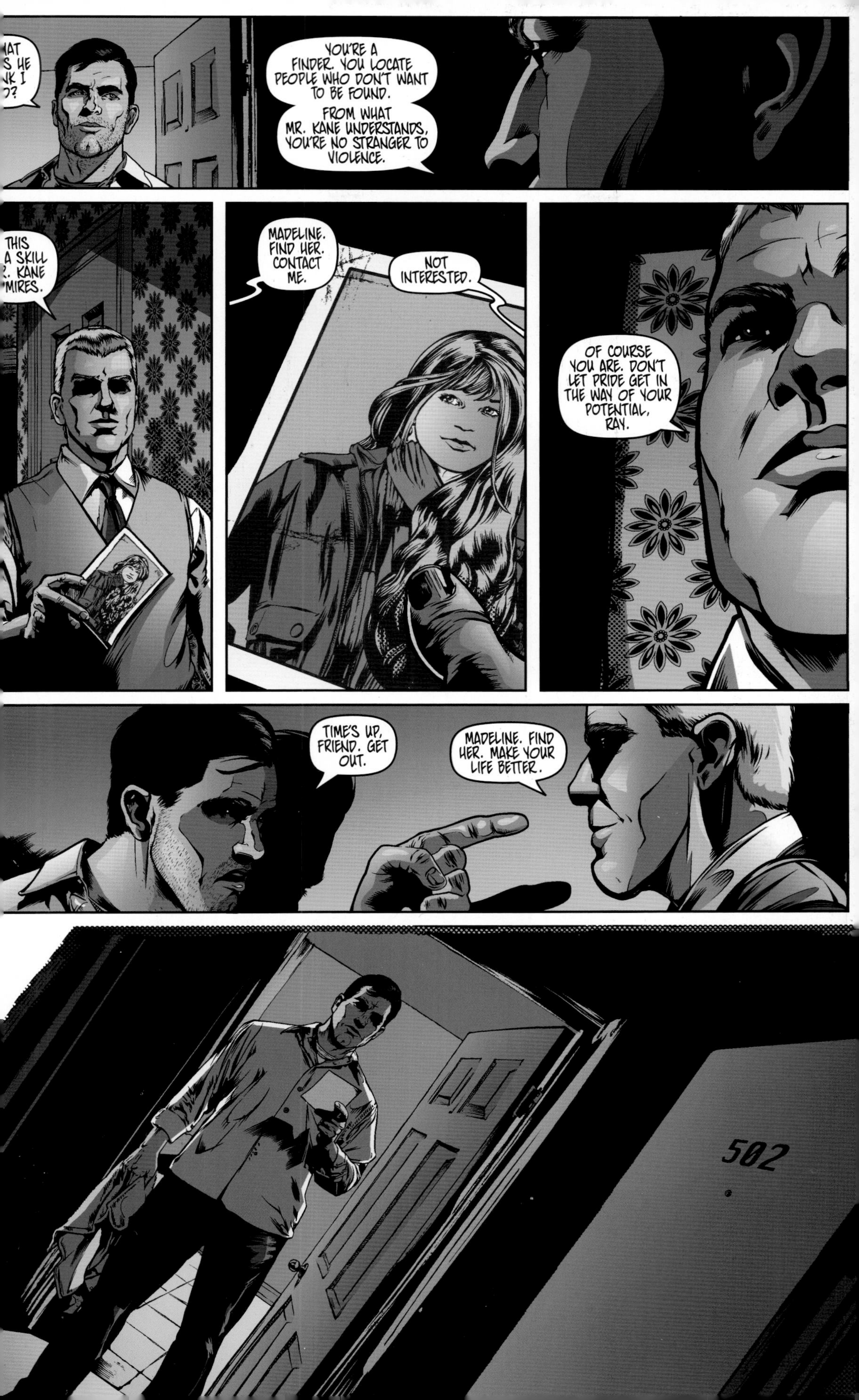
YOU'RE A FINDER. YOU LOCATE PEOPLE WHO DON'T WANT TO BE FOUND.
FROM WHAT MR. KANE UNDERSTANDS, YOU'RE NO STRANGER TO VIOLENCE.
MADELINE. FIND HER. CONTACT ME.
NOT INTERESTED.
OF COURSE YOU ARE. DON'T LET PRIDE GET IN THE WAY OF YOUR POTENTIAL, RAY.
TIME'S UP, FRIEND. GET OUT.
MADELINE. FIND HER. MAKE YOUR LIFE BETTER.
502

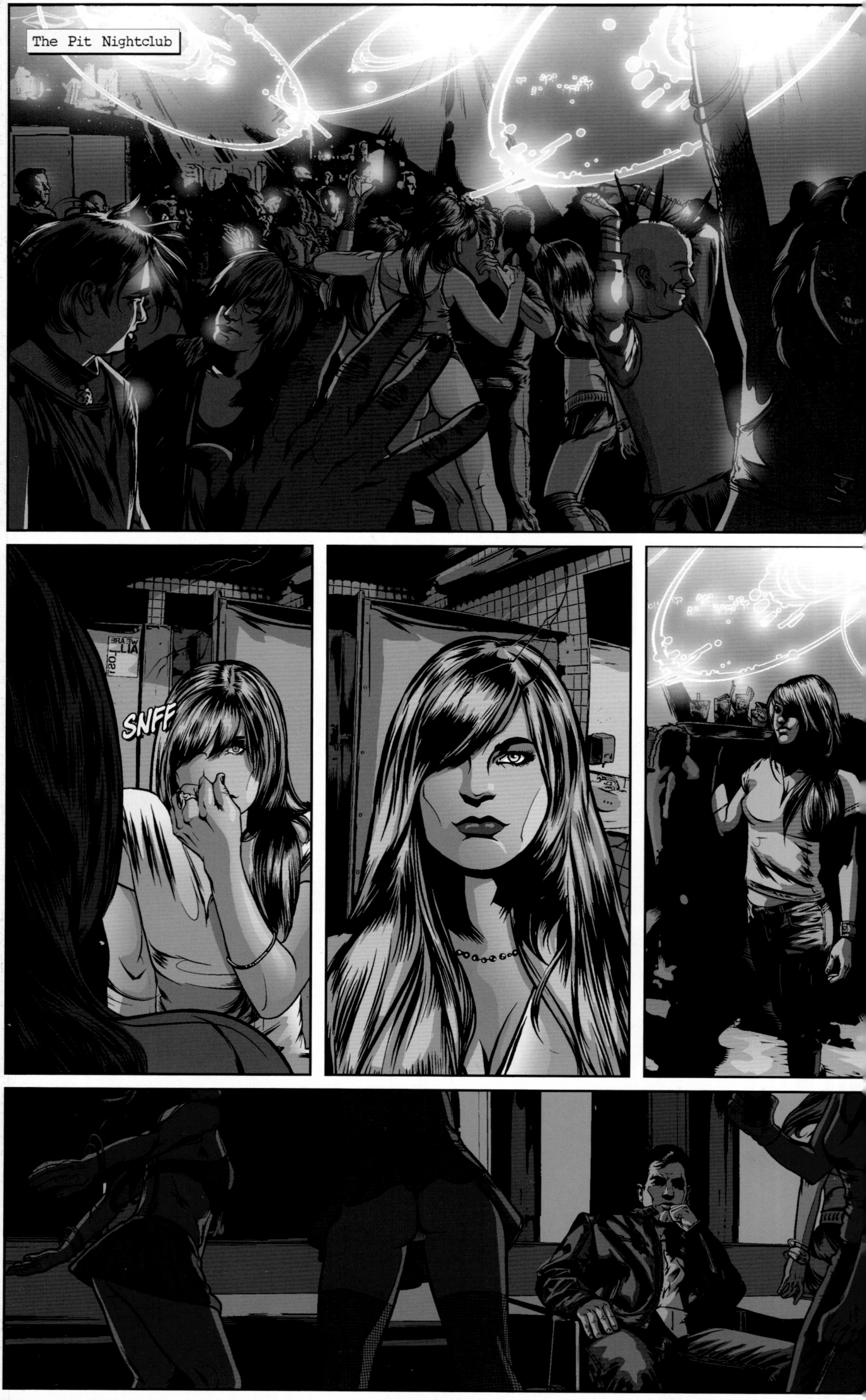
The Pit Nightclub
SNFF

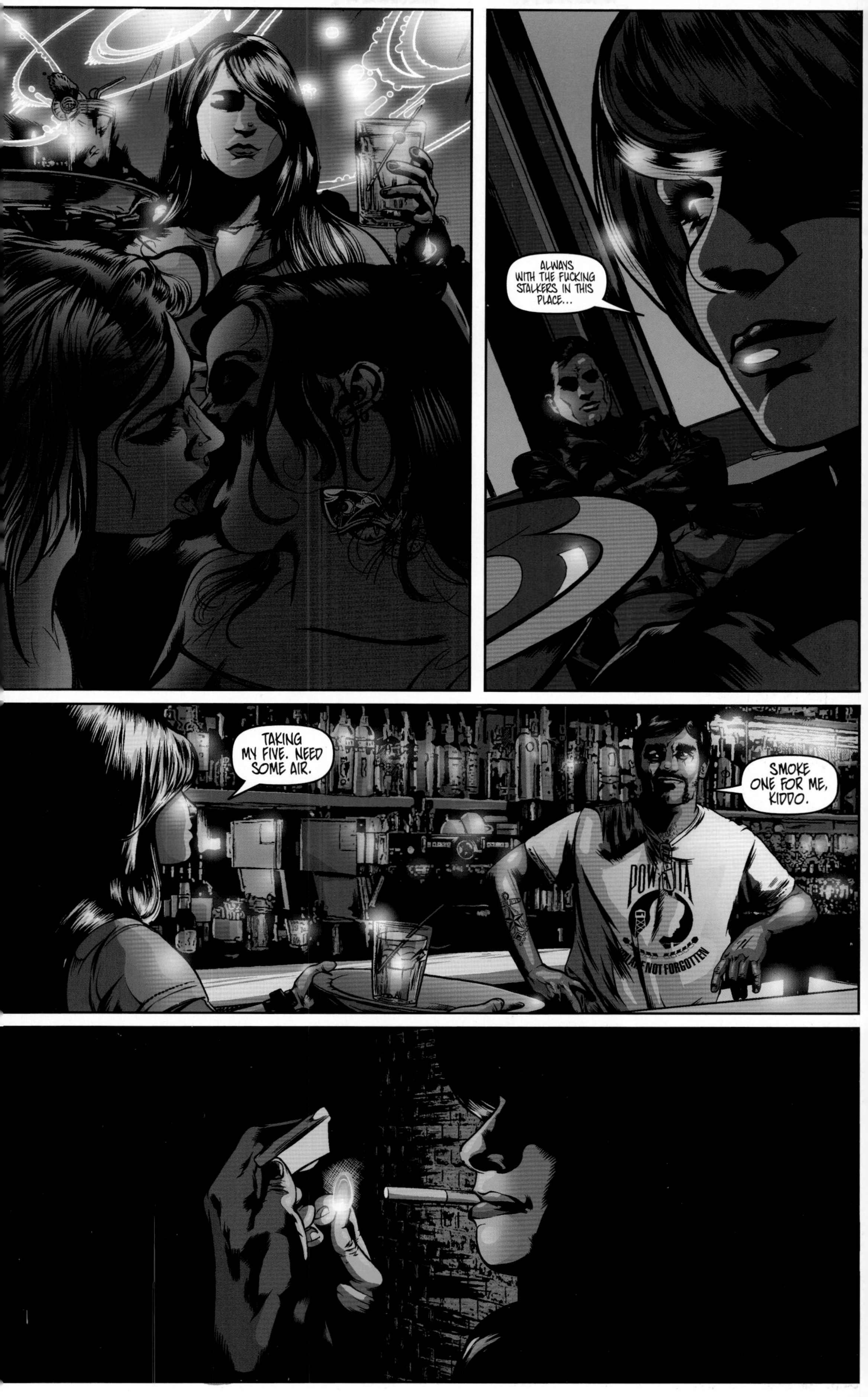
ALWAYS WITH THE FUCKING STALKERS IN THIS PLACE...
TAKING MY FIVE. NEED SOME AIR.
SMOKE ONE FOR ME, KIDDO.
YOU ARE NOT FORGOTTEN

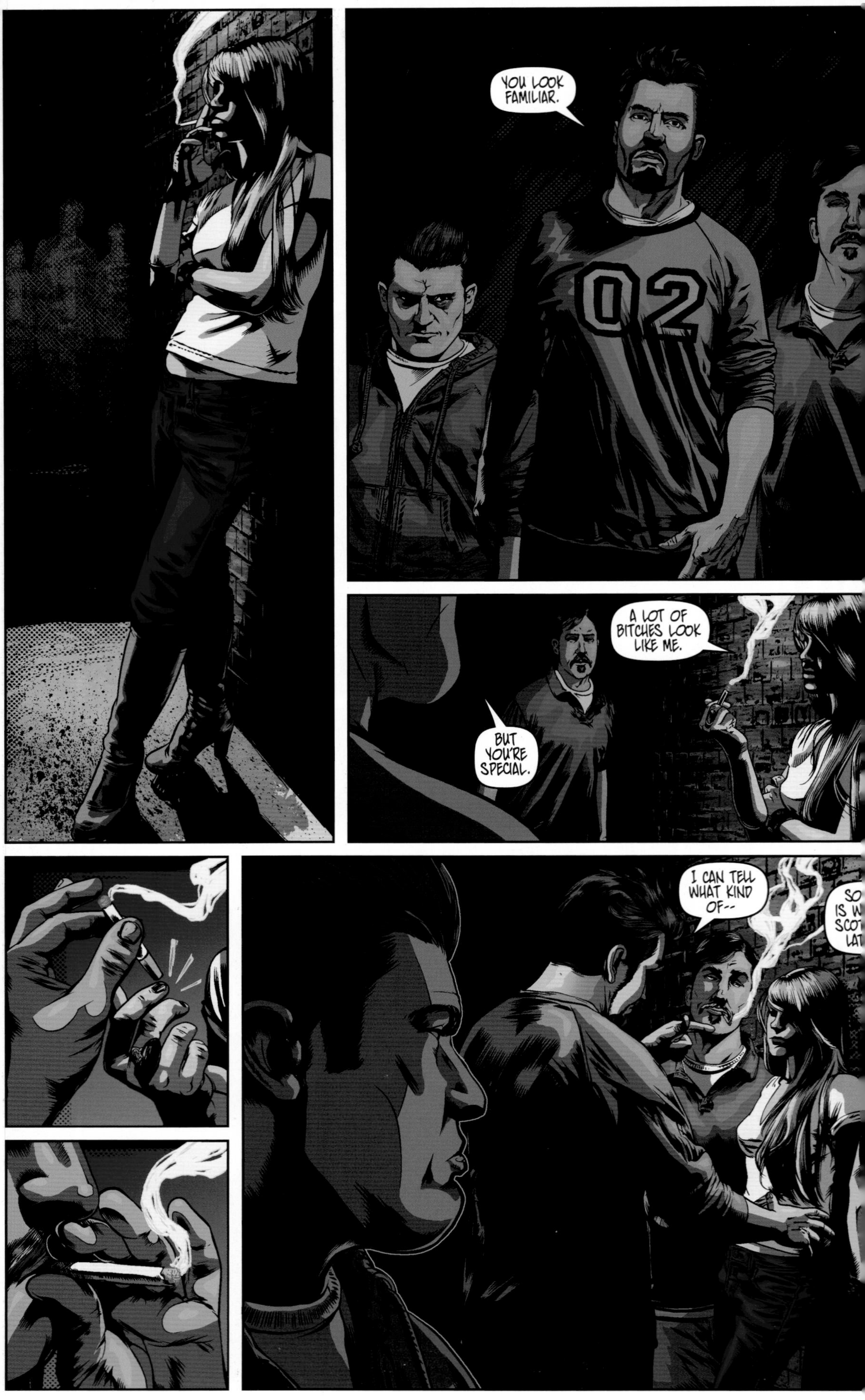
YOU LOOK FAMILIAR.
A LOT OF BITCHES LOOK LIKE ME.
BUT YOU'RE SPECIAL.
I CAN TELL WHAT KIND OF--

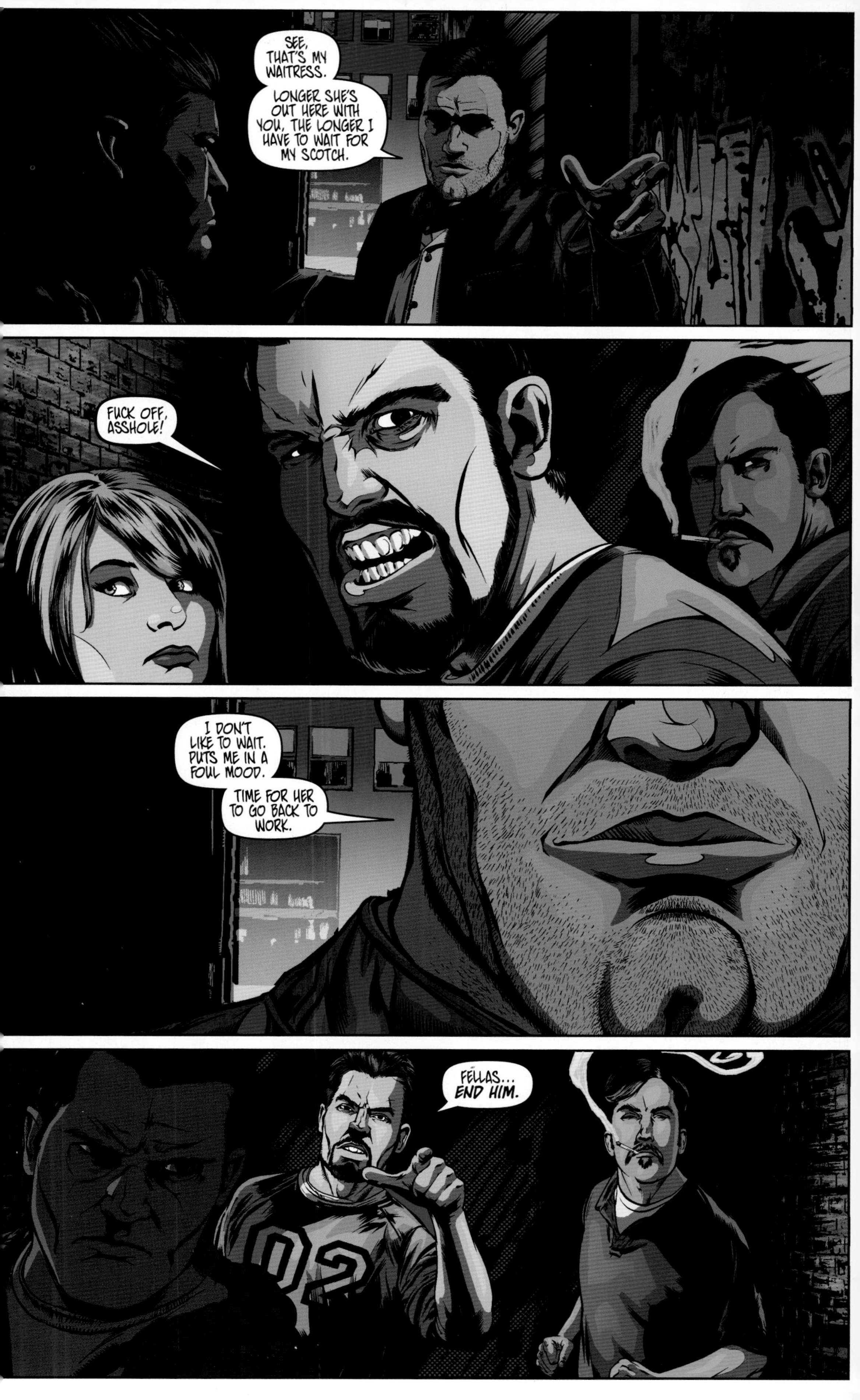
SEE, THAT'S MY WAITRESS.
LONGER SHE'S OUT HERE WITH YOU, THE LONGER I HAVE TO WAIT FOR MY SCOTCH.
FUCK OFF, ASSHOLE!
I DON'T LIKE TO WAIT. PUTS ME IN A FOUL MOOD.
TIME FOR HER TO GO BACK TO WORK.
FELLAS... END HIM.

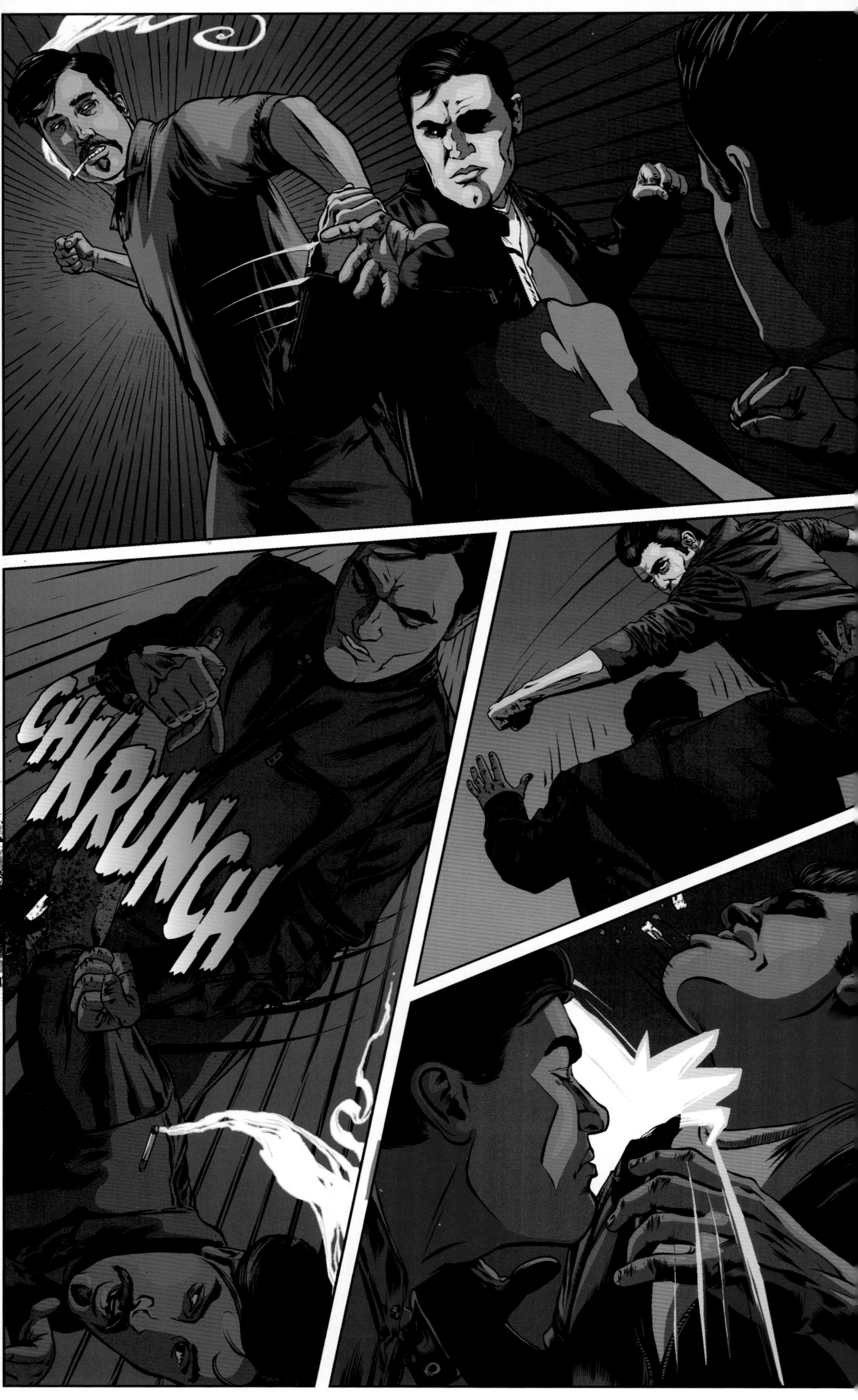
CHKRUNCH

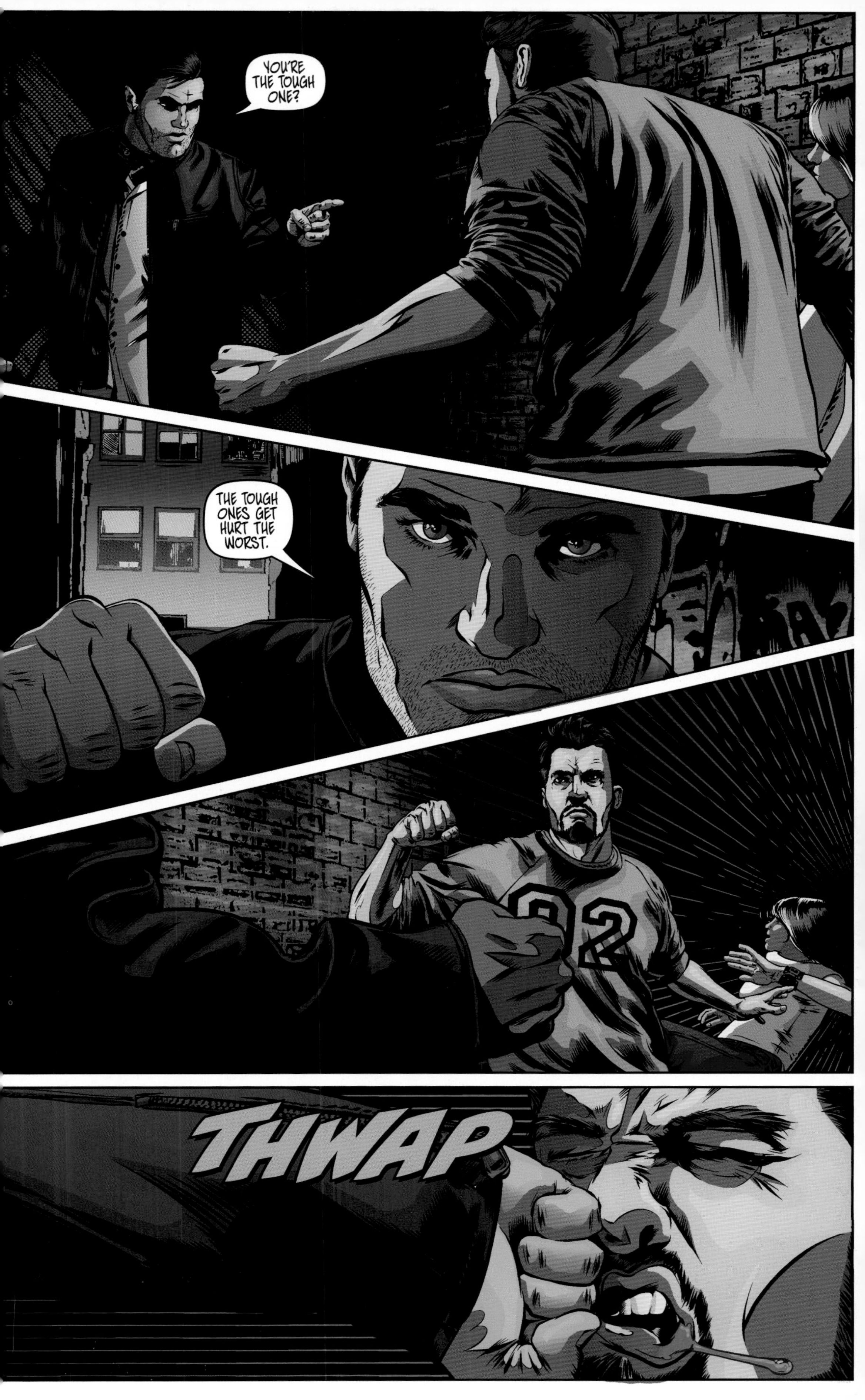
YOU'RE THE TOUGH ONE?
THE TOUGH ONES GET HURT THE WORST.
THWAP

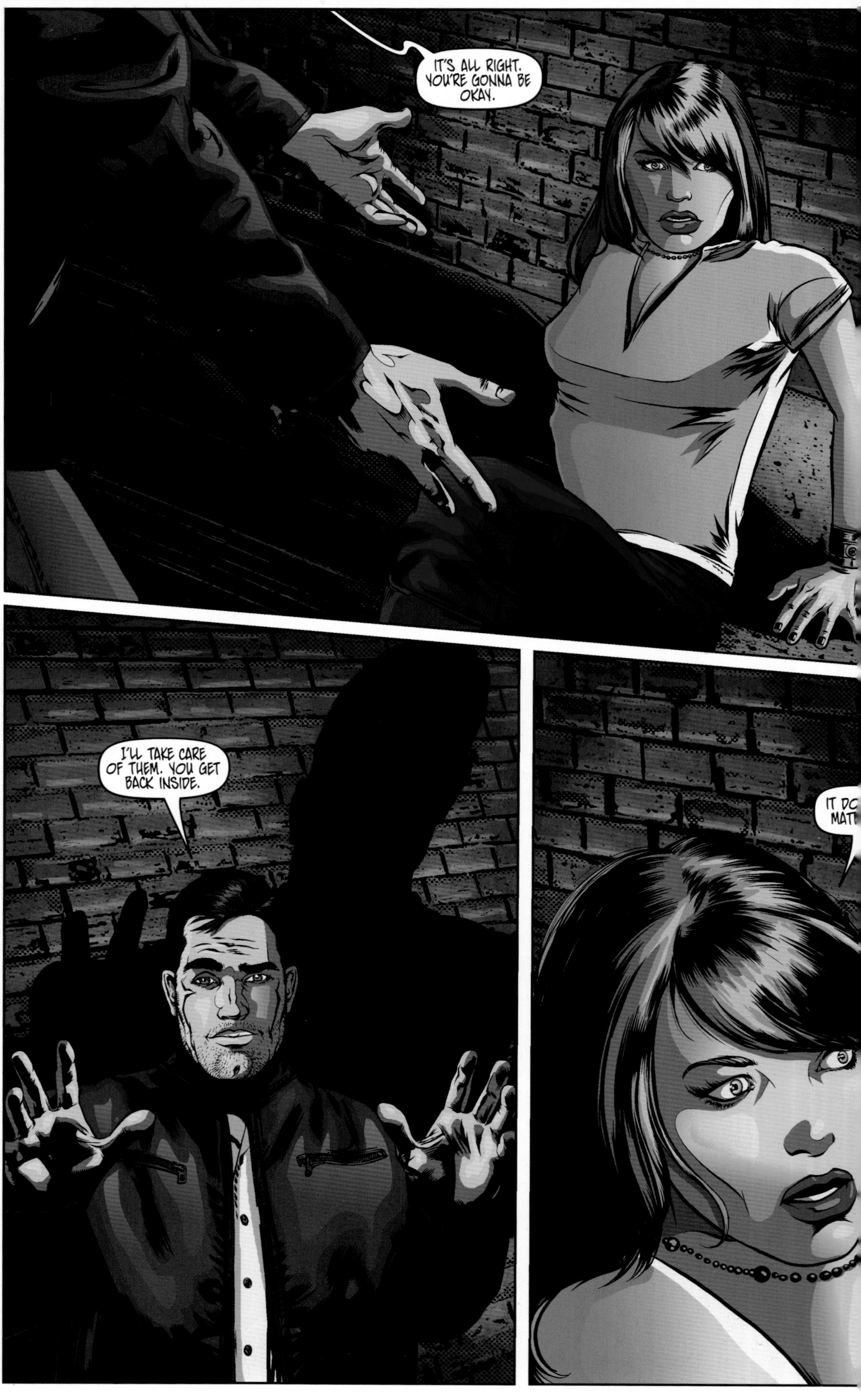
IT'S ALL RIGHT. YOU'RE GONNA BE OKAY.
I'LL TAKE CARE OF THEM. YOU GET BACK INSIDE.

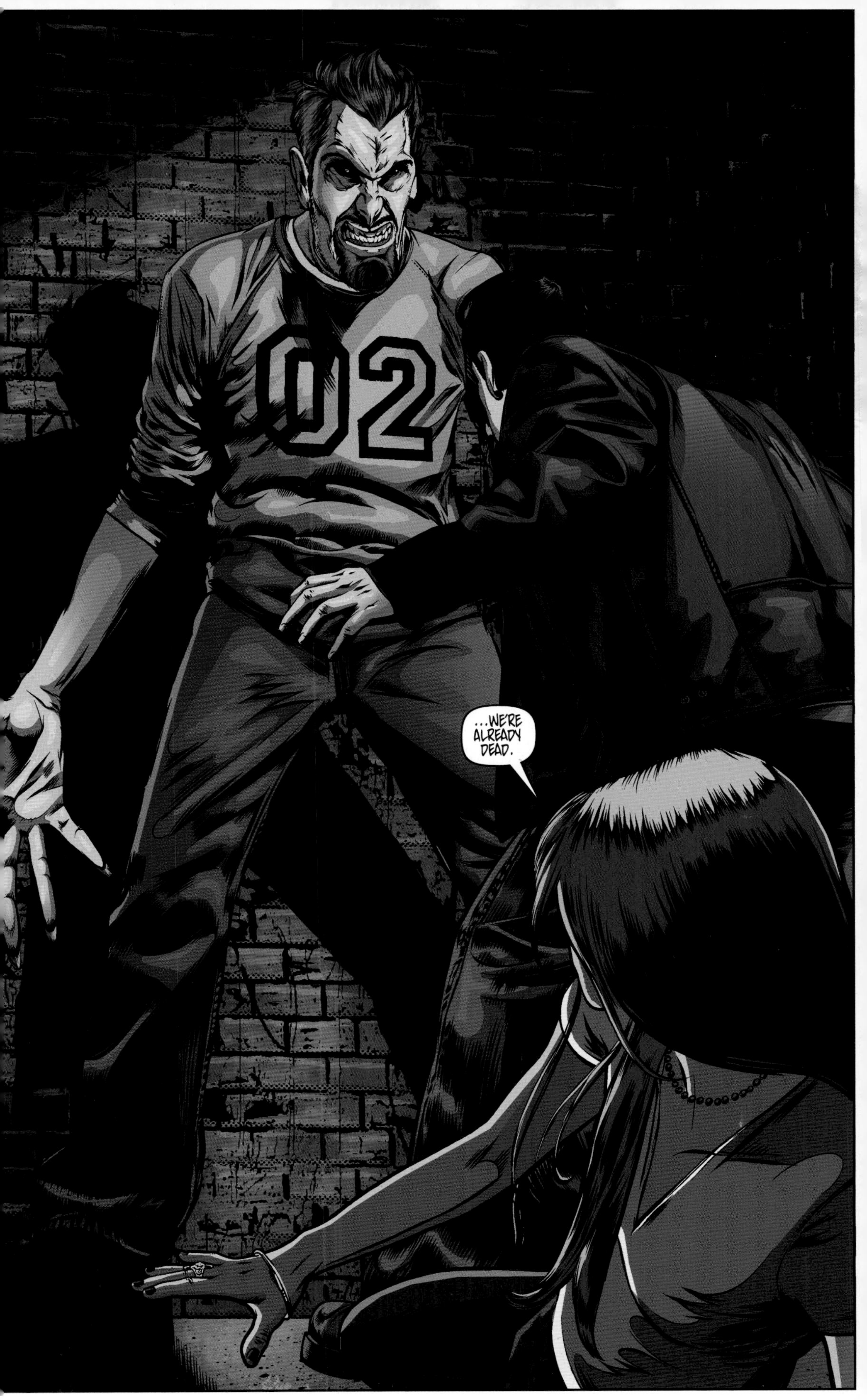
...WE'RE ALREADY DEAD.

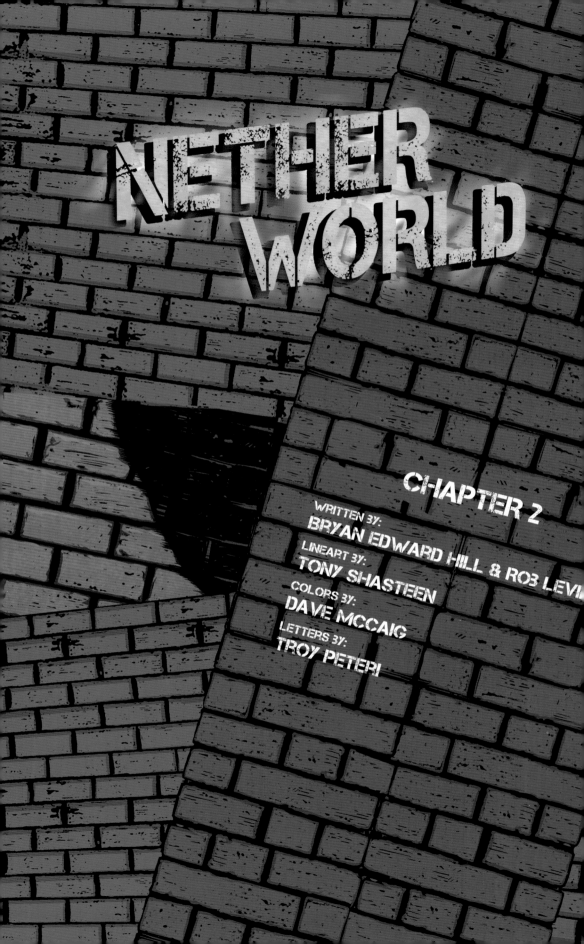

NETHER WORLD

CHAPTER 2

WRITTEN BY:
BRYAN EDWARD HILL & ROB LEVI

LINEART BY:
TONY SHASTEEN

COLORS BY:
DAVE MCCAIG

LETTERS BY:
TROY PETERI

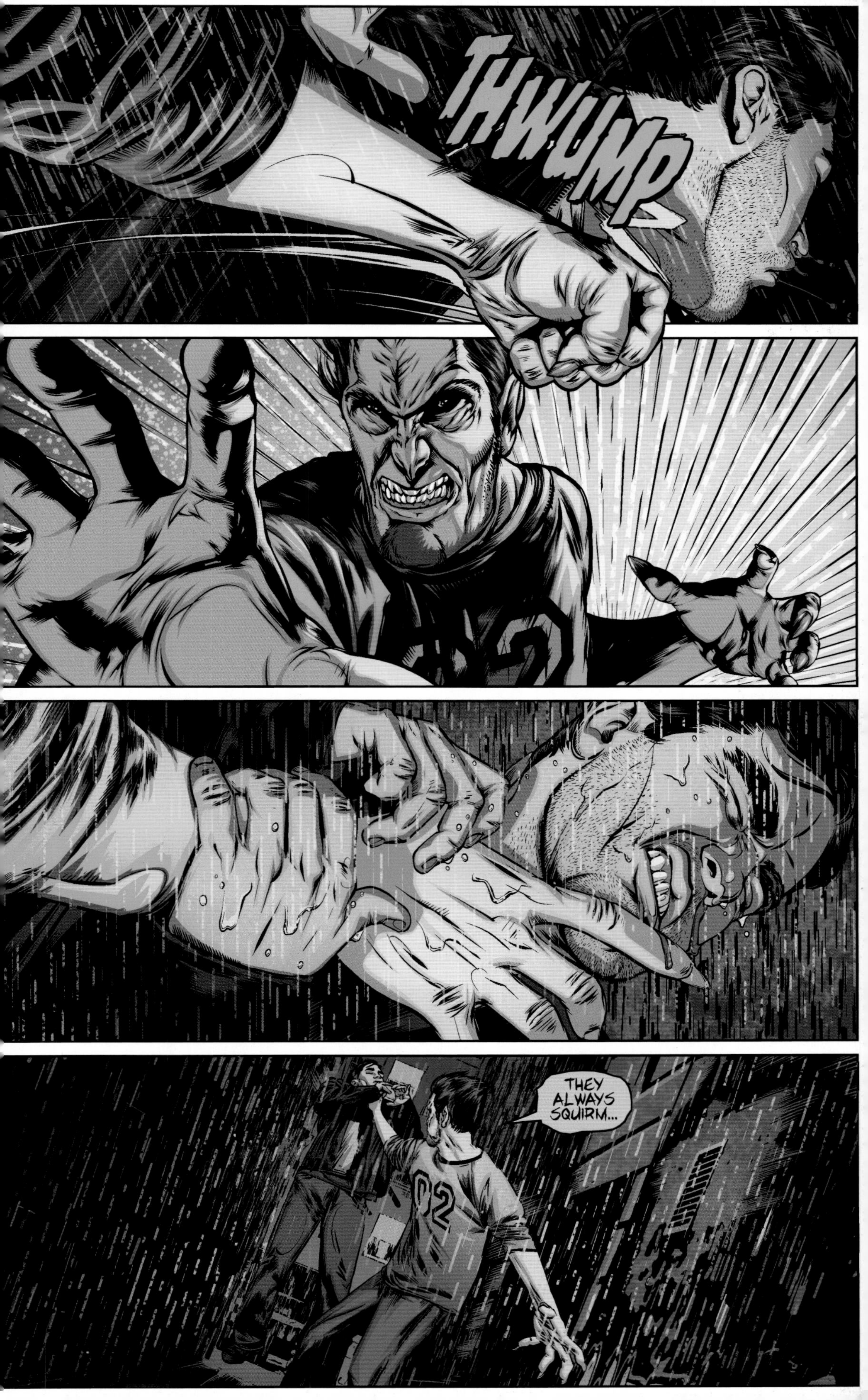
THWUMP
THEY ALWAYS SQUIRM...

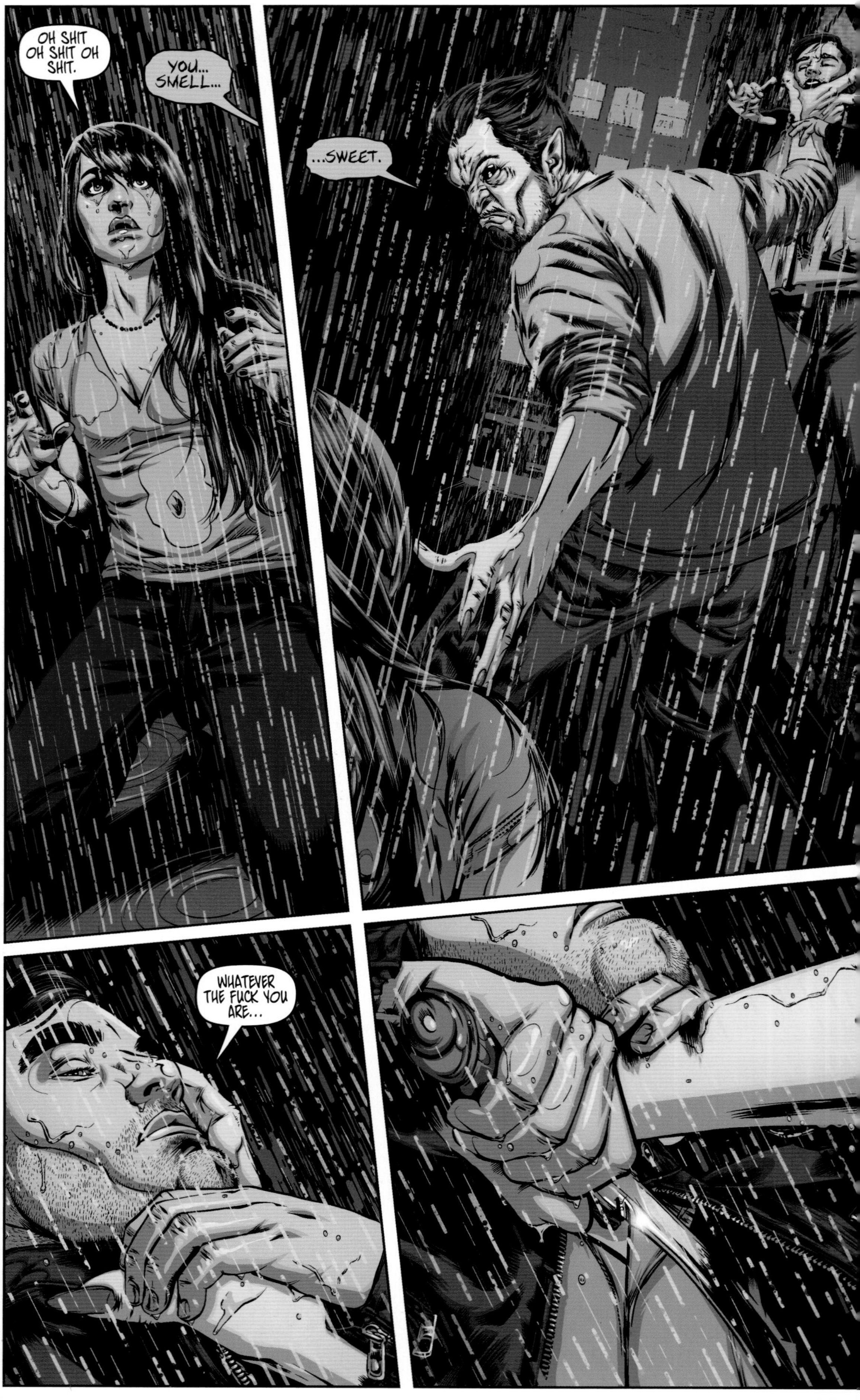
OH SHIT OH SHIT OH SHIT.
YOU... SMELL...
...SWEET.
WHATEVER THE FUCK YOU ARE...

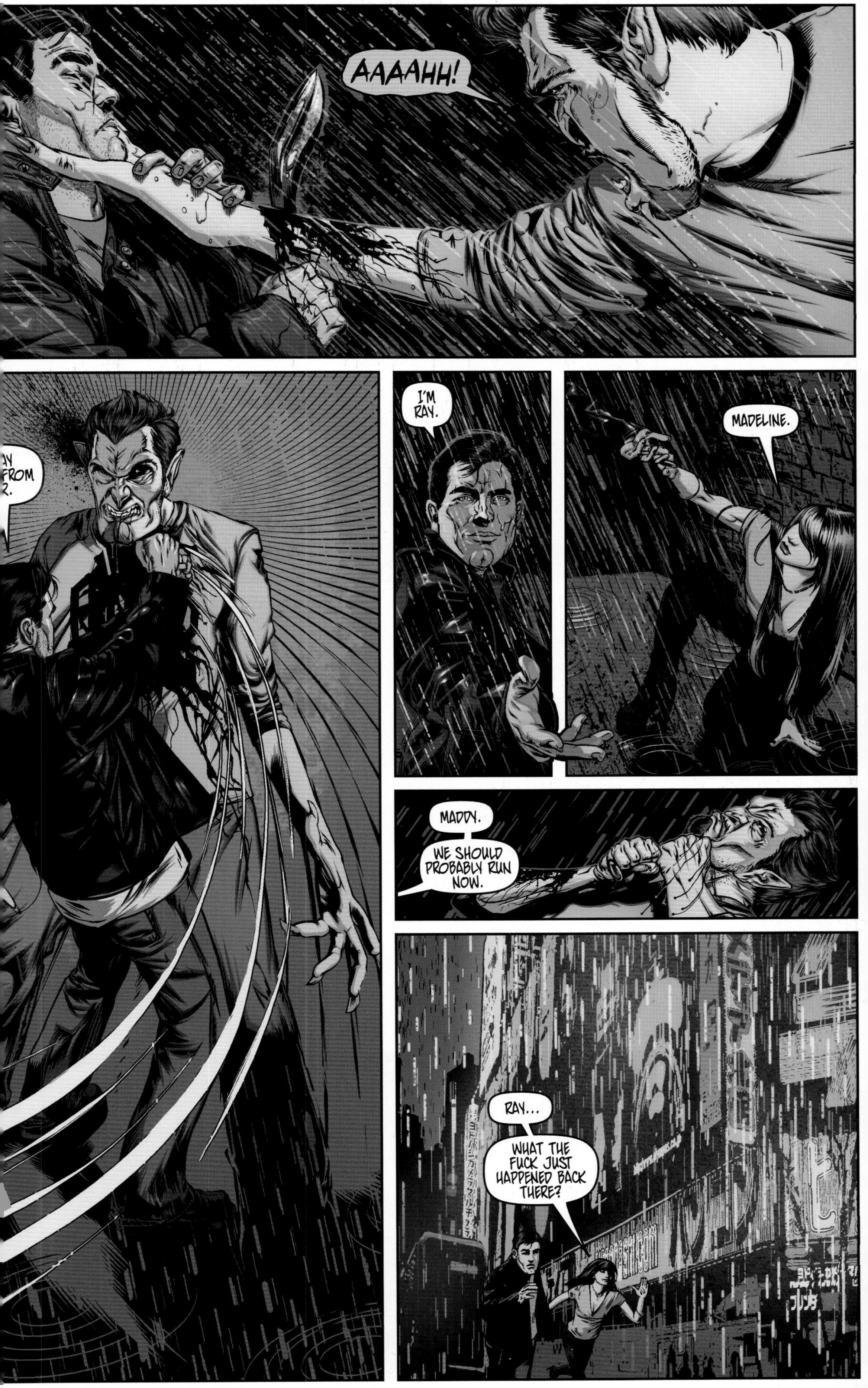
AAAAHH!
FROM
I'M RAY.
MADELINE.
MADDY.
WE SHOULD PROBABLY RUN NOW.
RAY...
WHAT THE FUCK JUST HAPPENED BACK THERE?

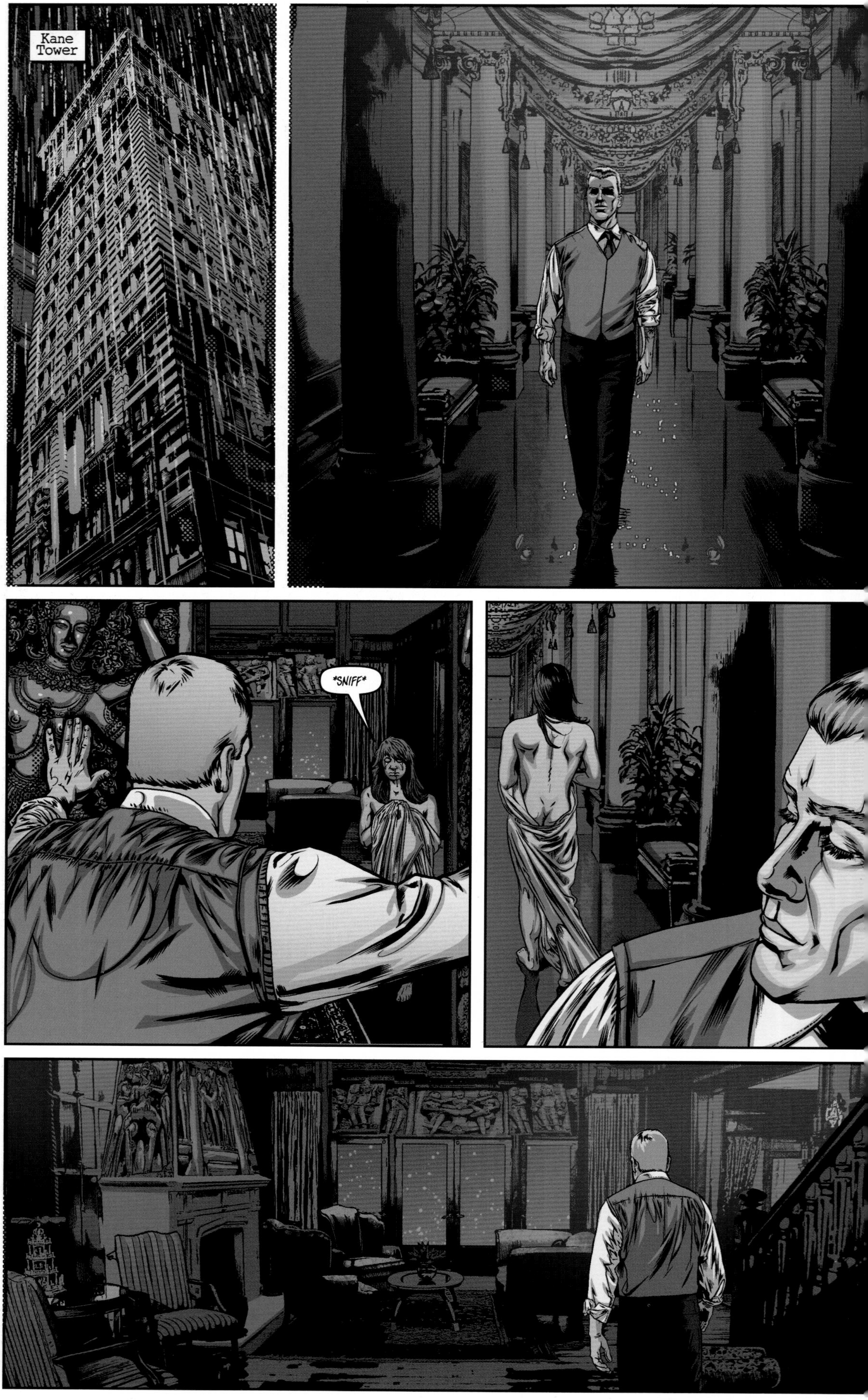
Kane Tower
SNIFF

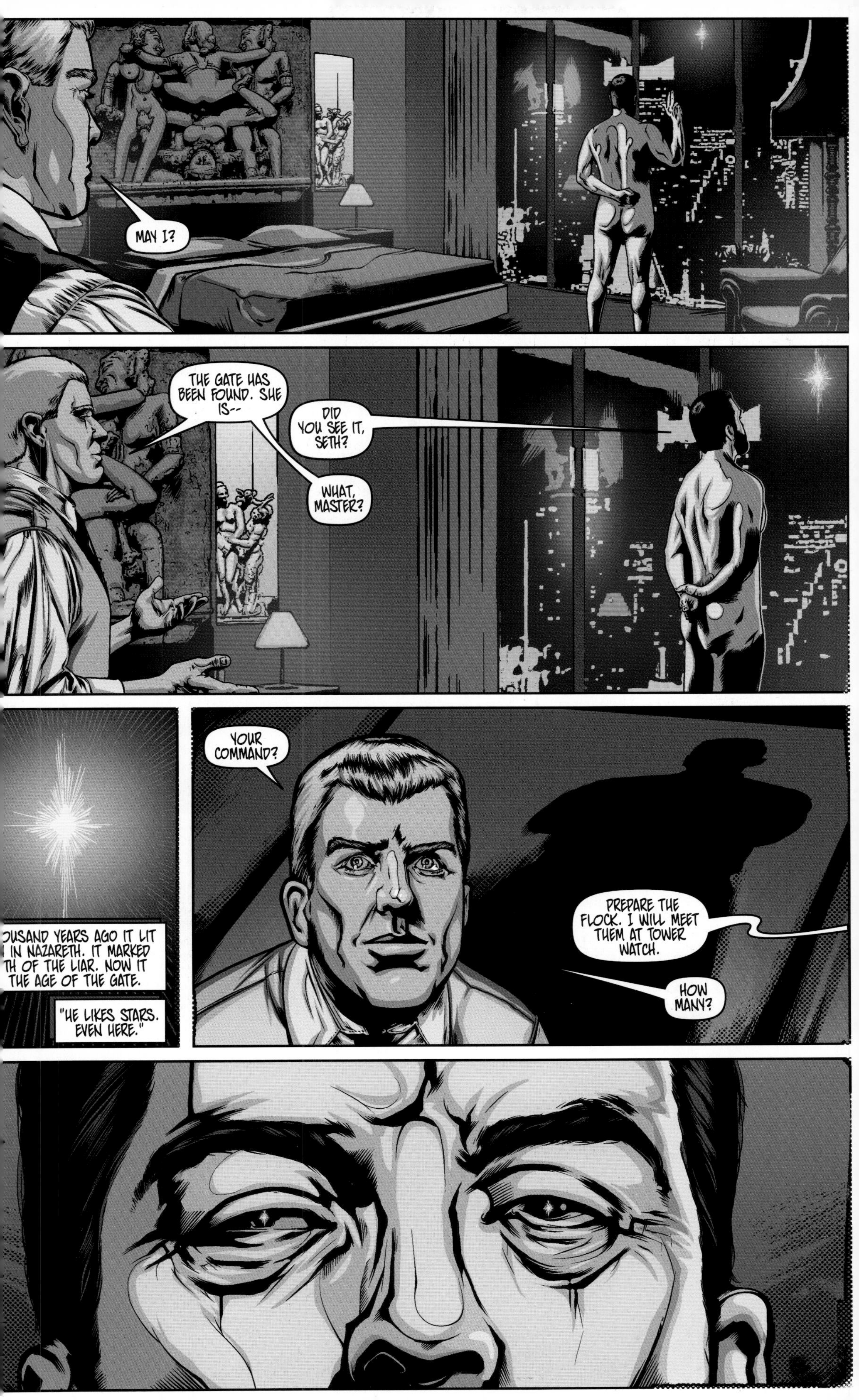
MAY I?
THE GATE HAS BEEN FOUND. SHE IS--
DID YOU SEE IT, SETH?
WHAT, MASTER?
OUSAND YEARS AGO IT LIT
IN NAZARETH. IT MARKED
TH OF THE LIAR. NOW IT
THE AGE OF THE GATE.
"HE LIKES STARS. EVEN HERE."
YOUR COMMAND?
PREPARE THE FLOCK. I WILL MEET THEM AT TOWER WATCH.
HOW MANY?

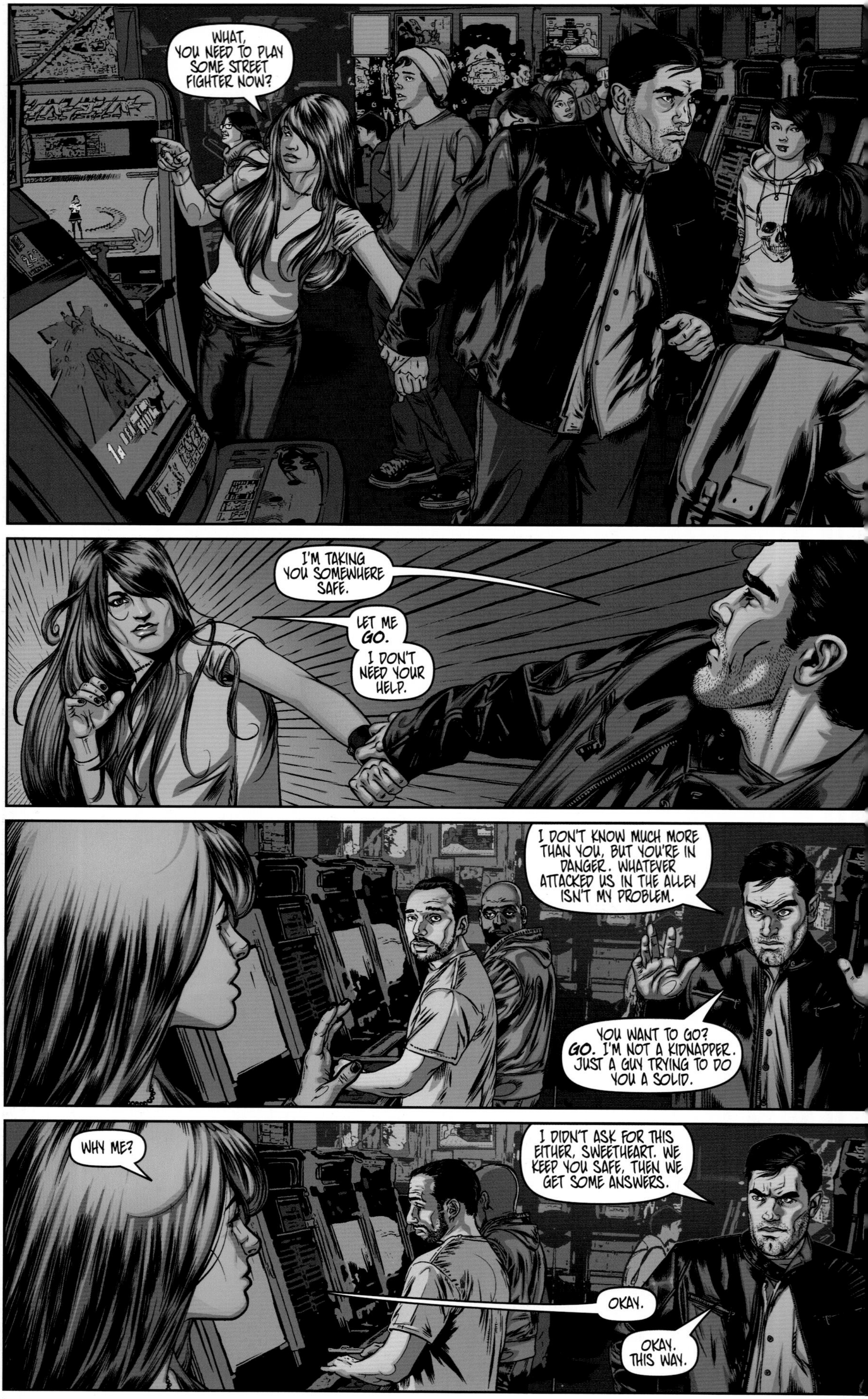
WHAT, YOU NEED TO PLAY SOME STREET FIGHTER NOW?
I'M TAKING YOU SOMEWHERE SAFE.
LET ME **GO.**
I DON'T NEED YOUR HELP.
I DON'T KNOW MUCH MORE THAN YOU, BUT YOU'RE IN DANGER. WHATEVER ATTACKED US IN THE ALLEY ISN'T MY PROBLEM.
YOU WANT TO GO? **GO.** I'M NOT A KIDNAPPER. JUST A GUY TRYING TO DO YOU A SOLID.
WHY ME?
I DIDN'T ASK FOR THIS EITHER, SWEETHEART. WE KEEP YOU SAFE, THEN WE GET SOME ANSWERS.
OKAY.
OKAY. THIS WAY.

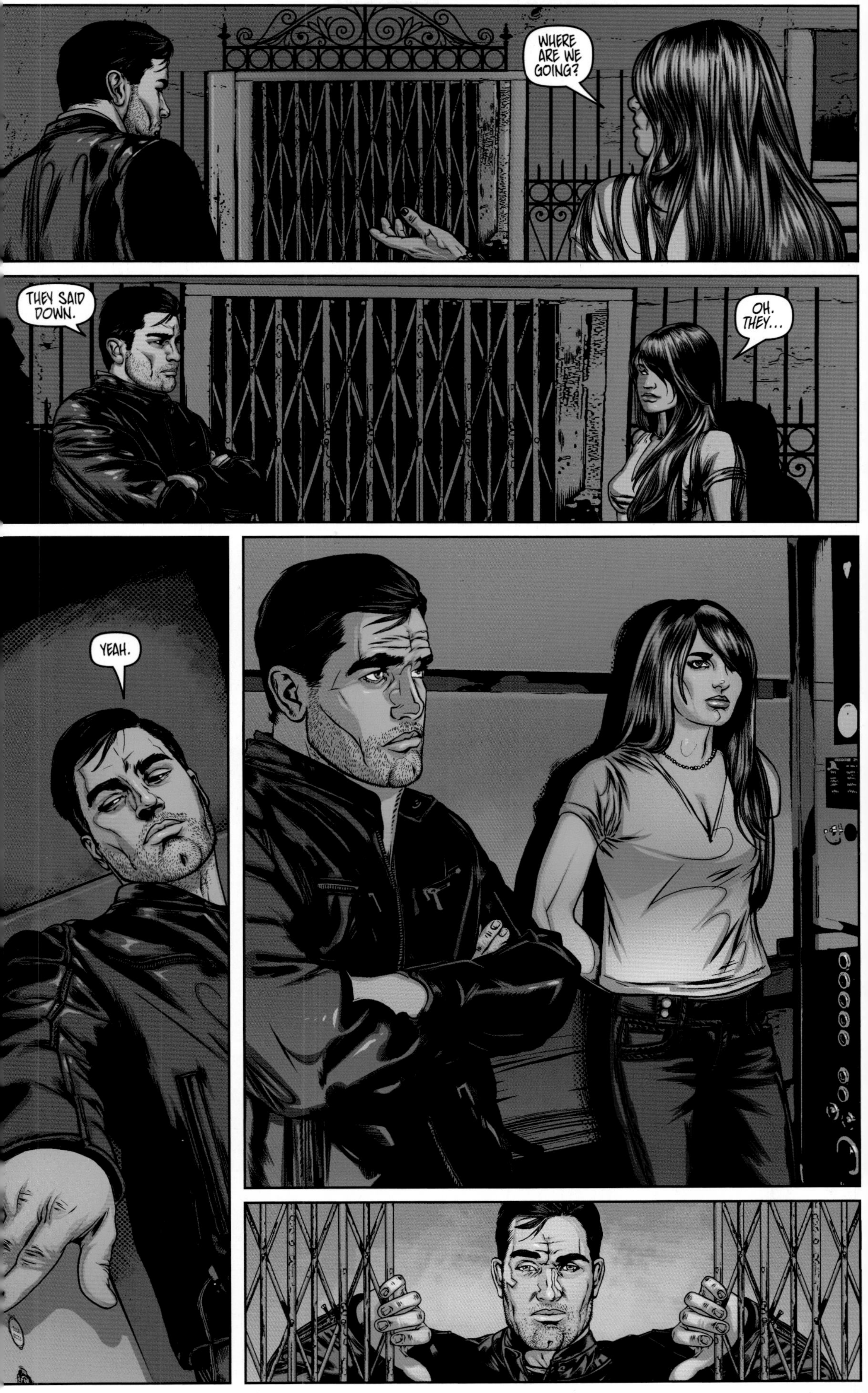
WHERE ARE WE GOING?
THEY SAID DOWN.
OH. THEY...
YEAH.

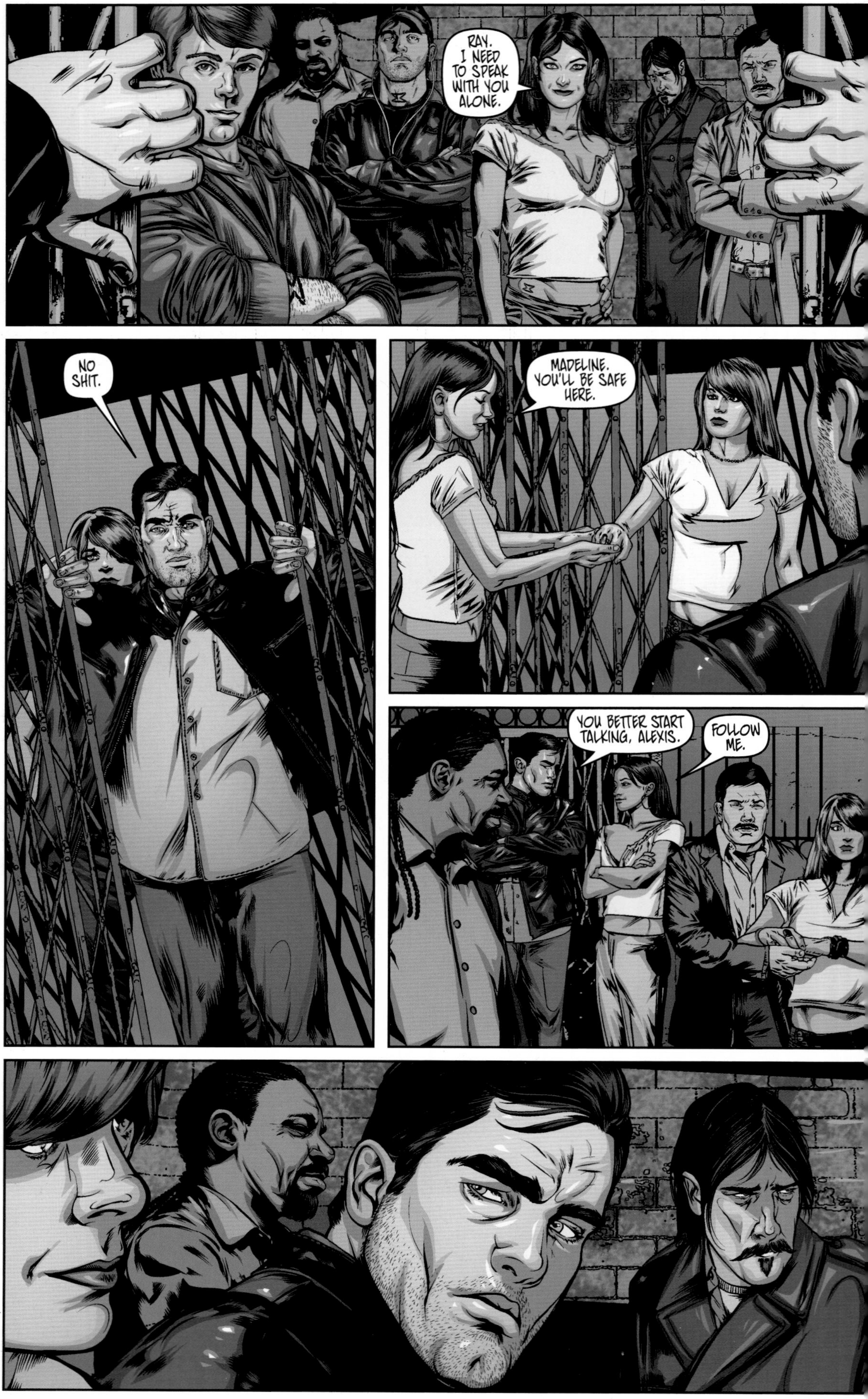
RAY. I NEED TO SPEAK WITH YOU ALONE.
NO SHIT.
MADELINE. YOU'LL BE SAFE HERE.
YOU BETTER START TALKING, ALEXIS.
FOLLOW ME.

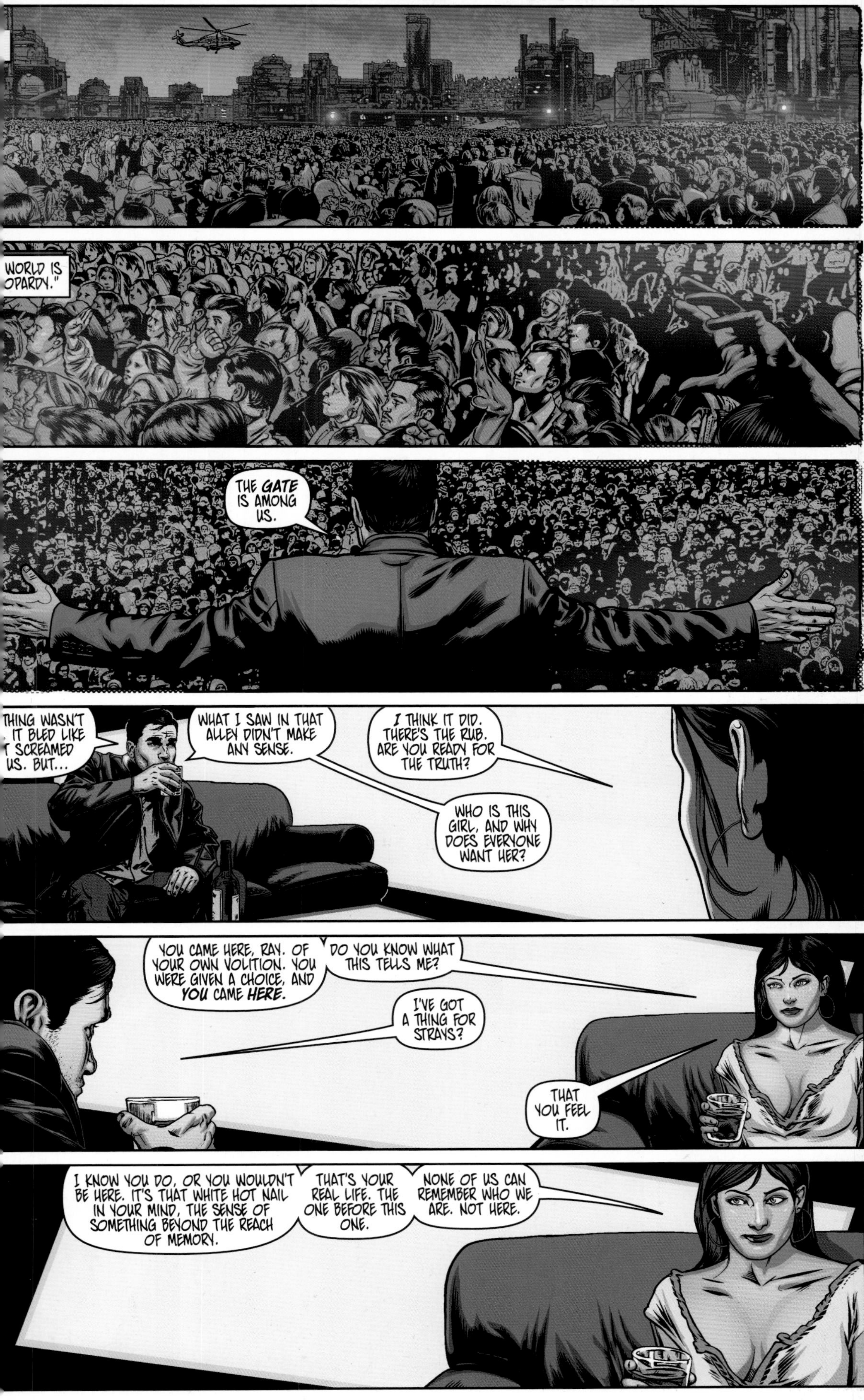
WORLD IS
OPARDY."
THE GATE IS AMONG US.
THING WASN'T , IT BLED LIKE T SCREAMED US. BUT...
WHAT I SAW IN THAT ALLEY DIDN'T MAKE ANY SENSE.
I THINK IT DID. THERE'S THE RUB. ARE YOU READY FOR THE TRUTH?
WHO IS THIS GIRL, AND WHY DOES EVERYONE WANT HER?
YOU CAME HERE, RAY. OF YOUR OWN VOLITION. YOU WERE GIVEN A CHOICE, AND YOU CAME HERE.
DO YOU KNOW WHAT THIS TELLS ME?
I'VE GOT A THING FOR STRAYS?
THAT YOU FEEL IT.
I KNOW YOU DO, OR YOU WOULDN'T BE HERE. IT'S THAT WHITE HOT NAIL IN YOUR MIND, THE SENSE OF SOMETHING BEYOND THE REACH OF MEMORY.
THAT'S YOUR REAL LIFE. THE ONE BEFORE THIS ONE.
NONE OF US CAN REMEMBER WHO WE ARE. NOT HERE.

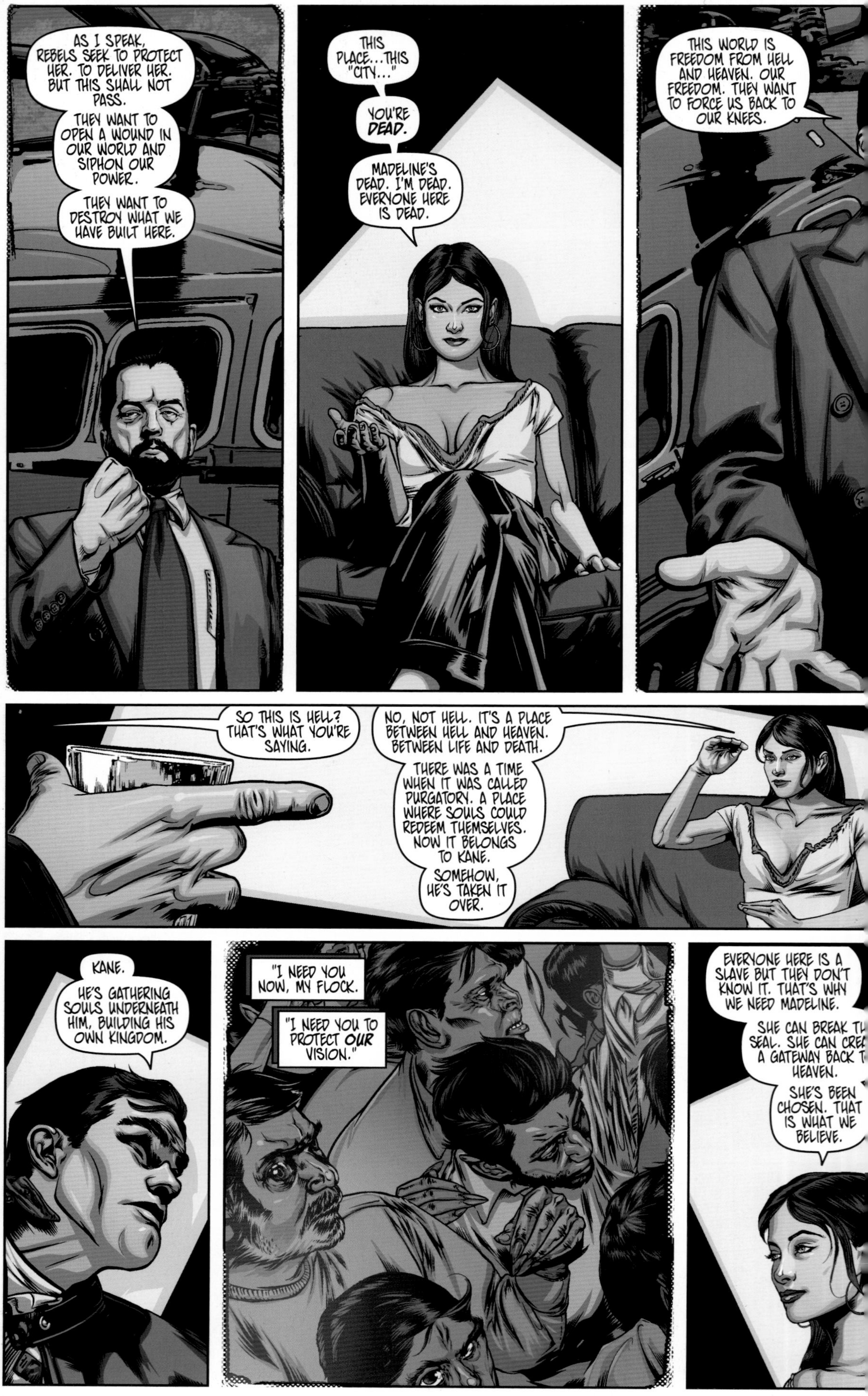
AS I SPEAK, REBELS SEEK TO PROTECT HER. TO DELIVER HER. BUT THIS SHALL NOT PASS.
THEY WANT TO OPEN A WOUND IN OUR WORLD AND SIPHON OUR POWER.
THEY WANT TO DESTROY WHAT WE HAVE BUILT HERE.
THIS PLACE...THIS "CITY..."
YOU'RE **DEAD.**
MADELINE'S DEAD. I'M DEAD. EVERYONE HERE IS DEAD.
THIS WORLD IS FREEDOM FROM HELL AND HEAVEN. OUR FREEDOM. THEY WANT TO FORCE US BACK TO OUR KNEES.
SO THIS IS HELL? THAT'S WHAT YOU'RE SAYING.
NO, NOT HELL. IT'S A PLACE BETWEEN HELL AND HEAVEN. BETWEEN LIFE AND DEATH.
THERE WAS A TIME WHEN IT WAS CALLED PURGATORY. A PLACE WHERE SOULS COULD REDEEM THEMSELVES. NOW IT BELONGS TO KANE.
SOMEHOW, HE'S TAKEN IT OVER.
KANE.
HE'S GATHERING SOULS UNDERNEATH HIM, BUILDING HIS OWN KINGDOM.
"I NEED YOU NOW, MY FLOCK.
"I NEED YOU TO PROTECT **OUR** VISION."
EVERYONE HERE IS A SLAVE BUT THEY DON'T KNOW IT. THAT'S WHY WE NEED MADELINE.
SHE CAN BREAK TH SEAL. SHE CAN CREA A GATEWAY BACK T HEAVEN.
SHE'S BEEN CHOSEN. THAT IS WHAT WE BELIEVE.

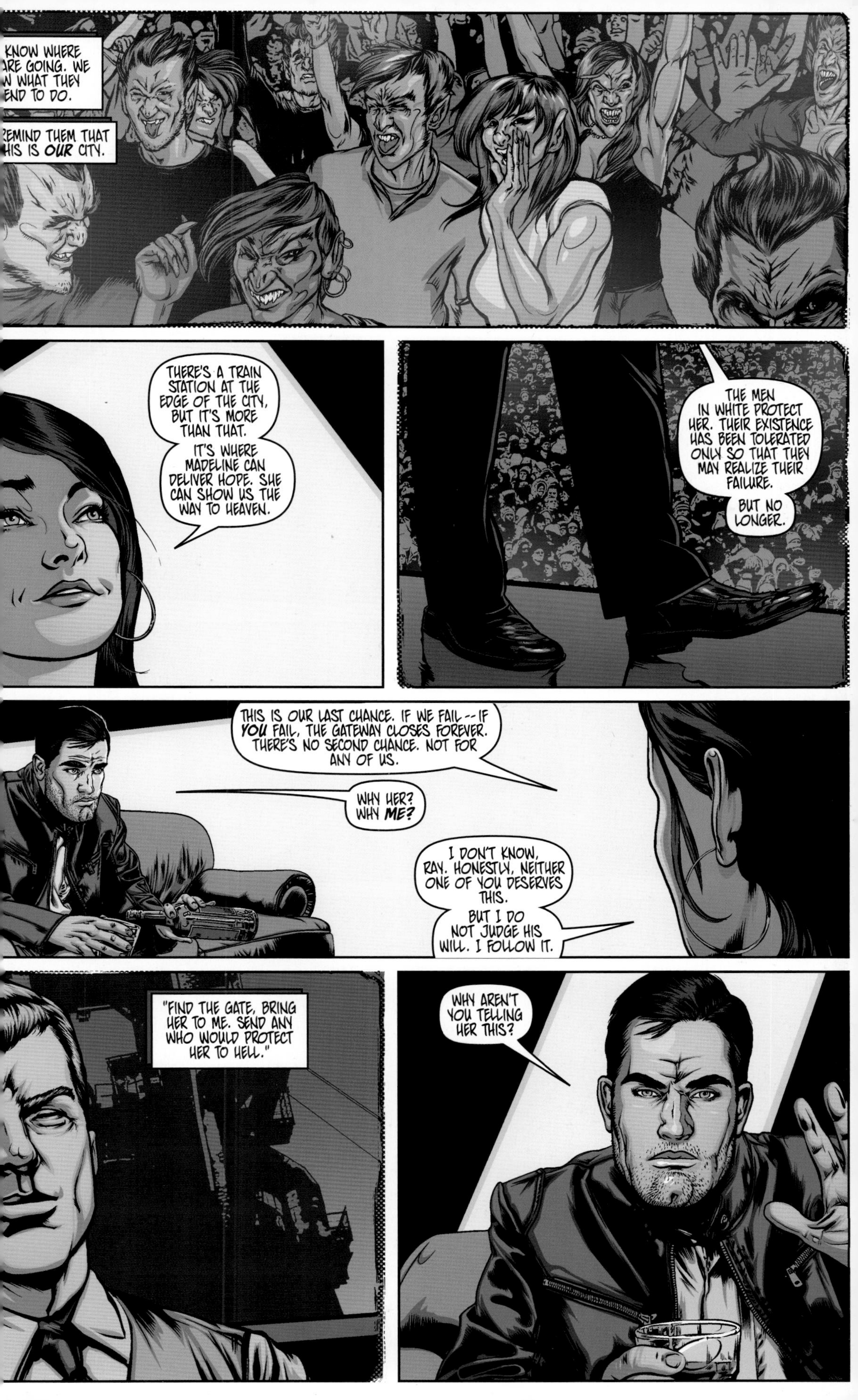
KNOW WHERE
ARE GOING. WE
W WHAT THEY
END TO DO.
REMIND THEM THAT
THIS IS OUR CITY.
THERE'S A TRAIN STATION AT THE EDGE OF THE CITY, BUT IT'S MORE THAN THAT.
IT'S WHERE MADELINE CAN DELIVER HOPE. SHE CAN SHOW US THE WAY TO HEAVEN.
THE MEN IN WHITE PROTECT HER. THEIR EXISTENCE HAS BEEN TOLERATED ONLY SO THAT THEY MAY REALIZE THEIR FAILURE.
BUT NO LONGER.
THIS IS OUR LAST CHANCE. IF WE FAIL -- IF YOU FAIL, THE GATEWAY CLOSES FOREVER. THERE'S NO SECOND CHANCE. NOT FOR ANY OF US.
WHY HER? WHY ME?
I DON'T KNOW, RAY. HONESTLY, NEITHER ONE OF YOU DESERVES THIS.
BUT I DO NOT JUDGE HIS WILL. I FOLLOW IT.
"FIND THE GATE, BRING HER TO ME. SEND ANY WHO WOULD PROTECT HER TO HELL."
WHY AREN'T YOU TELLING HER THIS?

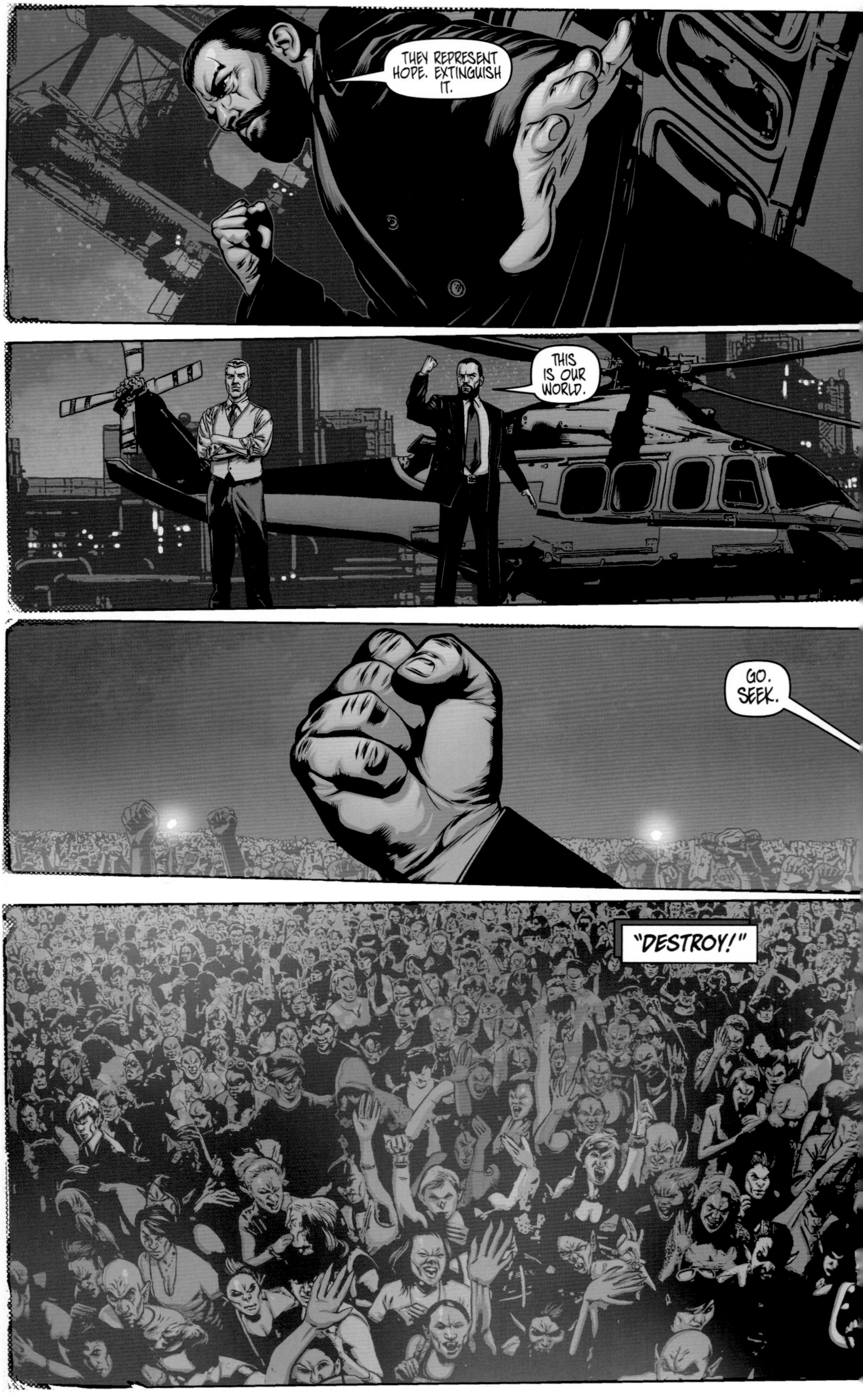
THEY REPRESENT HOPE. EXTINGUISH IT.
THIS IS OUR WORLD.
GO. SEEK.
"DESTROY!"

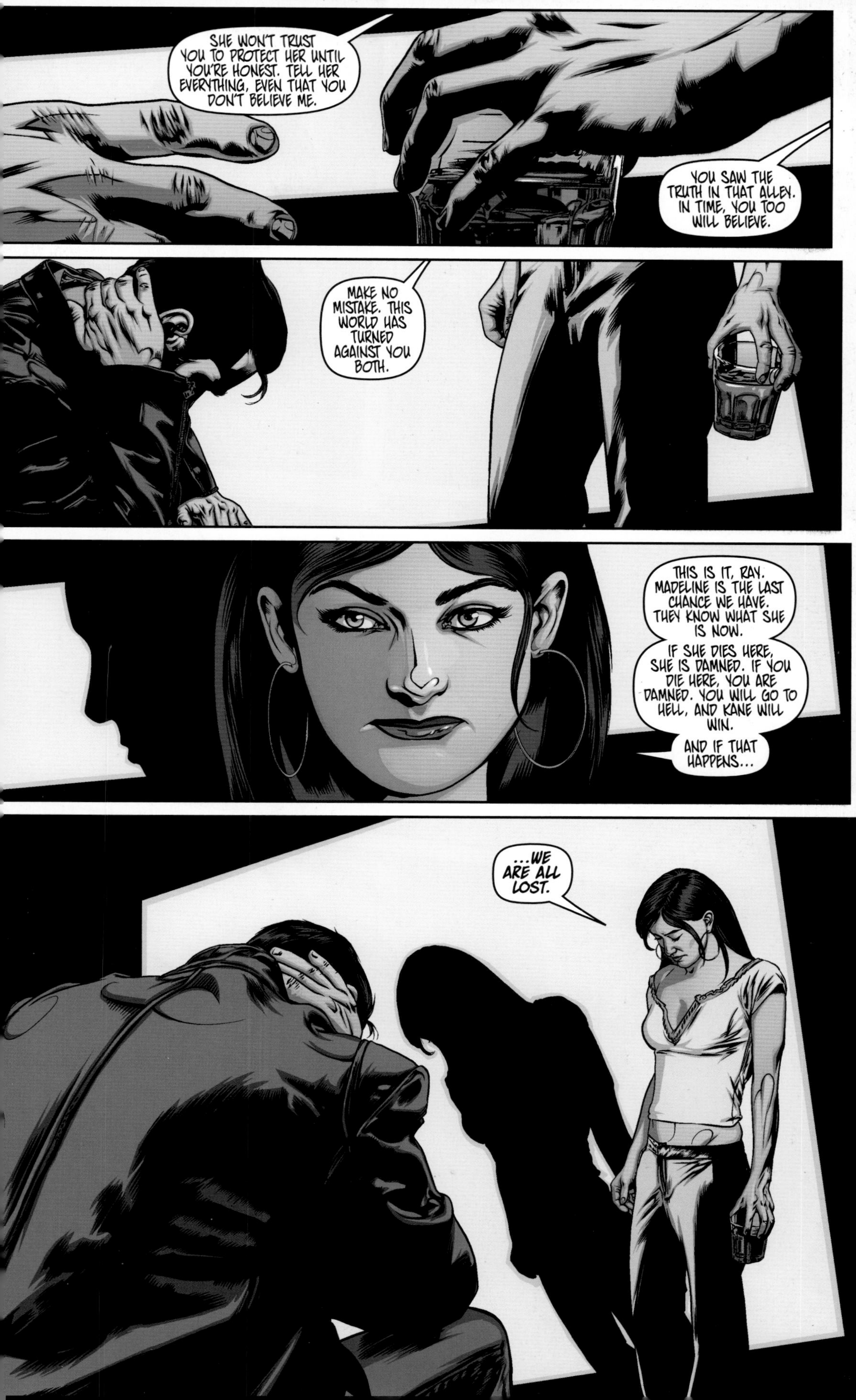
SHE WON'T TRUST YOU TO PROTECT HER UNTIL YOU'RE HONEST. TELL HER EVERYTHING, EVEN THAT YOU DON'T BELIEVE ME.
YOU SAW THE TRUTH IN THAT ALLEY. IN TIME, YOU TOO WILL BELIEVE.
MAKE NO MISTAKE. THIS WORLD HAS TURNED AGAINST YOU BOTH.
THIS IS IT, RAY. MADELINE IS THE LAST CHANCE WE HAVE. THEY KNOW WHAT SHE IS NOW.
IF SHE DIES HERE, SHE IS DAMNED. IF YOU DIE HERE, YOU ARE DAMNED. YOU WILL GO TO HELL, AND KANE WILL WIN.
AND IF THAT HAPPENS...
...WE ARE ALL LOST.

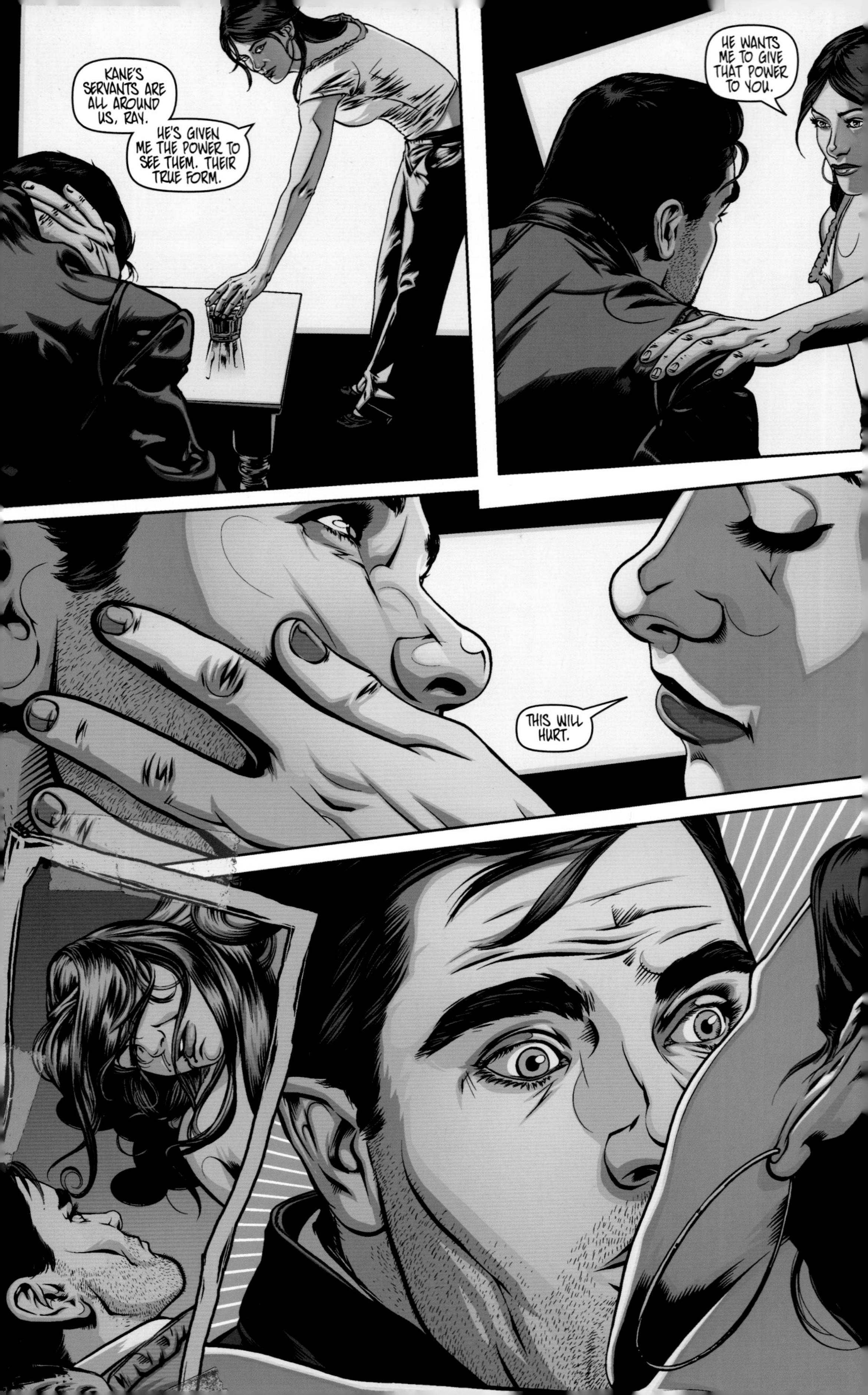
KANE'S SERVANTS ARE ALL AROUND US, RAY.
HE'S GIVEN ME THE POWER TO SEE THEM. THEIR TRUE FORM.
HE WANTS ME TO GIVE THAT POWER TO YOU.
THIS WILL HURT.

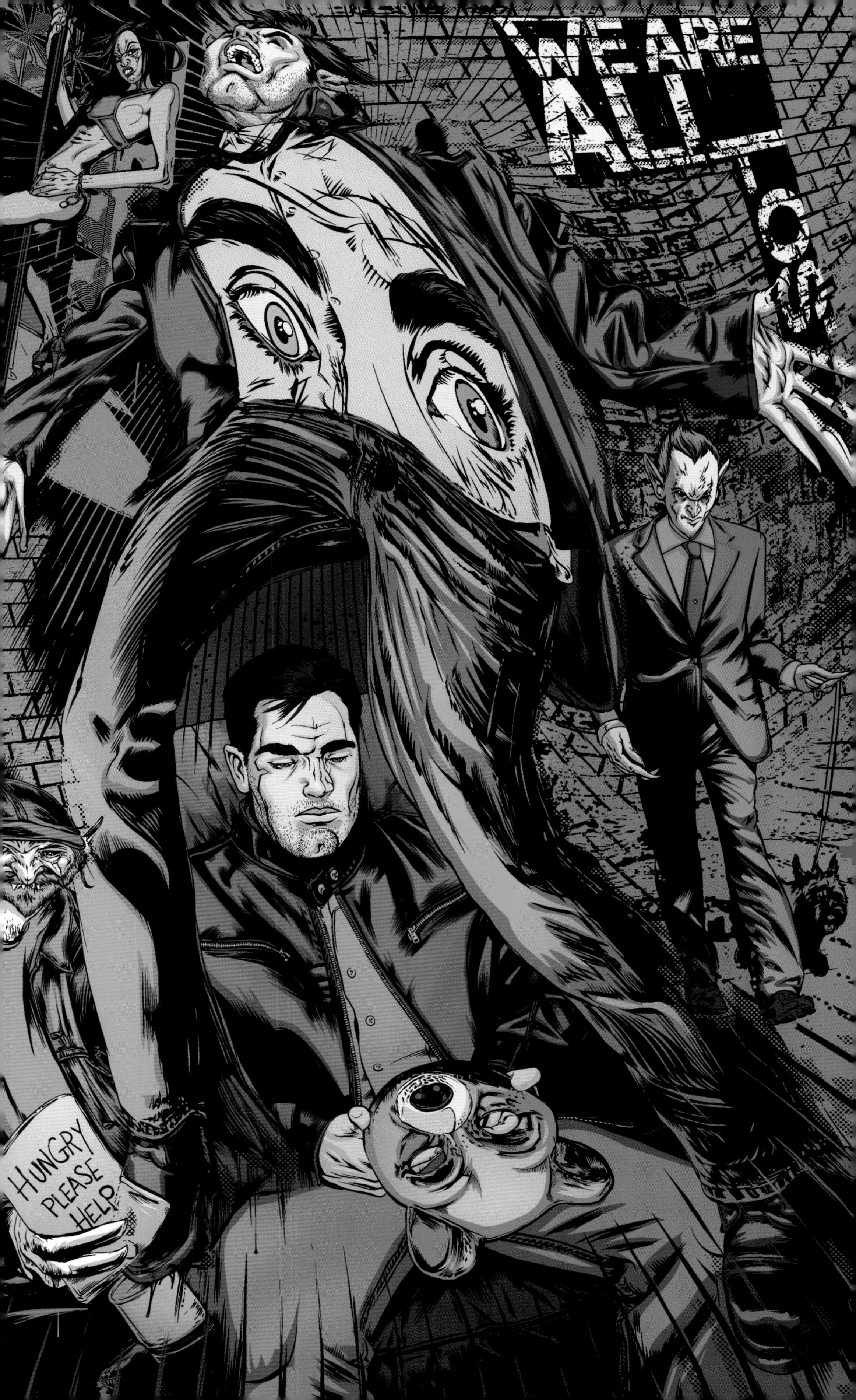
WE ARE ALL
HUNGRY PLEASE HELP

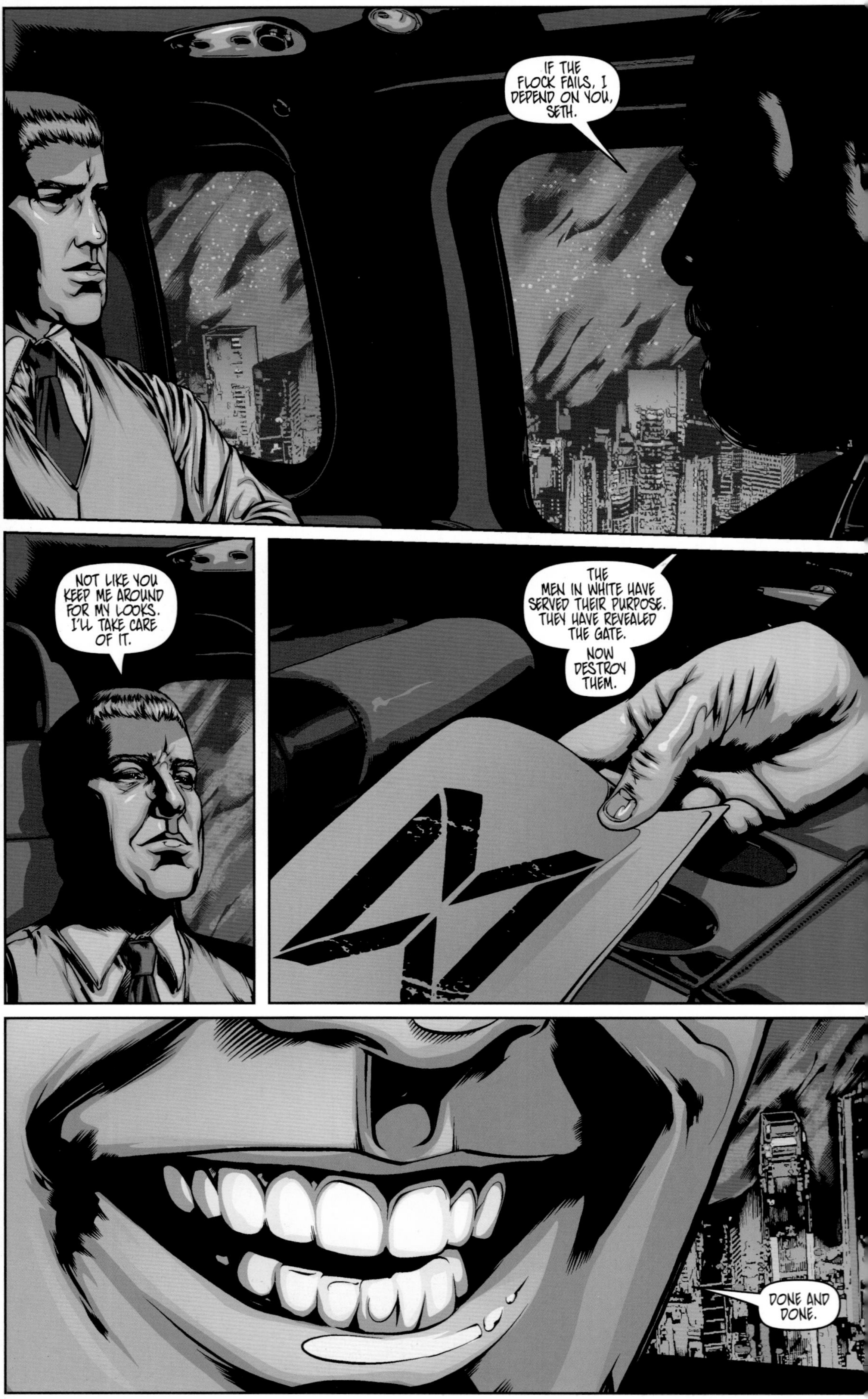
IF THE FLOCK FAILS, I DEPEND ON YOU, SETH.
NOT LIKE YOU KEEP ME AROUND FOR MY LOOKS. I'LL TAKE CARE OF IT.
THE MEN IN WHITE HAVE SERVED THEIR PURPOSE. THEY HAVE REVEALED THE GATE.
NOW DESTROY THEM.
DONE AND DONE.

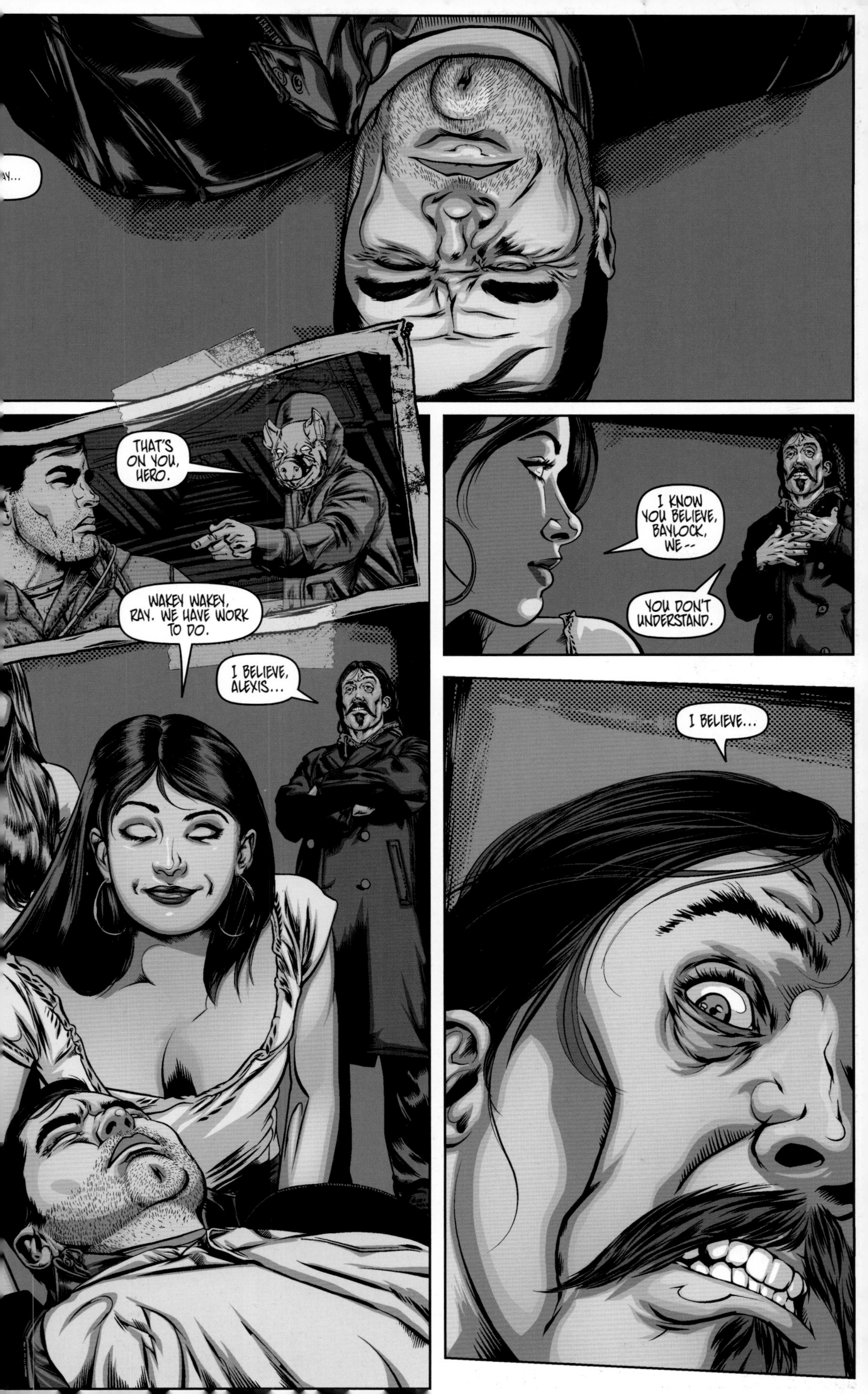
THAT'S ON YOU, HERO.
WAKEY WAKEY, RAY. WE HAVE WORK TO DO.
I BELIEVE, ALEXIS...
I KNOW YOU BELIEVE, BAYLOCK, WE--
YOU DON'T UNDERSTAND.
I BELIEVE...

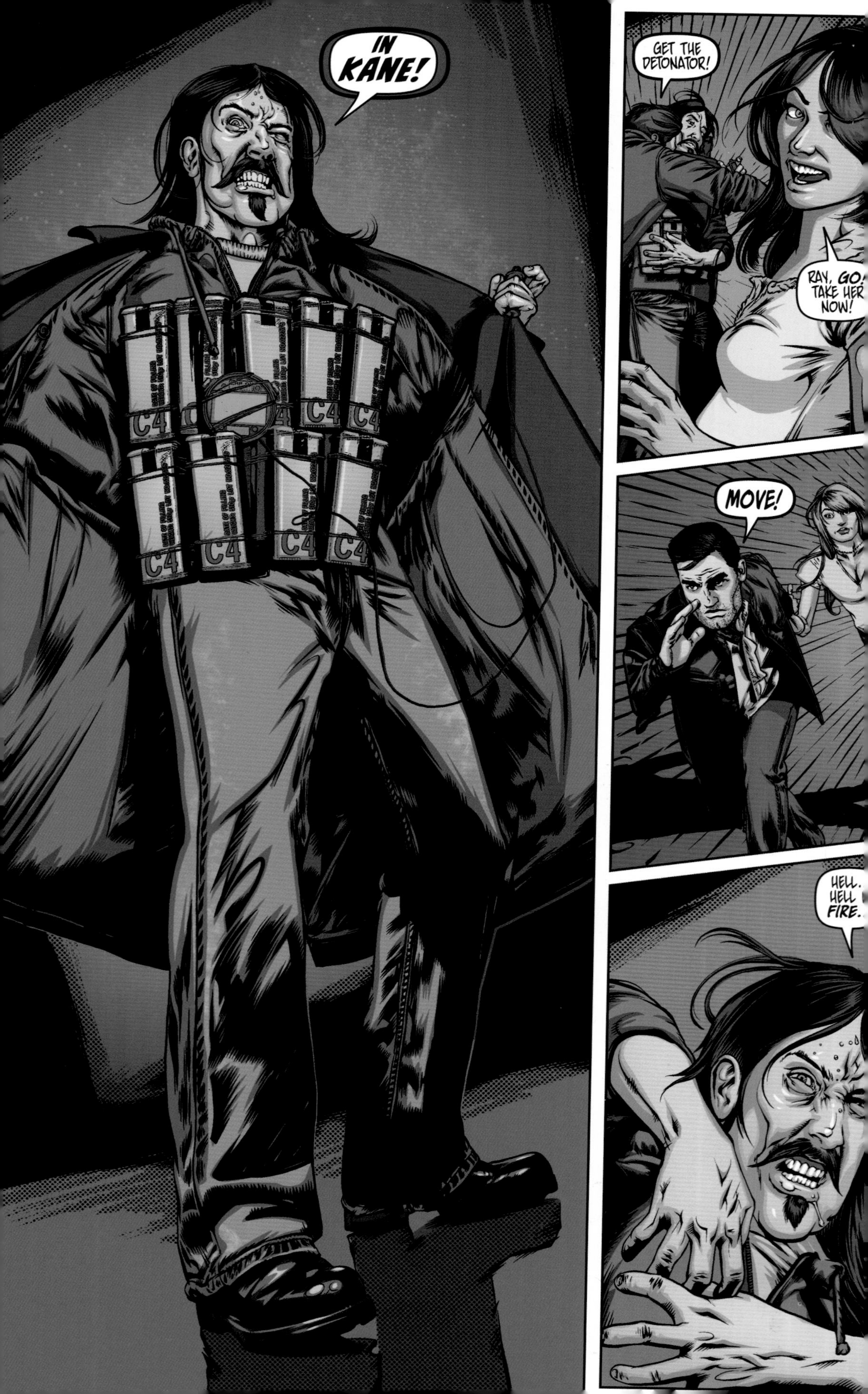
IN KANE!
GET THE DETONATOR!
RAY, GO! TAKE HER NOW!
MOVE!
HELL. HELL FIRE.

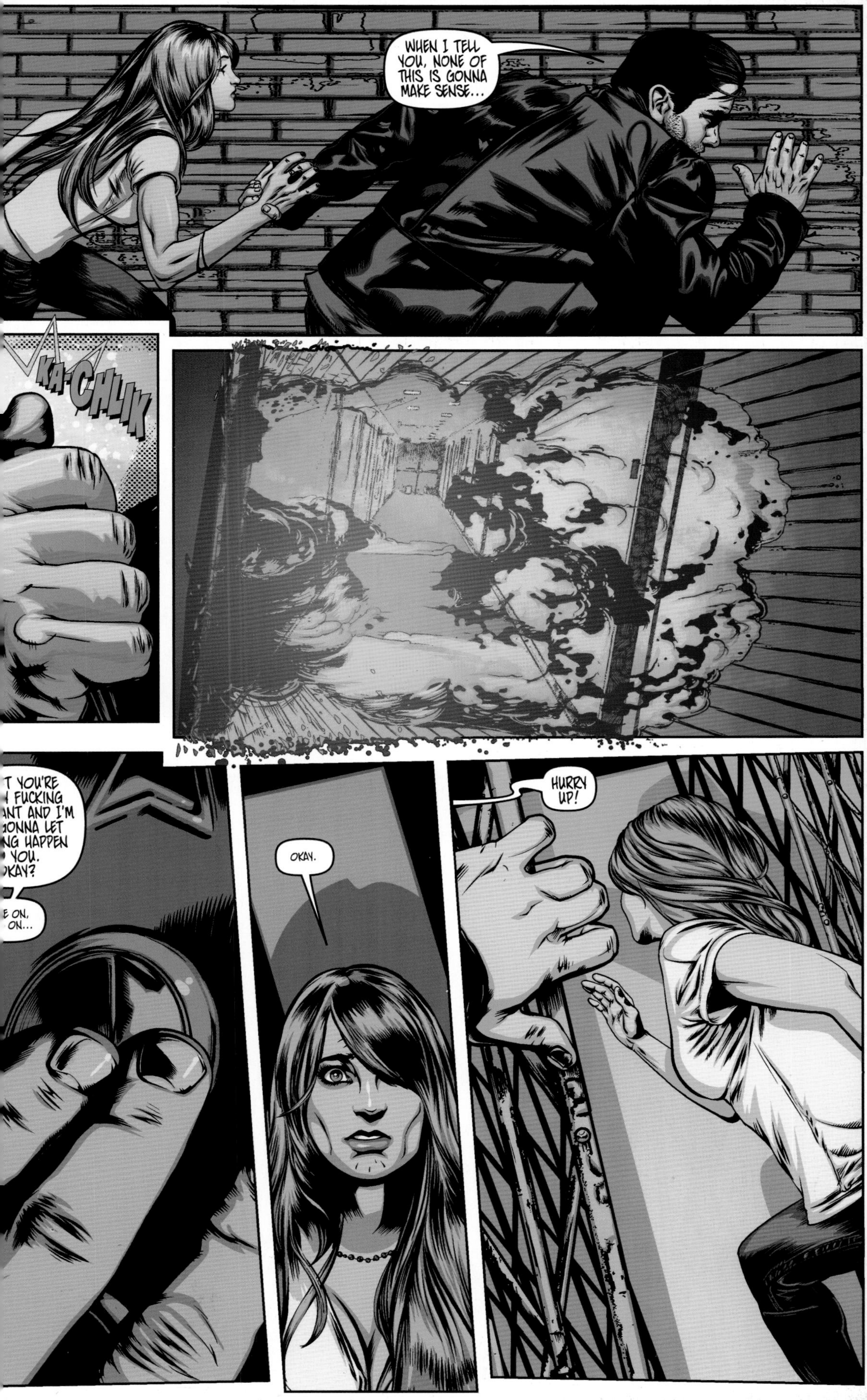
WHEN I TELL YOU, NONE OF THIS IS GONNA MAKE SENSE...
KA-CHLIK
T YOU'RE FUCKING ANT AND I'M ONNA LET NG HAPPEN YOU. OKAY?
E ON, ON...
OKAY.
HURRY UP!

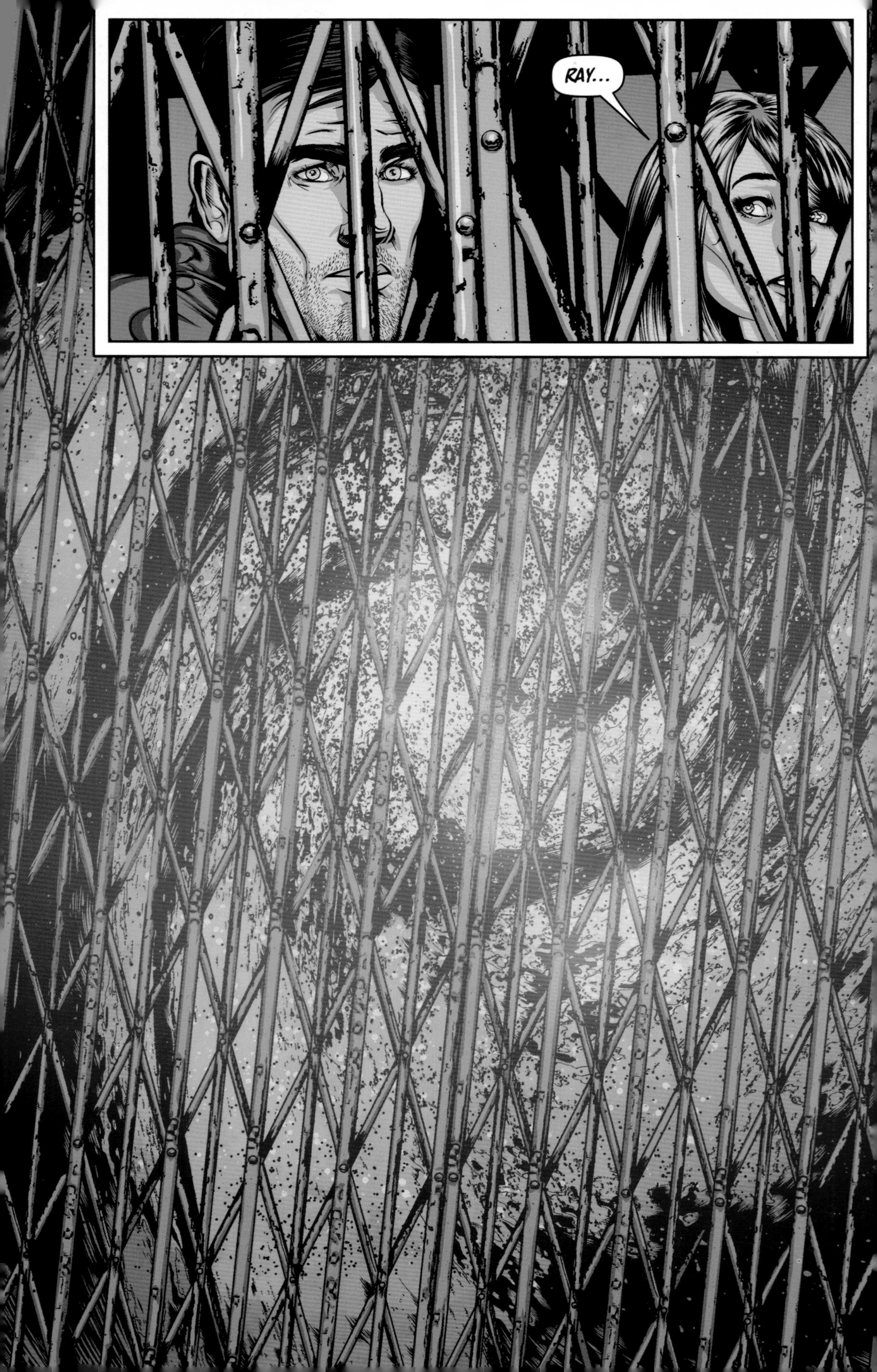
RAY...

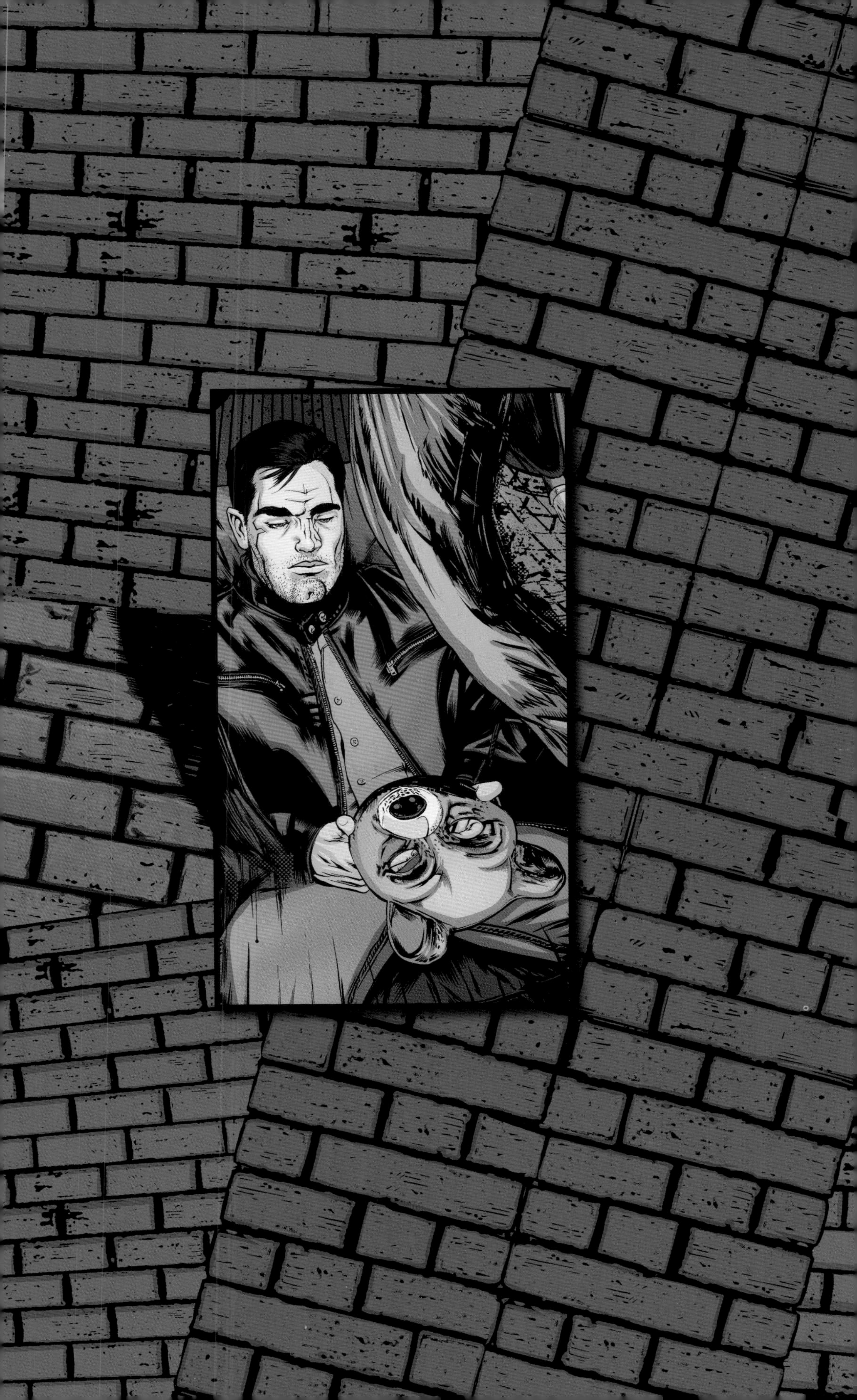

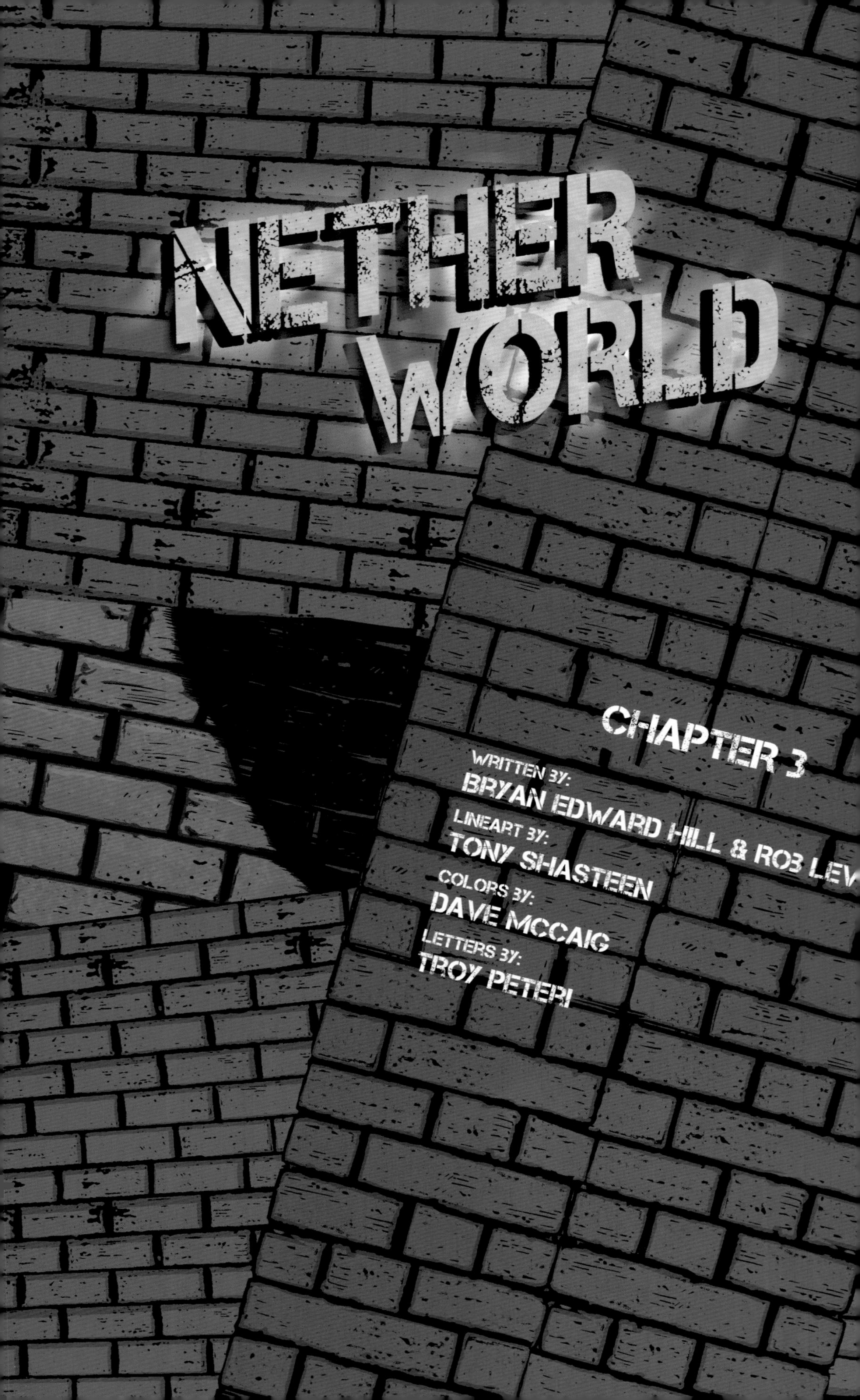
NETHER WORLD
CHAPTER 3
WRITTEN BY:
BRYAN EDWARD HILL & ROB LEV
LINEART BY:
TONY SHASTEEN
COLORS BY:
DAVE MCCAIG
LETTERS BY:
TROY PETERI

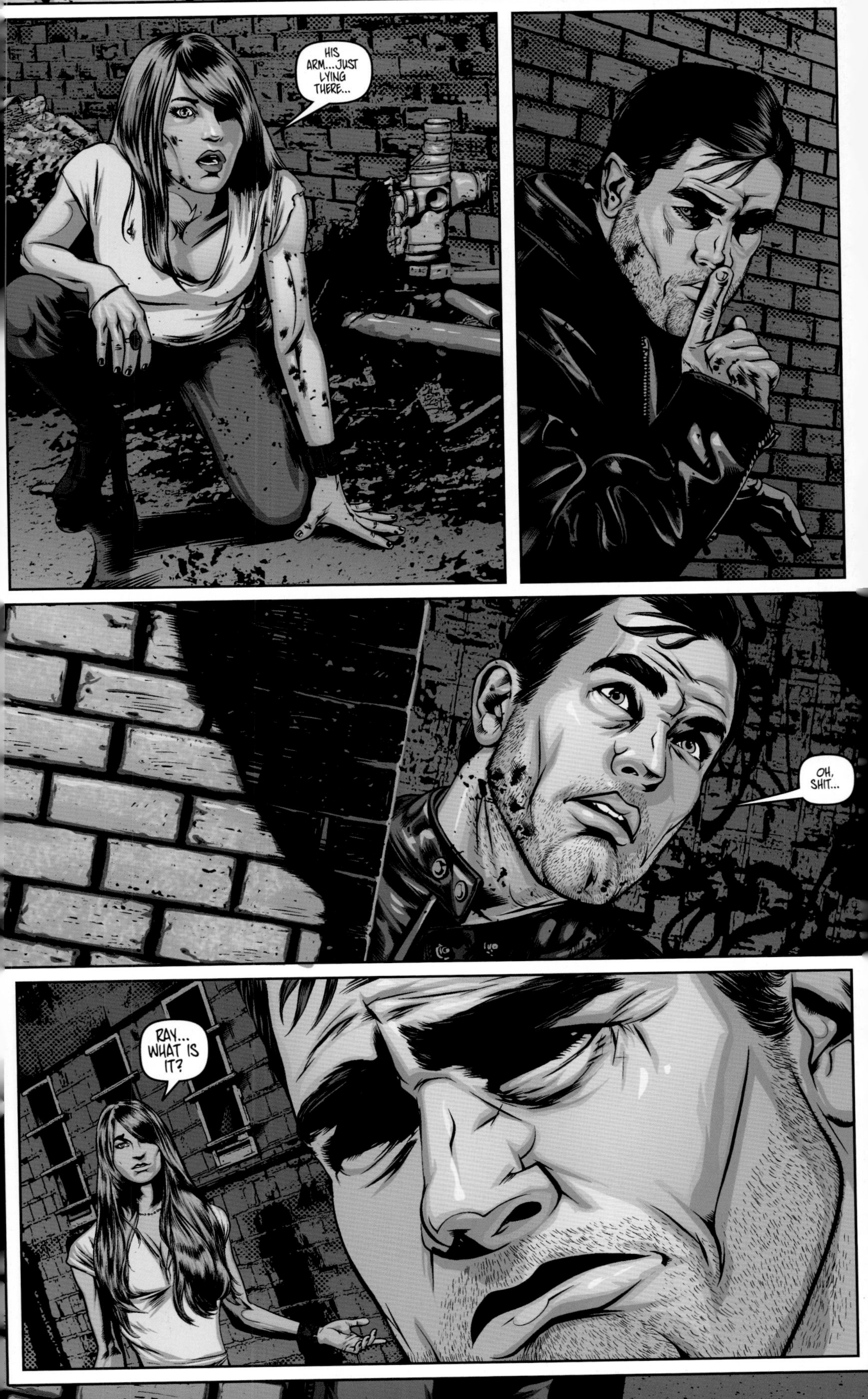
HIS ARM...JUST LYING THERE...
OH, SHIT...
RAY... WHAT IS IT?

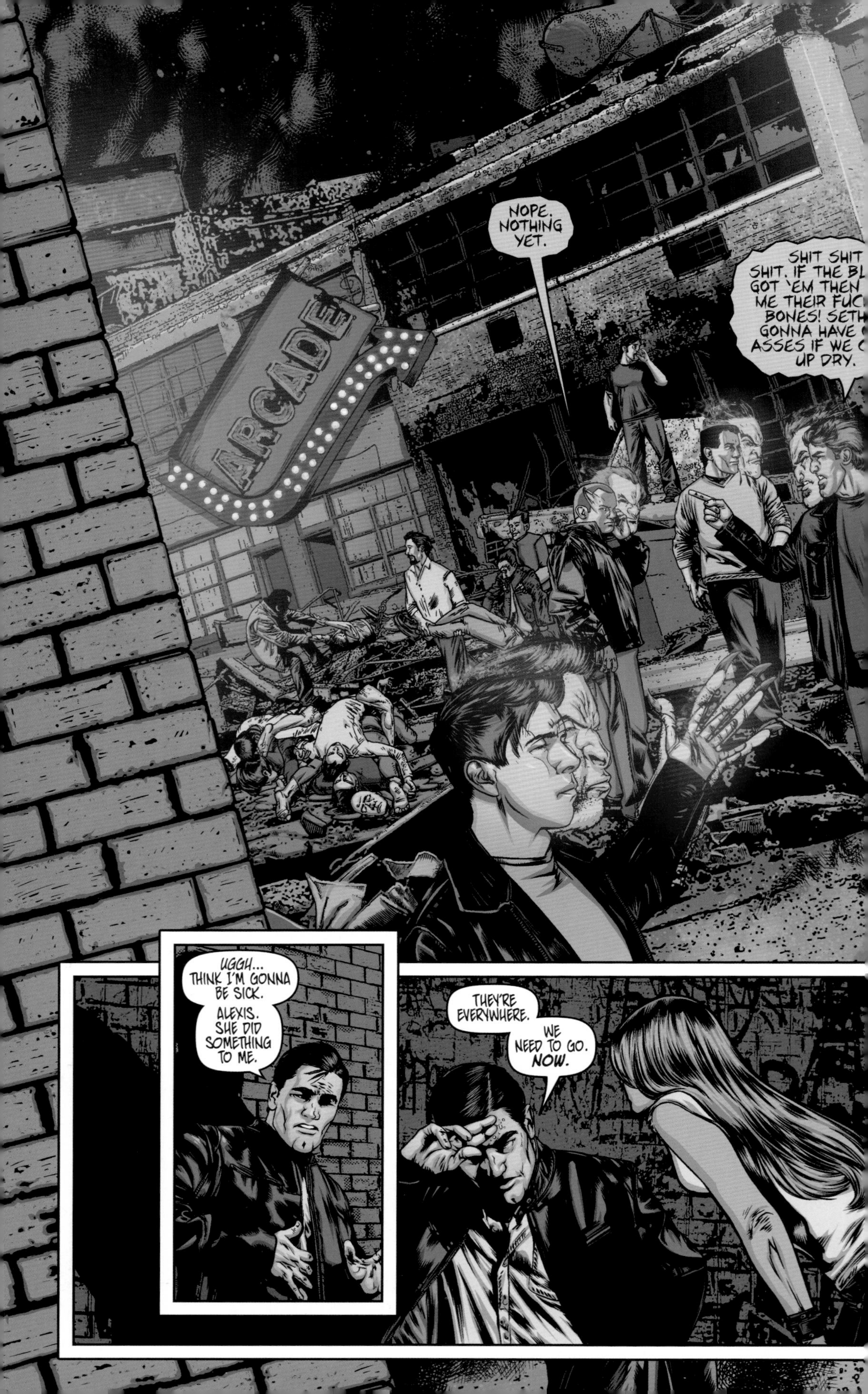

ARCADE
NOPE. NOTHING YET.
SHIT SHIT SHIT. IF THE BL GOT 'EM THEN ME THEIR FUC BONES! SETH GONNA HAVE ASSES IF WE UP DRY.
UGGH... THINK I'M GONNA BE SICK.
ALEXIS. SHE DID SOMETHING TO ME.
THEY'RE EVERYWHERE.
WE NEED TO GO. **NOW.**

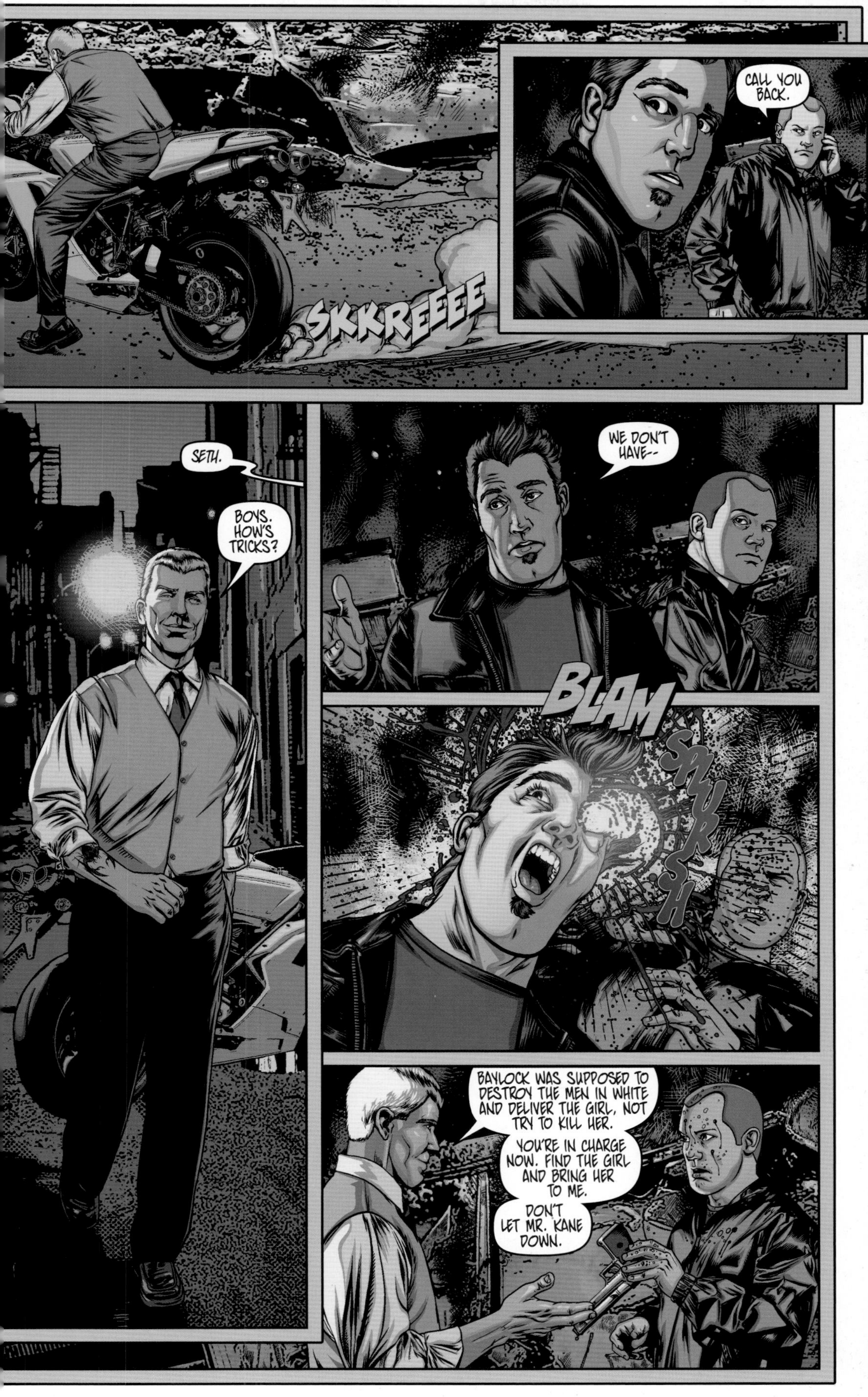
SKKREEEE
CALL YOU BACK.
SETH.
BOYS. HOW'S TRICKS?
WE DON'T HAVE--
BLAM
SPLURSH
BAYLOCK WAS SUPPOSED TO DESTROY THE MEN IN WHITE AND DELIVER THE GIRL, NOT TRY TO KILL HER.
YOU'RE IN CHARGE NOW. FIND THE GIRL AND BRING HER TO ME.
DON'T LET MR. KANE DOWN.

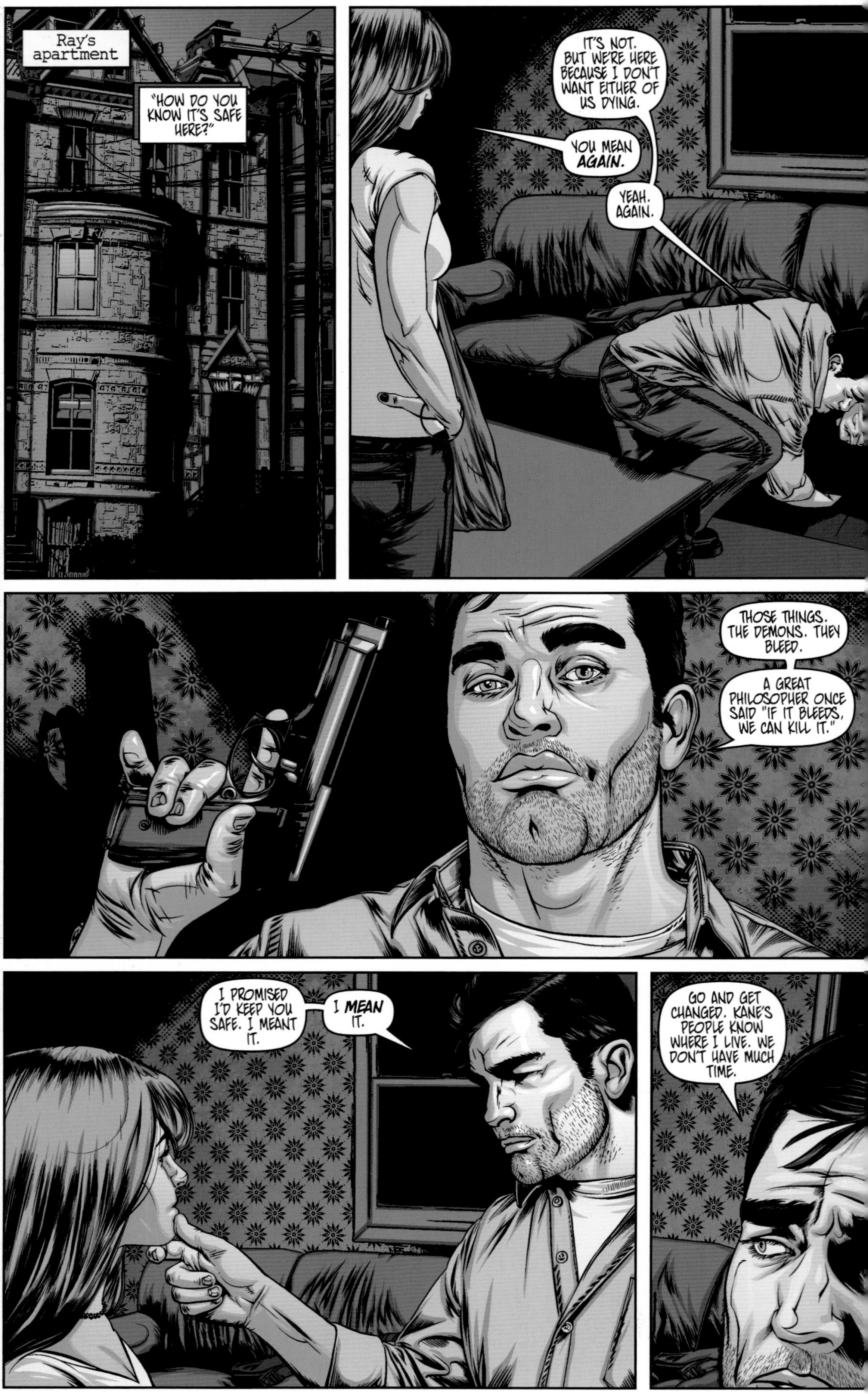
Ray's apartment
"HOW DO YOU KNOW IT'S SAFE HERE?"
IT'S NOT. BUT WE'RE HERE BECAUSE I DON'T WANT EITHER OF US DYING.
YOU MEAN **AGAIN.**
YEAH. AGAIN.
THOSE THINGS. THE DEMONS. THEY BLEED.
A GREAT PHILOSOPHER ONCE SAID "IF IT BLEEDS, WE CAN KILL IT."
I PROMISED I'D KEEP YOU SAFE. I MEANT IT.
I ***MEAN*** IT.
GO AND GET CHANGED. KANE'S PEOPLE KNOW WHERE I LIVE. WE DON'T HAVE MUCH TIME.

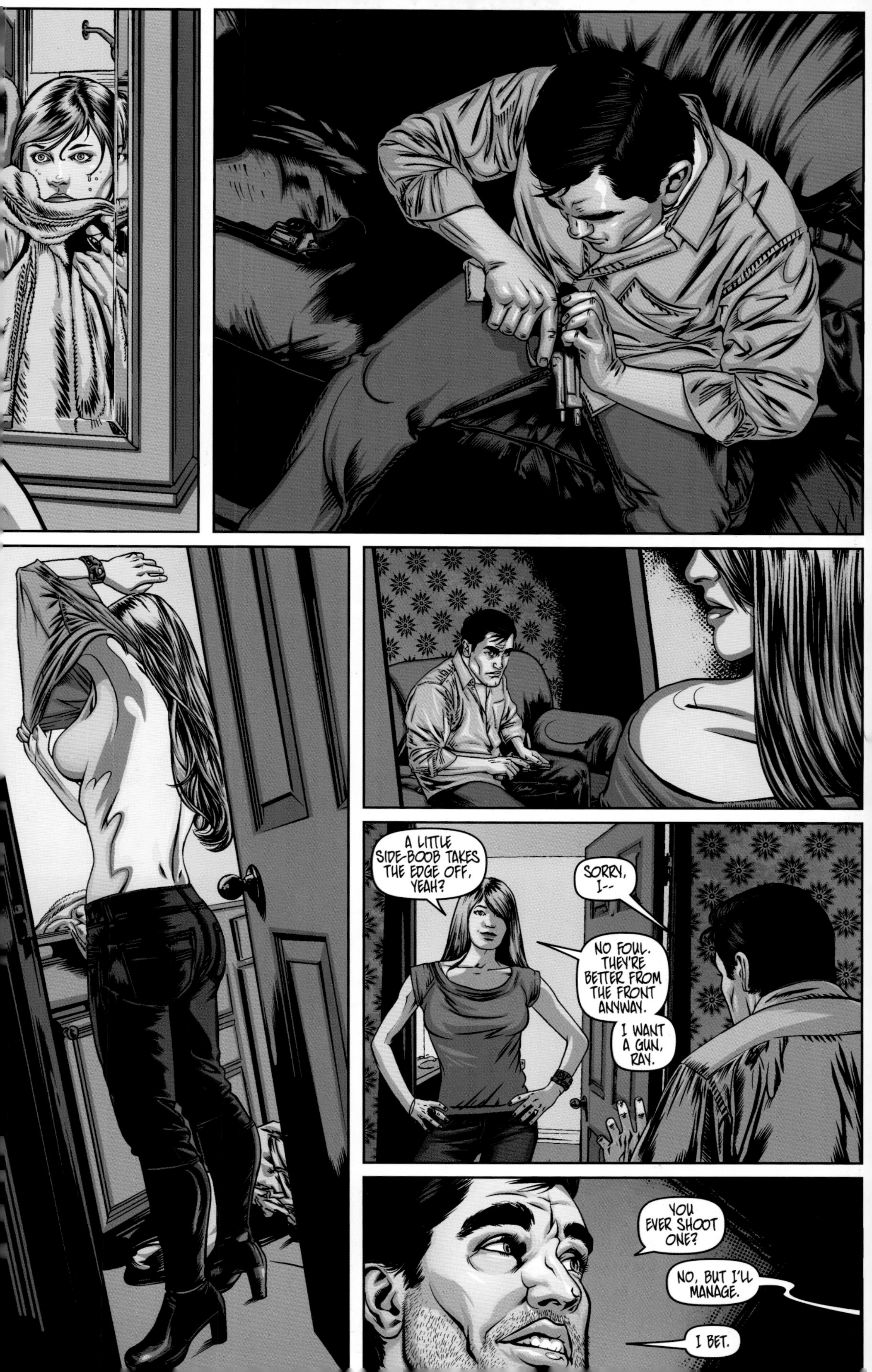
A LITTLE SIDE-BOOB TAKES THE EDGE OFF, YEAH?
SORRY, I--
NO FOUL. THEY'RE BETTER FROM THE FRONT ANYWAY.
I WANT A GUN, RAY.
YOU EVER SHOOT ONE?
NO, BUT I'LL MANAGE.
I BET.

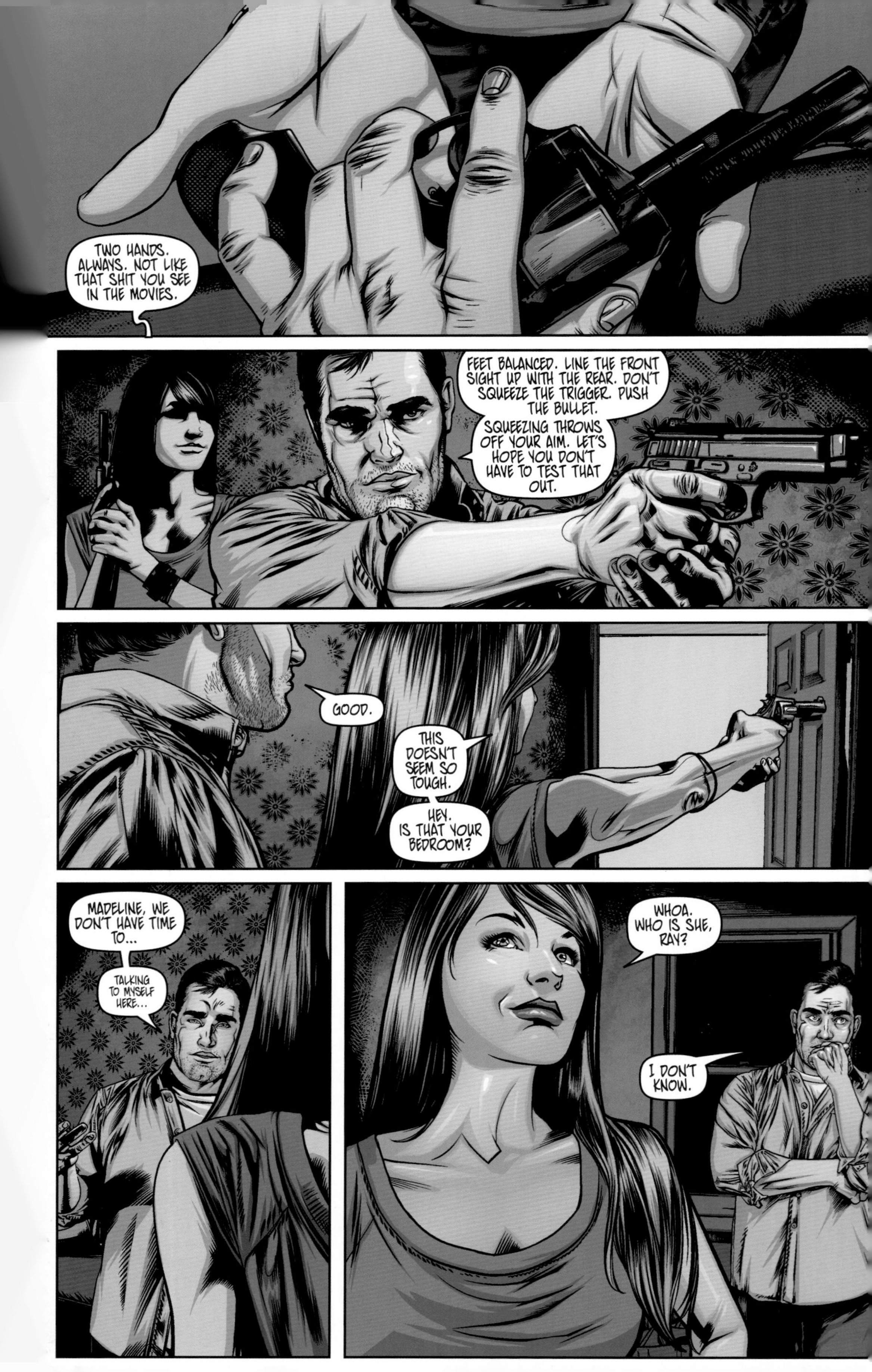
TWO HANDS. ALWAYS. NOT LIKE THAT SHIT YOU SEE IN THE MOVIES.
FEET BALANCED. LINE THE FRONT SIGHT UP WITH THE REAR. DON'T SQUEEZE THE TRIGGER. PUSH THE BULLET.
SQUEEZING THROWS OFF YOUR AIM. LET'S HOPE YOU DON'T HAVE TO TEST THAT OUT.
GOOD.
THIS DOESN'T SEEM SO TOUGH.
HEY. IS THAT YOUR BEDROOM?
MADELINE, WE DON'T HAVE TIME TO...
TALKING TO MYSELF HERE...
WHOA. WHO IS SHE, RAY?
I DON'T KNOW.

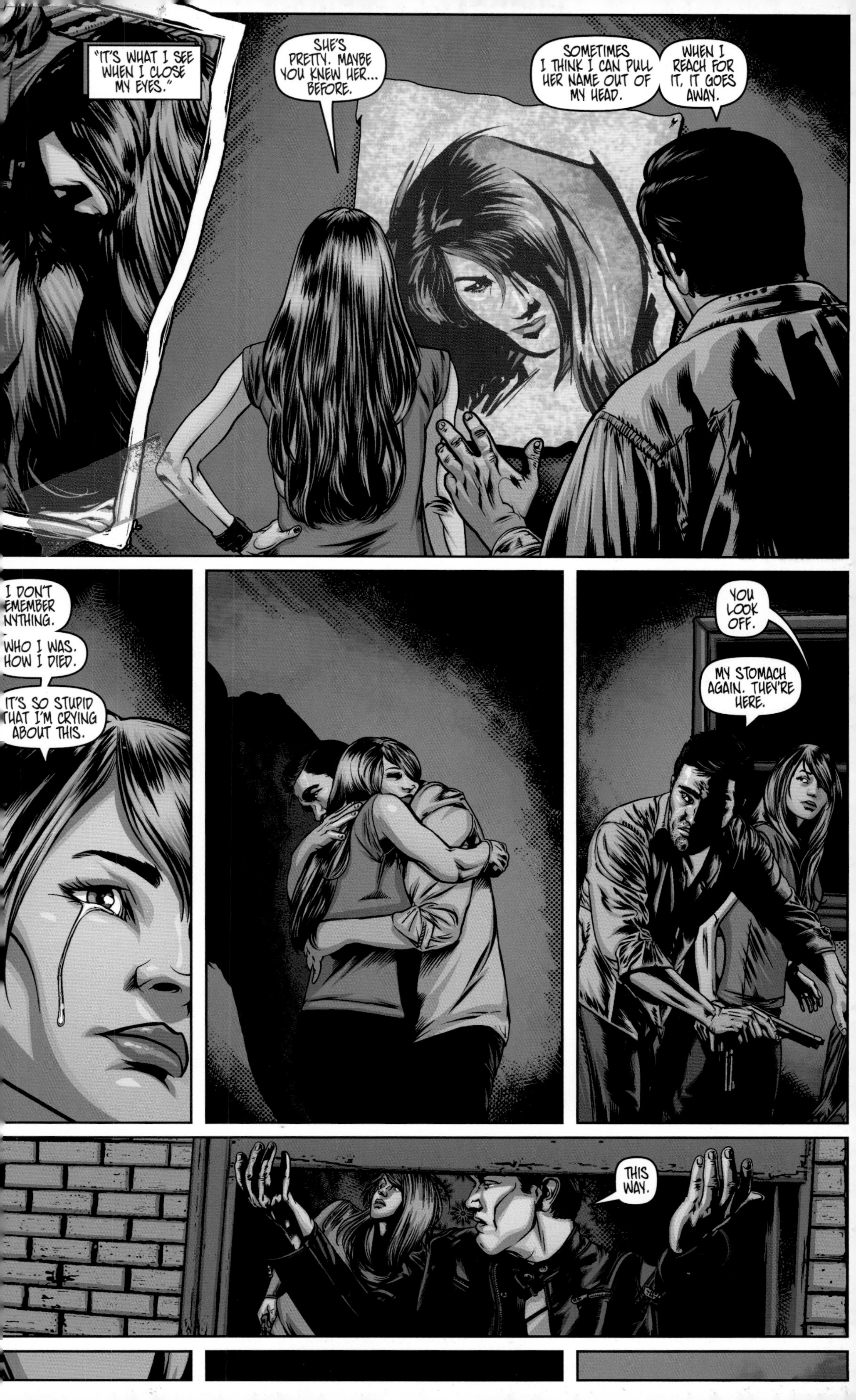
"IT'S WHAT I SEE WHEN I CLOSE MY EYES."
SHE'S PRETTY. MAYBE YOU KNEW HER... BEFORE.
SOMETIMES I THINK I CAN PULL HER NAME OUT OF MY HEAD.
WHEN I REACH FOR IT, IT GOES AWAY.
I DON'T EMEMBER NYTHING.
WHO I WAS. HOW I DIED.
IT'S SO STUPID THAT I'M CRYING ABOUT THIS.
YOU LOOK OFF.
MY STOMACH AGAIN. THEY'RE HERE.
THIS WAY.

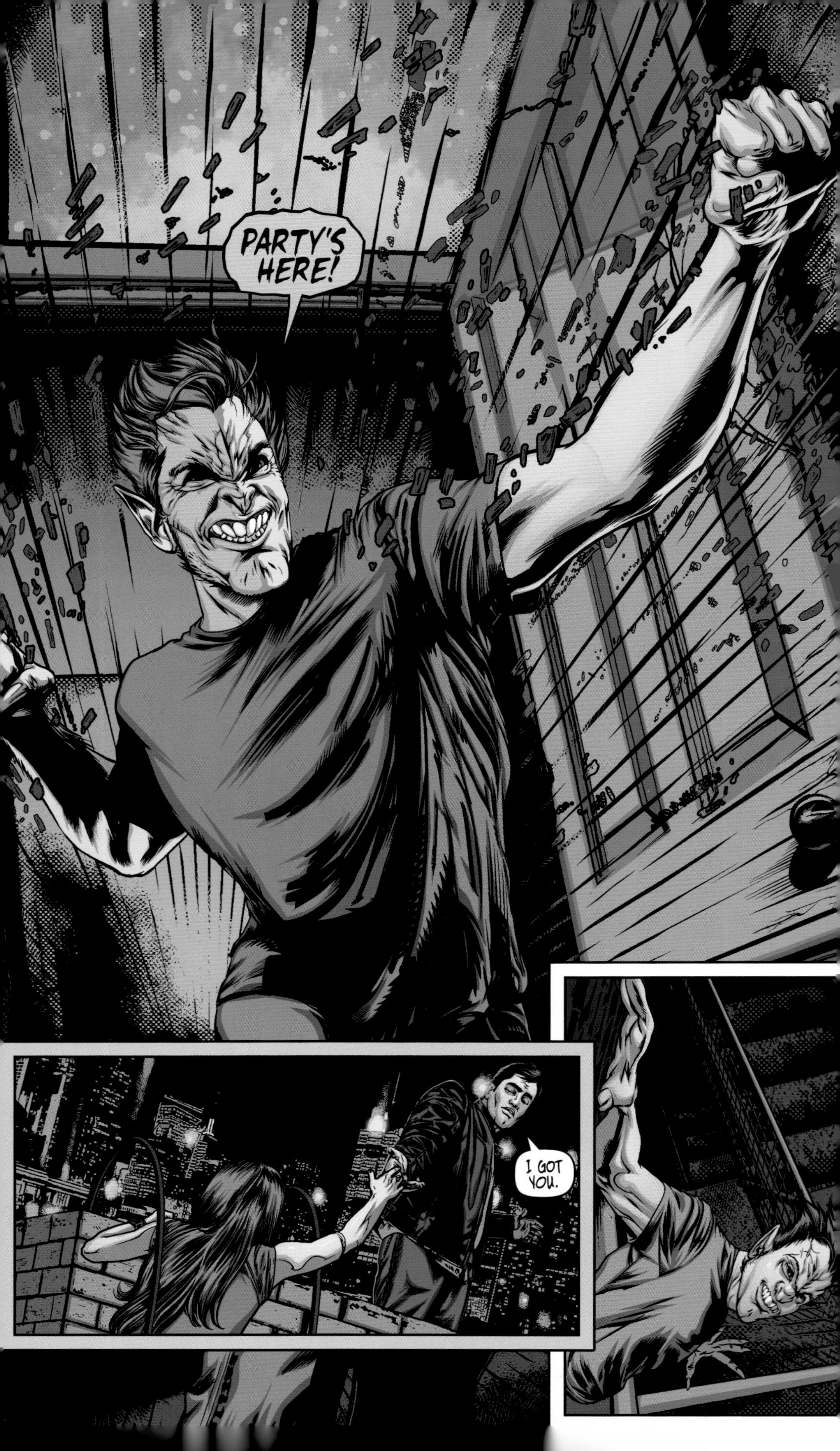
PARTY'S HERE!
I GOT YOU.

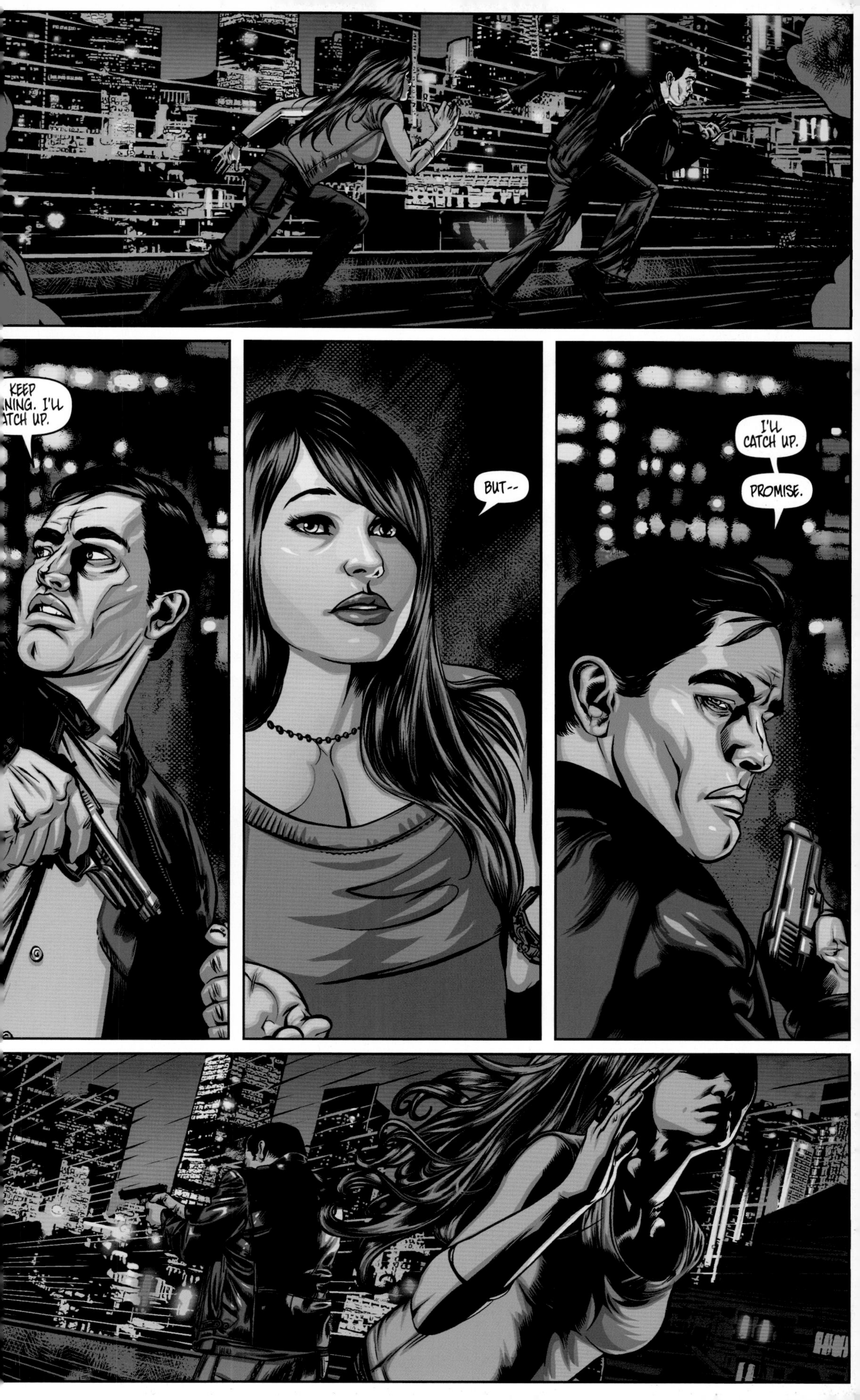
KEEP
NING. I'LL
ATCH UP.
BUT--
I'LL CATCH UP.
PROMISE.

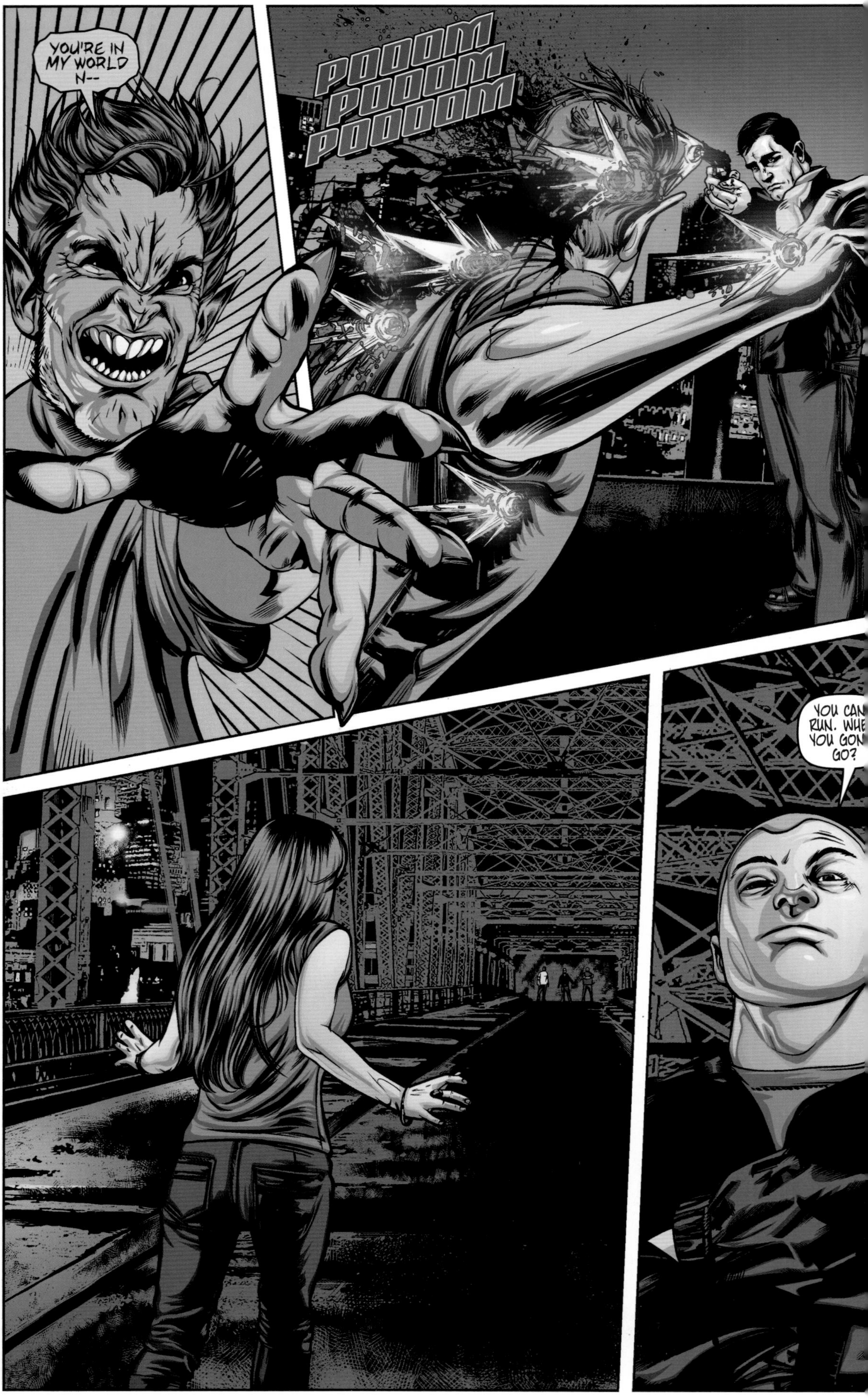

YOU'RE IN MY WORLD N--
POOOOM POOOOM POOOOM
YOU CAN
RUN. WHE
YOU GON
GO?

FUUUUUUUCK...

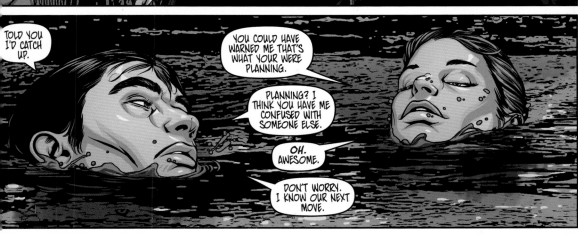

TOLD YOU I'D CATCH UP.

YOU COULD HAVE WARNED ME THAT'S WHAT YOUR WERE PLANNING.

PLANNING? I THINK YOU HAVE ME CONFUSED WITH SOMEONE ELSE.

OH. AWESOME.

DON'T WORRY. I KNOW OUR NEXT MOVE.

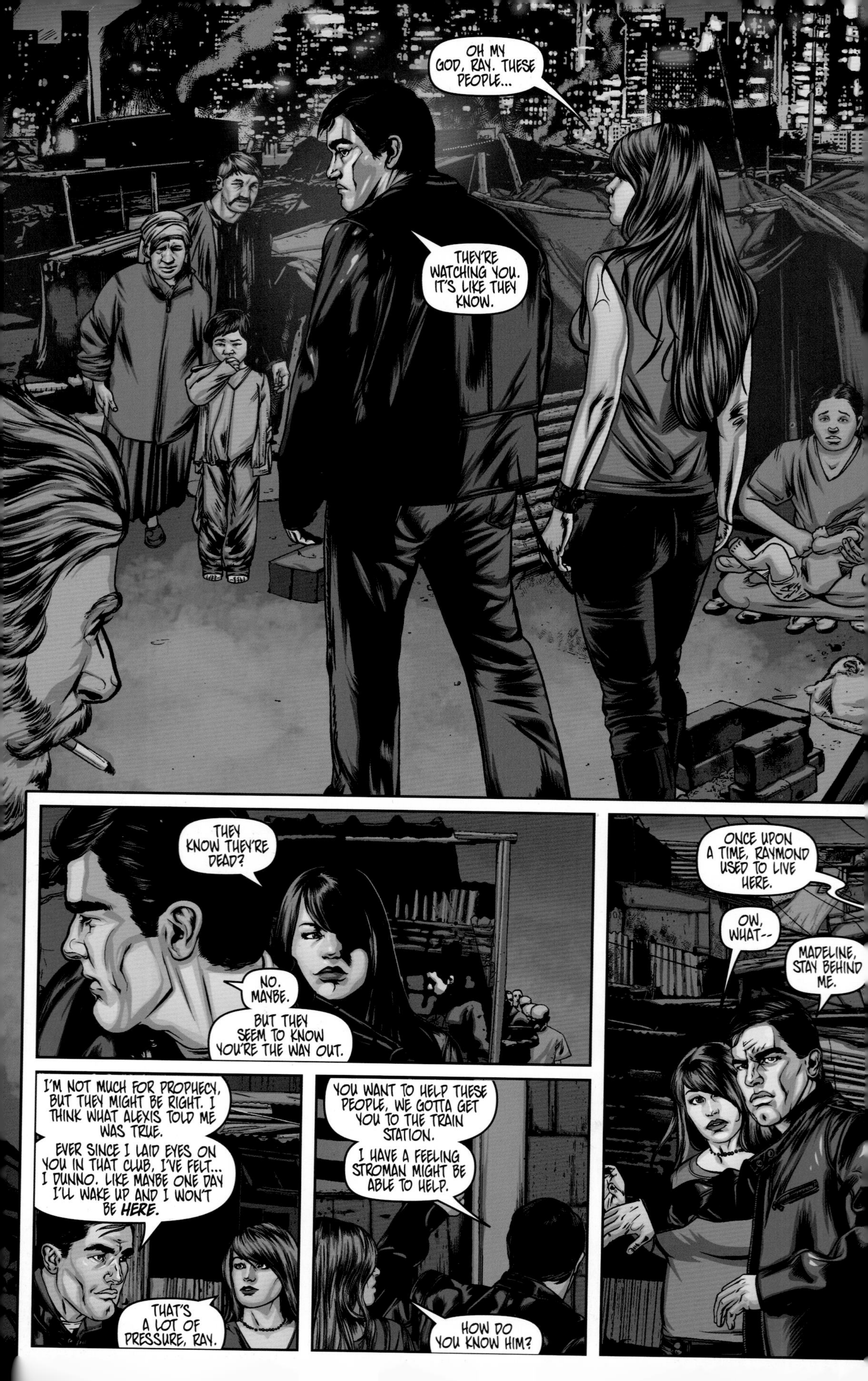
OH MY GOD, RAY. THESE PEOPLE...
THEY'RE WATCHING YOU. IT'S LIKE THEY KNOW.
THEY KNOW THEY'RE DEAD?
NO. MAYBE.
BUT THEY SEEM TO KNOW YOU'RE THE WAY OUT.
ONCE UPON A TIME, RAYMOND USED TO LIVE HERE.
OW, WHAT--
MADELINE, STAY BEHIND ME.
I'M NOT MUCH FOR PROPHECY, BUT THEY MIGHT BE RIGHT. I THINK WHAT ALEXIS TOLD ME WAS TRUE.
EVER SINCE I LAID EYES ON YOU IN THAT CLUB, I'VE FELT... I DUNNO. LIKE MAYBE ONE DAY I'LL WAKE UP AND I WON'T BE **HERE**.
THAT'S A LOT OF PRESSURE, RAY.
YOU WANT TO HELP THESE PEOPLE, WE GOTTA GET YOU TO THE TRAIN STATION.
I HAVE A FEELING STROMAN MIGHT BE ABLE TO HELP.
HOW DO YOU KNOW HIM?

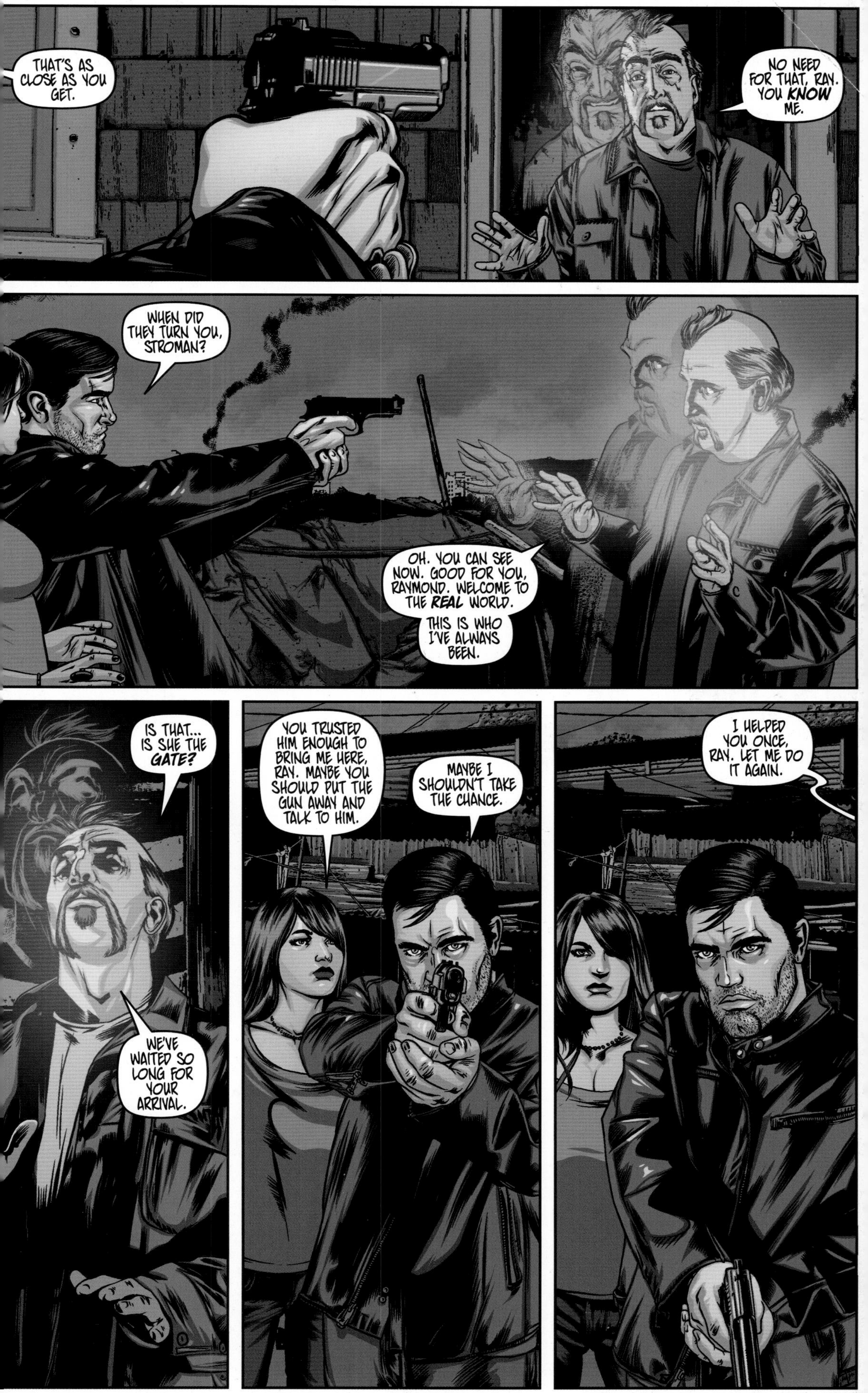
THAT'S AS CLOSE AS YOU GET.
NO NEED FOR THAT, RAY. YOU KNOW ME.
WHEN DID THEY TURN YOU, STROMAN?
OH. YOU CAN SEE NOW. GOOD FOR YOU, RAYMOND. WELCOME TO THE REAL WORLD.
THIS IS WHO I'VE ALWAYS BEEN.
IS THAT... IS SHE THE GATE?
WE'VE WAITED SO LONG FOR YOUR ARRIVAL.
YOU TRUSTED HIM ENOUGH TO BRING ME HERE, RAY. MAYBE YOU SHOULD PUT THE GUN AWAY AND TALK TO HIM.
MAYBE I SHOULDN'T TAKE THE CHANCE.
I HELPED YOU ONCE, RAY. LET ME DO IT AGAIN.

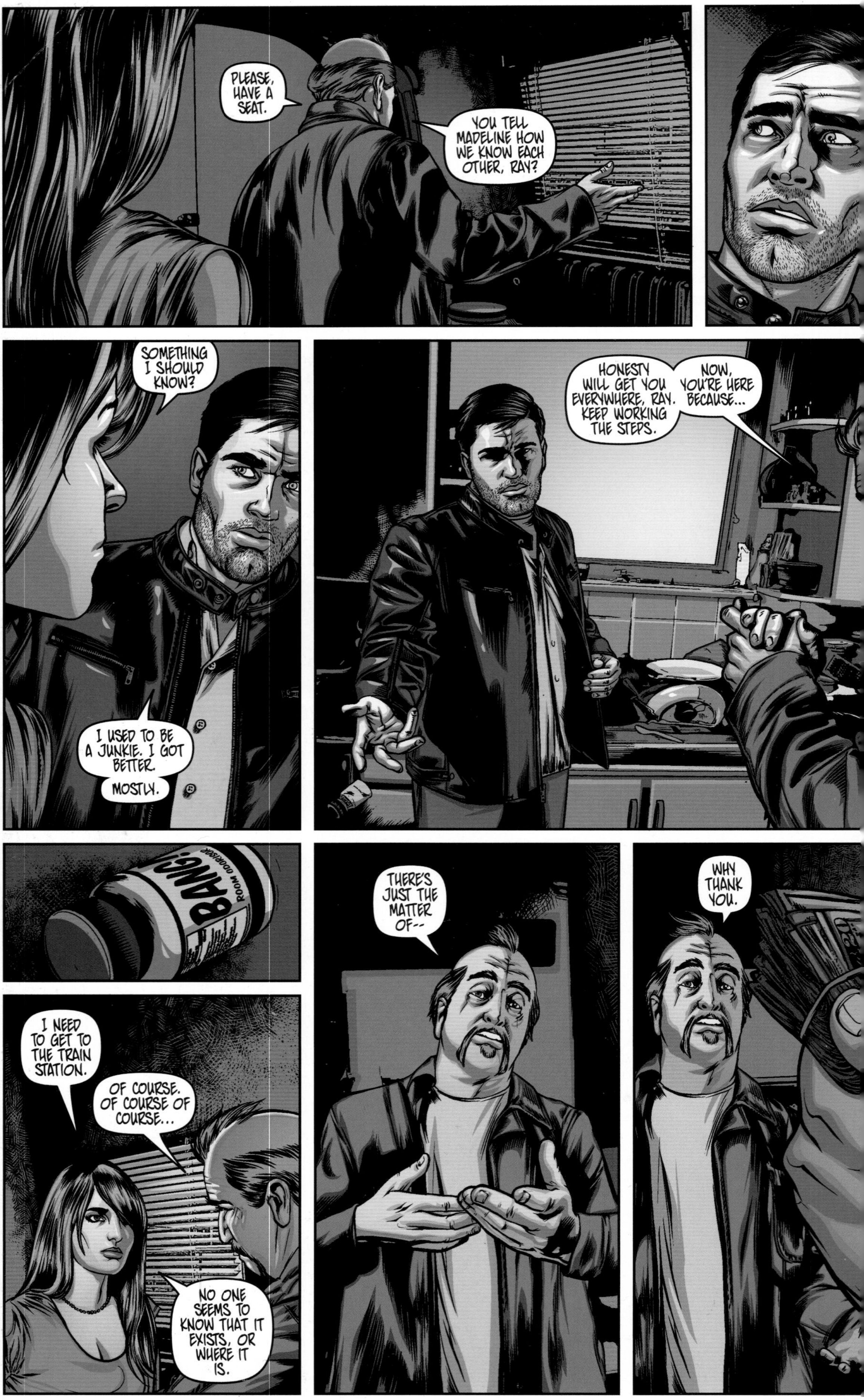
PLEASE, HAVE A SEAT.
YOU TELL MADELINE HOW WE KNOW EACH OTHER, RAY?
SOMETHING I SHOULD KNOW?
I USED TO BE A JUNKIE. I GOT BETTER.
MOSTLY.
HONESTY WILL GET YOU EVERYWHERE, RAY. KEEP WORKING THE STEPS.
NOW, YOU'RE HERE BECAUSE...
BANG!
I NEED TO GET TO THE TRAIN STATION.
OF COURSE. OF COURSE OF COURSE...
NO ONE SEEMS TO KNOW THAT IT EXISTS, OR WHERE IT IS.
THERE'S JUST THE MATTER OF--
WHY THANK YOU.

JUST A MOMENT...

DAMN... I REMEMBER WHEN SHE ACTUALLY LOOKED LIKE THIS. THIS WAS BEFORE.

BEFORE *KANE*. WHEN THIS PLACE FUNCTIONED THE WAY IT WAS SUPPOSED TO.

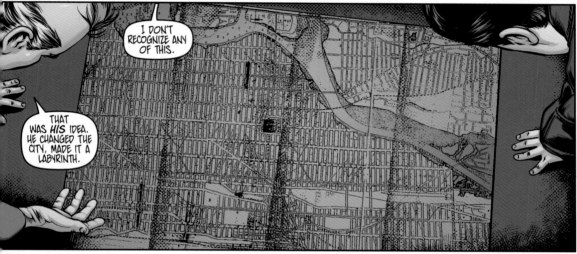

I DON'T RECOGNIZE ANY OF THIS.

THAT WAS *HIS* IDEA. HE CHANGED THE CITY, MADE IT A LABYRINTH.

THANKS, STROMAN. WE'LL FIGURE IT OUT FROM HERE.

I UNDERSTAND, RAYMOND. AND REMEMBER...

ONE DAY AT A TIME.

REDEMPTION IS POSSIBLE FOR ANYONE. EVEN *YOU.*

RAY!

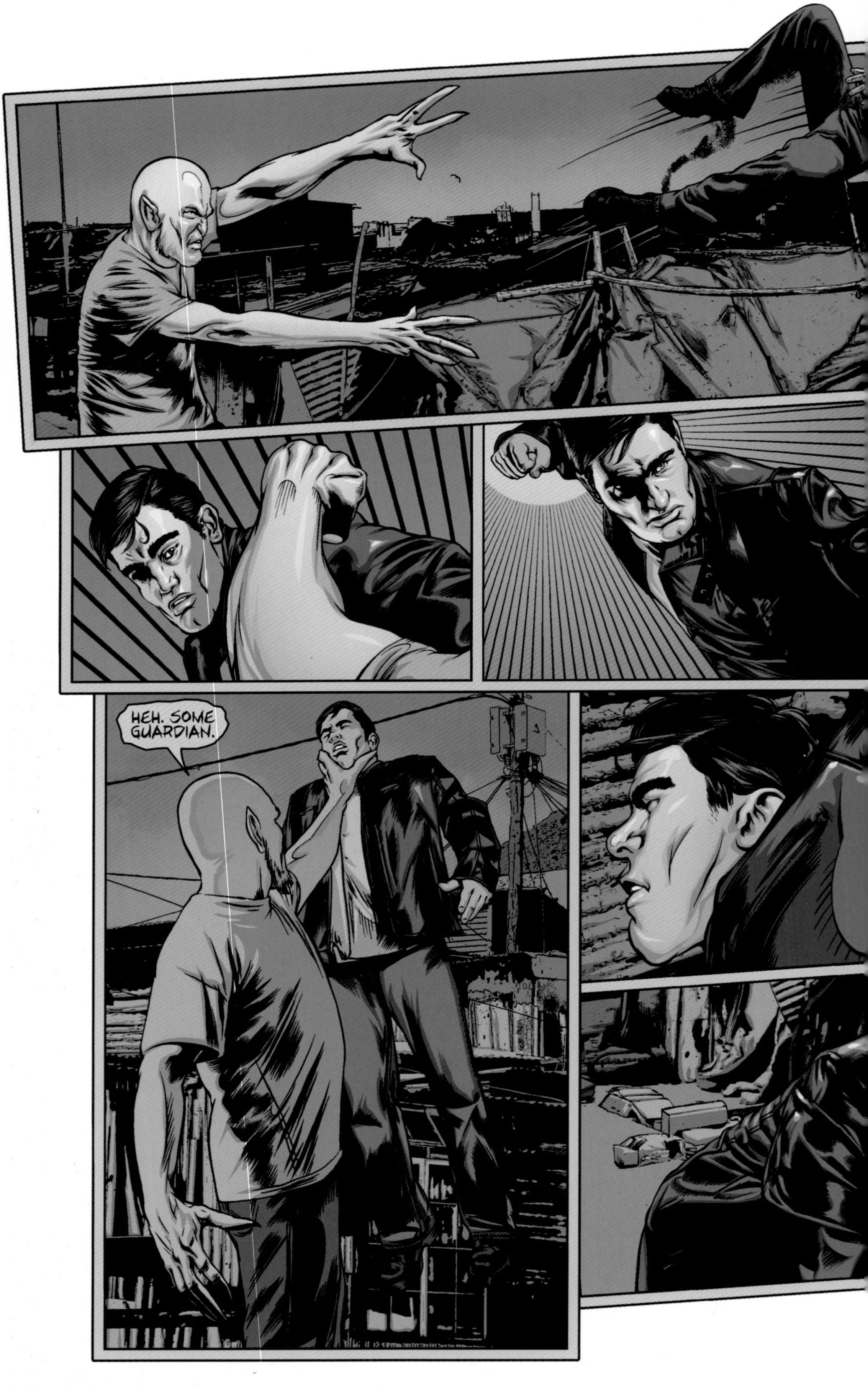
HEH. SOME GUARDIAN.

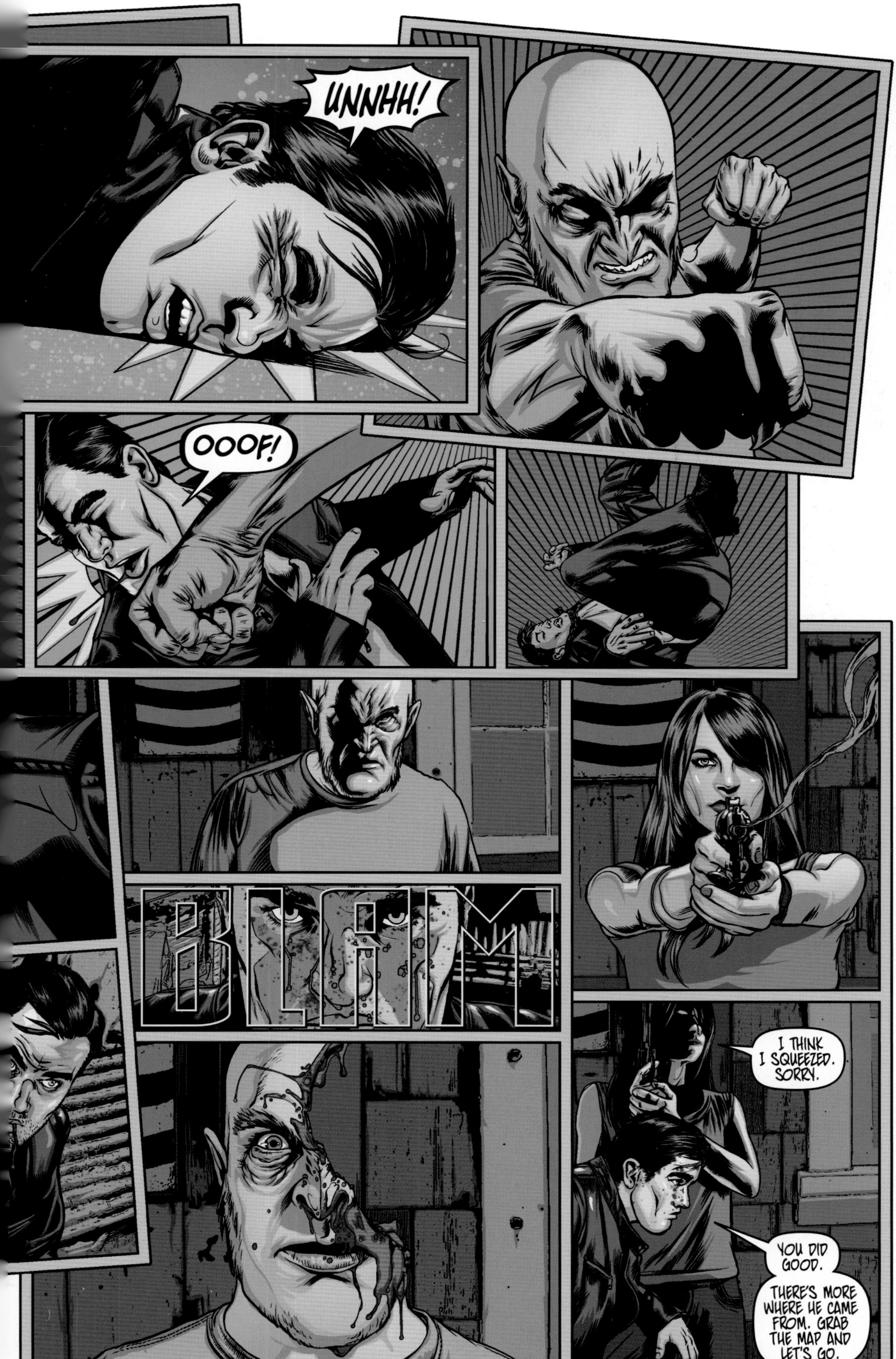
UNNHH!
OOOF!
BLAM
I THINK I SQUEEZED. SORRY.
YOU DID GOOD.
THERE'S MORE WHERE HE CAME FROM. GRAB THE MAP AND LET'S GO.

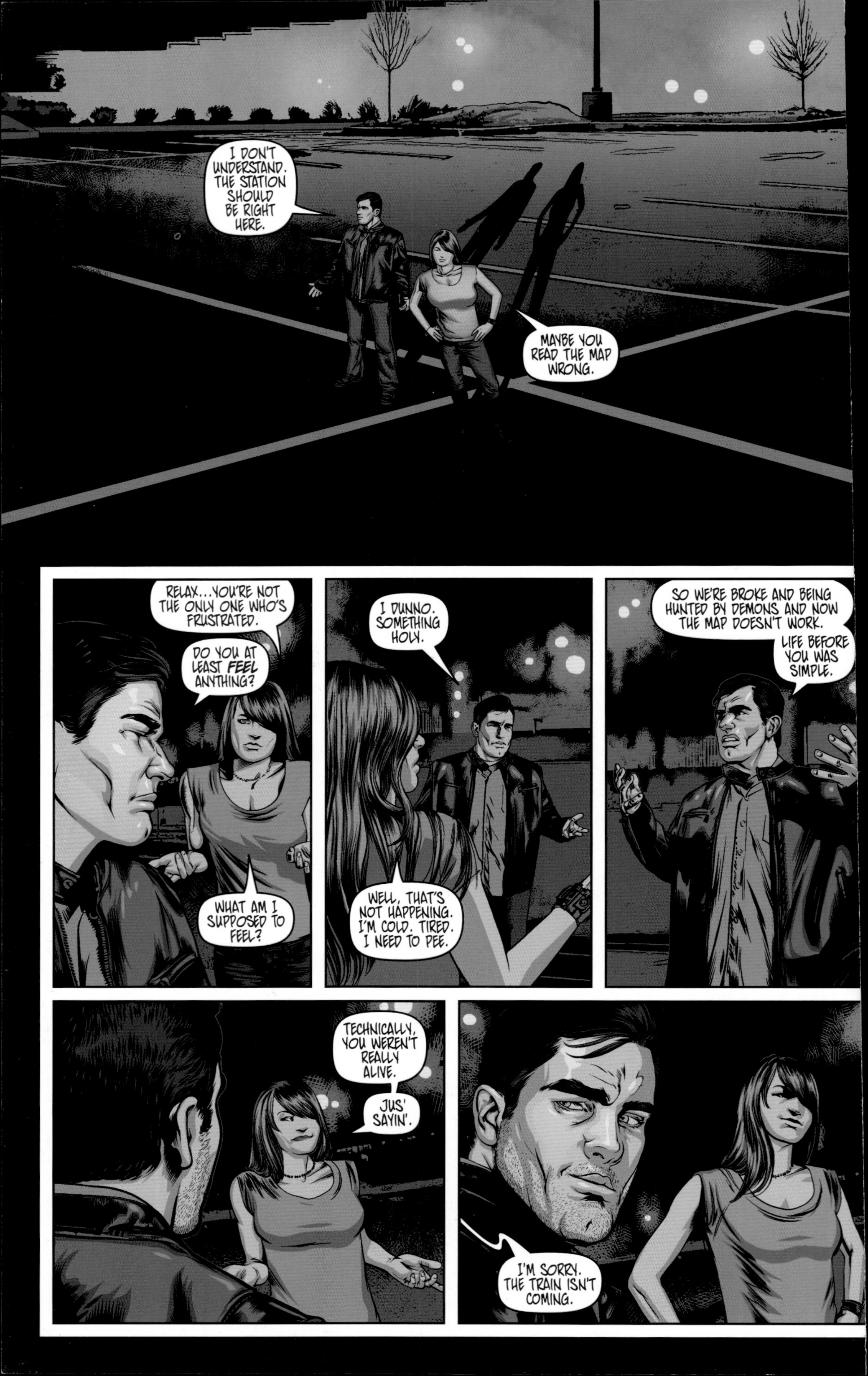
I DON'T UNDERSTAND. THE STATION SHOULD BE RIGHT HERE.
MAYBE YOU READ THE MAP WRONG.
RELAX...YOU'RE NOT THE ONLY ONE WHO'S FRUSTRATED.
DO YOU AT LEAST FEEL ANYTHING?
WHAT AM I SUPPOSED TO FEEL?
I DUNNO. SOMETHING HOLY.
WELL, THAT'S NOT HAPPENING. I'M COLD. TIRED. I NEED TO PEE.
SO WE'RE BROKE AND BEING HUNTED BY DEMONS AND NOW THE MAP DOESN'T WORK.
LIFE BEFORE YOU WAS SIMPLE.
TECHNICALLY, YOU WEREN'T REALLY ALIVE.
JUS' SAYIN'.
I'M SORRY. THE TRAIN ISN'T COMING.

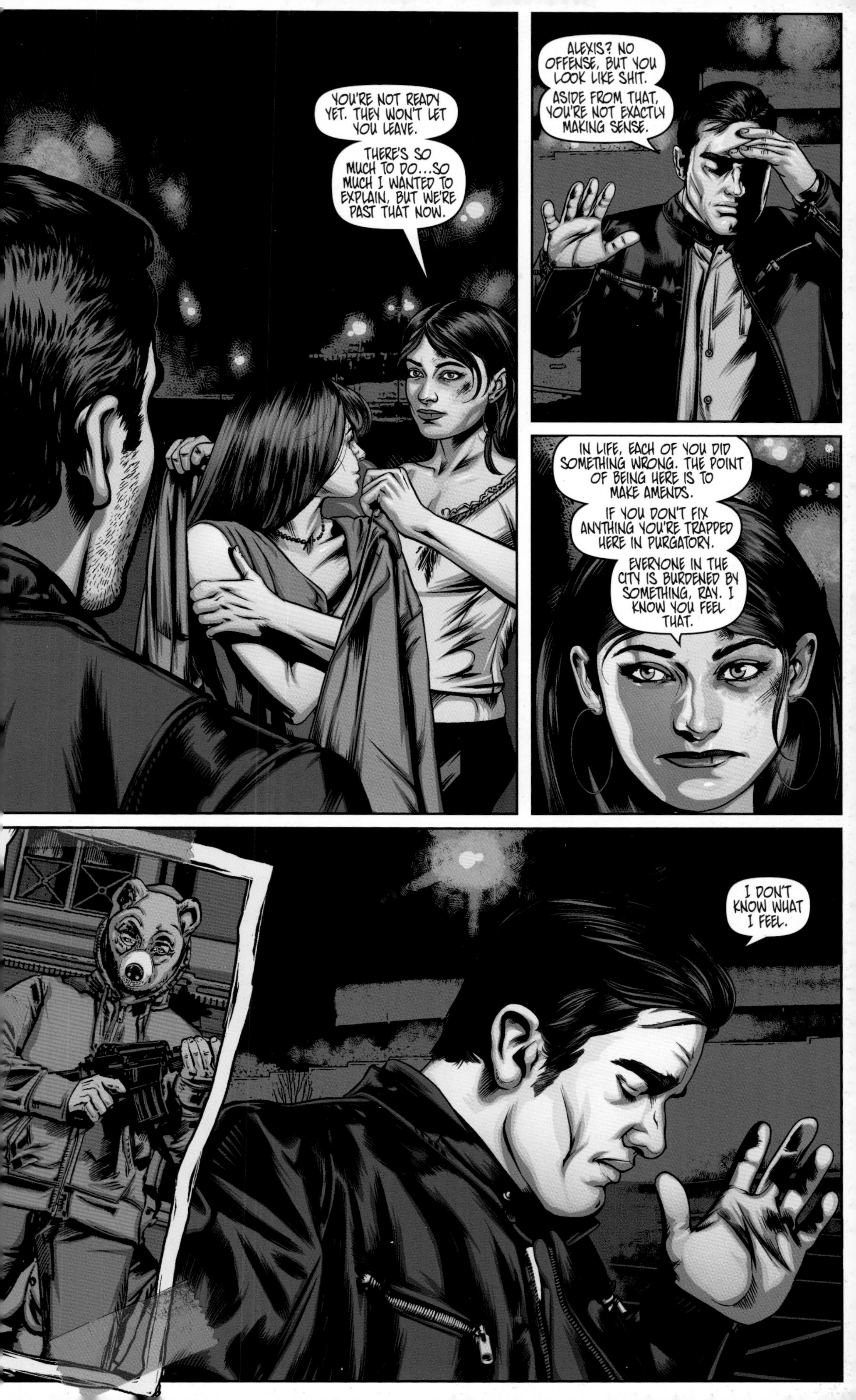
YOU'RE NOT READY YET. THEY WON'T LET YOU LEAVE.
THERE'S SO MUCH TO DO...SO MUCH I WANTED TO EXPLAIN, BUT WE'RE PAST THAT NOW.
ALEXIS? NO OFFENSE, BUT YOU LOOK LIKE SHIT.
ASIDE FROM THAT, YOU'RE NOT EXACTLY MAKING SENSE.
IN LIFE, EACH OF YOU DID SOMETHING WRONG. THE POINT OF BEING HERE IS TO MAKE AMENDS.
IF YOU DON'T FIX ANYTHING YOU'RE TRAPPED HERE IN PURGATORY.
EVERYONE IN THE CITY IS BURDENED BY SOMETHING, RAY. I KNOW YOU FEEL THAT.
I DON'T KNOW WHAT I FEEL.

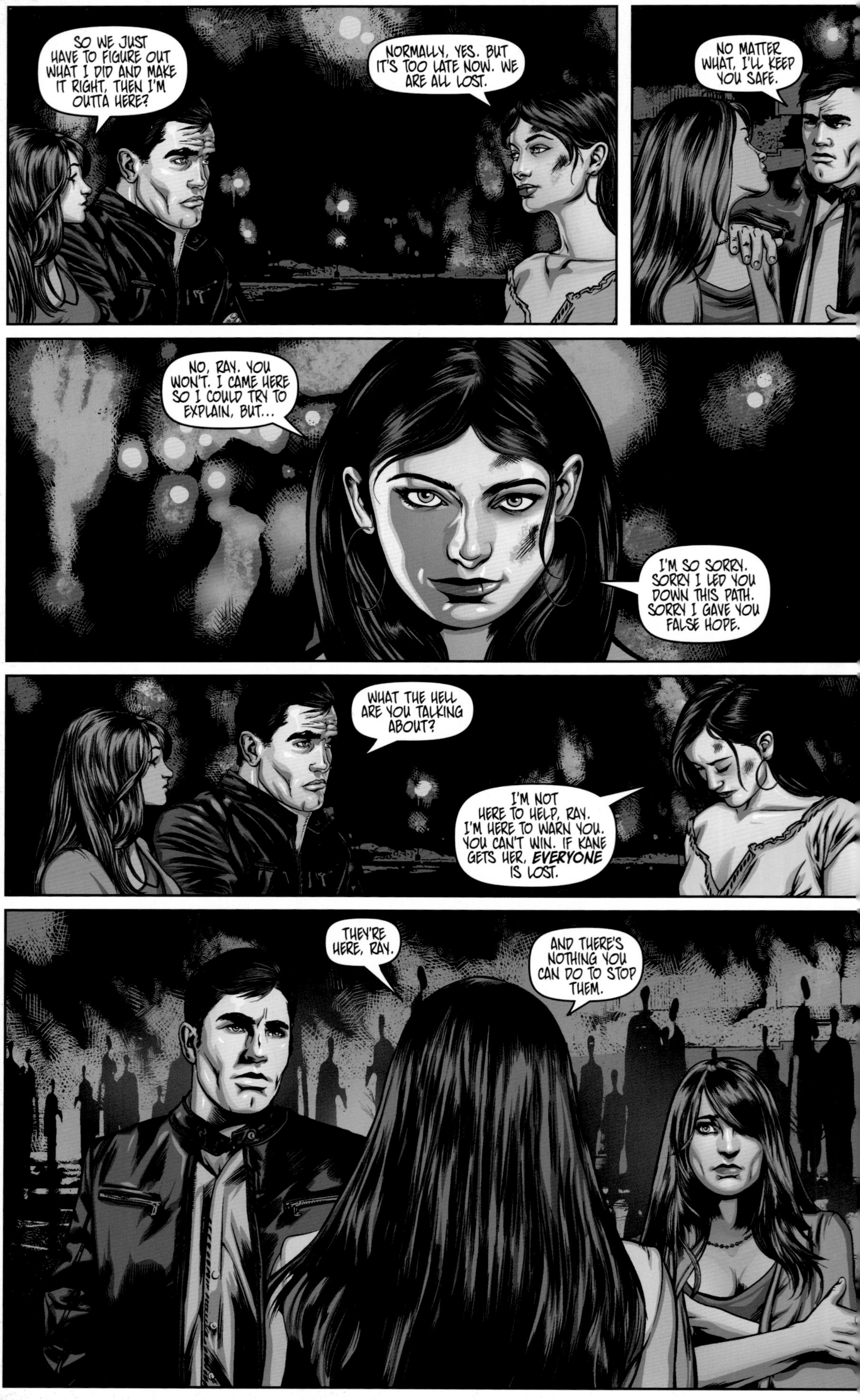
SO WE JUST HAVE TO FIGURE OUT WHAT I DID AND MAKE IT RIGHT, THEN I'M OUTTA HERE?
NORMALLY, YES. BUT IT'S TOO LATE NOW. WE ARE ALL LOST.
NO MATTER WHAT, I'LL KEEP YOU SAFE.
NO, RAY. YOU WON'T. I CAME HERE SO I COULD TRY TO EXPLAIN, BUT...
I'M SO SORRY. SORRY I LED YOU DOWN THIS PATH. SORRY I GAVE YOU FALSE HOPE.
WHAT THE HELL ARE YOU TALKING ABOUT?
I'M NOT HERE TO HELP, RAY. I'M HERE TO WARN YOU. YOU CAN'T WIN. IF KANE GETS HER, EVERYONE IS LOST.
THEY'RE HERE, RAY.
AND THERE'S NOTHING YOU CAN DO TO STOP THEM.

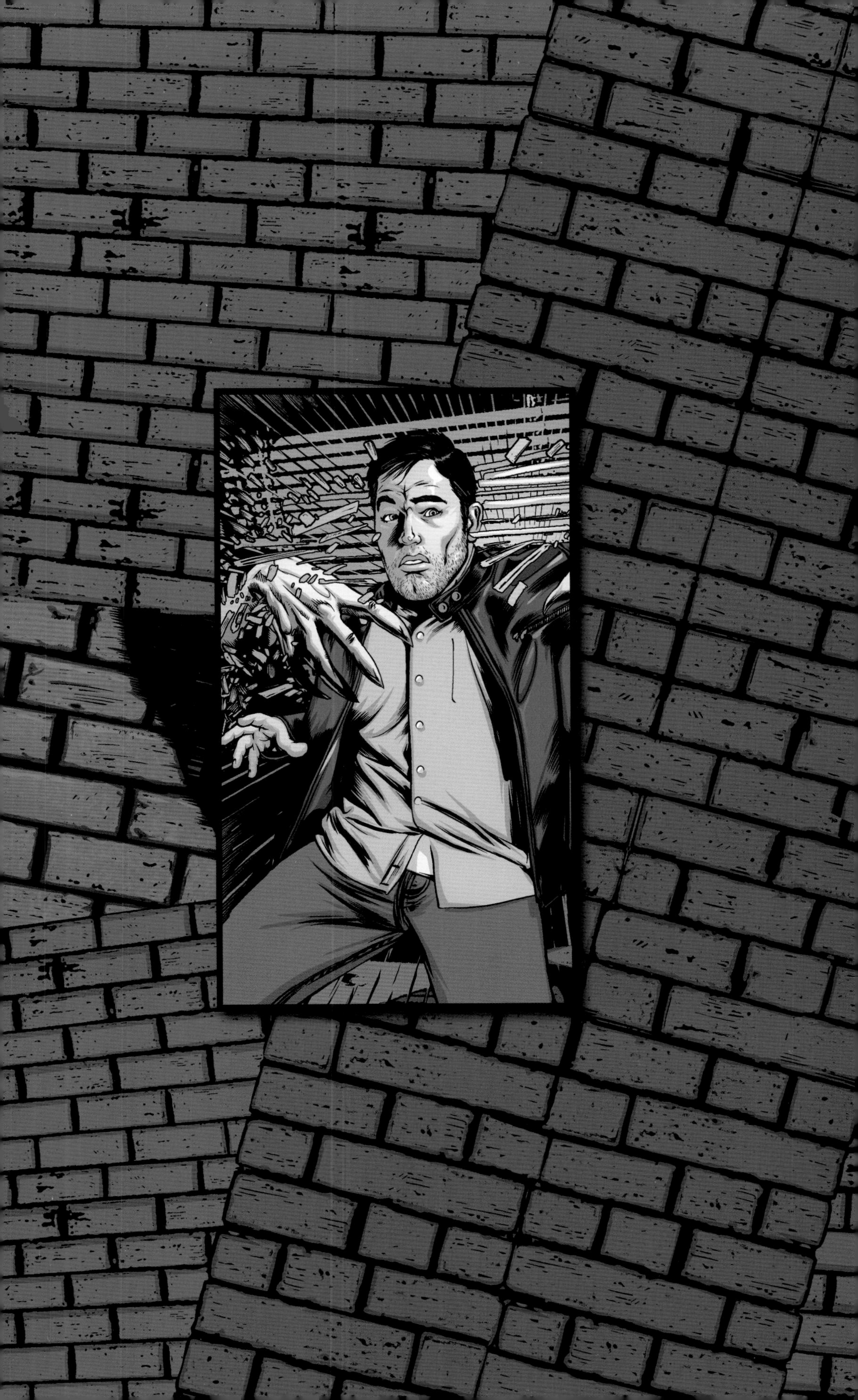

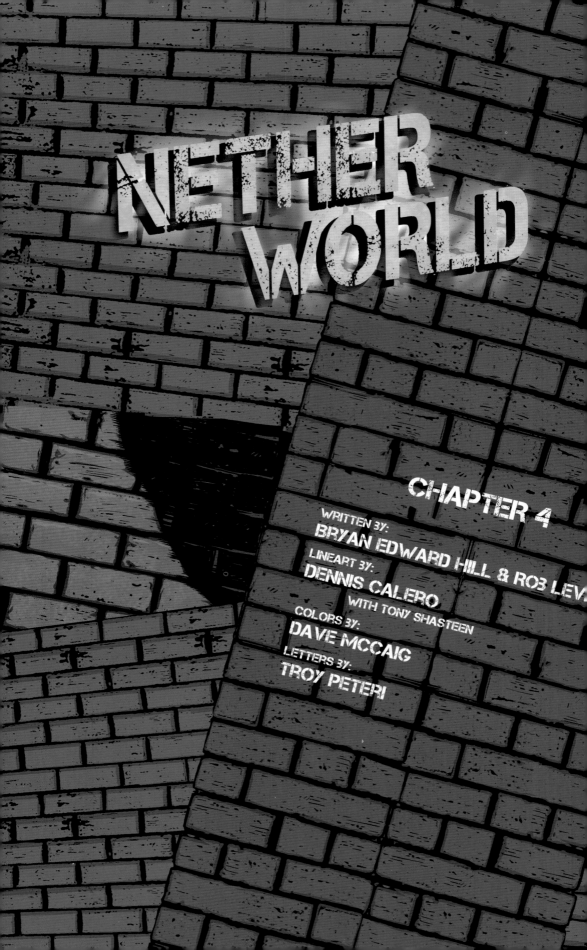

NETHER WORLD

CHAPTER 4

WRITTEN BY:
BRYAN EDWARD HILL & ROB LEV

LINEART BY:
DENNIS CALERO
WITH TONY SHASTEEN

COLORS BY:
DAVE MCCAIG

LETTERS BY:
TROY PETERI

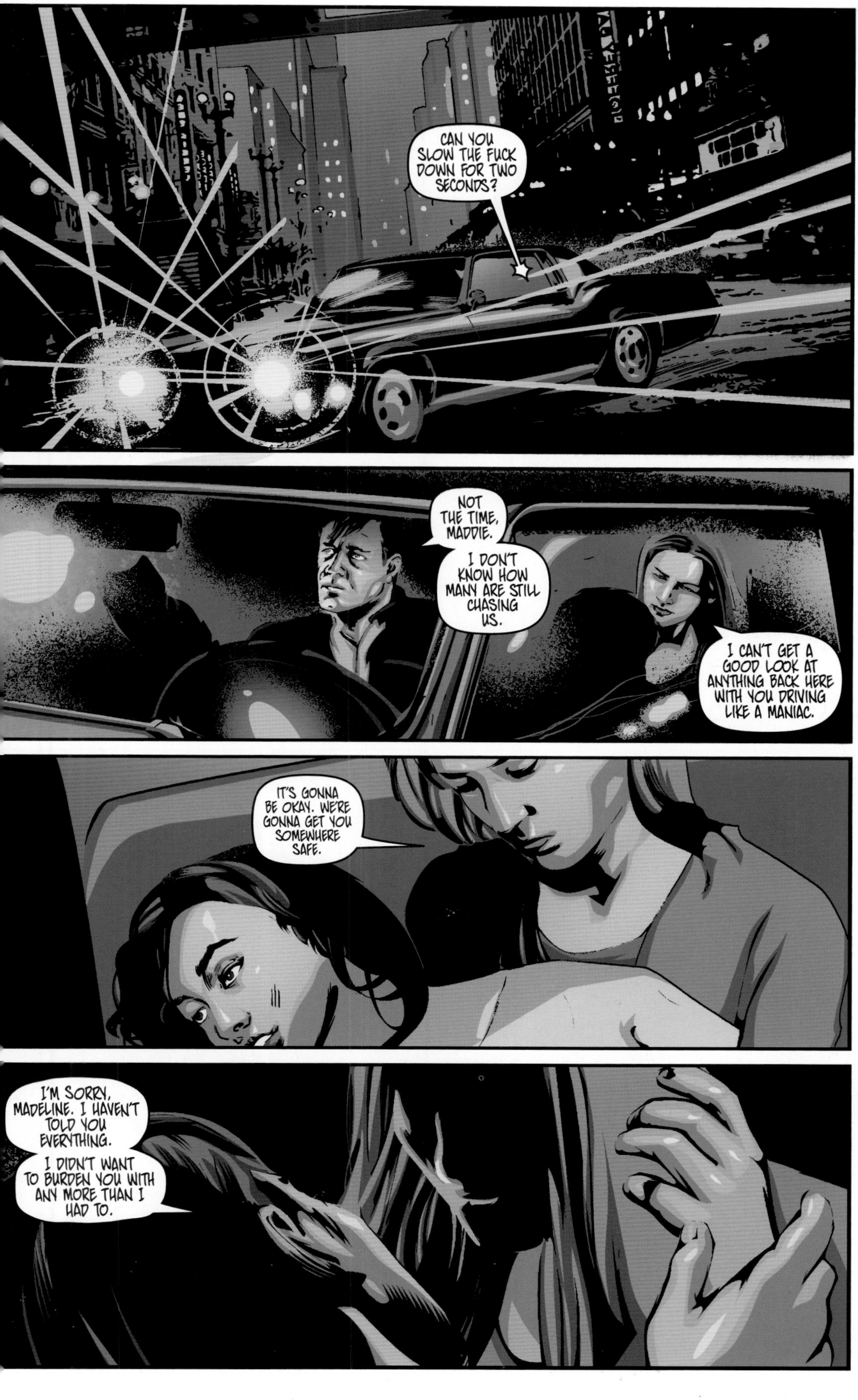
CAN YOU SLOW THE FUCK DOWN FOR TWO SECONDS?
NOT THE TIME, MADDIE.
I DON'T KNOW HOW MANY ARE STILL CHASING US.
I CAN'T GET A GOOD LOOK AT ANYTHING BACK HERE WITH YOU DRIVING LIKE A MANIAC.
IT'S GONNA BE OKAY. WE'RE GONNA GET YOU SOMEWHERE SAFE.
I'M SORRY, MADELINE. I HAVEN'T TOLD YOU EVERYTHING.
I DIDN'T WANT TO BURDEN YOU WITH ANY MORE THAN I HAD TO.

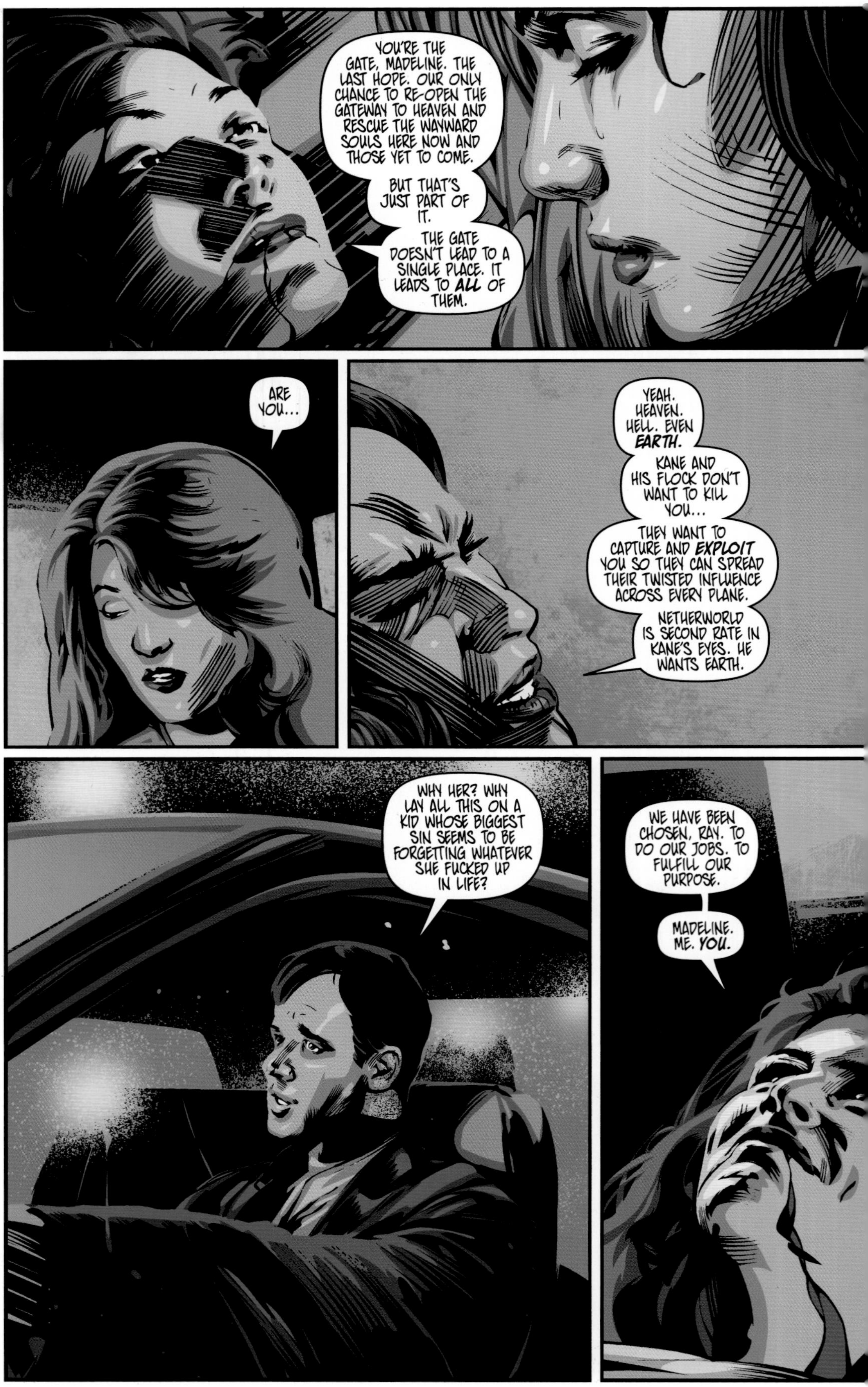
YOU'RE THE GATE, MADELINE. THE LAST HOPE. OUR ONLY CHANCE TO RE-OPEN THE GATEWAY TO HEAVEN AND RESCUE THE WAYWARD SOULS HERE NOW AND THOSE YET TO COME.
BUT THAT'S JUST PART OF IT.
THE GATE DOESN'T LEAD TO A SINGLE PLACE. IT LEADS TO **ALL** OF THEM.
ARE YOU...
YEAH. HEAVEN. HELL. EVEN **EARTH**.
KANE AND HIS FLOCK DON'T WANT TO KILL YOU...
THEY WANT TO CAPTURE AND **EXPLOIT** YOU SO THEY CAN SPREAD THEIR TWISTED INFLUENCE ACROSS EVERY PLANE.
NETHERWORLD IS SECOND RATE IN KANE'S EYES. HE WANTS EARTH.
WHY HER? WHY LAY ALL THIS ON A KID WHOSE BIGGEST SIN SEEMS TO BE FORGETTING WHATEVER SHE FUCKED UP IN LIFE?
WE HAVE BEEN CHOSEN, RAY. TO DO OUR JOBS. TO FULFILL OUR PURPOSE.
MADELINE. ME. **YOU**.

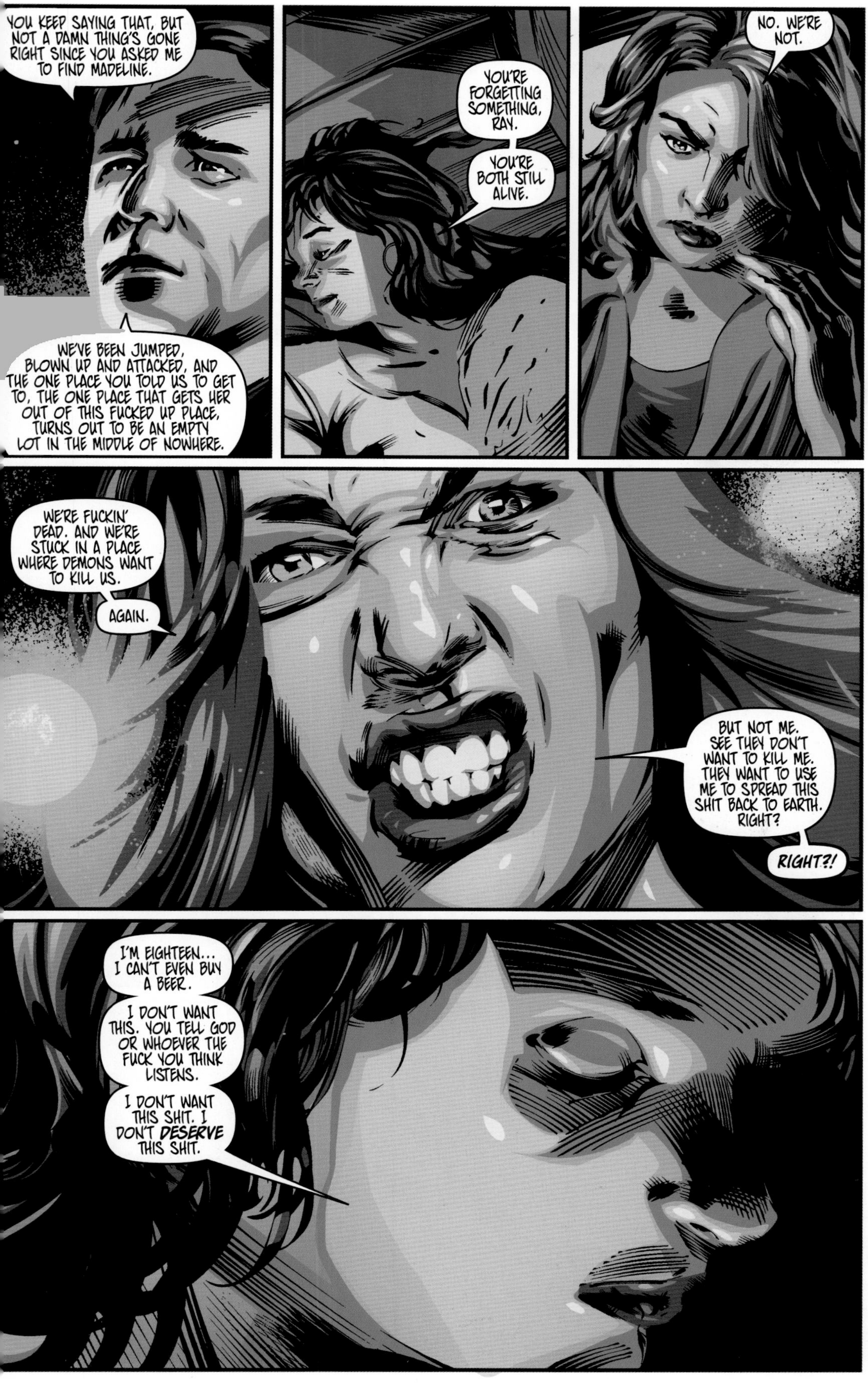

YOU KEEP SAYING THAT, BUT NOT A DAMN THING'S GONE RIGHT SINCE YOU ASKED ME TO FIND MADELINE.
WE'VE BEEN JUMPED, BLOWN UP AND ATTACKED, AND THE ONE PLACE YOU TOLD US TO GET TO, THE ONE PLACE THAT GETS HER OUT OF THIS FUCKED UP PLACE, TURNS OUT TO BE AN EMPTY LOT IN THE MIDDLE OF NOWHERE.
YOU'RE FORGETTING SOMETHING, RAY.
YOU'RE BOTH STILL ALIVE.
NO. WE'RE NOT.
WE'RE FUCKIN' DEAD. AND WE'RE STUCK IN A PLACE WHERE DEMONS WANT TO KILL US.
AGAIN.
BUT NOT ME. SEE THEY DON'T WANT TO KILL ME. THEY WANT TO USE ME TO SPREAD THIS SHIT BACK TO EARTH. RIGHT?
RIGHT?!
I'M EIGHTEEN... I CAN'T EVEN BUY A BEER.
I DON'T WANT THIS. YOU TELL GOD OR WHOEVER THE FUCK YOU THINK LISTENS.
I DON'T WANT THIS SHIT. I DON'T *DESERVE* THIS SHIT.

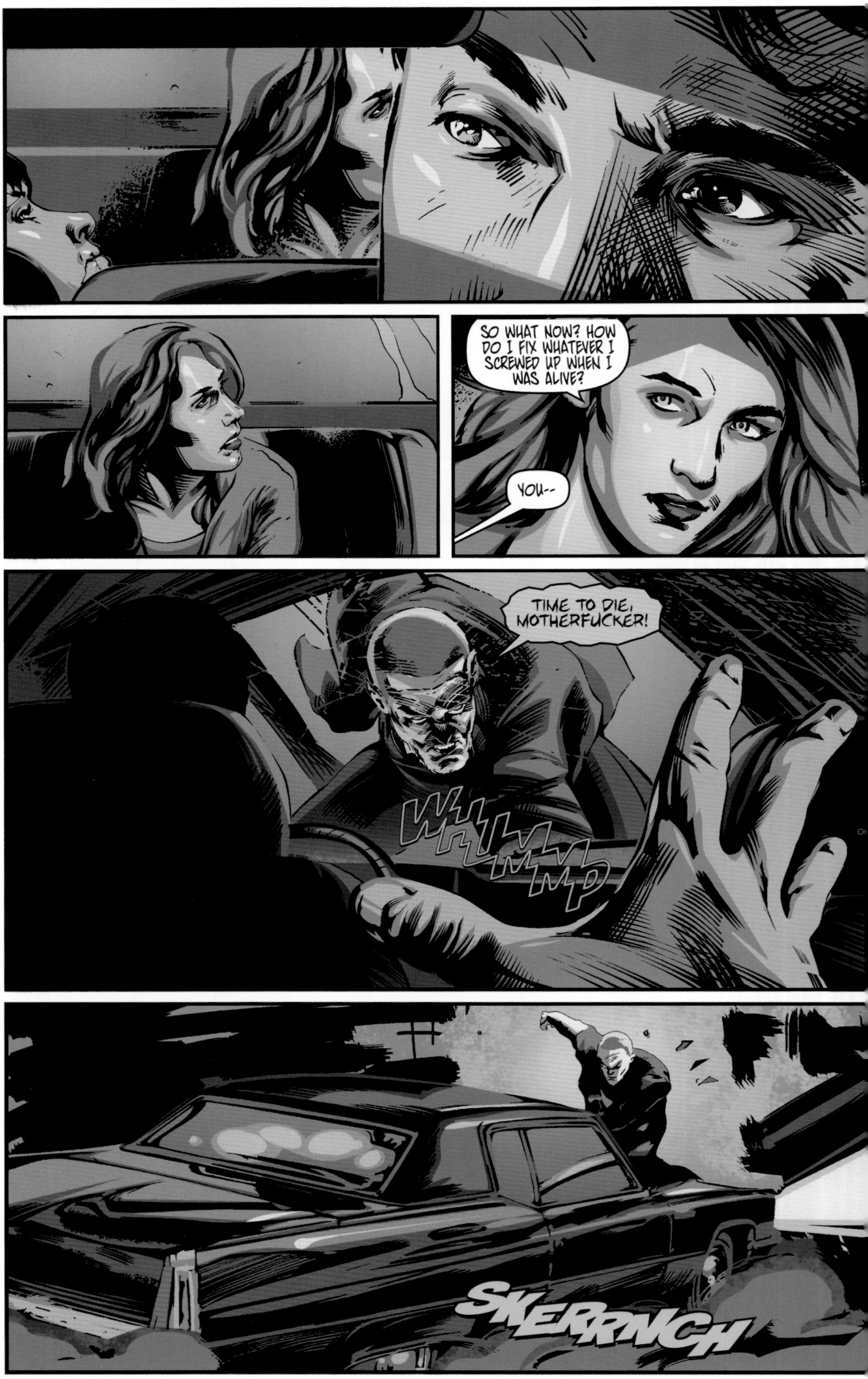
SO WHAT NOW? HOW DO I FIX WHATEVER I SCREWED UP WHEN I WAS ALIVE?
YOU--
TIME TO DIE, MOTHERFUCKER!
WHUMMMP
SKERRNCH

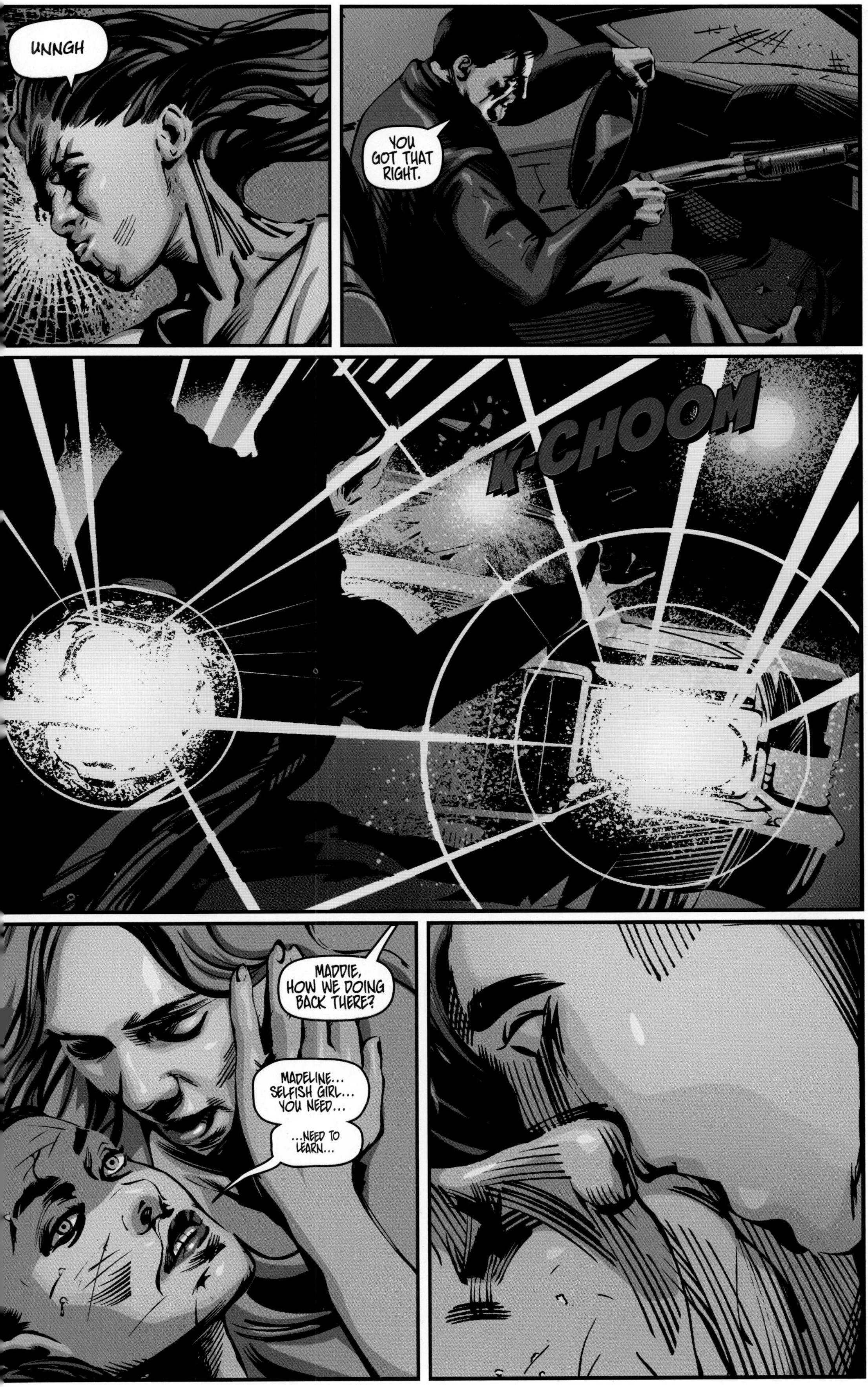
UNNGH
YOU GOT THAT RIGHT.
K-CHOOM
MADDIE, HOW WE DOING BACK THERE?
MADELINE... SELFISH GIRL... YOU NEED...
...NEED TO LEARN...

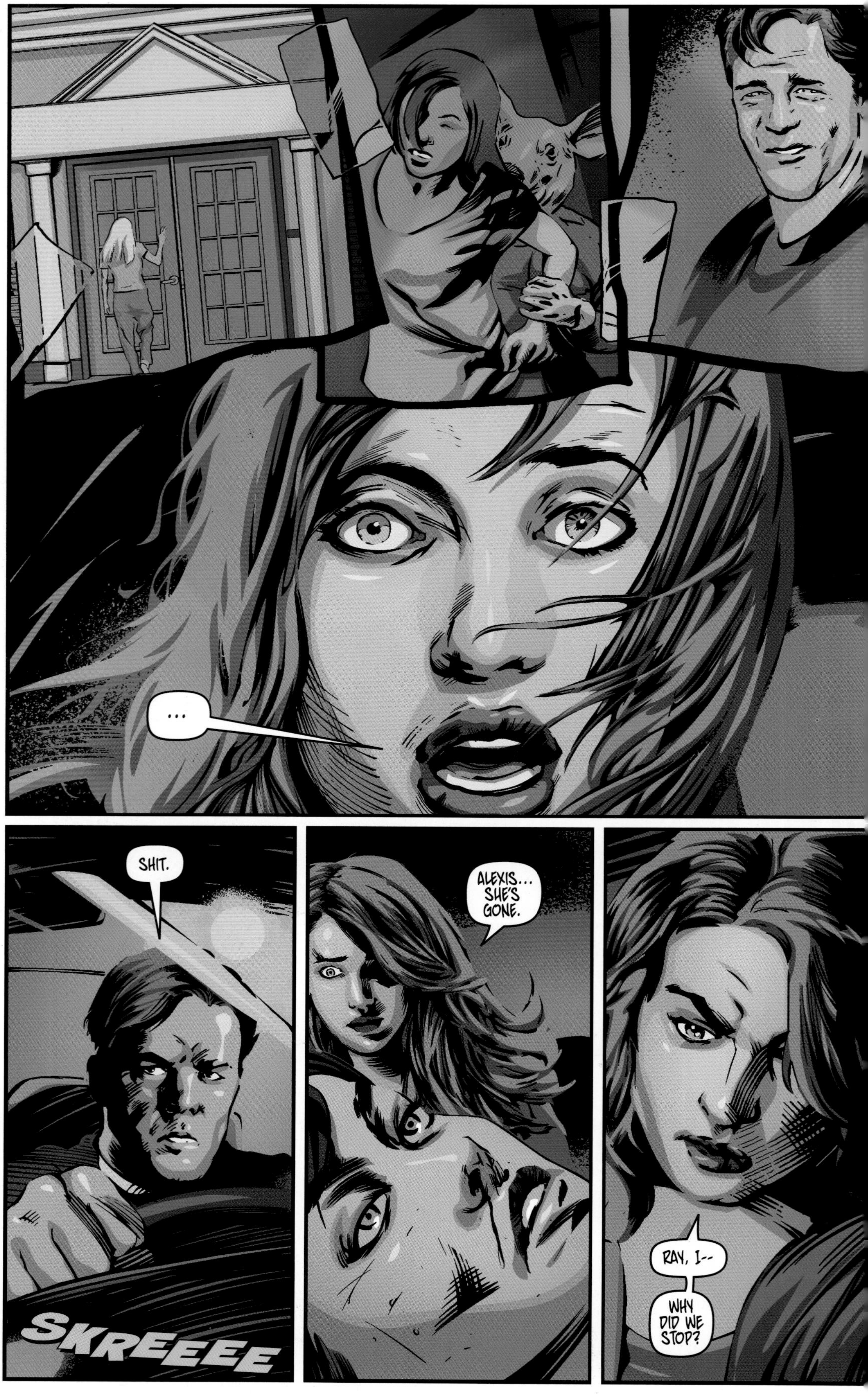
...
SHIT.
SKREEEEE
ALEXIS... SHE'S GONE.
RAY, I--
WHY DID WE STOP?

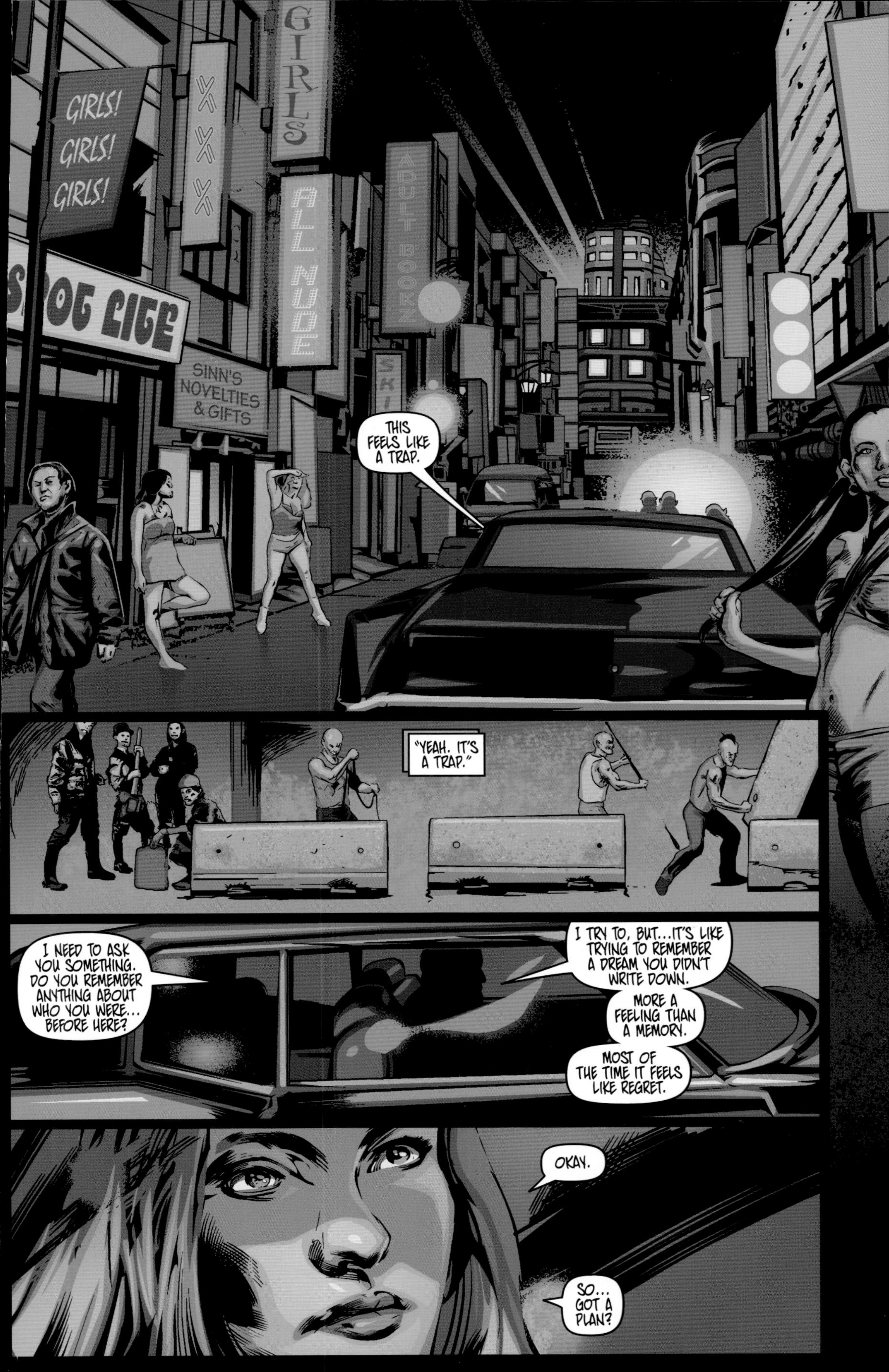
GIRLS
GIRLS! GIRLS! GIRLS!
XXXX
ALL NUDE
ADULT BOOKZ
SINN'S NOVELTIES & GIFTS
THIS FEELS LIKE A TRAP.
"YEAH. IT'S A TRAP."
I NEED TO ASK YOU SOMETHING. DO YOU REMEMBER ANYTHING ABOUT WHO YOU WERE... BEFORE HERE?
I TRY TO, BUT...IT'S LIKE TRYING TO REMEMBER A DREAM YOU DIDN'T WRITE DOWN.
MORE A FEELING THAN A MEMORY.
MOST OF THE TIME IT FEELS LIKE REGRET.
OKAY.
SO... GOT A PLAN?

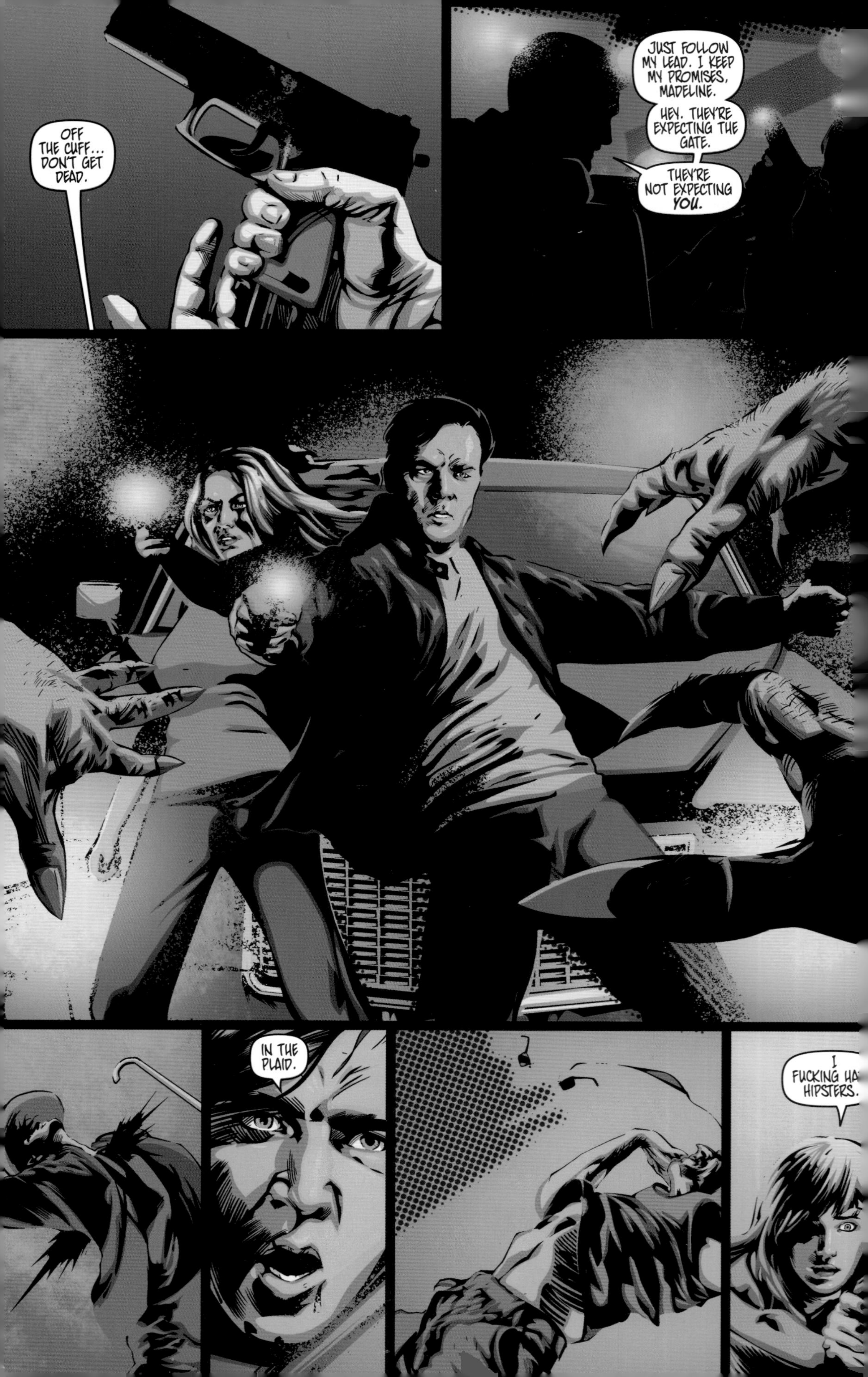
OFF THE CUFF... DON'T GET DEAD.
JUST FOLLOW MY LEAD. I KEEP MY PROMISES, MADELINE.
HEY. THEY'RE EXPECTING THE GATE.
THEY'RE NOT EXPECTING YOU.
IN THE PLAID.
I FUCKING HA
HIPSTERS.

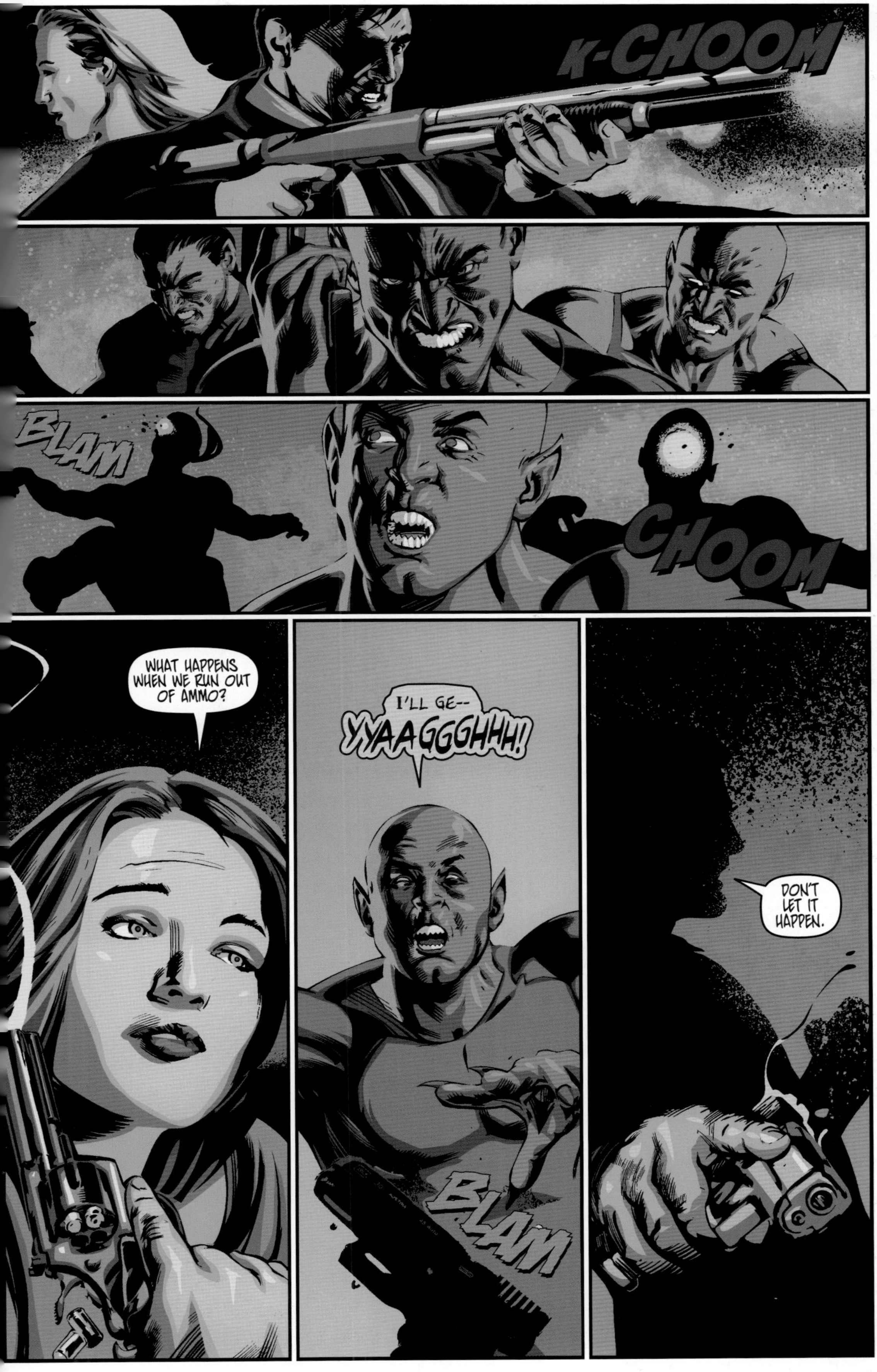
K-CHOOM
BLAM
CHOOM
WHAT HAPPENS WHEN WE RUN OUT OF AMMO?
I'LL GE--
YYAAGGGHHH!
BLAM
DON'T LET IT HAPPEN.

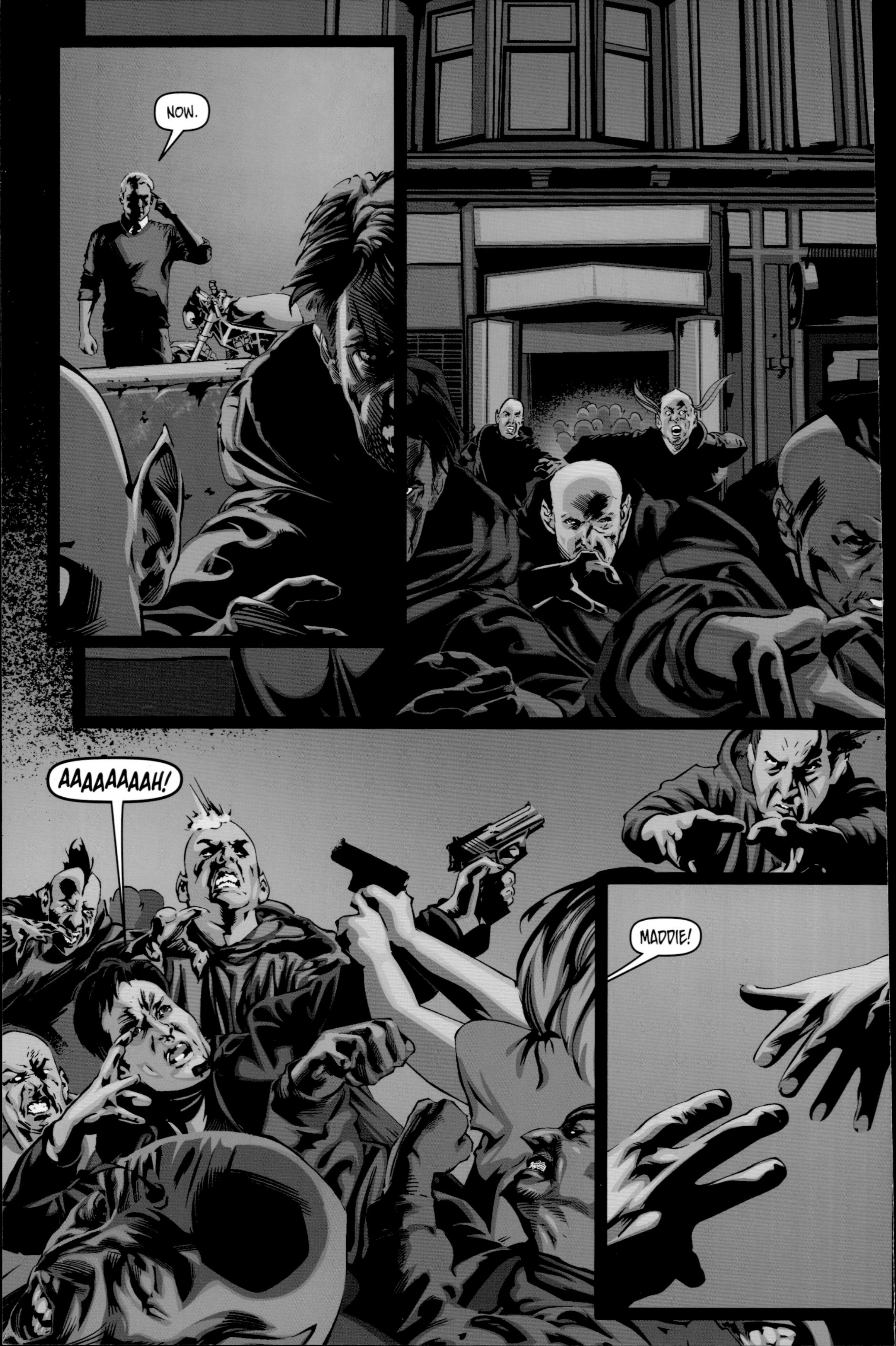
NOW.
AAAAAAAAH!
MADDIE!

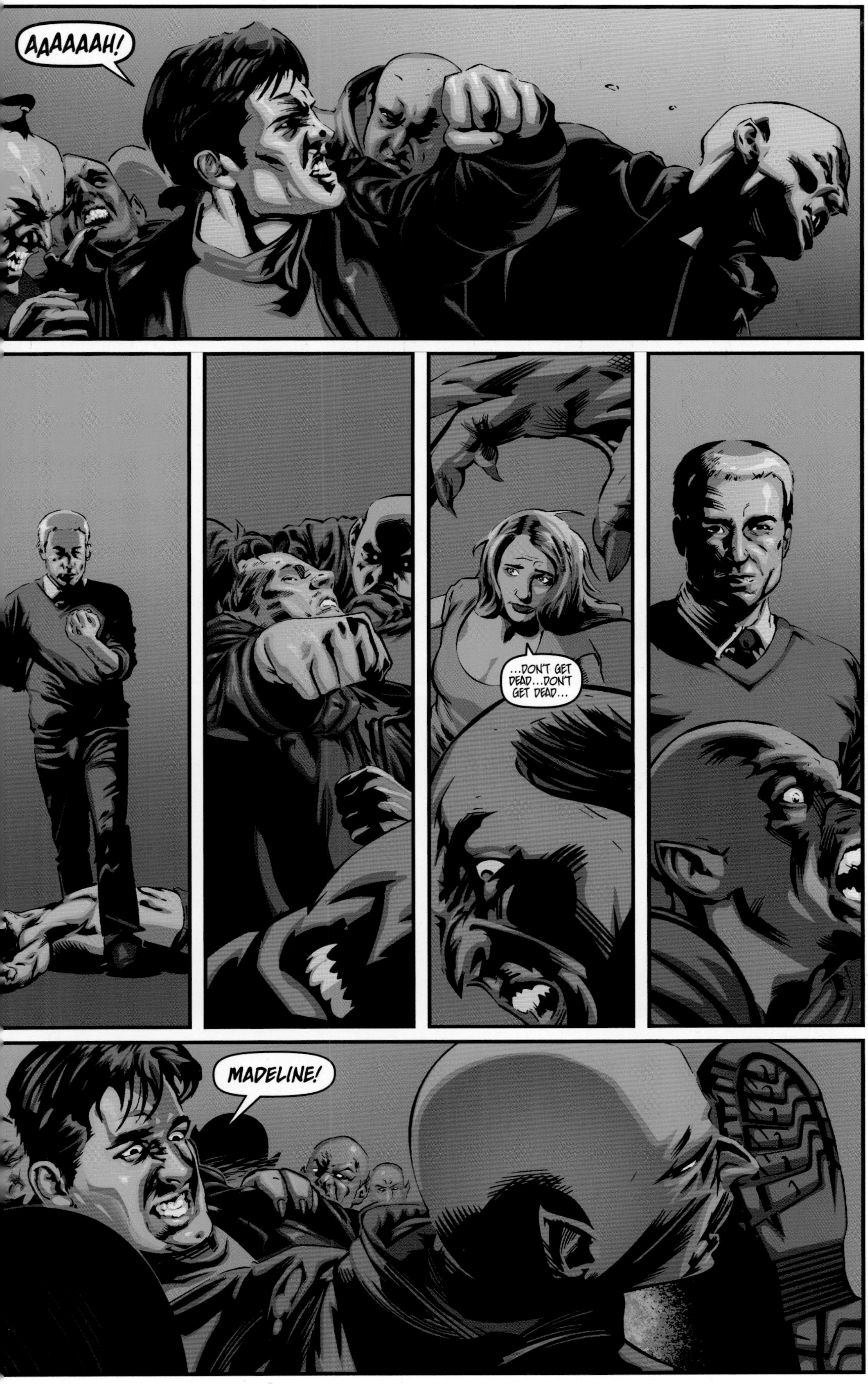
AAAAAAH!
...DON'T GET DEAD...DON'T GET DEAD...
MADELINE!

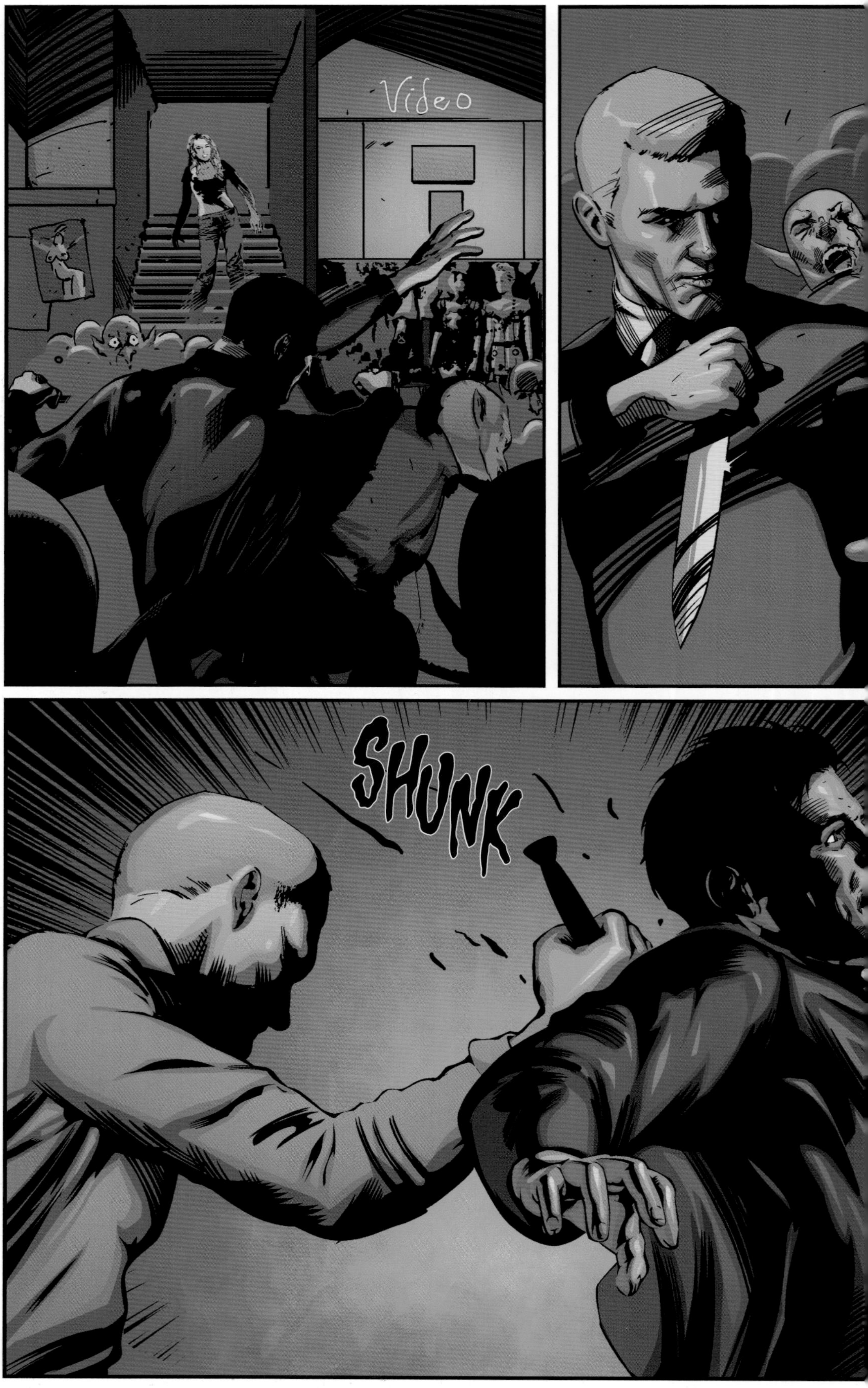
Video
SHUNK

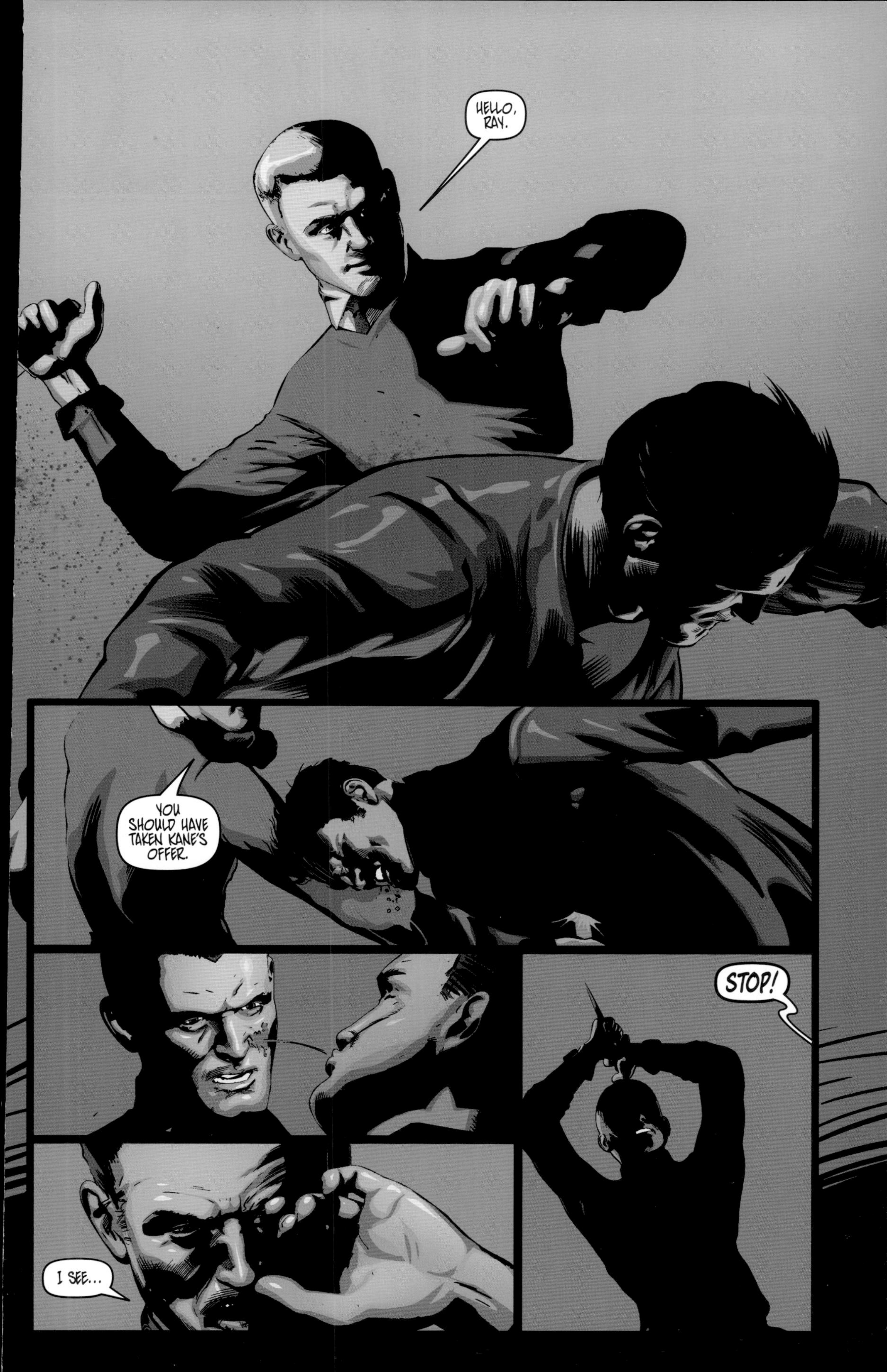
HELLO, RAY.
YOU SHOULD HAVE TAKEN KANE'S OFFER.
STOP!
I SEE...

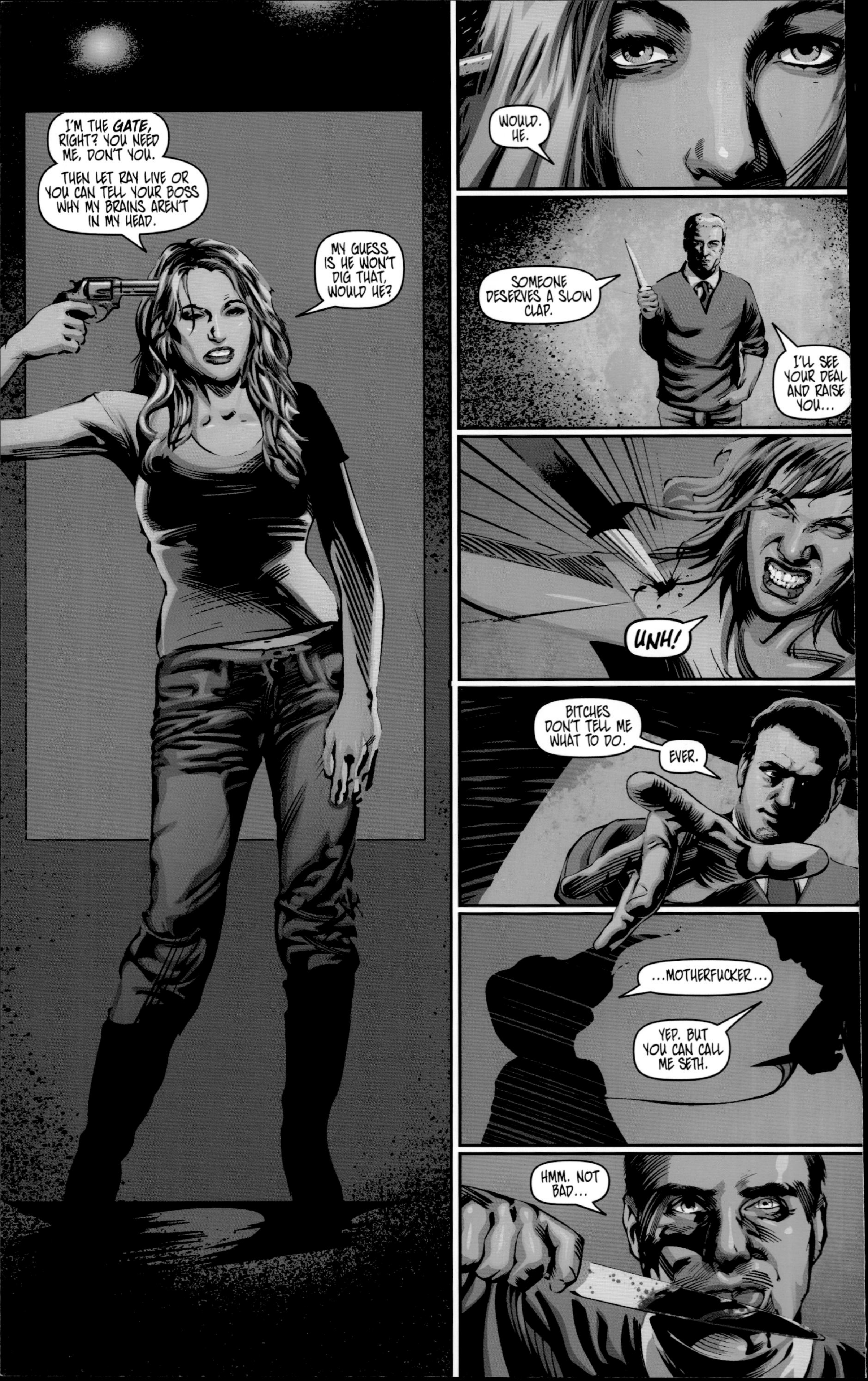
I'M THE GATE, RIGHT? YOU NEED ME, DON'T YOU.
THEN LET RAY LIVE OR YOU CAN TELL YOUR BOSS WHY MY BRAINS AREN'T IN MY HEAD.
MY GUESS IS HE WON'T DIG THAT, WOULD HE?
WOULD. HE.
SOMEONE DESERVES A SLOW CLAP.
I'LL SEE YOUR DEAL AND RAISE YOU...
UNH!
BITCHES DON'T TELL ME WHAT TO DO.
EVER.
...MOTHERFUCKER...
YEP. BUT YOU CAN CALL ME SETH.
HMM. NOT BAD...

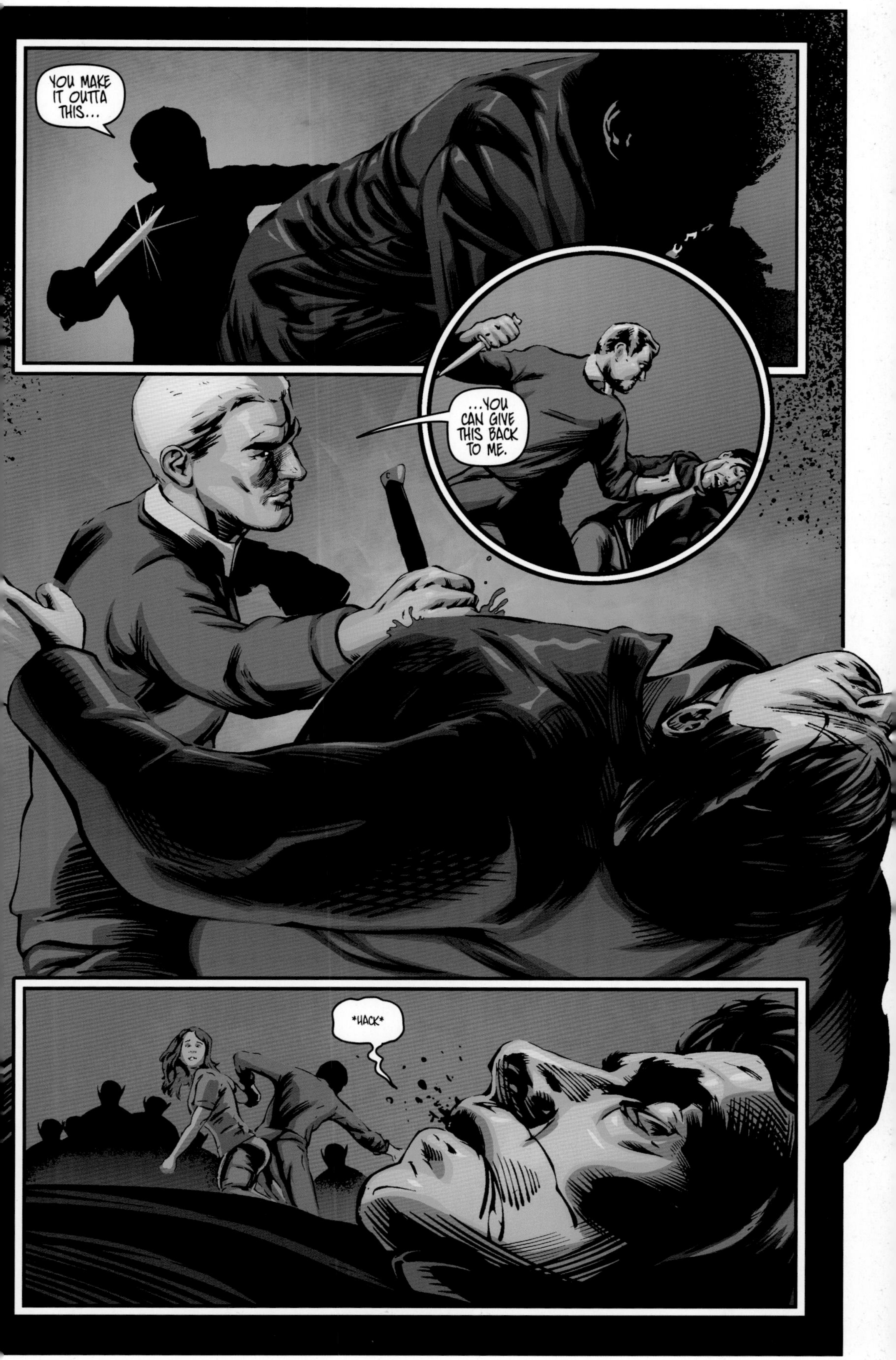
YOU MAKE IT OUTTA THIS...
...YOU CAN GIVE THIS BACK TO ME.
HACK

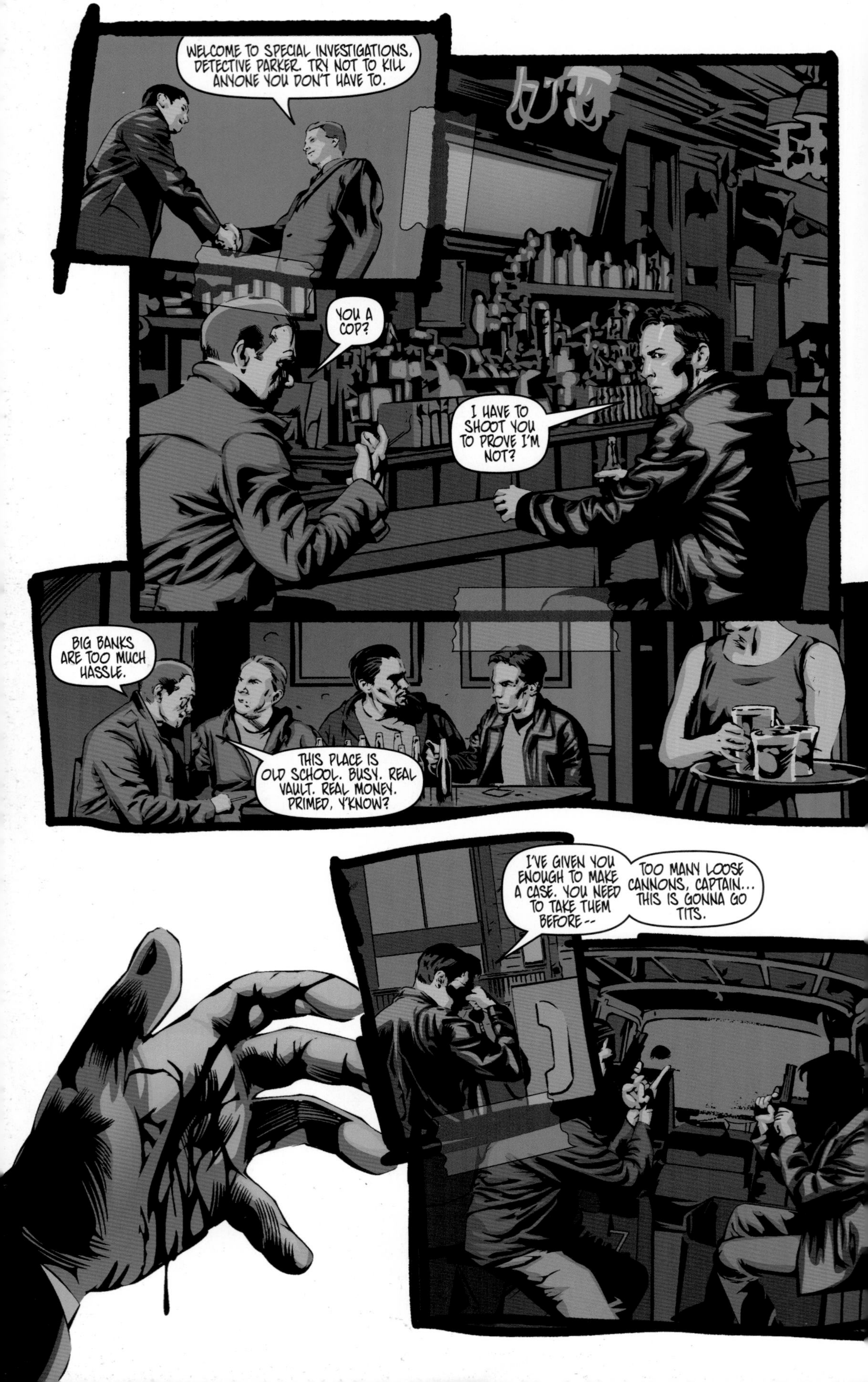
WELCOME TO SPECIAL INVESTIGATIONS, DETECTIVE PARKER. TRY NOT TO KILL ANYONE YOU DON'T HAVE TO.
YOU A COP?
I HAVE TO SHOOT YOU TO PROVE I'M NOT?
BIG BANKS ARE TOO MUCH HASSLE.
THIS PLACE IS OLD SCHOOL. BUSY. REAL VAULT. REAL MONEY. PRIMED, Y'KNOW?
I'VE GIVEN YOU ENOUGH TO MAKE A CASE. YOU NEED TO TAKE THEM BEFORE--
TOO MANY LOOSE CANNONS, CAPTAIN... THIS IS GONNA GO TITS.

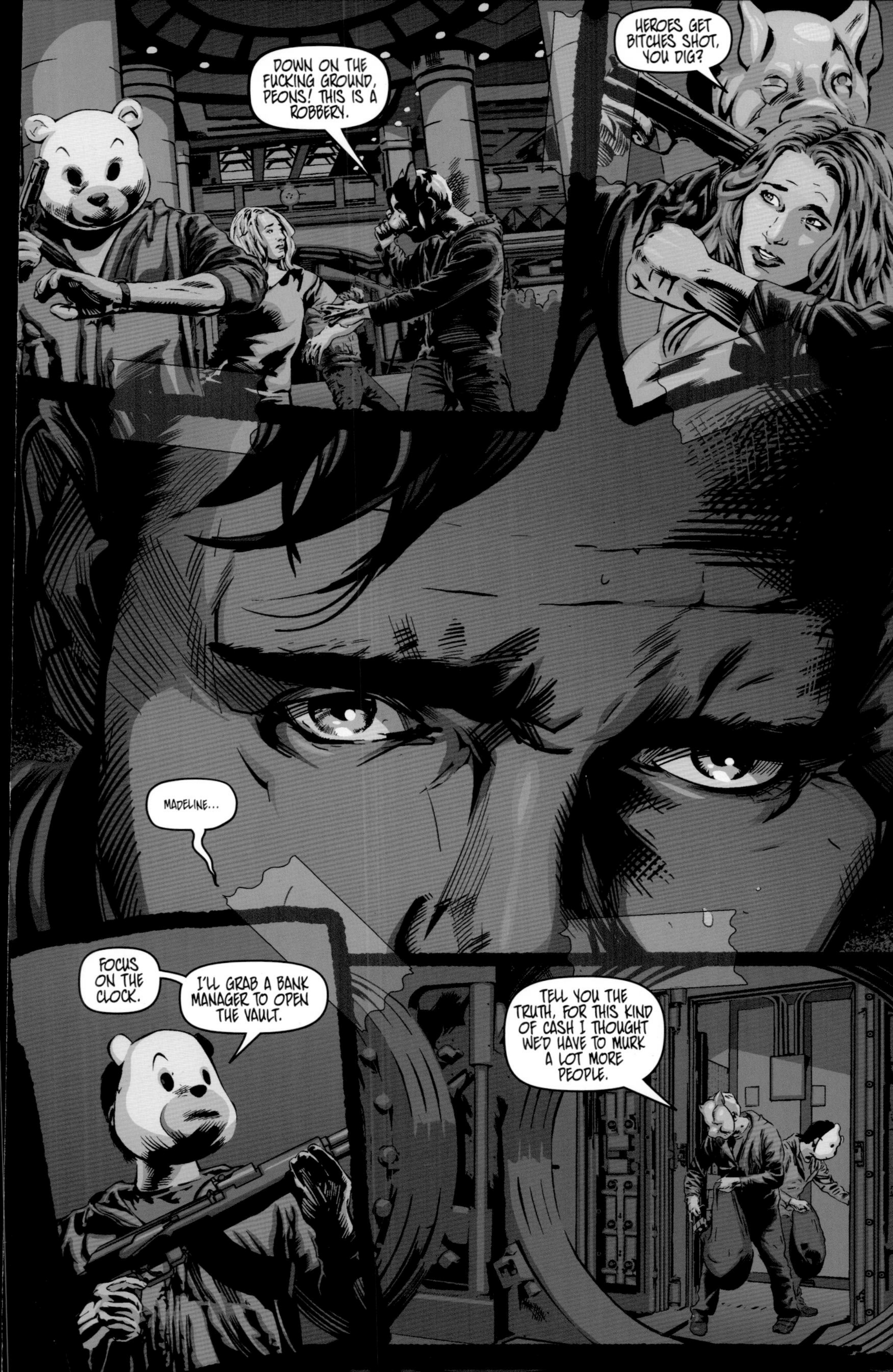
DOWN ON THE FUCKING GROUND, PEONS! THIS IS A ROBBERY.
HEROES GET BITCHES SHOT, YOU DIG?
MADELINE...
FOCUS ON THE CLOCK.
I'LL GRAB A BANK MANAGER TO OPEN THE VAULT.
TELL YOU THE TRUTH, FOR THIS KIND OF CASH I THOUGHT WE'D HAVE TO MURK A LOT MORE PEOPLE.

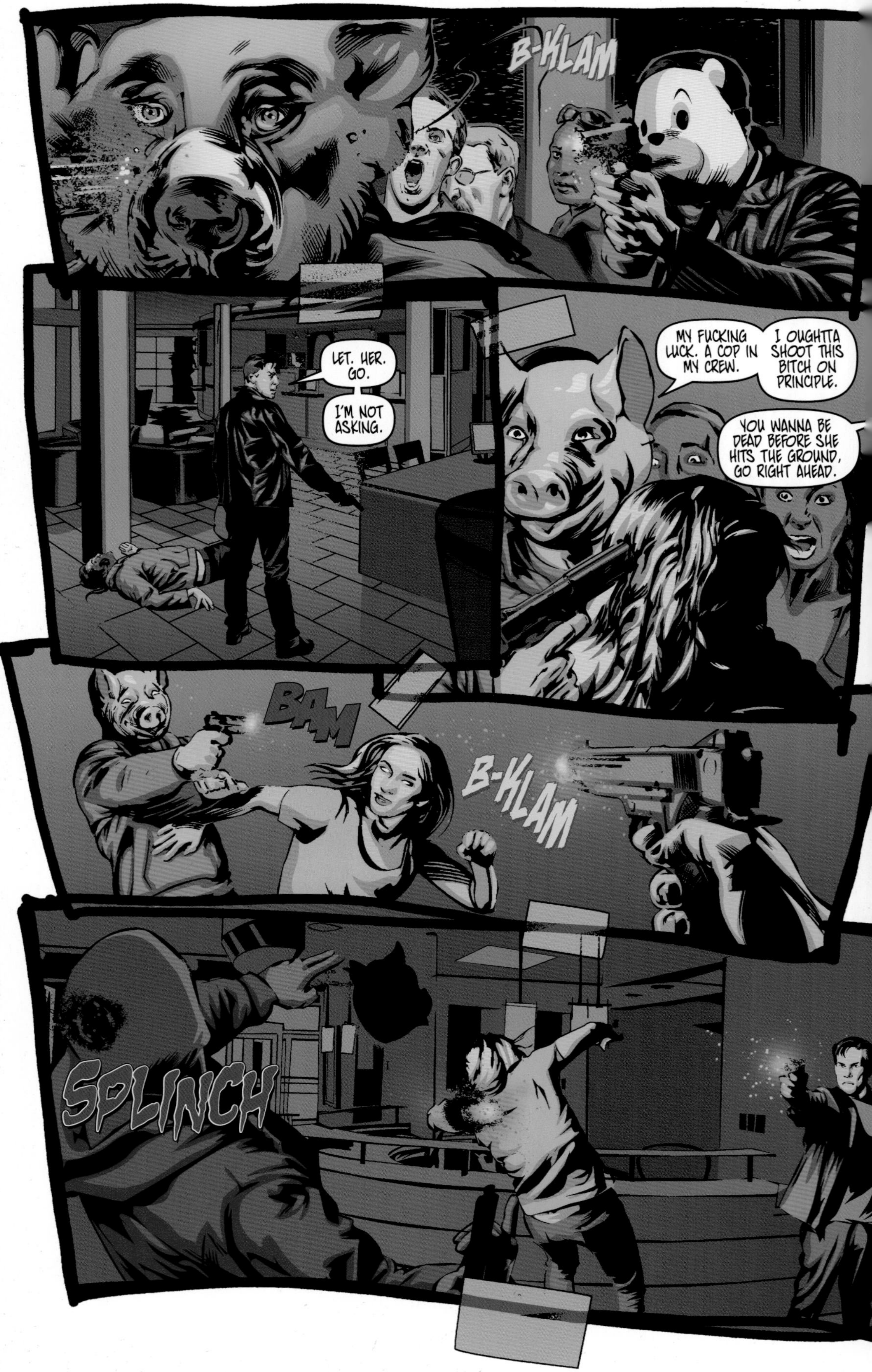

B-KLAM
LET. HER. GO.
I'M NOT ASKING.
MY FUCKING LUCK. A COP IN MY CREW.
I OUGHTTA SHOOT THIS BITCH ON PRINCIPLE.
YOU WANNA BE DEAD BEFORE SHE HITS THE GROUND, GO RIGHT AHEAD.
BAM
B-KLAM
SPLINCH

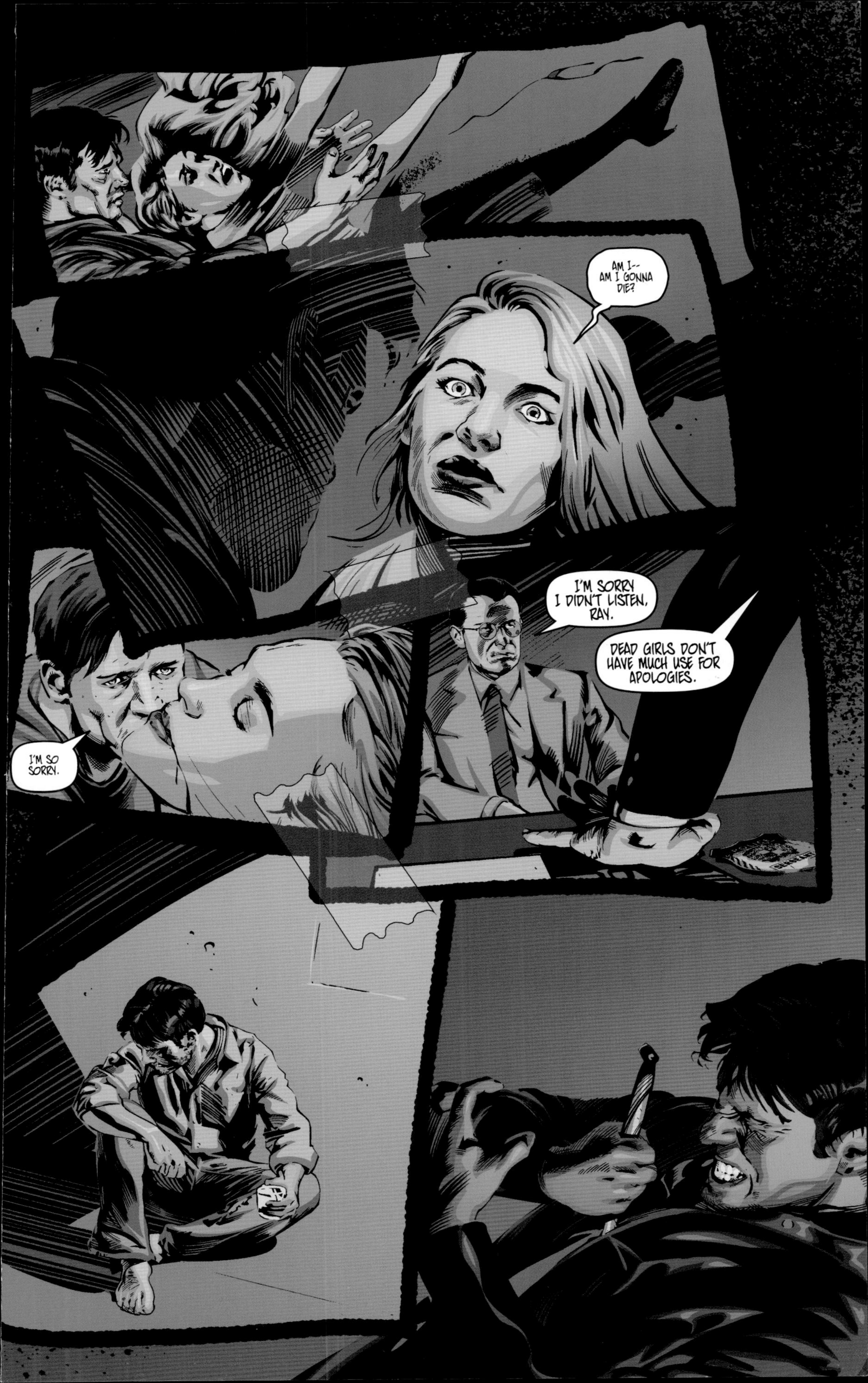
AM I-- AM I GONNA DIE?
I'M SO SORRY.
I'M SORRY I DIDN'T LISTEN, RAY.
DEAD GIRLS DON'T HAVE MUCH USE FOR APOLOGIES.

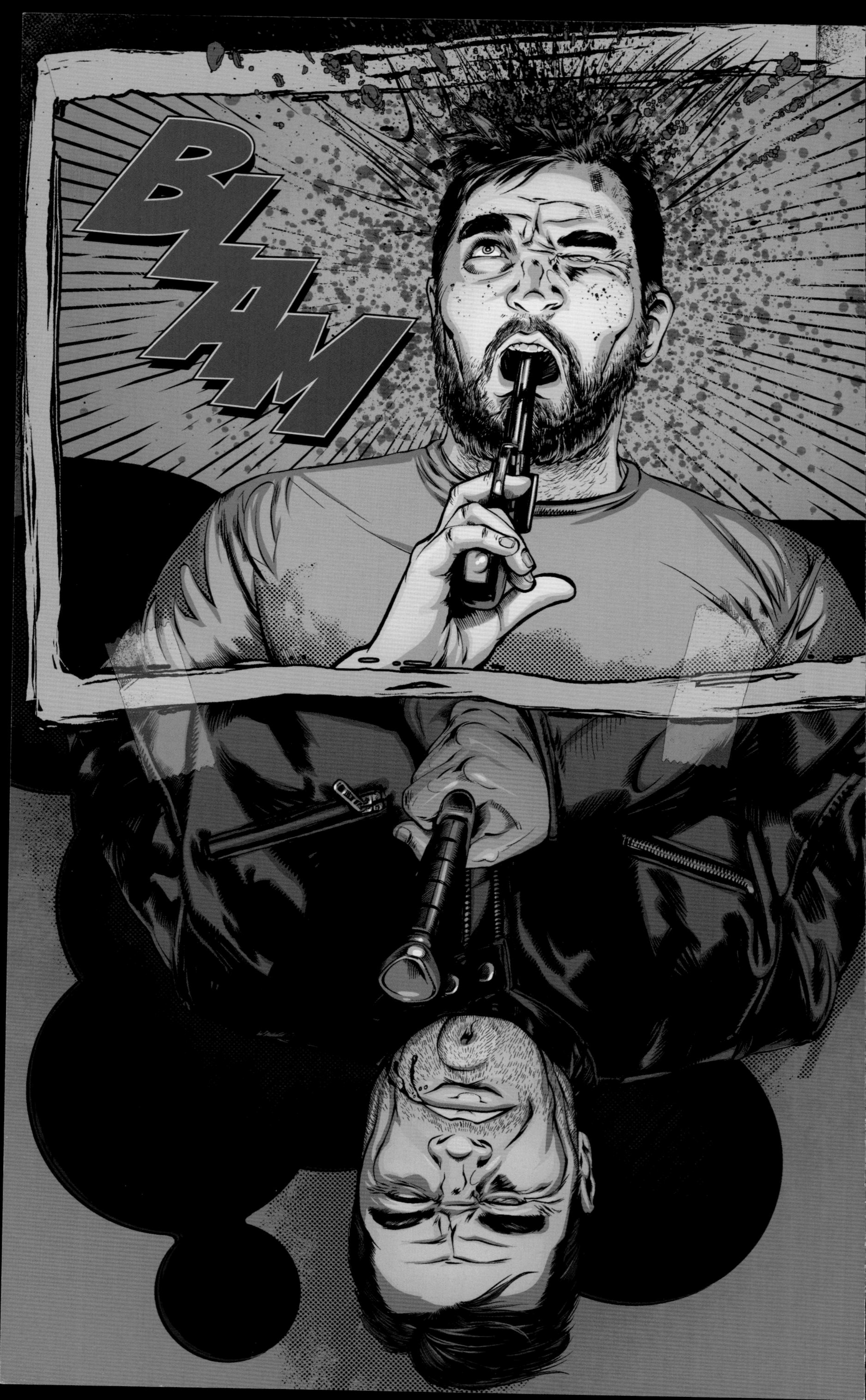
BLAM

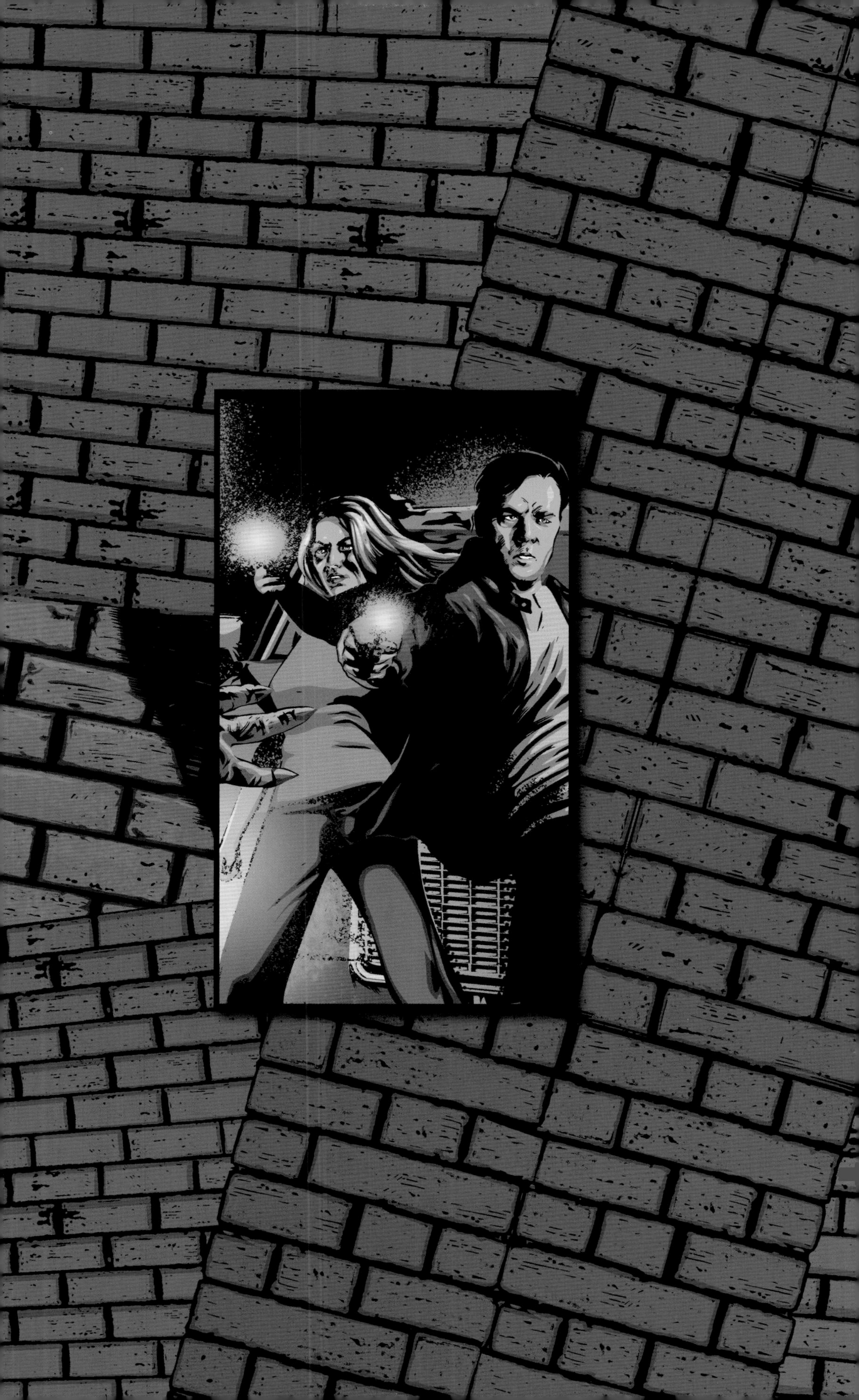

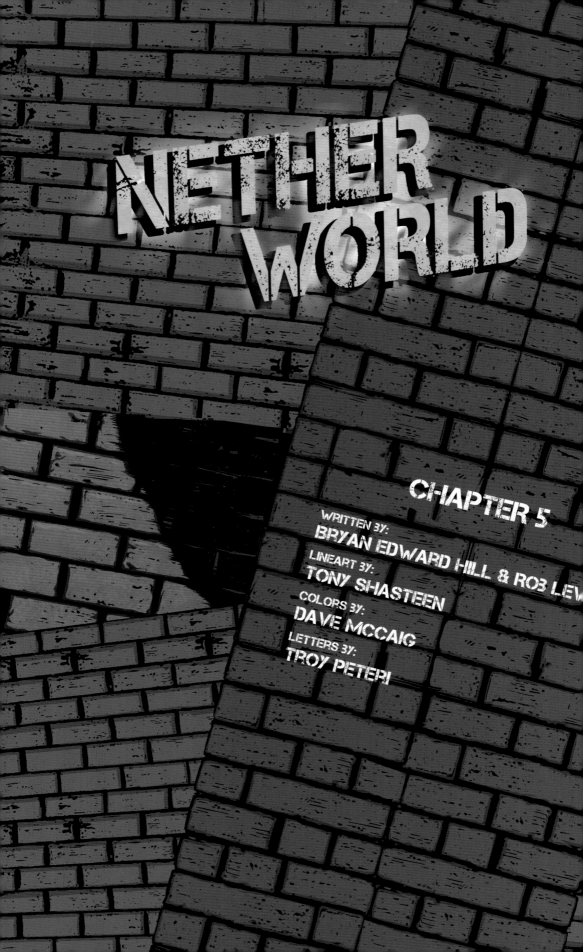

NETHER WORLD

CHAPTER 5

WRITTEN BY:
BRYAN EDWARD HILL & ROB LEV

LINEART BY:
TONY SHASTEEN

COLORS BY:
DAVE MCCAIG

LETTERS BY:
TROY PETERI

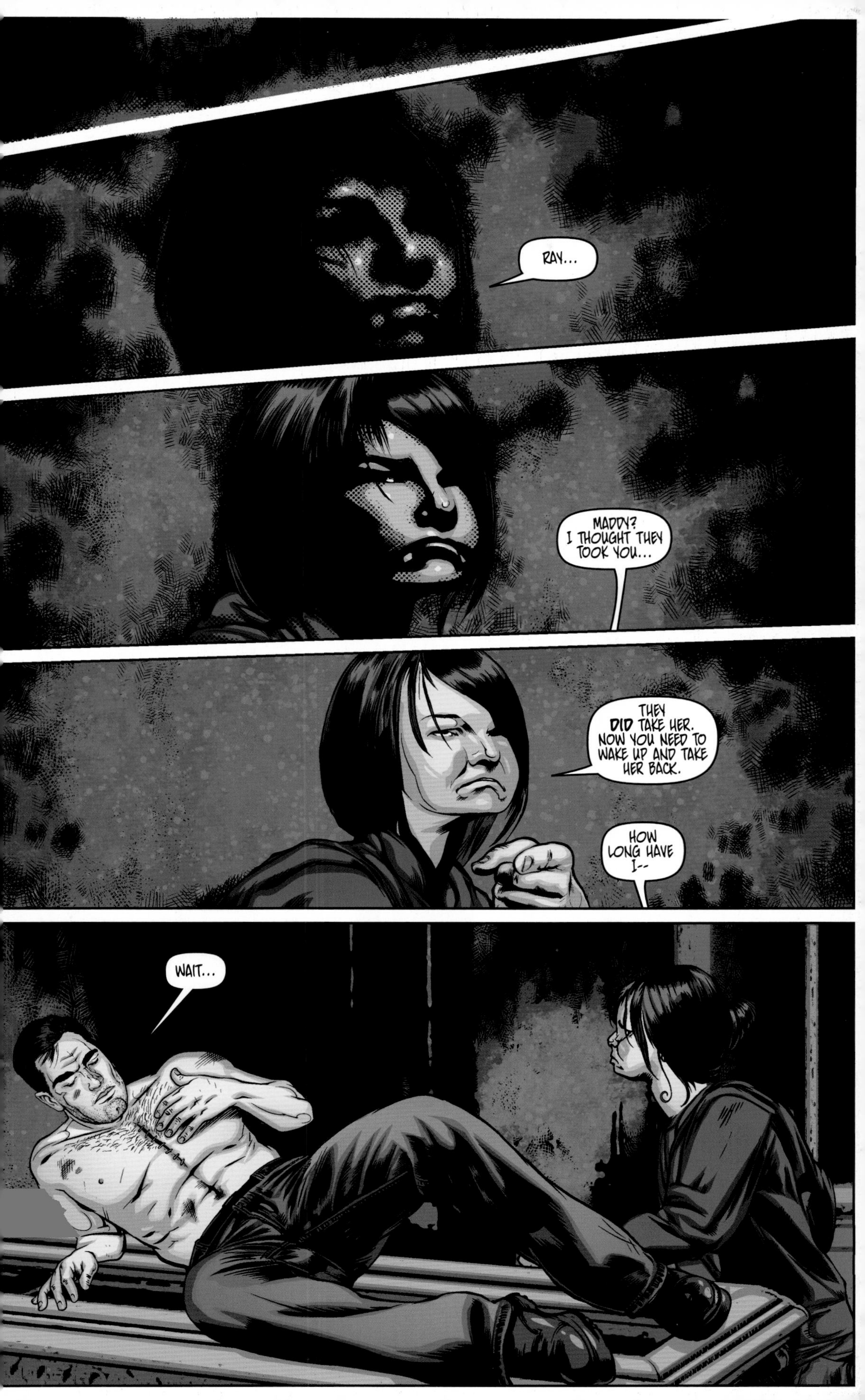
RAY...
MADDY? I THOUGHT THEY TOOK YOU...
THEY DID TAKE HER. NOW YOU NEED TO WAKE UP AND TAKE HER BACK.
HOW LONG HAVE I--
WAIT...

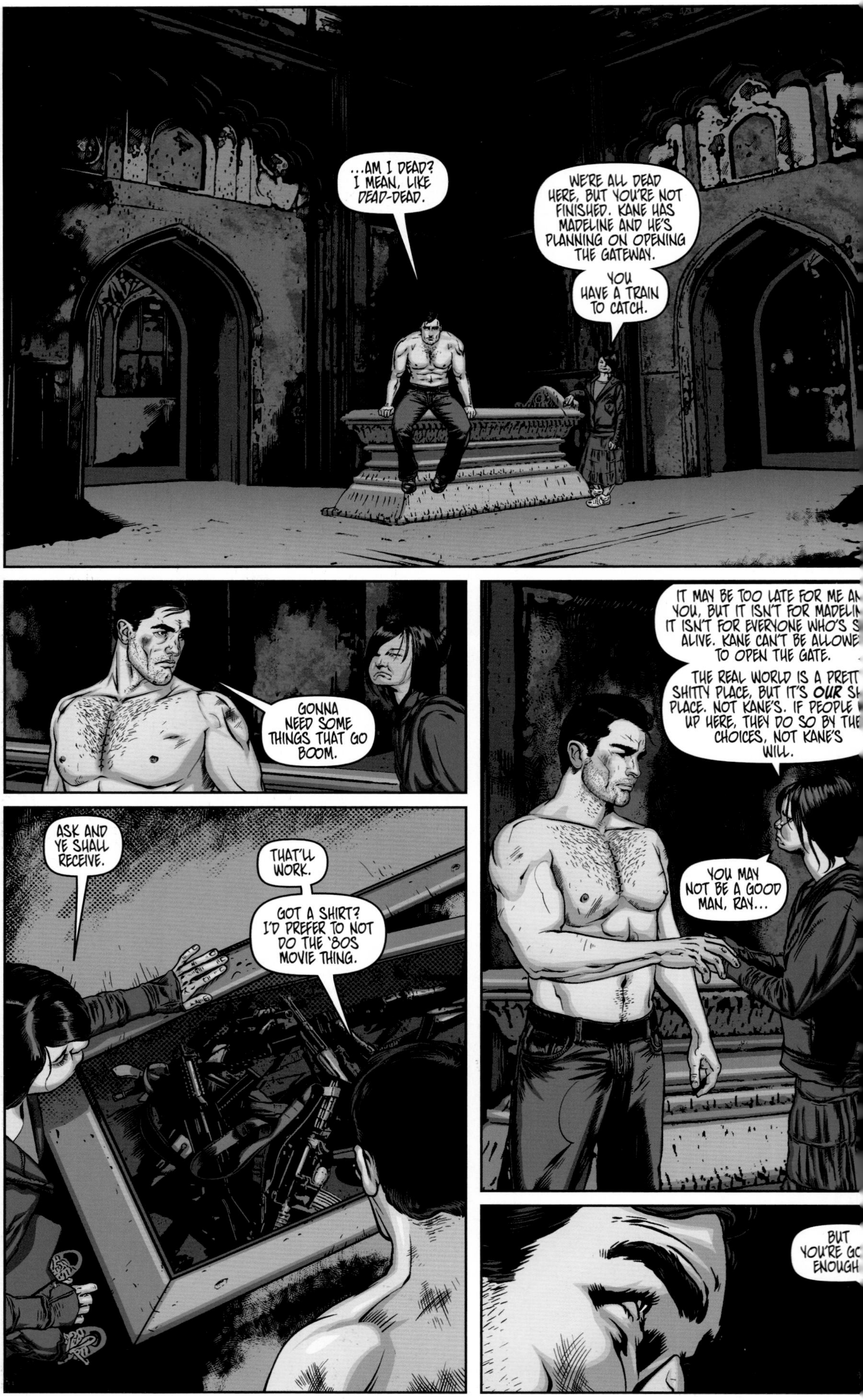

...AM I DEAD? I MEAN, LIKE DEAD-DEAD.
WE'RE ALL DEAD HERE, BUT YOU'RE NOT FINISHED. KANE HAS MADELINE AND HE'S PLANNING ON OPENING THE GATEWAY.
YOU HAVE A TRAIN TO CATCH.
GONNA NEED SOME THINGS THAT GO BOOM.
ASK AND YE SHALL RECEIVE.
THAT'LL WORK.
GOT A SHIRT? I'D PREFER TO NOT DO THE '80S MOVIE THING.
IT MAY BE TOO LATE FOR ME AN YOU, BUT IT ISN'T FOR MADELIN IT ISN'T FOR EVERYONE WHO'S S ALIVE. KANE CAN'T BE ALLOWE TO OPEN THE GATE.
THE REAL WORLD IS A PRETT SHITTY PLACE, BUT IT'S **OUR** S PLACE. NOT KANE'S. IF PEOPLE UP HERE, THEY DO SO BY THE CHOICES, NOT KANE'S WILL.
YOU MAY NOT BE A GOOD MAN, RAY...
BUT YOU'RE GO ENOUGH

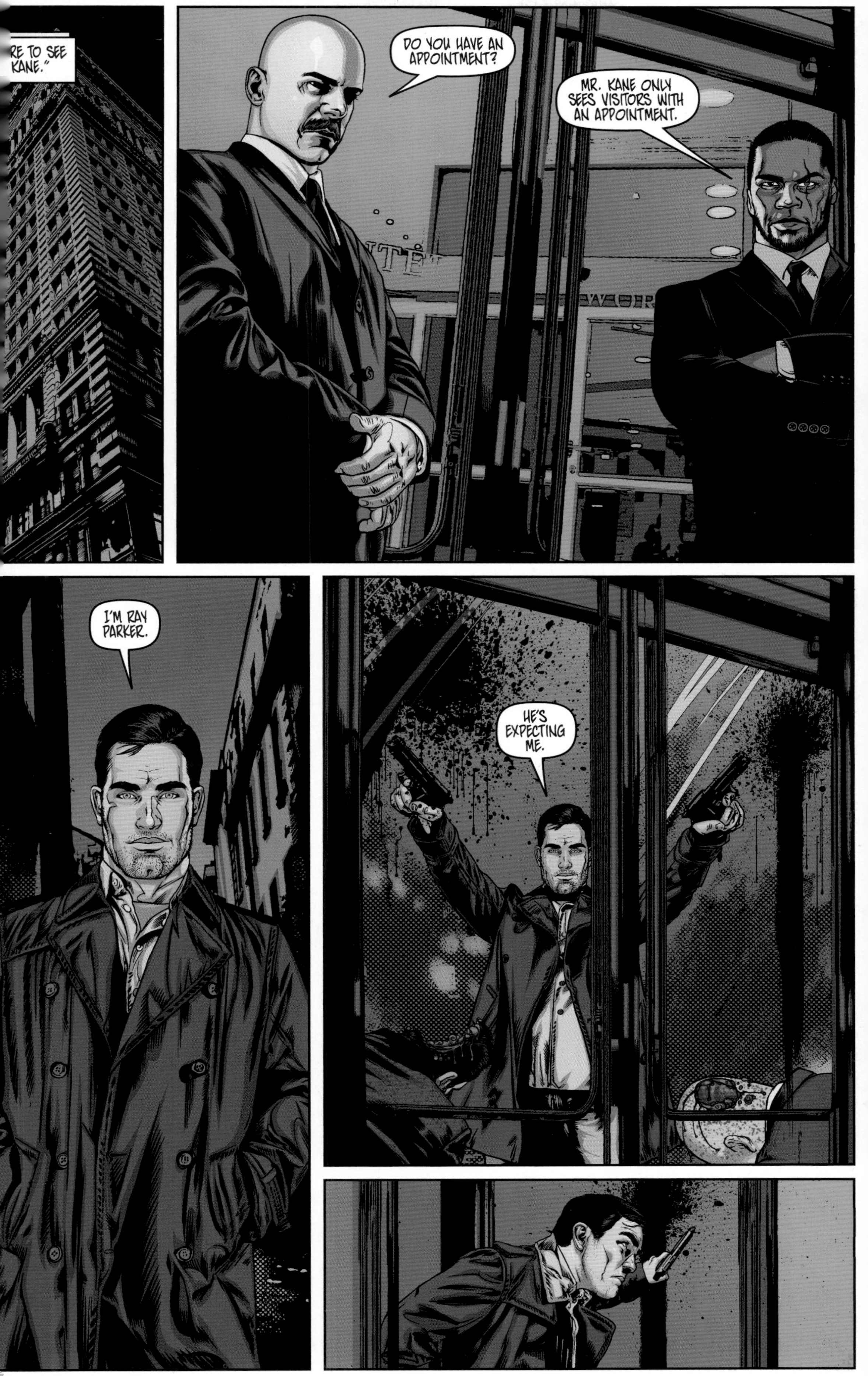
RE TO SEE
KANE."
DO YOU HAVE AN APPOINTMENT?
MR. KANE ONLY SEES VISITORS WITH AN APPOINTMENT.
I'M RAY PARKER.
HE'S EXPECTING ME.

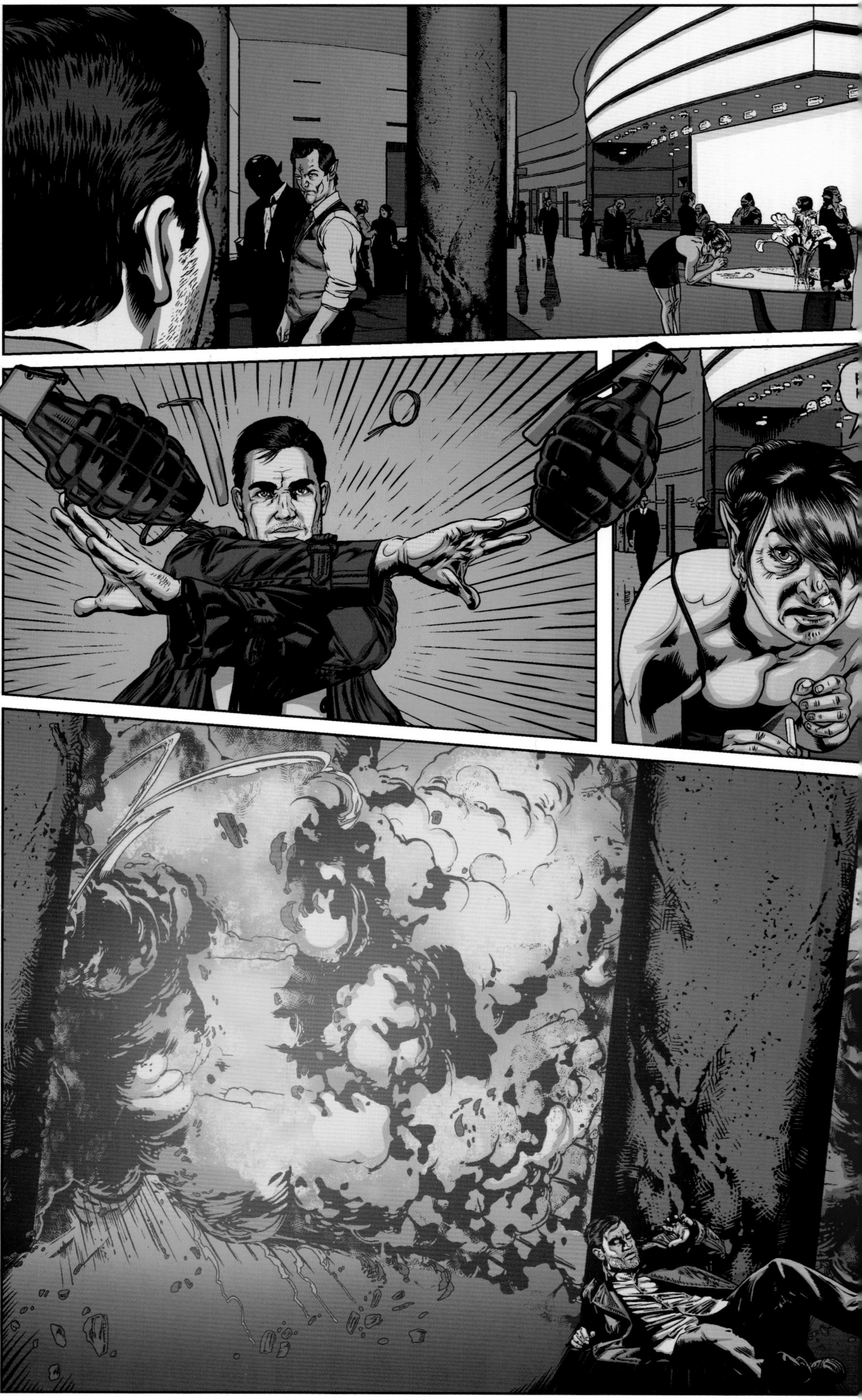

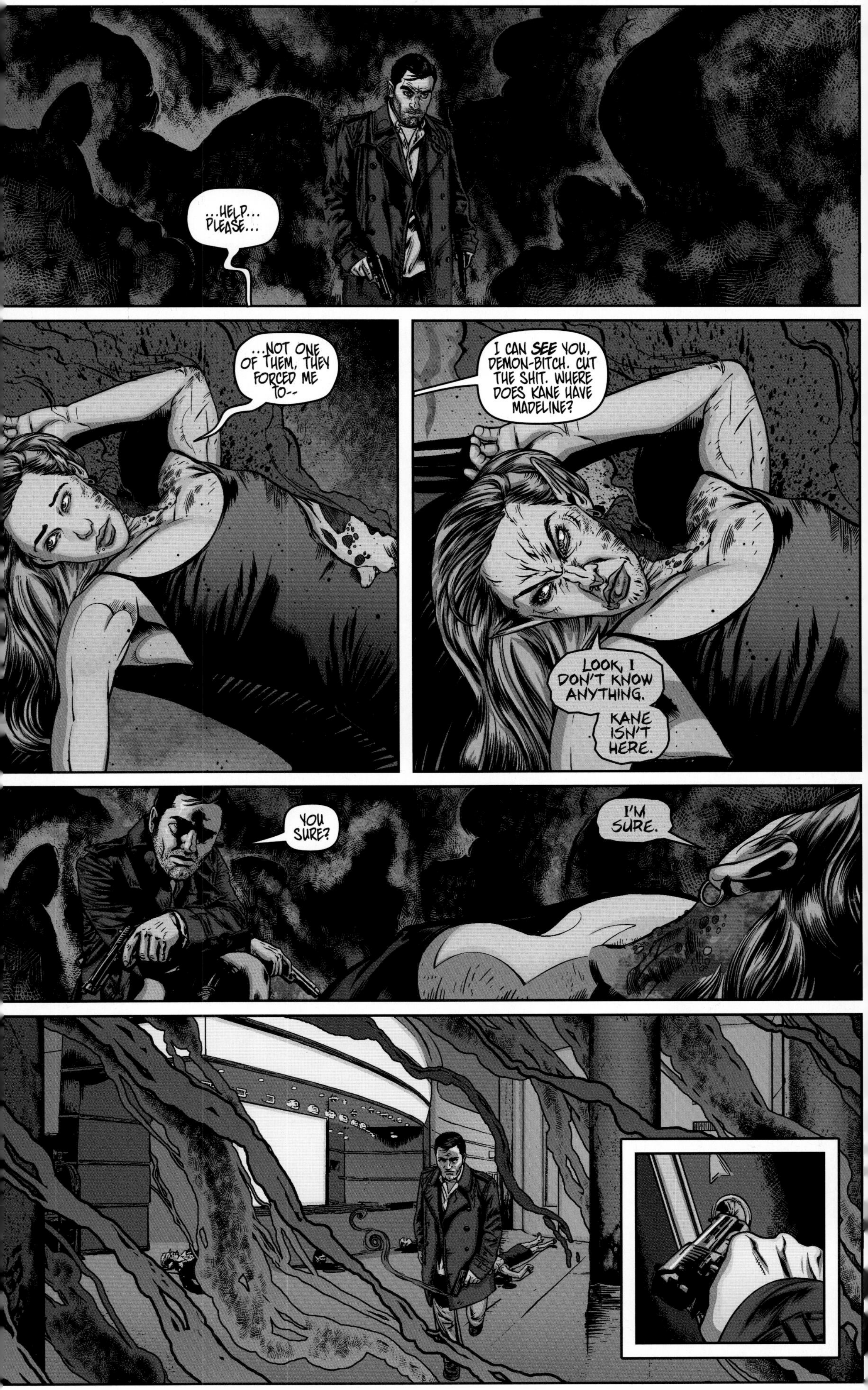
...HELP... PLEASE...
...NOT ONE OF THEM, THEY FORCED ME TO--
I CAN SEE YOU, DEMON-BITCH. CUT THE SHIT. WHERE DOES KANE HAVE MADELINE?
LOOK, I DON'T KNOW ANYTHING.
KANE ISN'T HERE.
YOU SURE?
I'M SURE.

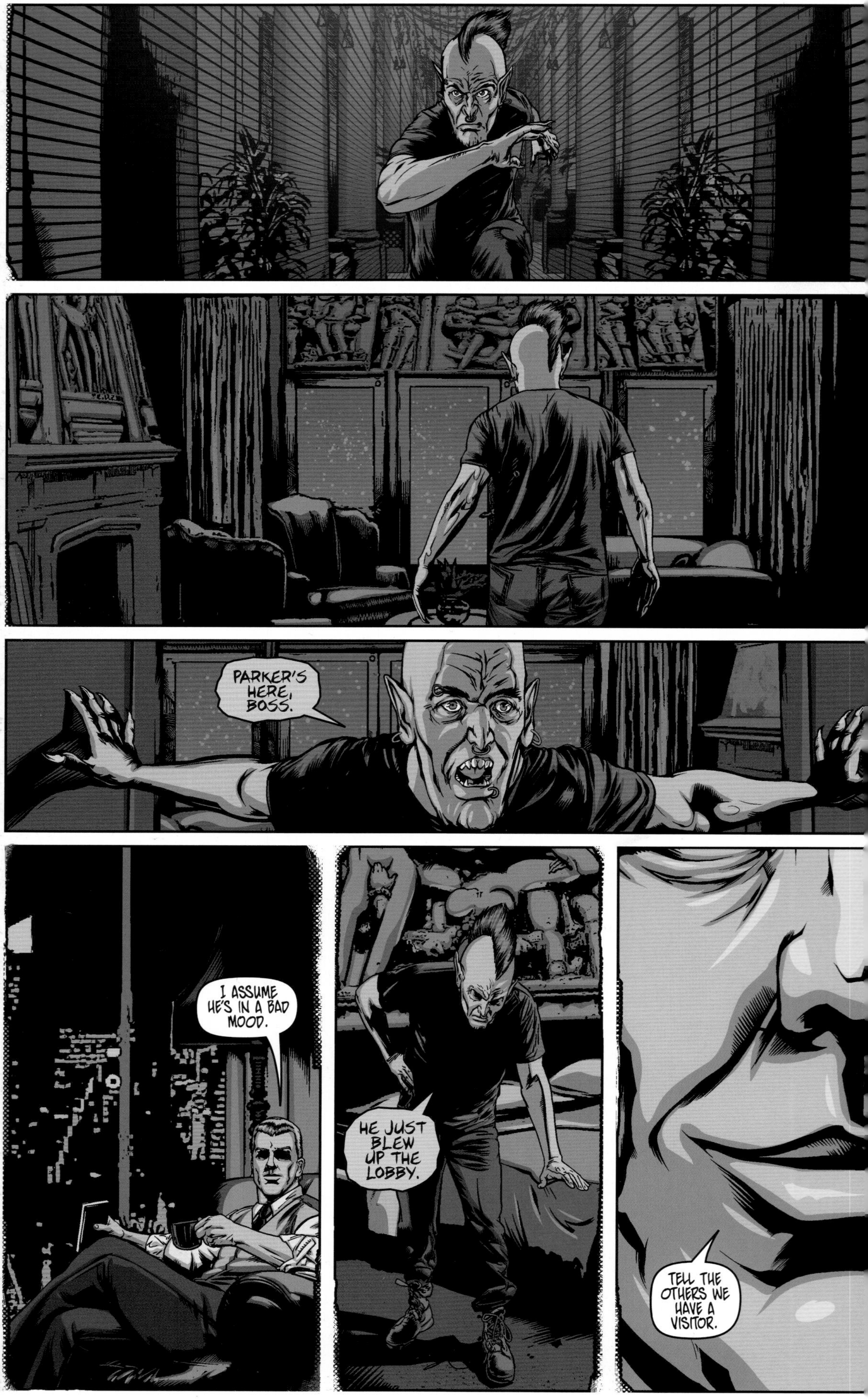
PARKER'S HERE, BOSS.
I ASSUME HE'S IN A BAD MOOD.
HE JUST BLEW UP THE LOBBY.
TELL THE OTHERS WE HAVE A VISITOR.

EASY DOES IT, BOYS. I DON'T WANT ANY OF YOU BLOWING THE BACK OF MY HEAD OFF WHEN THE DOORS OPEN.

DING

MOTHER... PUSS... BUCKET...

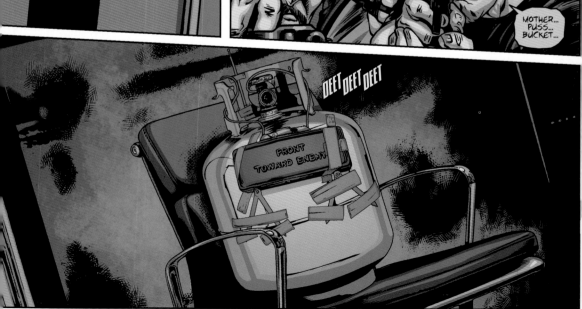

DEET DEET DEET

FRONT TOWARD ENEMY

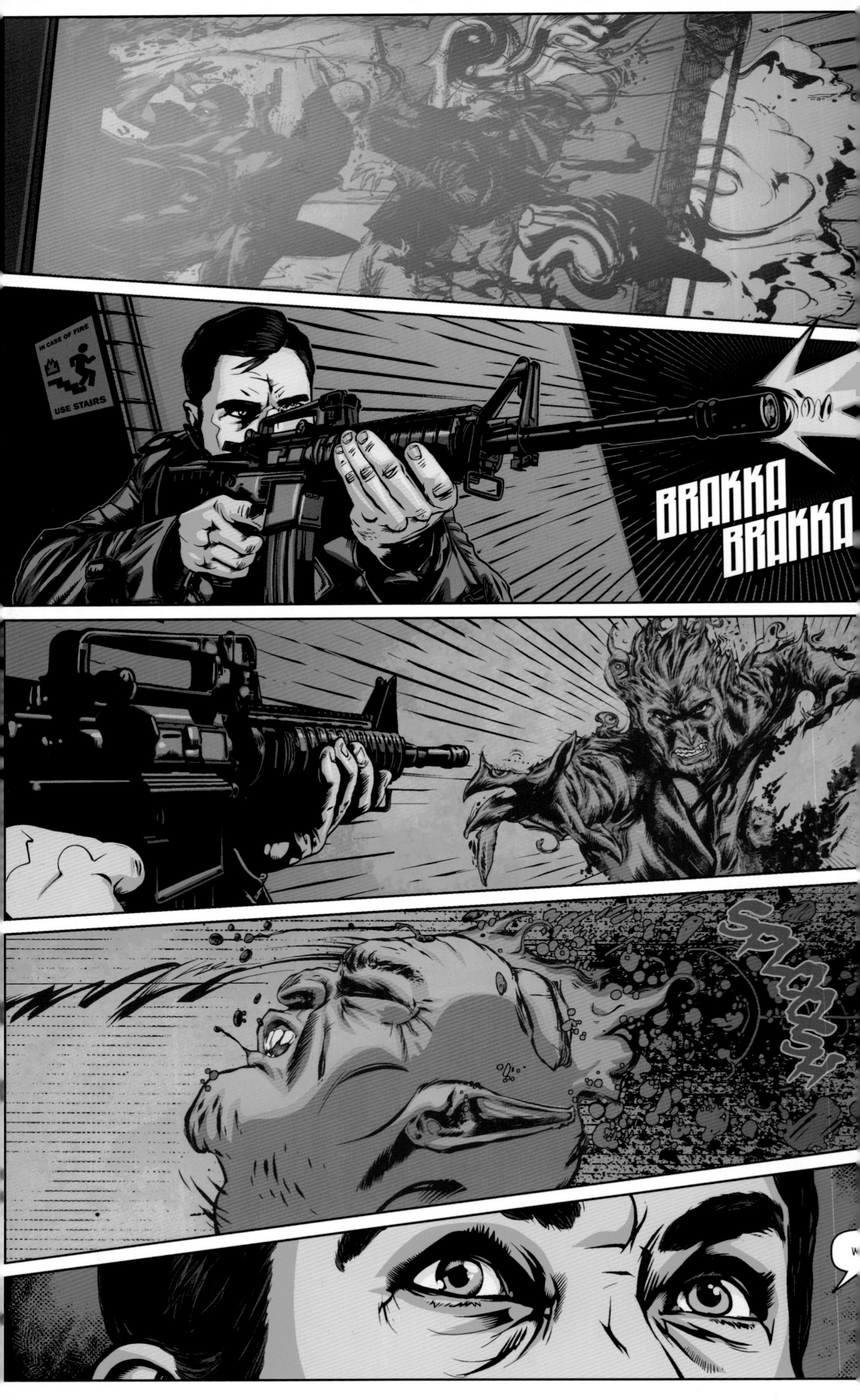
IN CASE OF FIRE
USE STAIRS
BRAKKA BRAKKA
SPLOOSH

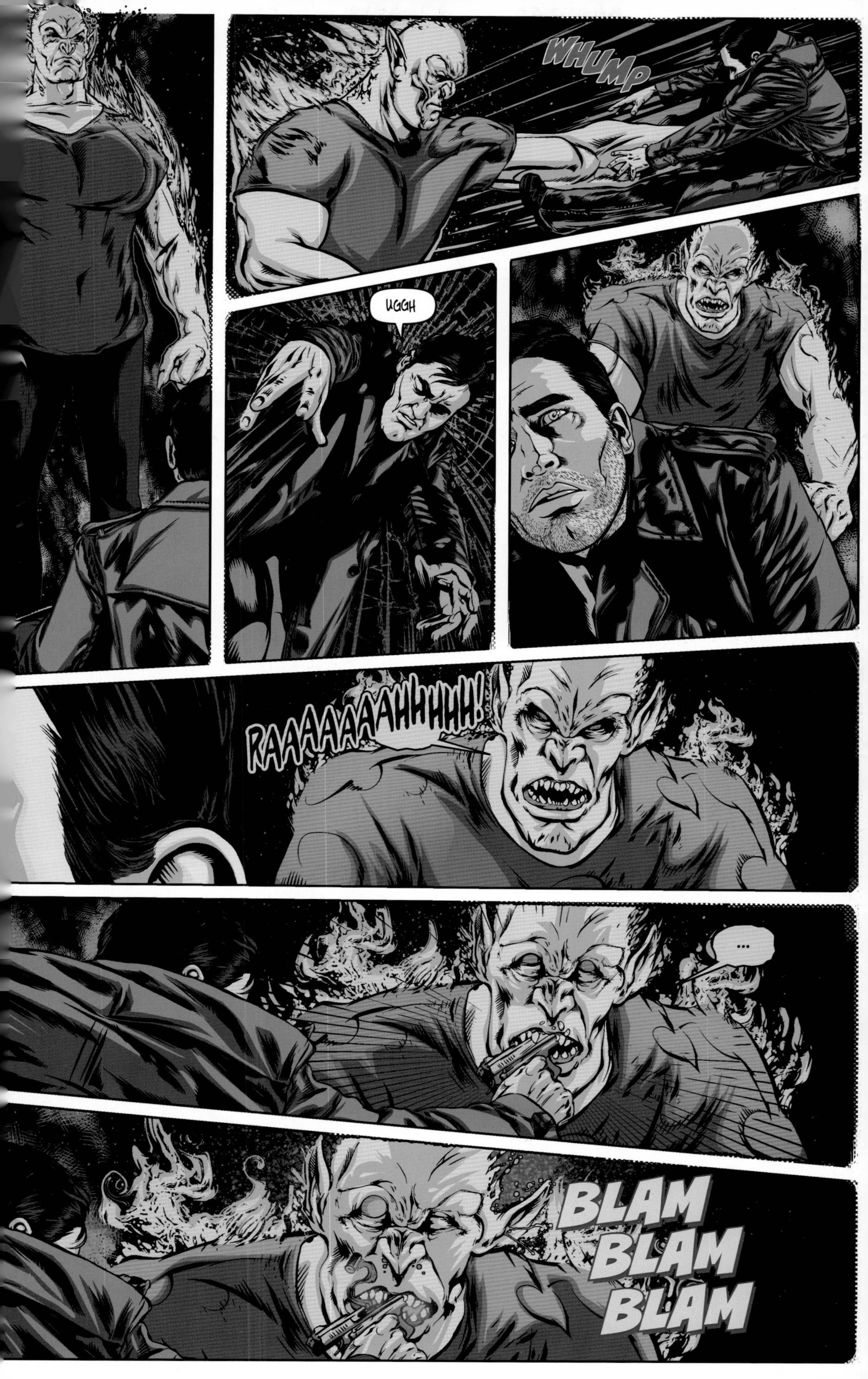
WHUMP
UGGH
RAAAAAAAHHHHH!
...
BLAM
BLAM
BLAM

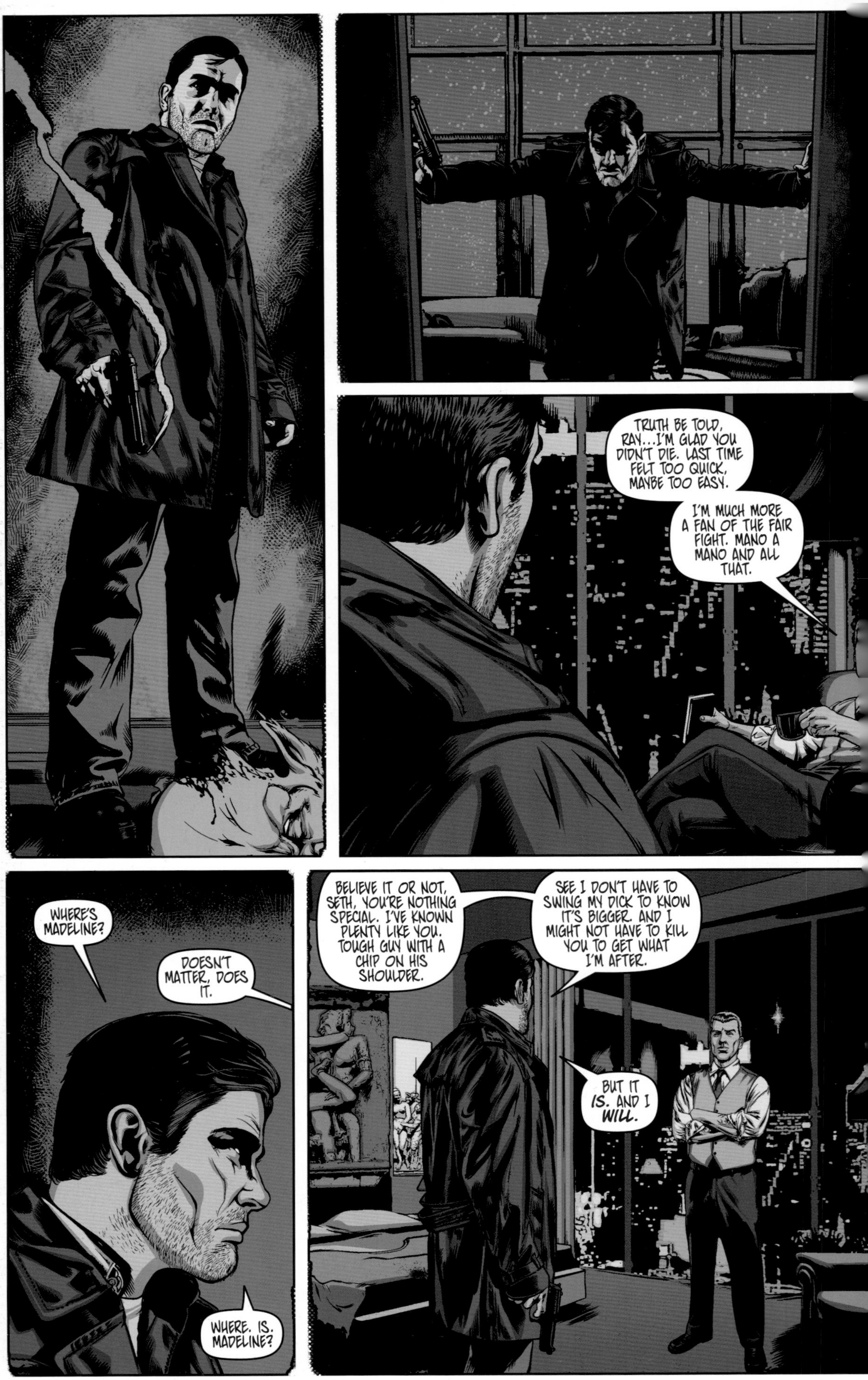
TRUTH BE TOLD, RAY... I'M GLAD YOU DIDN'T DIE. LAST TIME FELT TOO QUICK, MAYBE TOO EASY.
I'M MUCH MORE A FAN OF THE FAIR FIGHT. MANO A MANO AND ALL THAT.
WHERE'S MADELINE?
DOESN'T MATTER, DOES IT.
WHERE. IS. MADELINE?
BELIEVE IT OR NOT, SETH, YOU'RE NOTHING SPECIAL. I'VE KNOWN PLENTY LIKE YOU. TOUGH GUY WITH A CHIP ON HIS SHOULDER.
SEE I DON'T HAVE TO SWING MY DICK TO KNOW IT'S BIGGER. AND I MIGHT NOT HAVE TO KILL YOU TO GET WHAT I'M AFTER.
BUT IT *IS*. AND I ***WILL***.

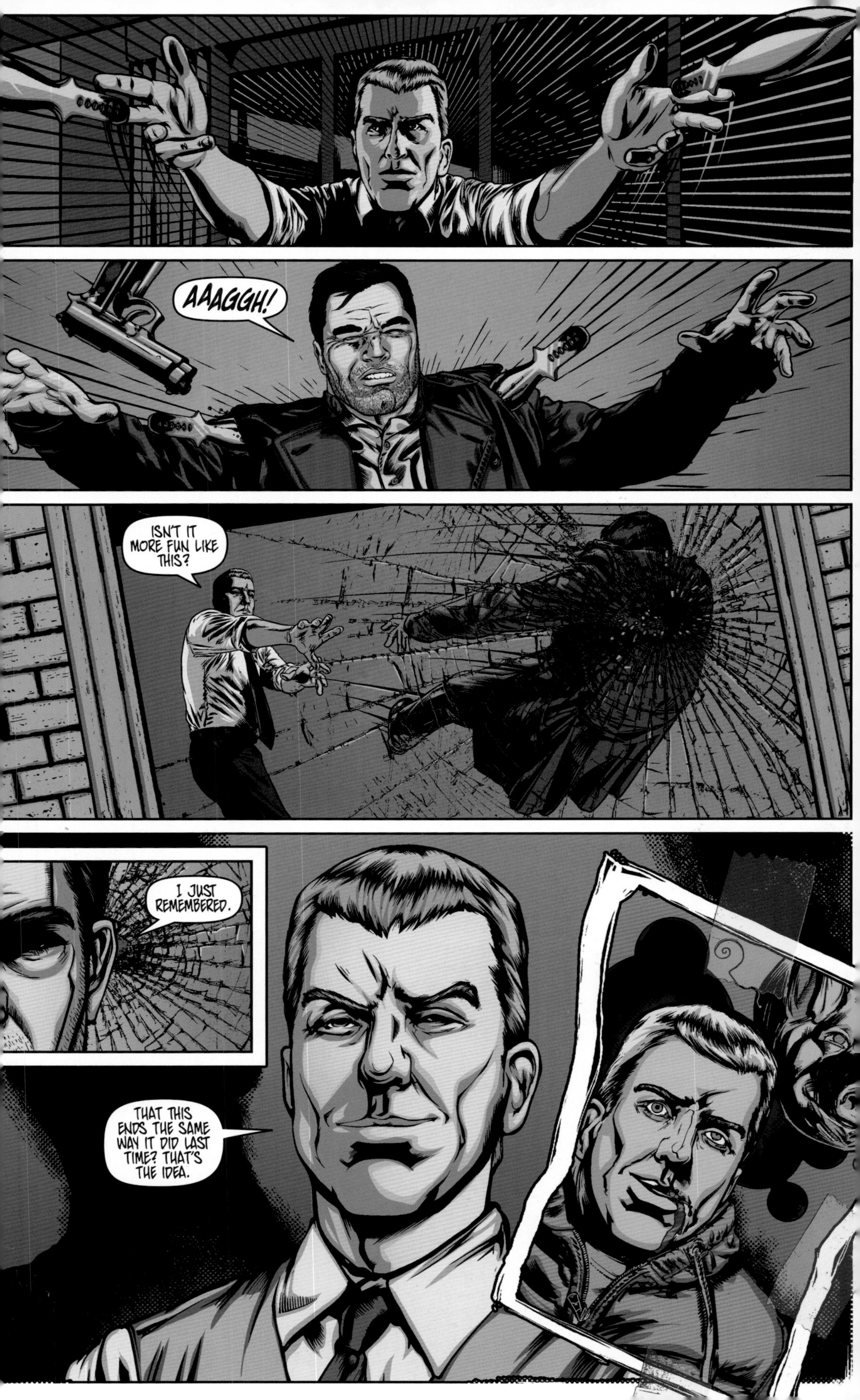
AAAGGH!
ISN'T IT MORE FUN LIKE THIS?
I JUST REMEMBERED.
THAT THIS ENDS THE SAME WAY IT DID LAST TIME? THAT'S THE IDEA.

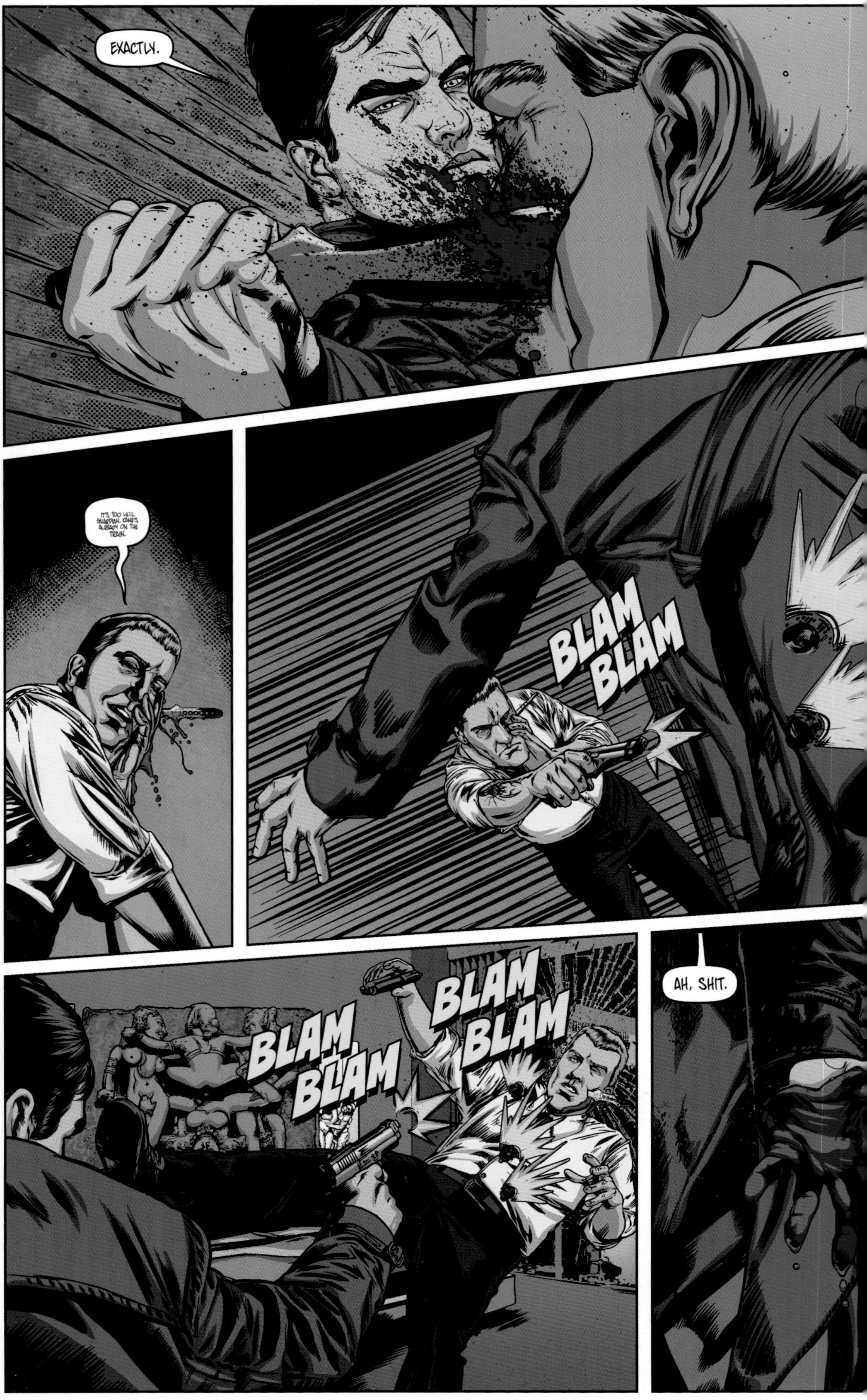
EXACTLY.
IT'S TOO LATE, GUARDIAN. KANE'S ALREADY ON THE TRAIN.
BLAM BLAM
BLAM BLAM
BLAM BLAM
AH, SHIT.

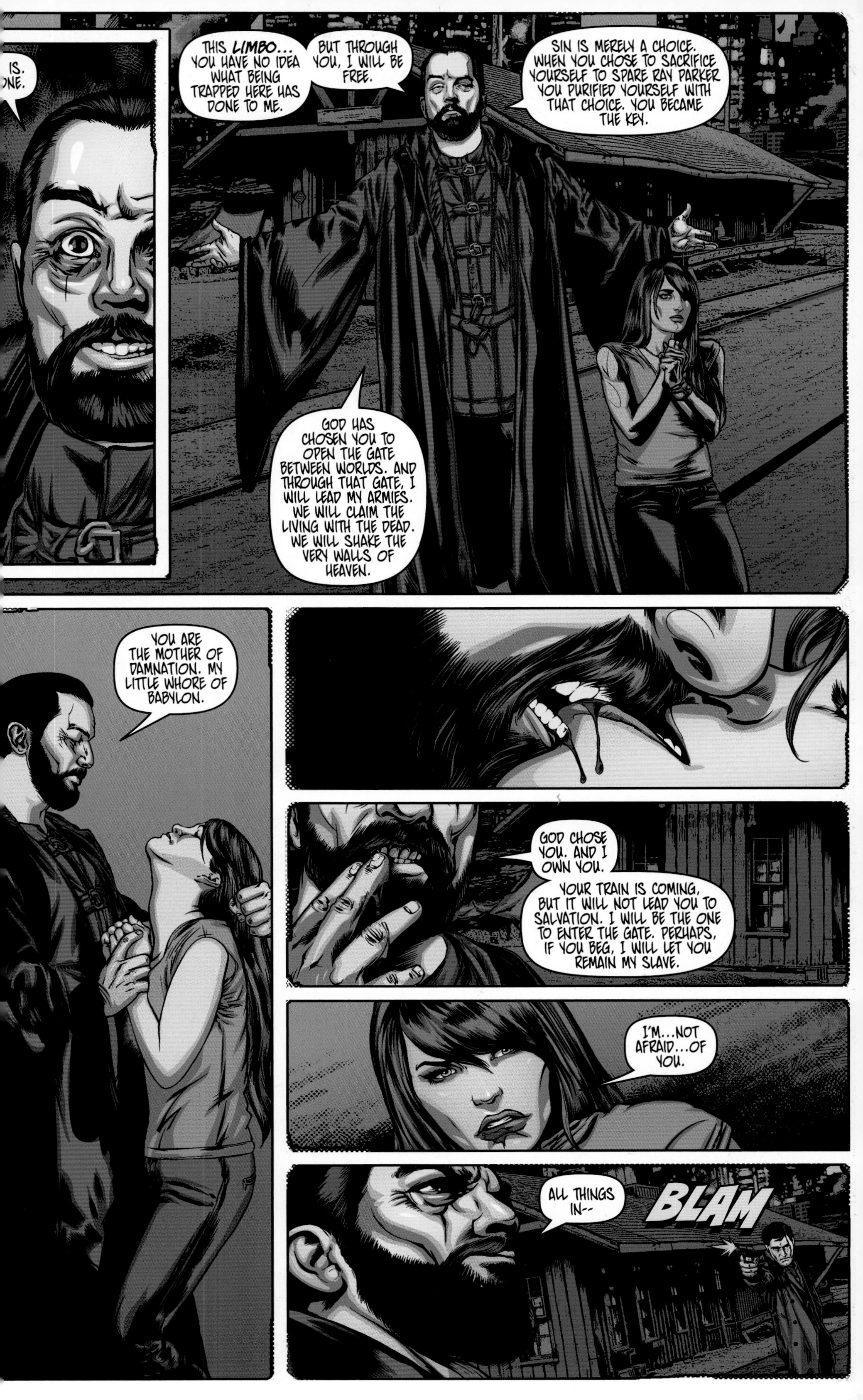
IS.
THIS LIMBO... YOU HAVE NO IDEA WHAT BEING TRAPPED HERE HAS DONE TO ME.
BUT THROUGH YOU, I WILL BE FREE.
SIN IS MERELY A CHOICE. WHEN YOU CHOSE TO SACRIFICE YOURSELF TO SPARE RAY PARKER YOU PURIFIED YOURSELF WITH THAT CHOICE. YOU BECAME THE KEY.
GOD HAS CHOSEN YOU TO OPEN THE GATE BETWEEN WORLDS. AND THROUGH THAT GATE, I WILL LEAD MY ARMIES. WE WILL CLAIM THE LIVING WITH THE DEAD. WE WILL SHAKE THE VERY WALLS OF HEAVEN.
YOU ARE THE MOTHER OF DAMNATION. MY LITTLE WHORE OF BABYLON.
GOD CHOSE YOU. AND I OWN YOU.
YOUR TRAIN IS COMING, BUT IT WILL NOT LEAD YOU TO SALVATION. I WILL BE THE ONE TO ENTER THE GATE. PERHAPS, IF YOU BEG, I WILL LET YOU REMAIN MY SLAVE.
I'M...NOT AFRAID...OF YOU.
ALL THINGS IN--
BLAM

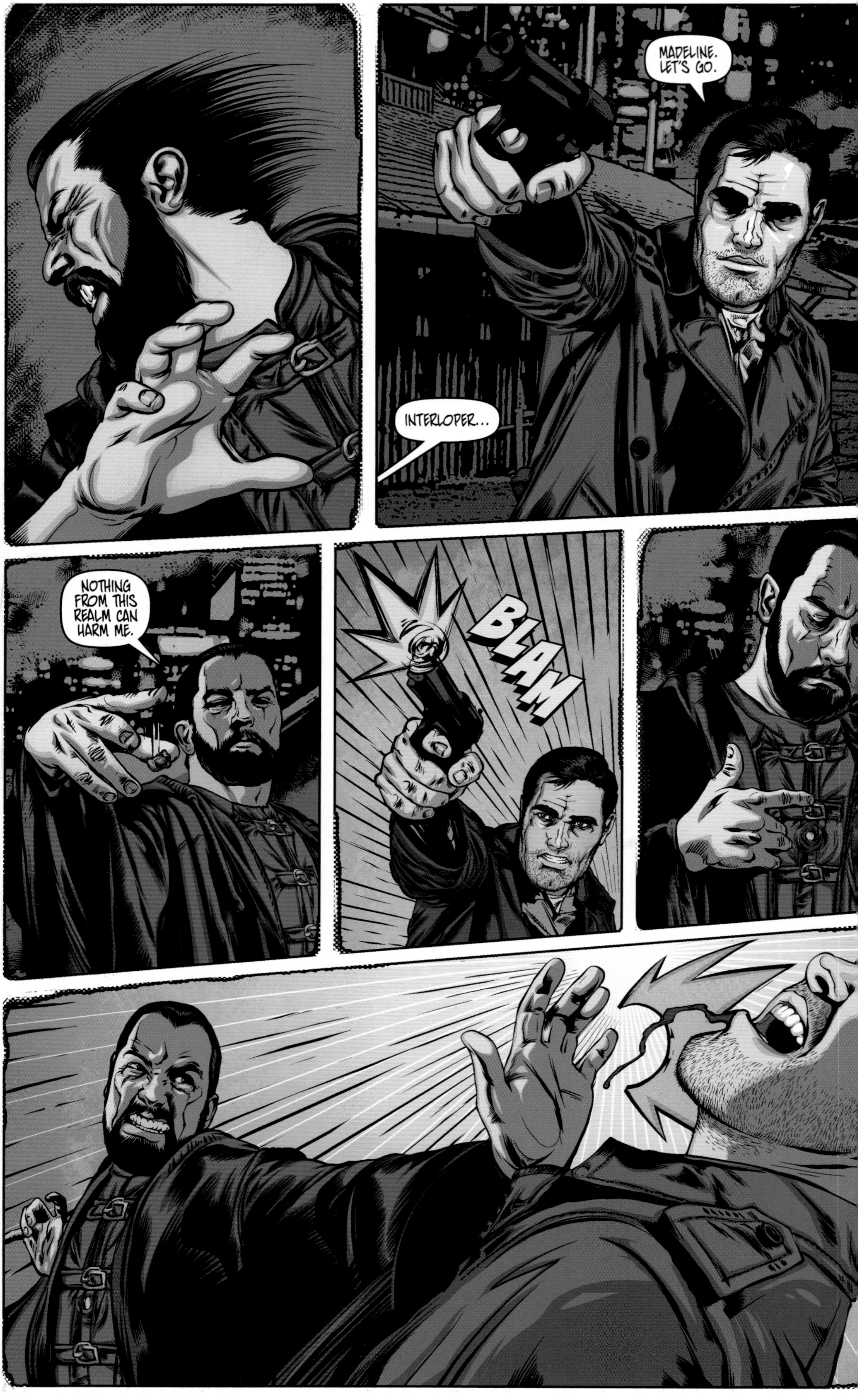
MADELINE. LET'S GO.
INTERLOPER...
NOTHING FROM THIS REALM CAN HARM ME.
BLAM

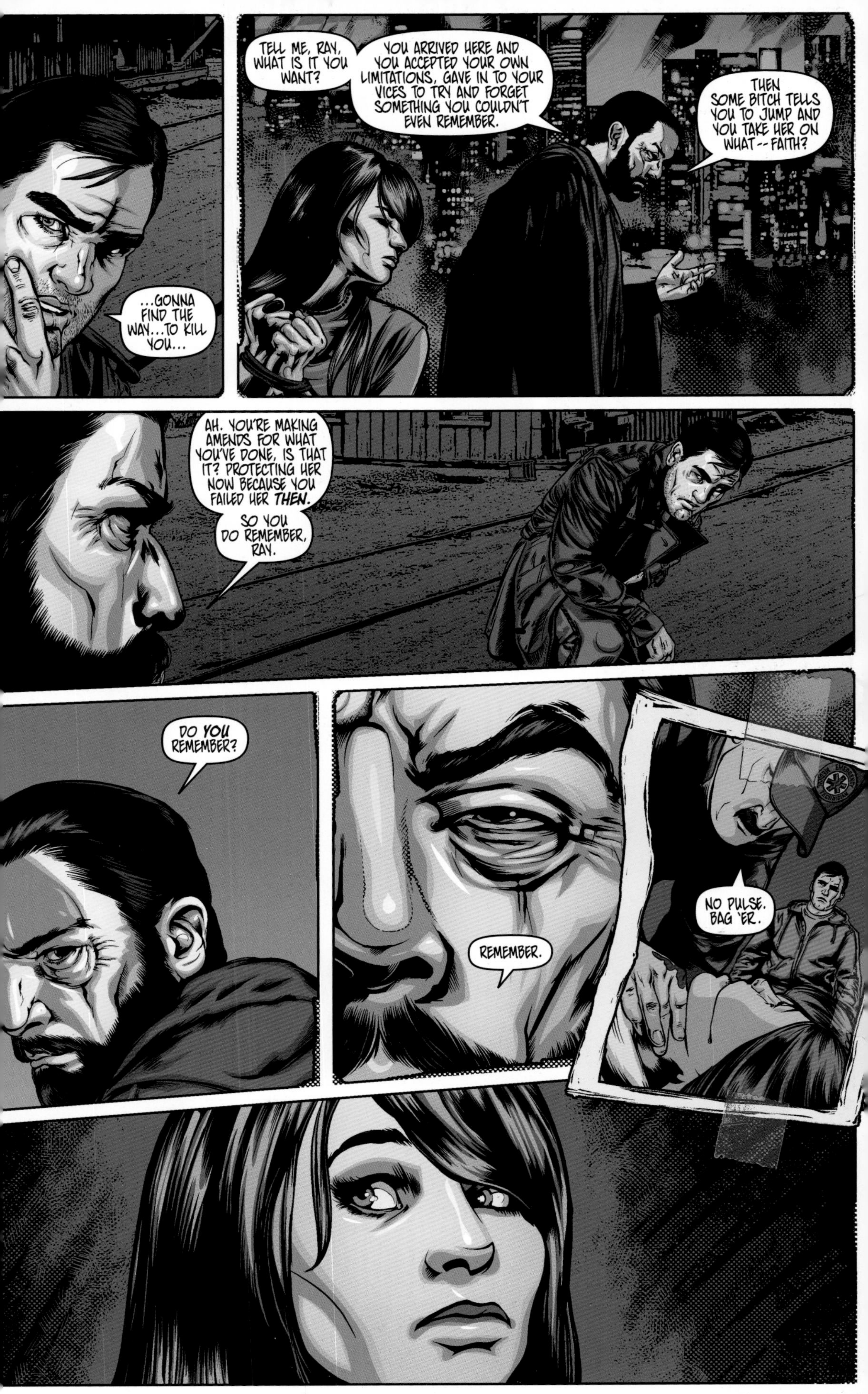
...GONNA FIND THE WAY...TO KILL YOU...
TELL ME, RAY, WHAT IS IT YOU WANT?
YOU ARRIVED HERE AND YOU ACCEPTED YOUR OWN LIMITATIONS, GAVE IN TO YOUR VICES TO TRY AND FORGET SOMETHING YOU COULDN'T EVEN REMEMBER.
THEN SOME BITCH TELLS YOU TO JUMP AND YOU TAKE HER ON WHAT--FAITH?
AH. YOU'RE MAKING AMENDS FOR WHAT YOU'VE DONE, IS THAT IT? PROTECTING HER NOW BECAUSE YOU FAILED HER ***THEN.***
SO YOU DO REMEMBER, RAY.
DO ***YOU*** REMEMBER?
REMEMBER.
NO PULSE. BAG 'ER.

I KNOW HOW YOU DIED, MADELINE.

I DON'T UNDERSTAND...

I RECOGNIZED YOU, WHEN I FIRST SAW YOU HERE, I JUST COULDN'T REMEMBER.

RAY--

I'M SORRY... YOU'RE HERE BECAUSE OF ME. *I'M* RESPONSIBLE, MADDIE. I KILLED YOU.

WELL, THAT'S NOT *ENTIRELY* TRUE. YOUR ACTIONS PUT A BULLET IN HER, RAY, BUT HER CHOICES, HER *SIN*, LED HER HERE. PLENTY OF FRESH BLAME TO GO 'ROUND.

WHATTDYA THINK, LITTLE MADELINE? SHOULD YOUR KILLER BURN?

I THINK SHOUL

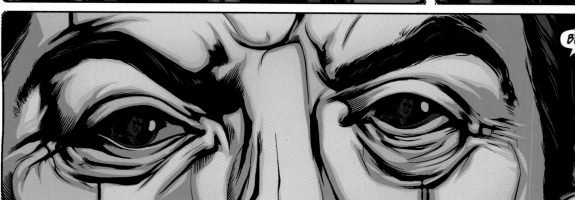

B

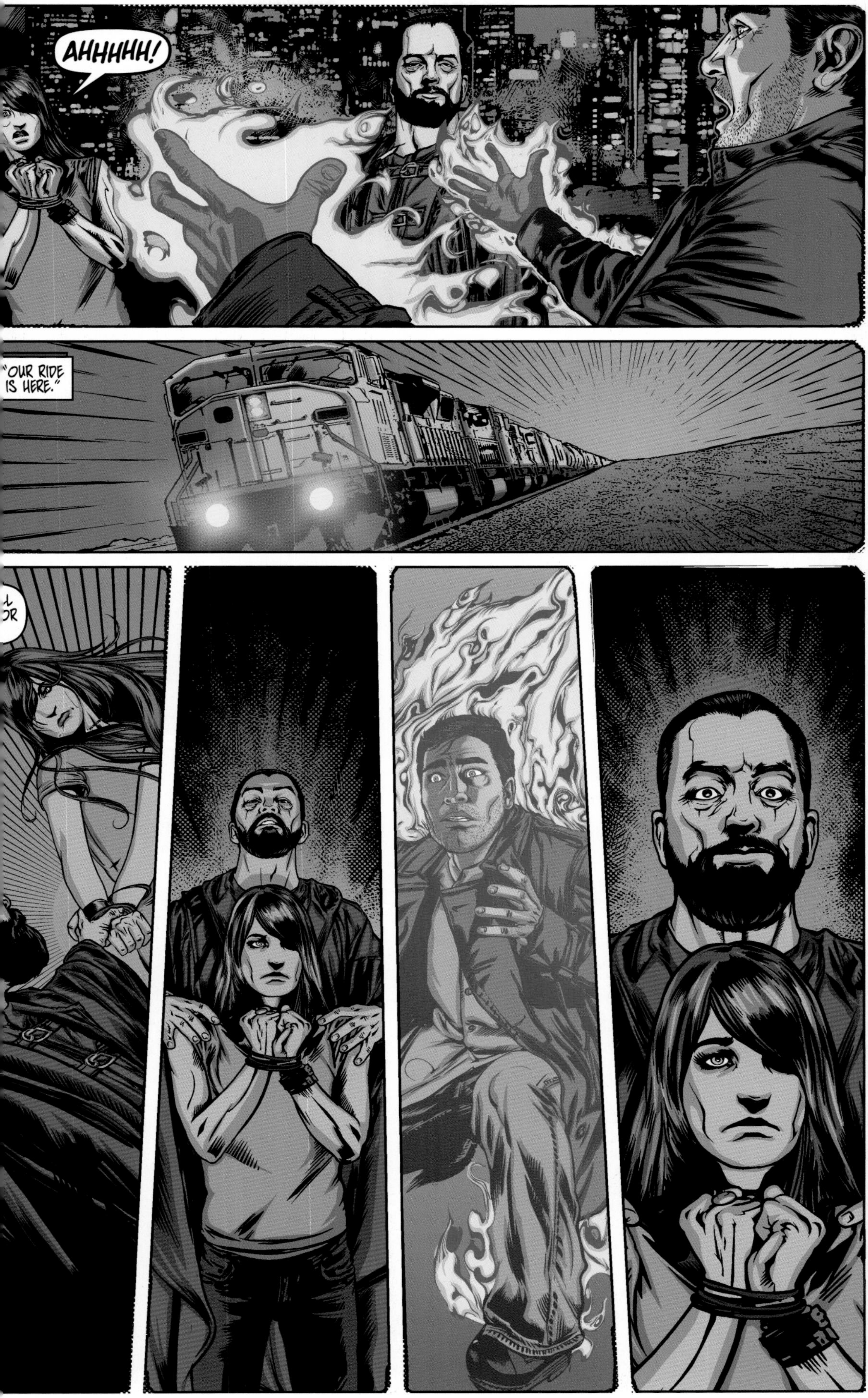
AHHHHH!
"OUR RIDE IS HERE."

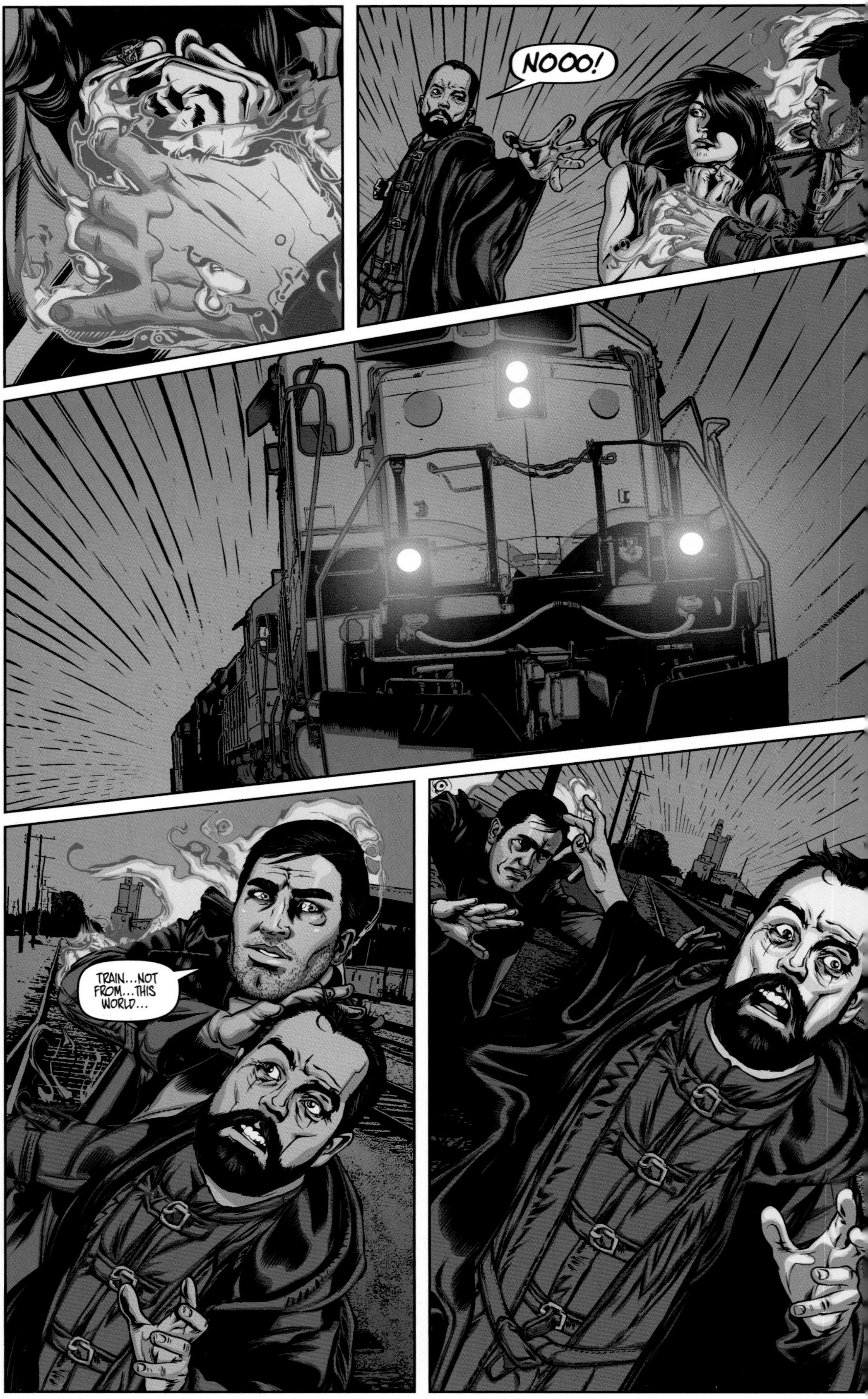
NOOO!
TRAIN...NOT FROM...THIS WORLD...

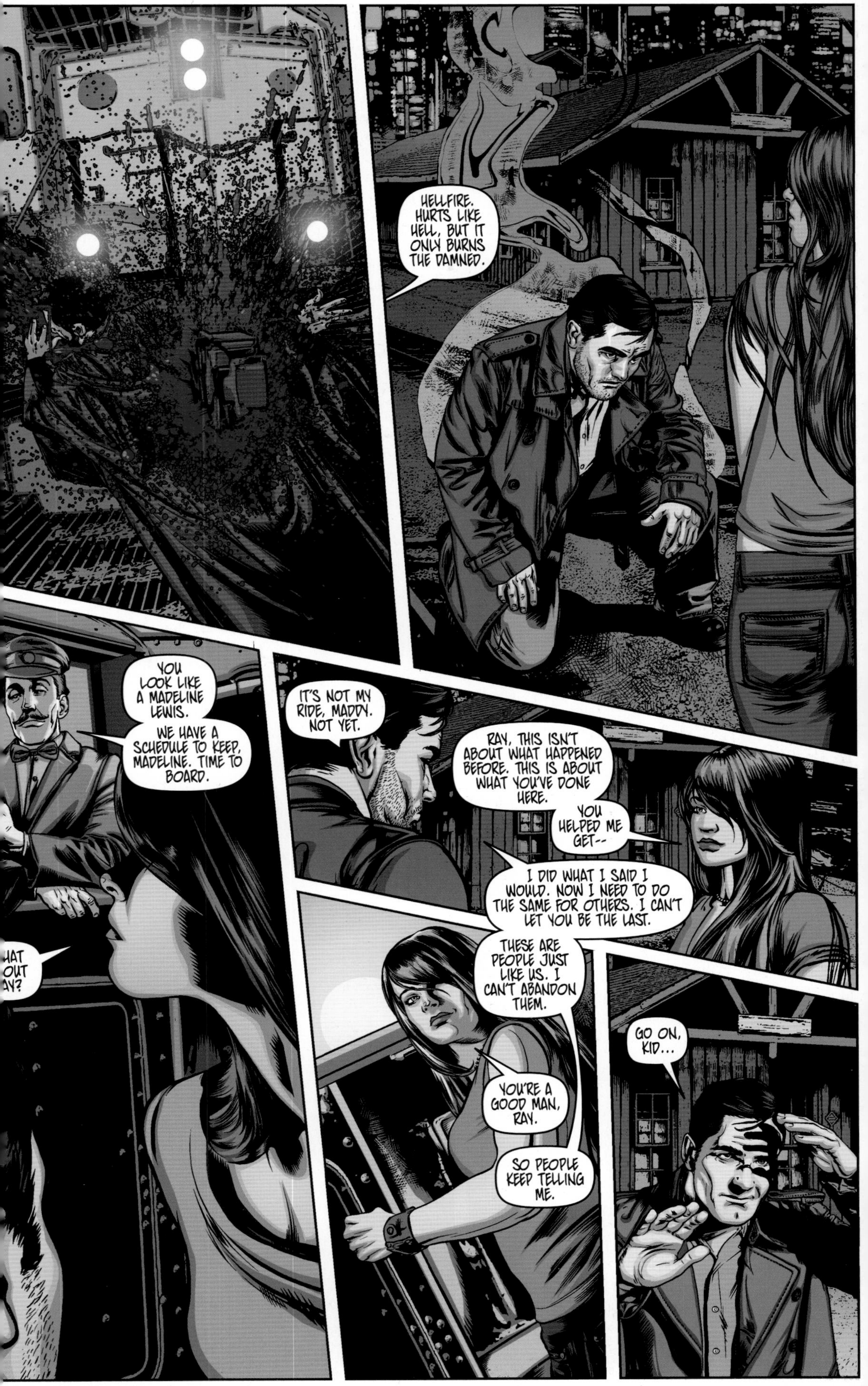
HELLFIRE. HURTS LIKE HELL, BUT IT ONLY BURNS THE DAMNED.
YOU LOOK LIKE A MADELINE LEWIS.
WE HAVE A SCHEDULE TO KEEP, MADELINE. TIME TO BOARD.
IT'S NOT MY RIDE, MADDY. NOT YET.
RAY, THIS ISN'T ABOUT WHAT HAPPENED BEFORE. THIS IS ABOUT WHAT YOU'VE DONE HERE.
YOU HELPED ME GET--
I DID WHAT I SAID I WOULD. NOW I NEED TO DO THE SAME FOR OTHERS. I CAN'T LET YOU BE THE LAST.
THESE ARE PEOPLE JUST LIKE US. I CAN'T ABANDON THEM.
YOU'RE A GOOD MAN, RAY.
SO PEOPLE KEEP TELLING ME.
GO ON, KID...

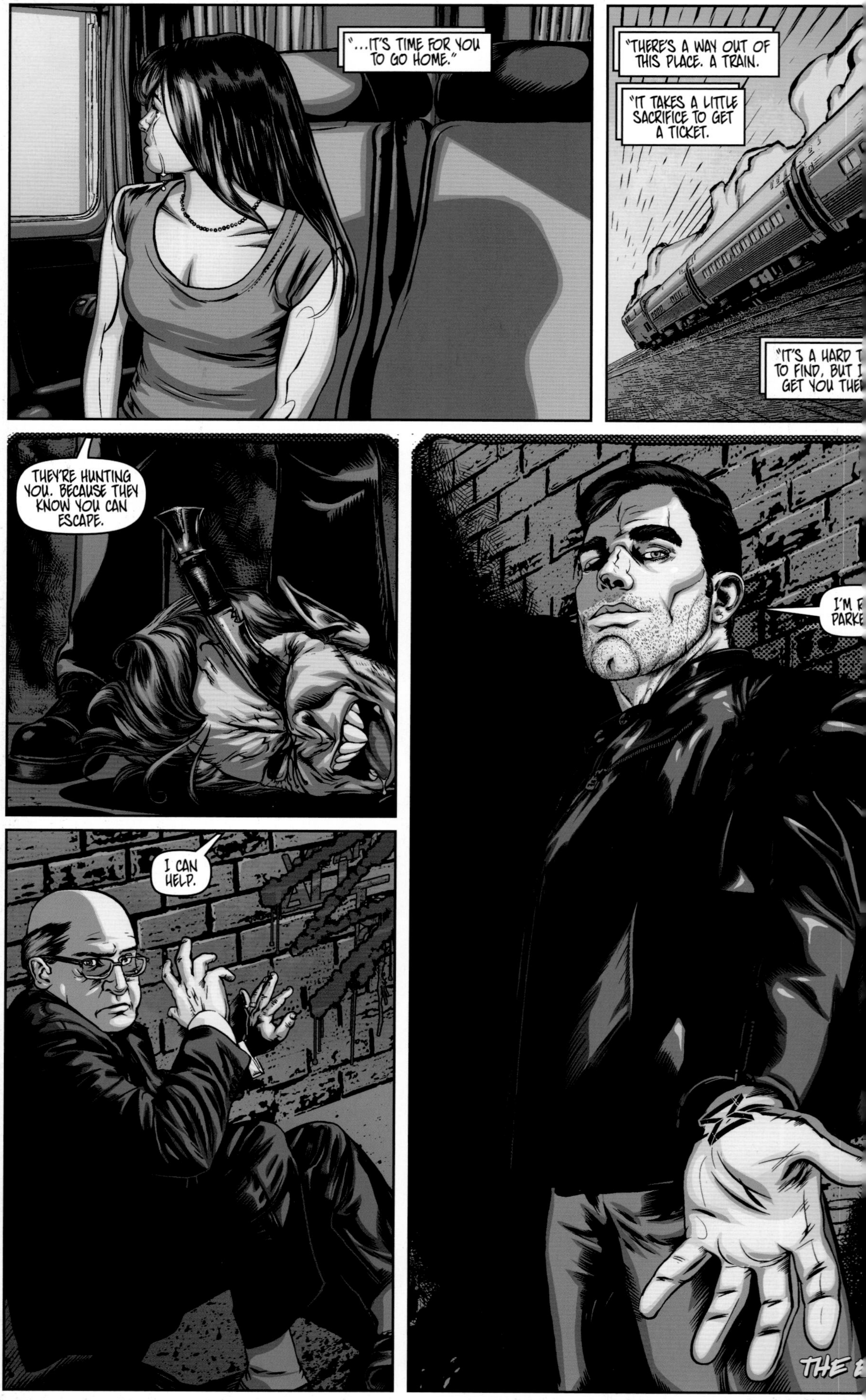
"...IT'S TIME FOR YOU TO GO HOME."
"THERE'S A WAY OUT OF THIS PLACE. A TRAIN.
"IT TAKES A LITTLE SACRIFICE TO GET A TICKET.
"IT'S A HARD TO FIND, BUT I GET YOU
THEY'RE HUNTING YOU. BECAUSE THEY KNOW YOU CAN ESCAPE.
I'M
I CAN HELP.
THE

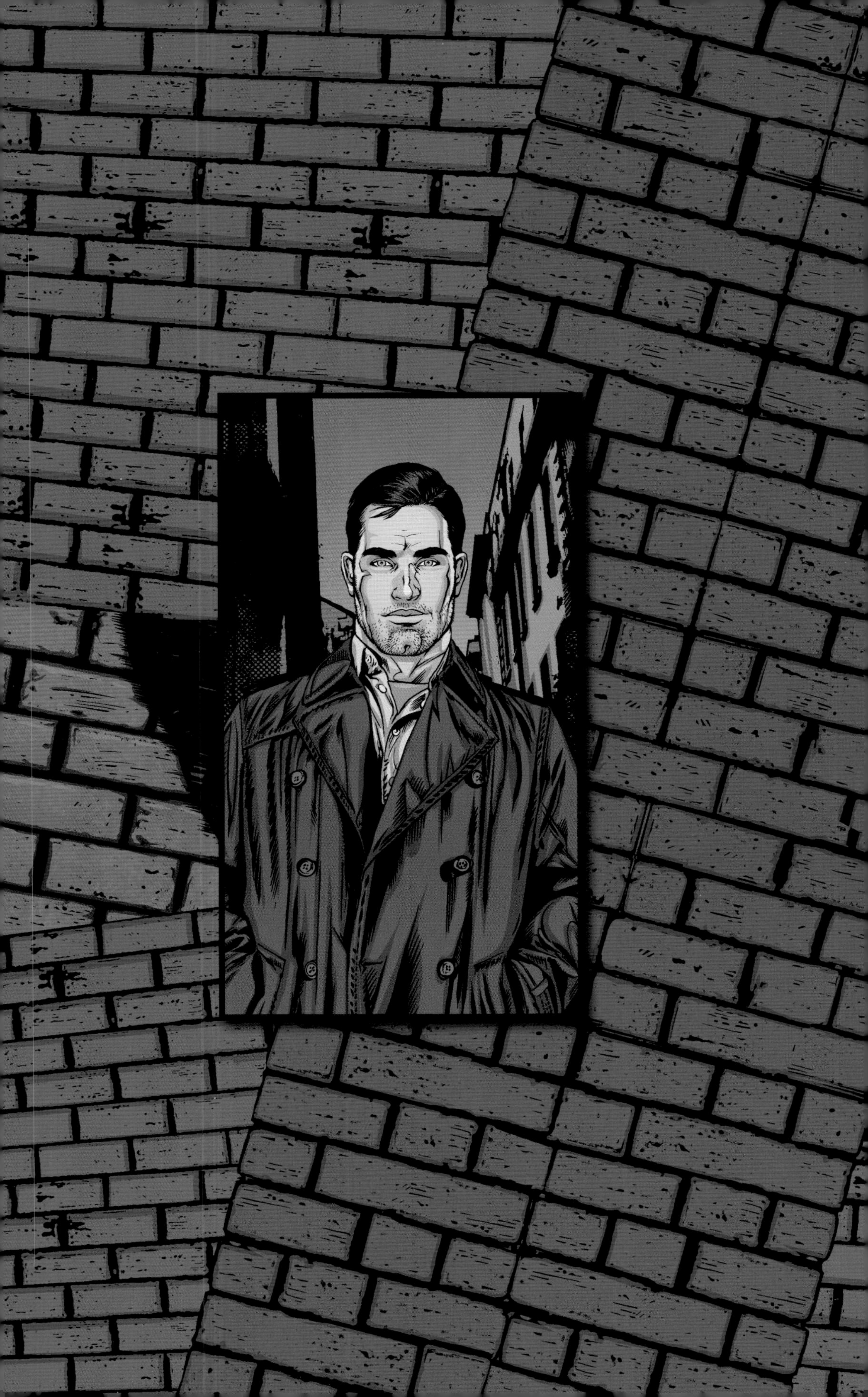

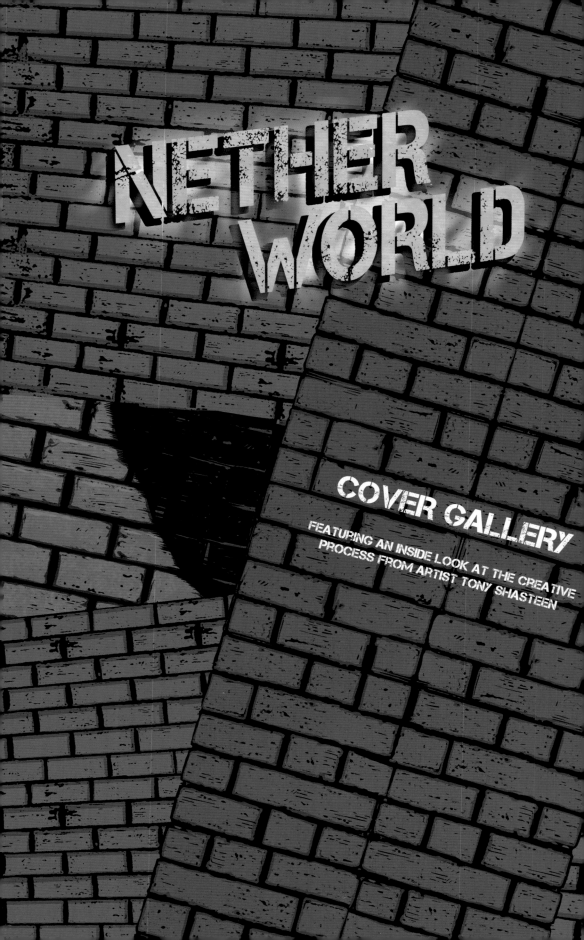

NETHER WORLD

COVER GALLERY

FEATURING AN INSIDE LOOK AT THE CREATIVE
PROCESS FROM ARTIST TONY SHASTEEN

NETHERWORLD ISSUE #1 COVER B
ART BY: BOZHIDAR SAVOV

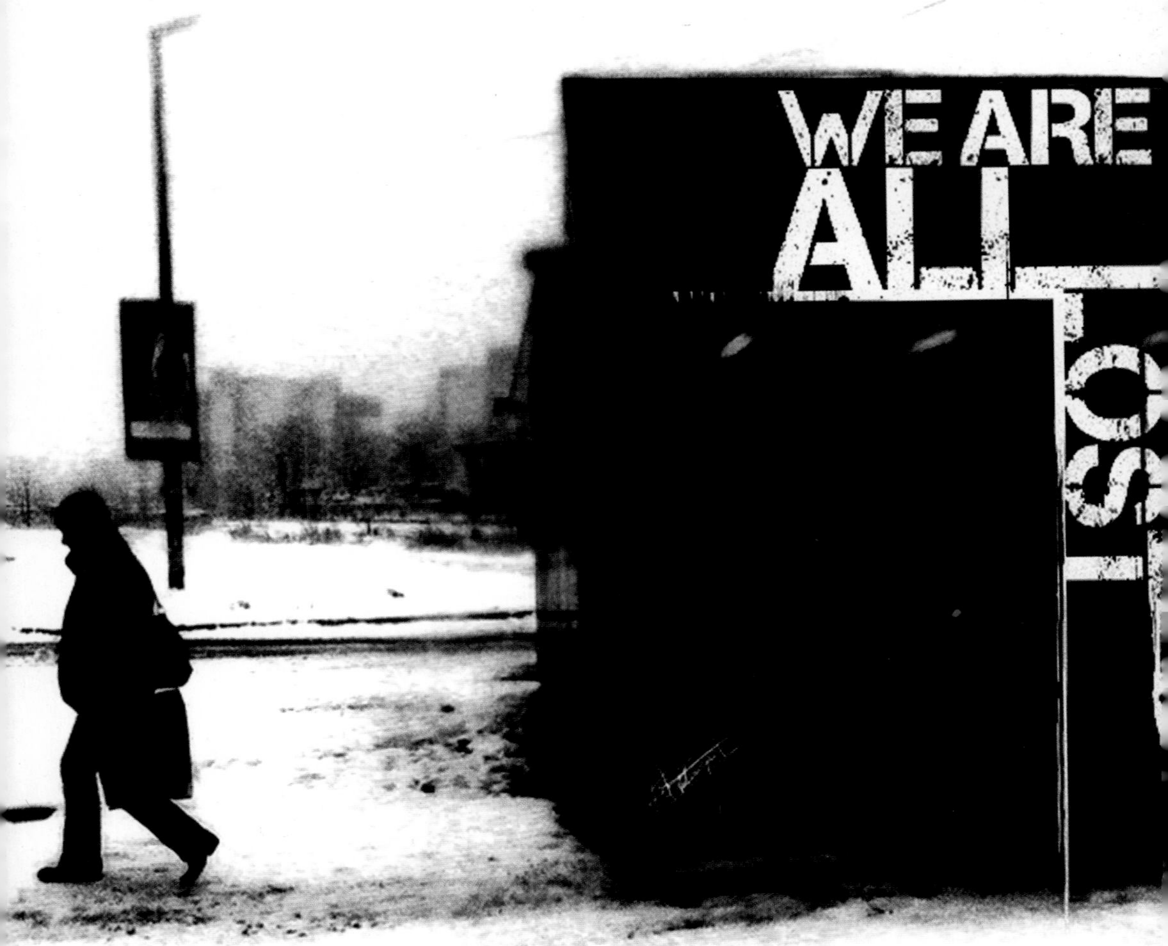
WE ARE
ALL

NETHERWORLD ISSUE #1 COVER A LAYOUTS AND INKS

ART BY: TONY SHASTEEN

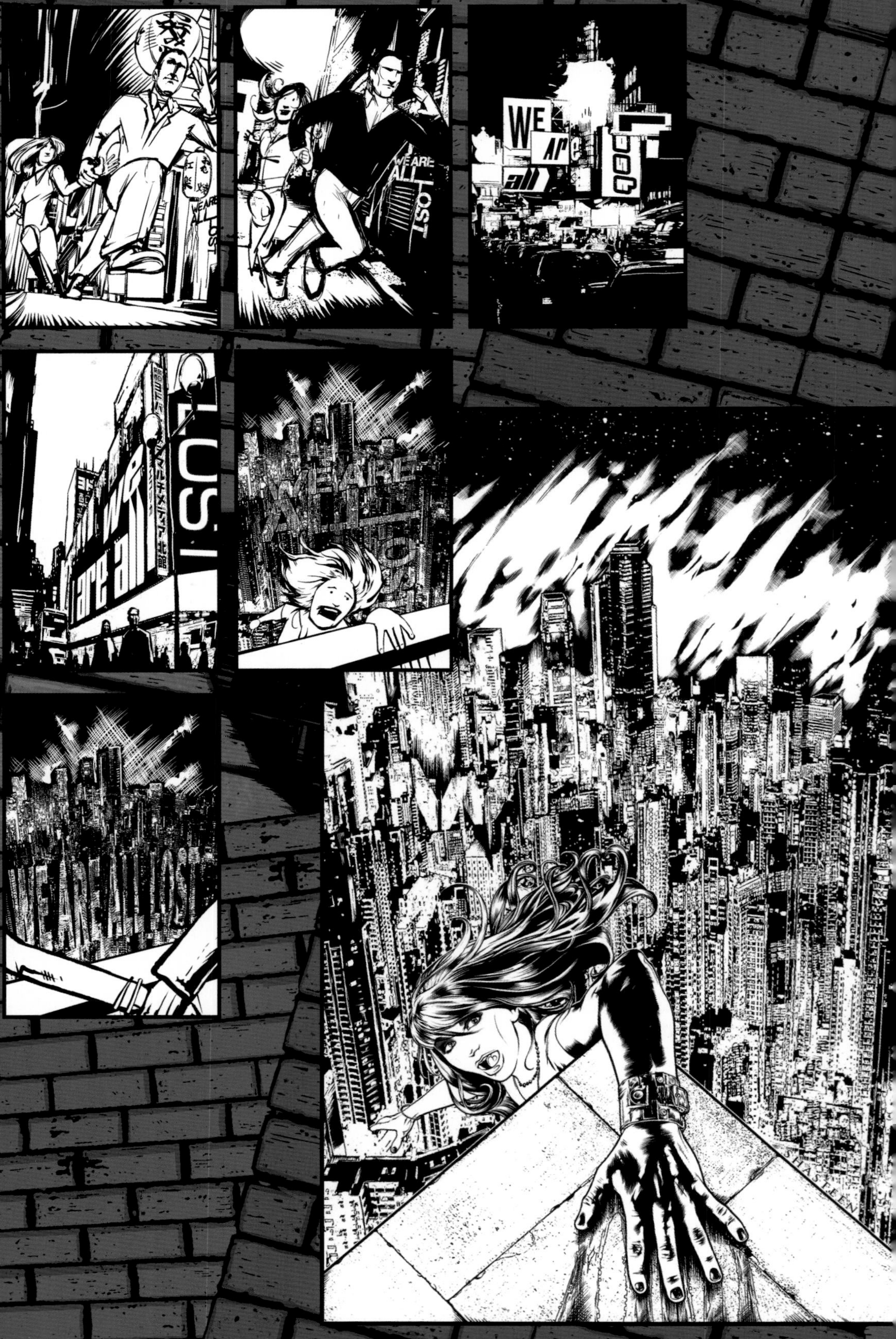
WE ARE ALL LOST
SHASTEEN

NETHERWORLD ISSUE #1 COVER A

ART BY: TONY SHASTEEN

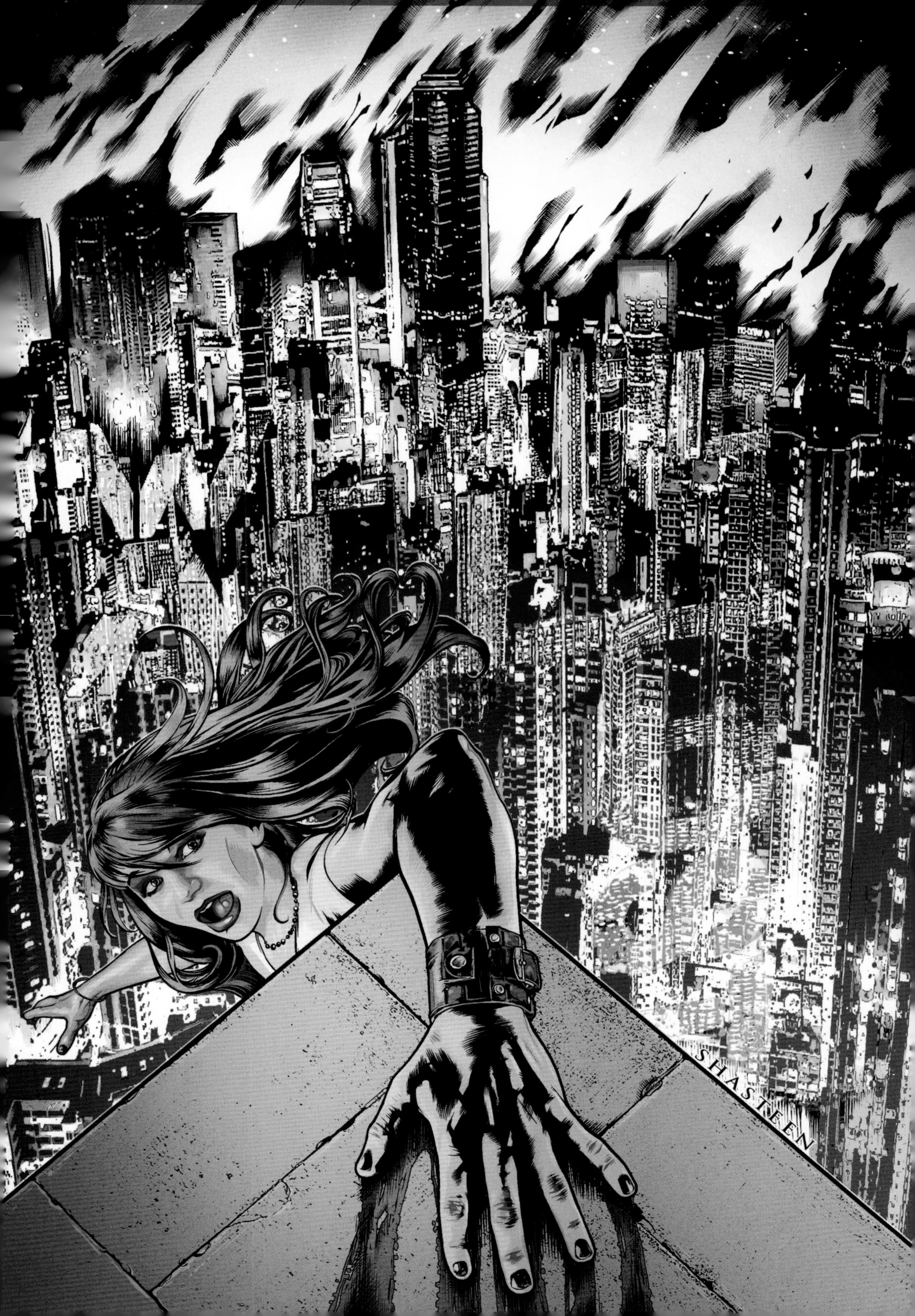
SHASTEEN

NETHERWORLD ISSUE #2 LAYOUTS AND INKS

ART BY: TONY SHASTEEN

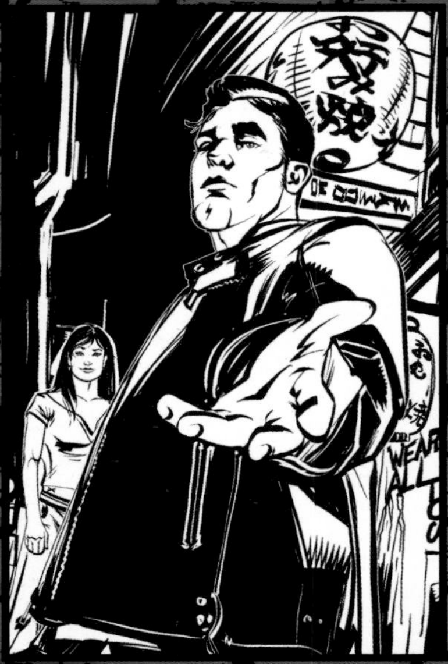

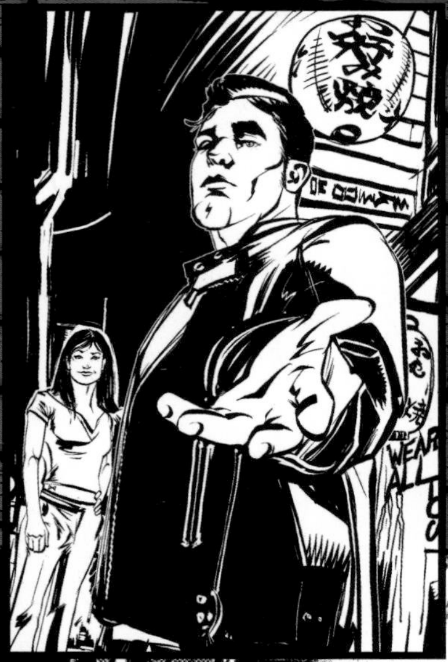

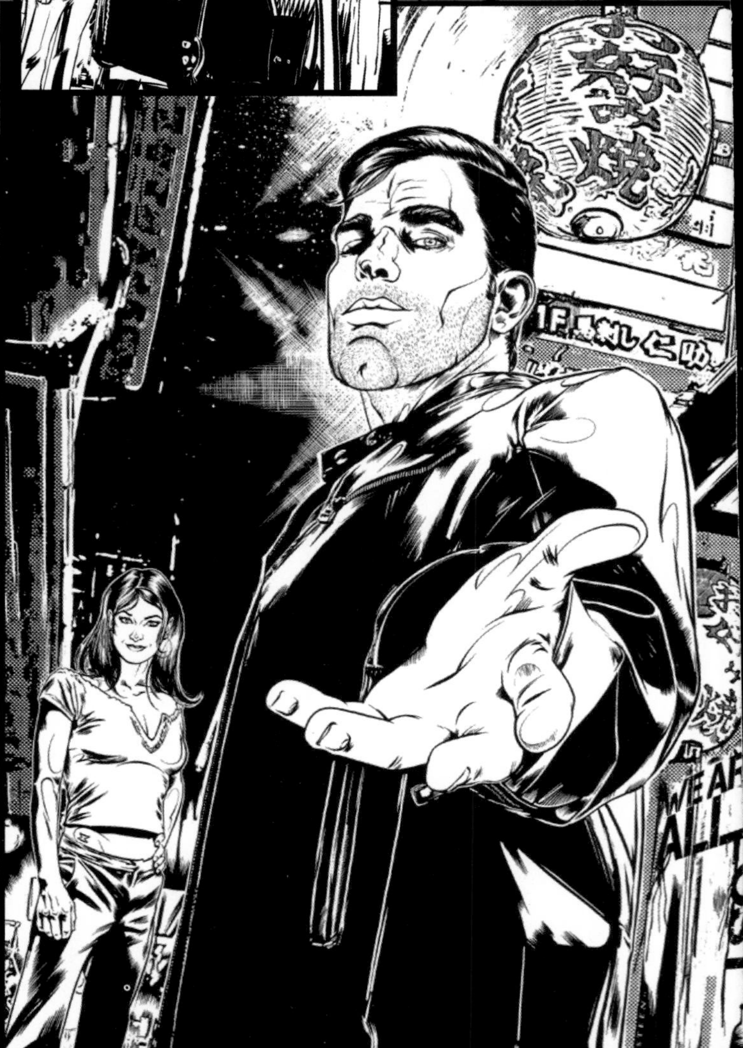

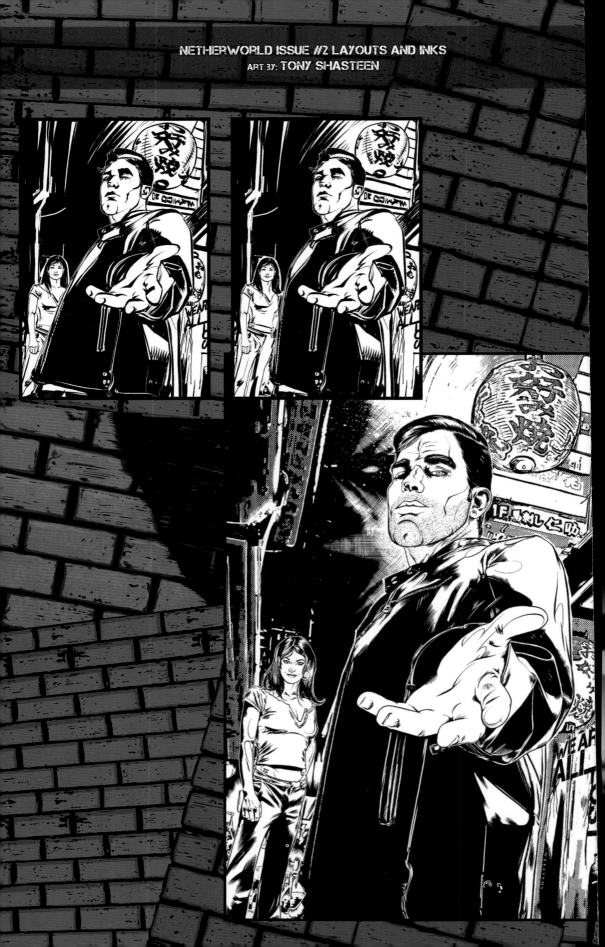

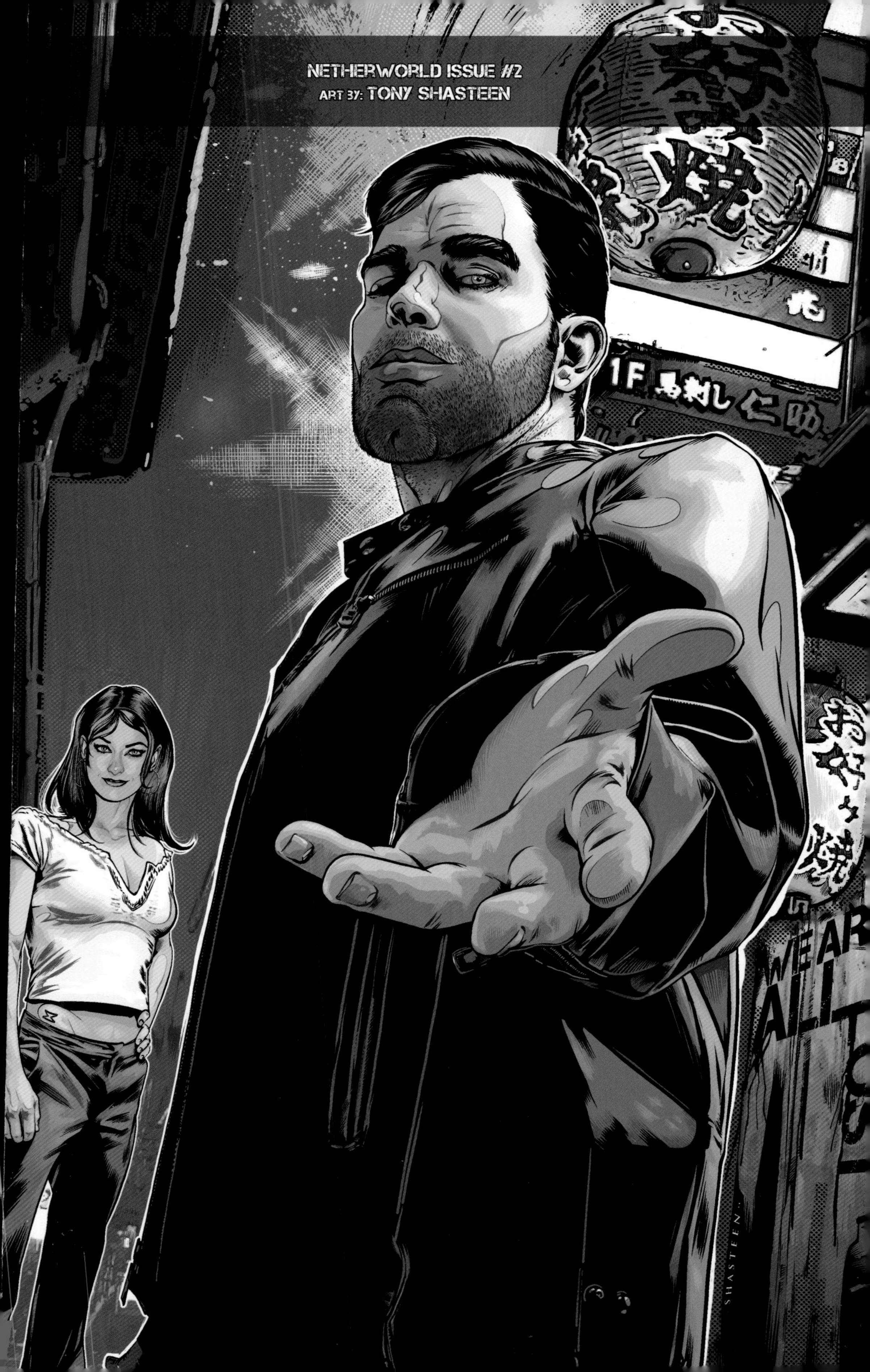
1F
WEAR
ALL
SHASTEEN

NETHERWORLD ISSUE #2
ART BY: TONY SHASTEEN

NETHERWORLD ISSUE #3 LAYOUTS AND INKS

ART BY: TONY SHASTEEN

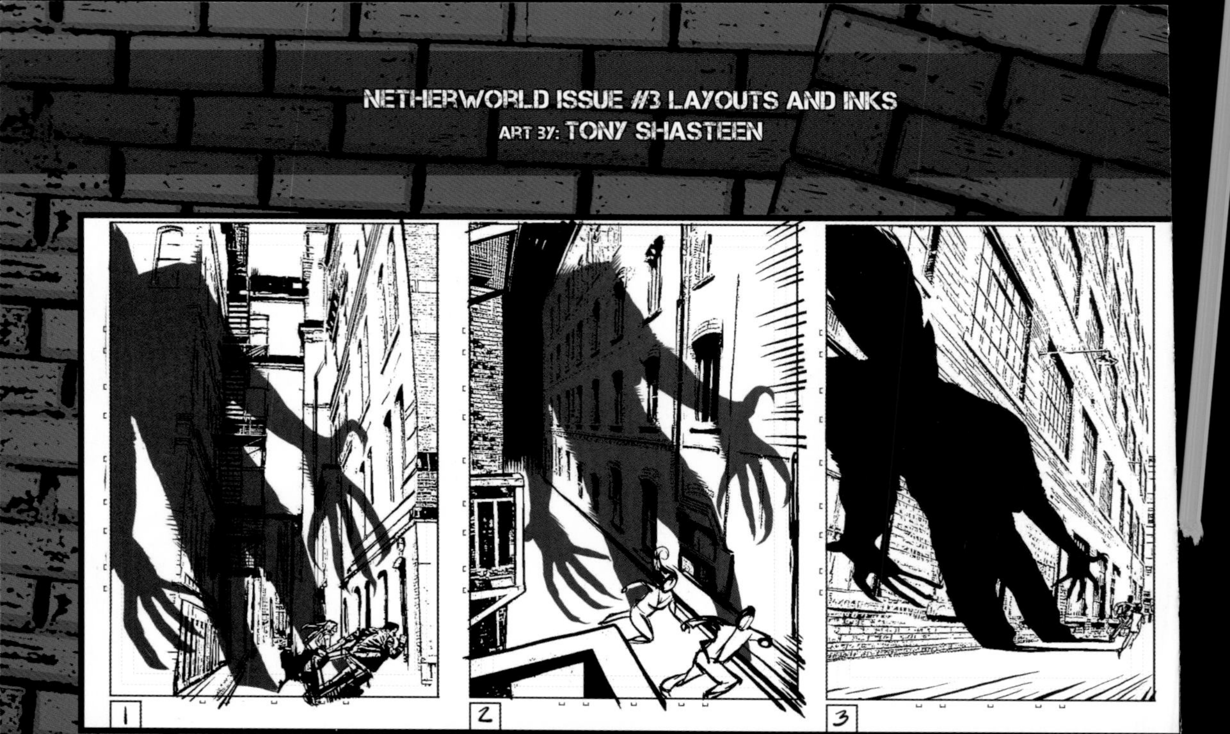
1
2
3

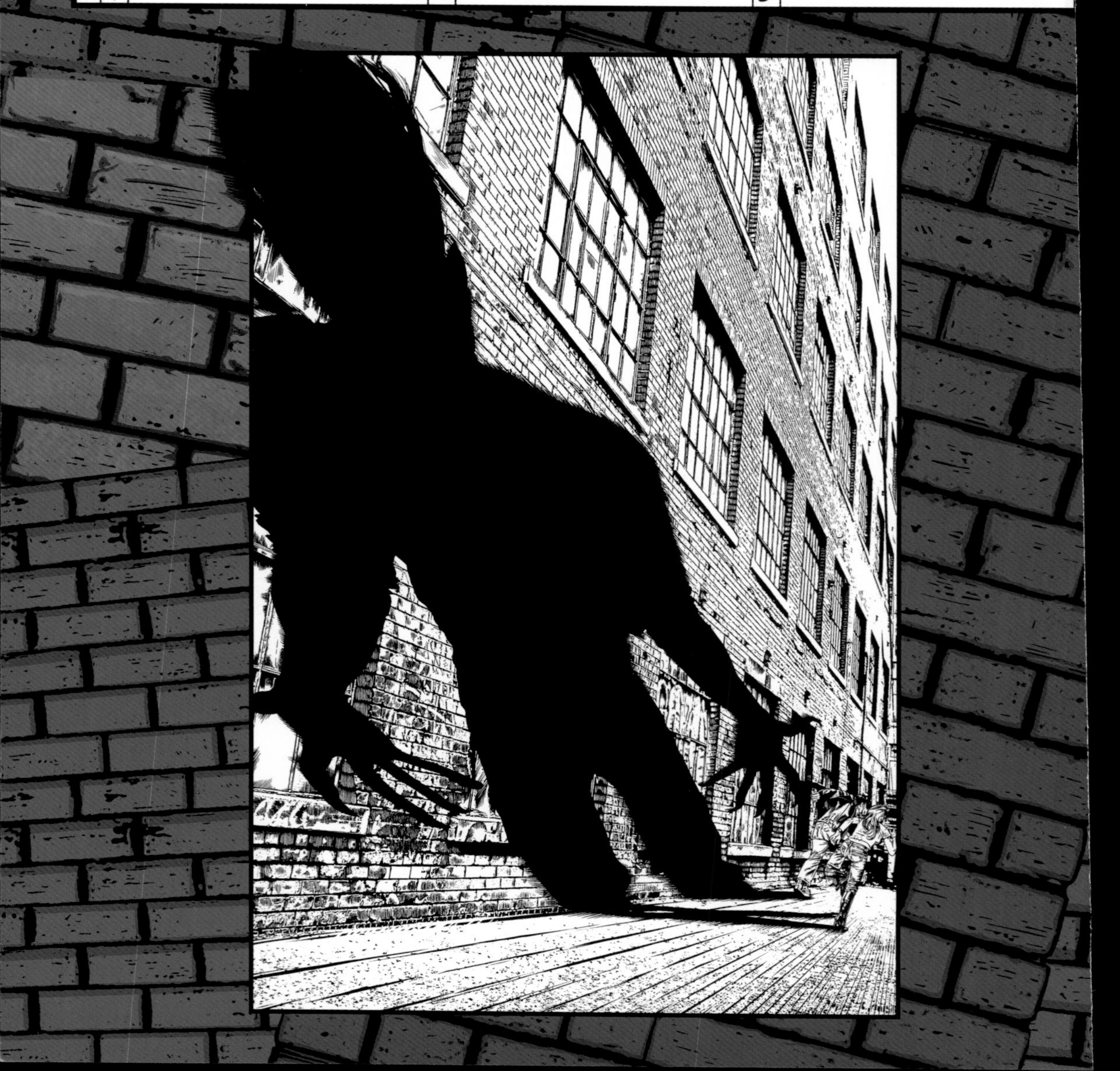

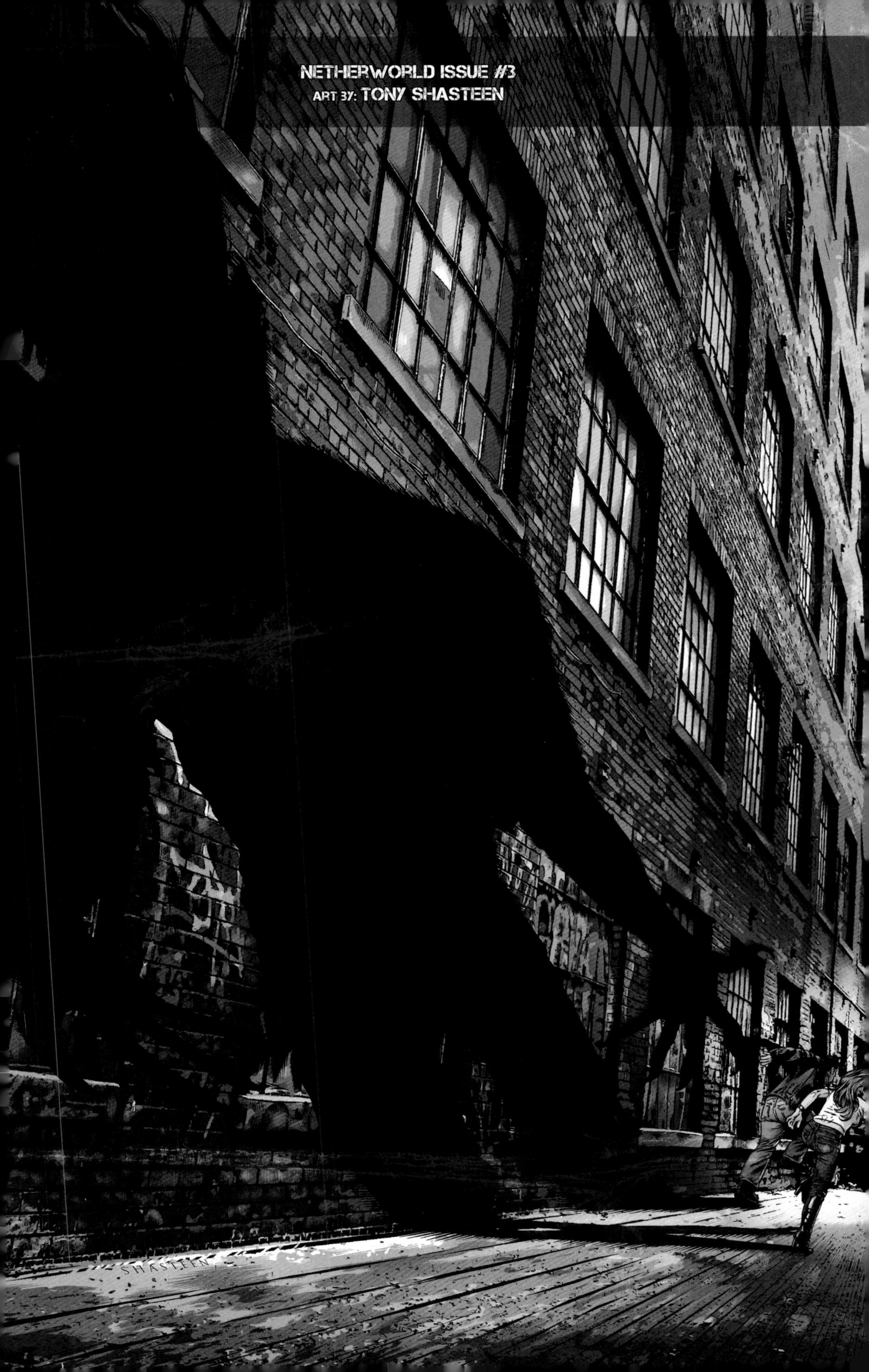
SHASTEEN

NETHERWORLD ISSUE #3
ART BY: TONY SHASTEEN

NETHERWORLD ISSUE #4 LAYOUTS AND INKS

ART BY: TONY SHASTEEN

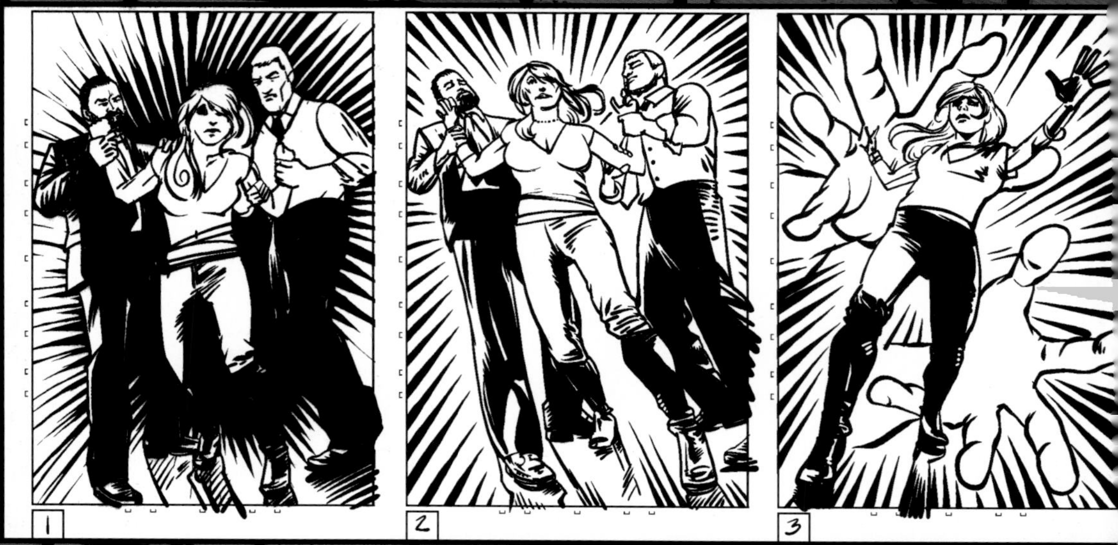
1
2
3

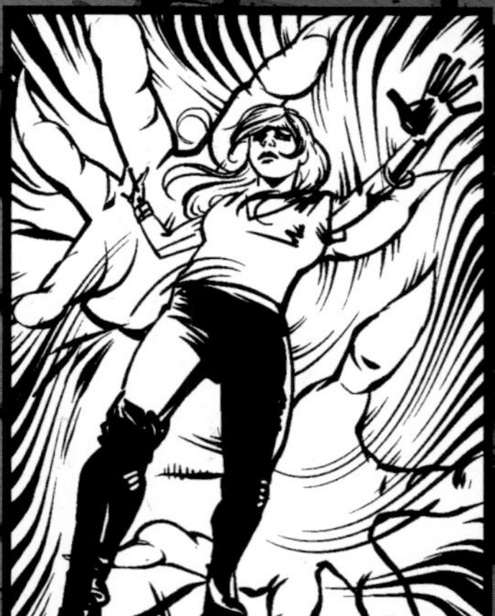

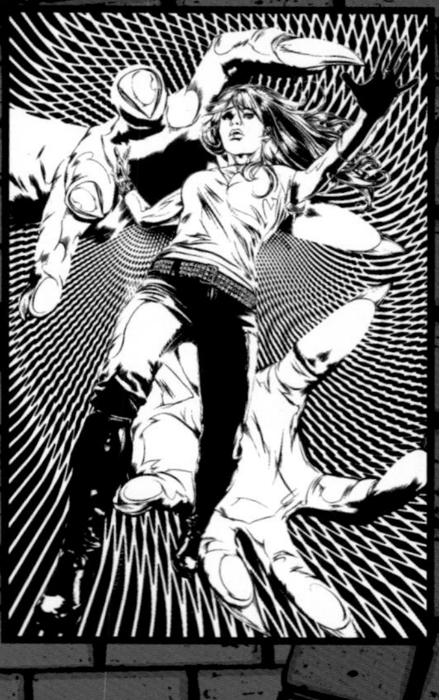

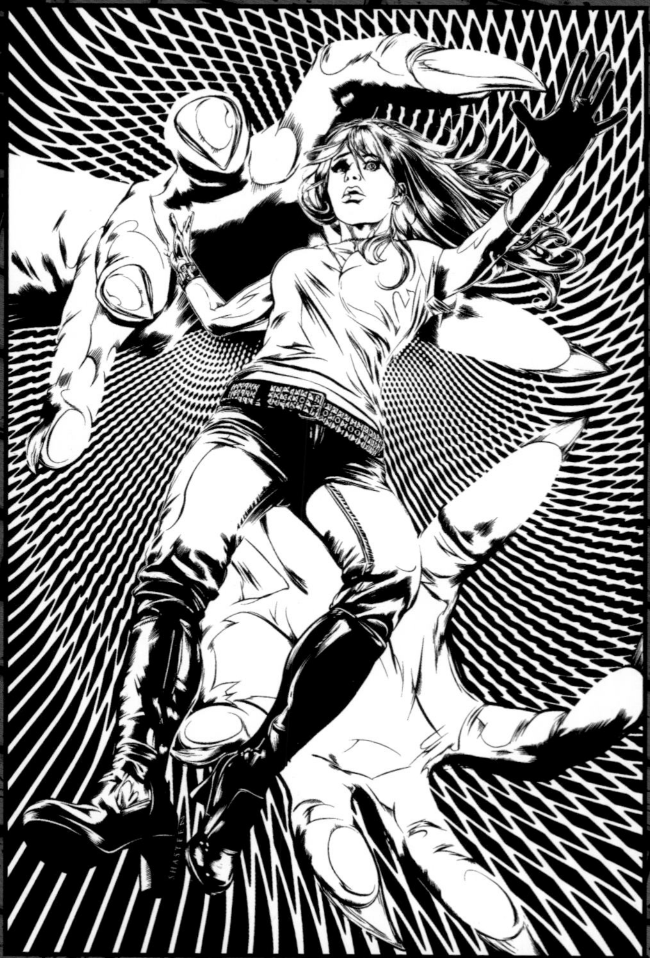

NETHERWORLD ISSUE #4

ART BY: TONY SHASTEEN

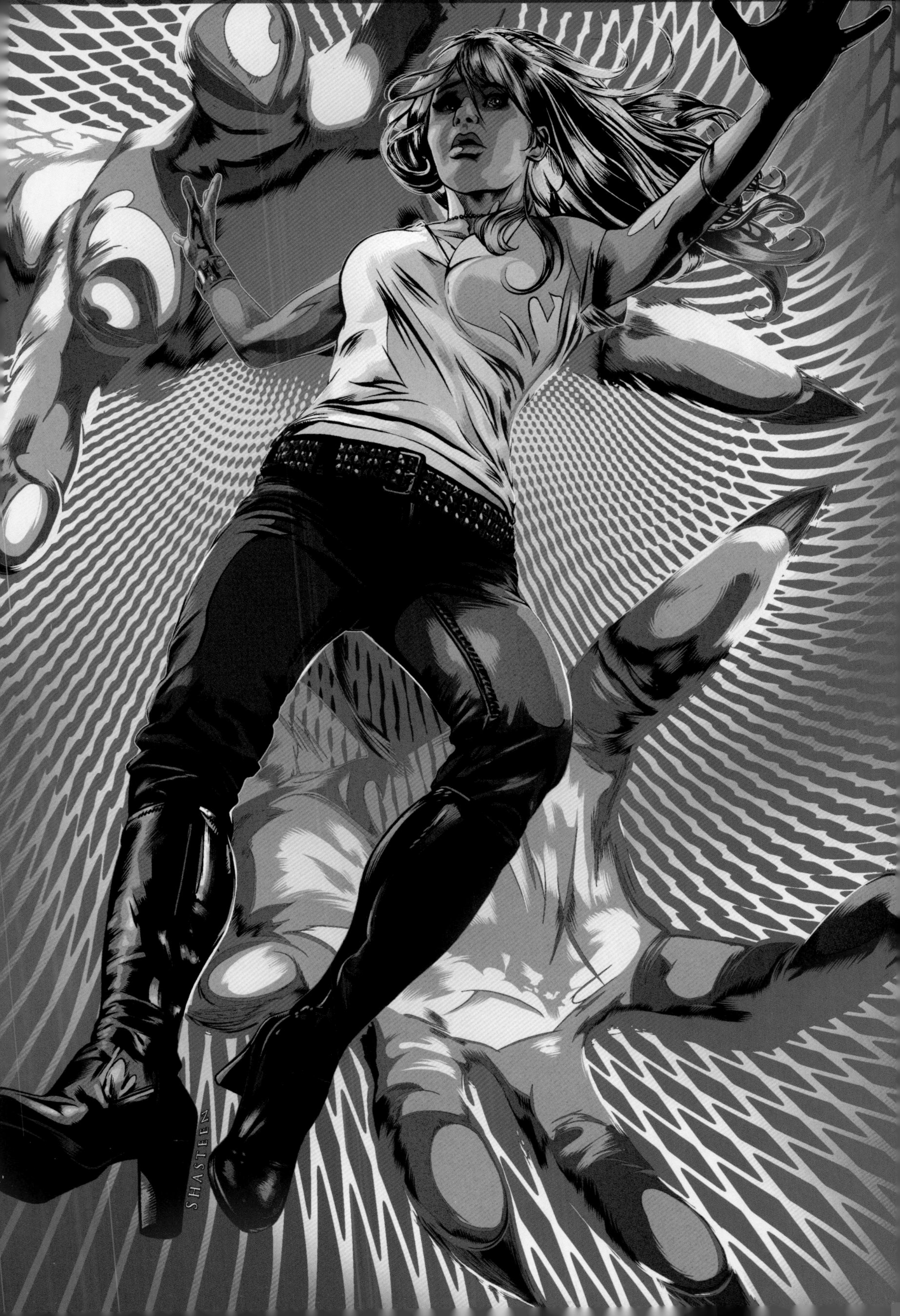
SHASTEEN

NETHERWORLD ISSUE #5 LAYOUTS AND INKS

ART BY: TONY SHASTEEN

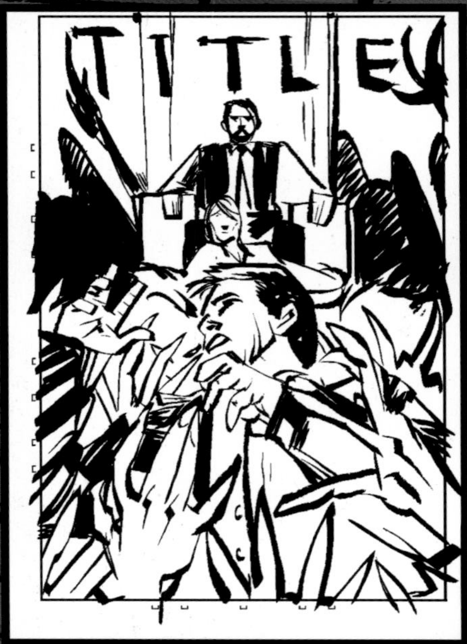
TITLE

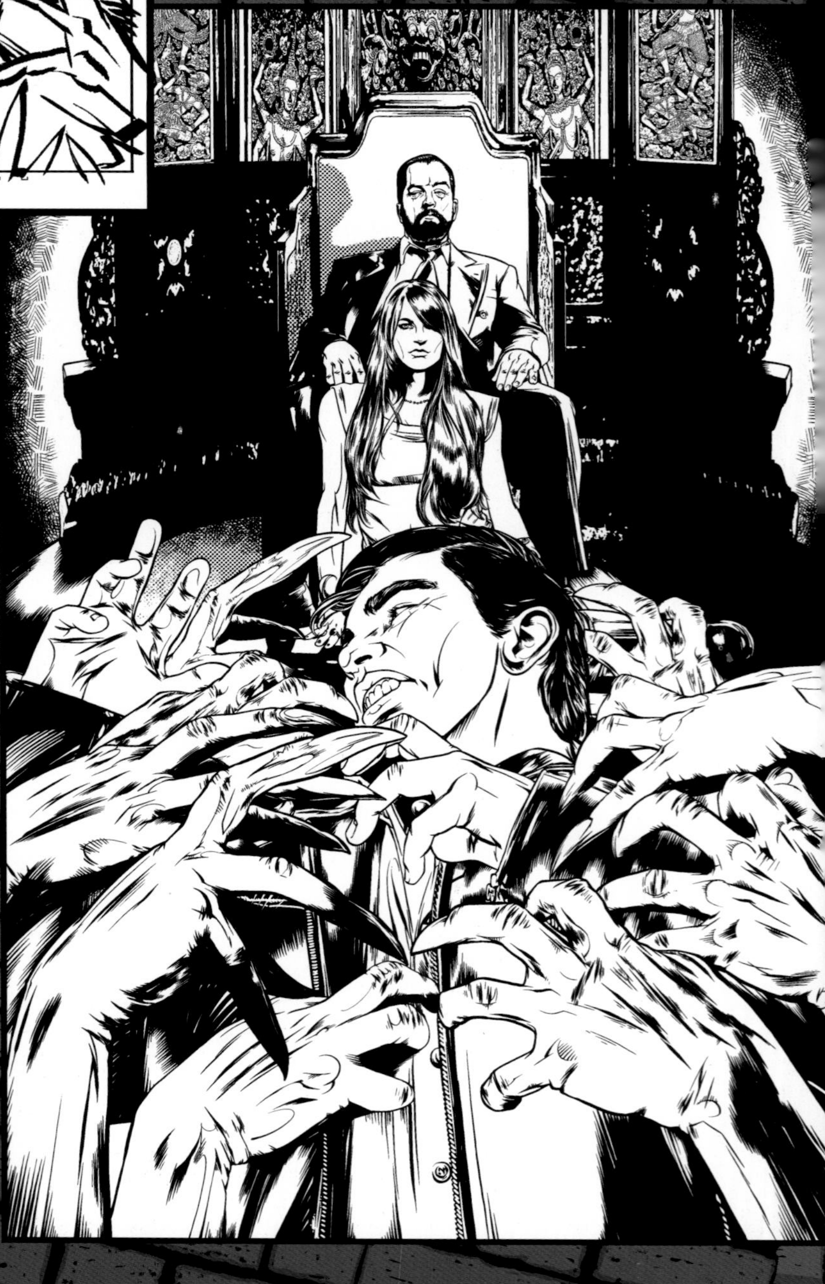

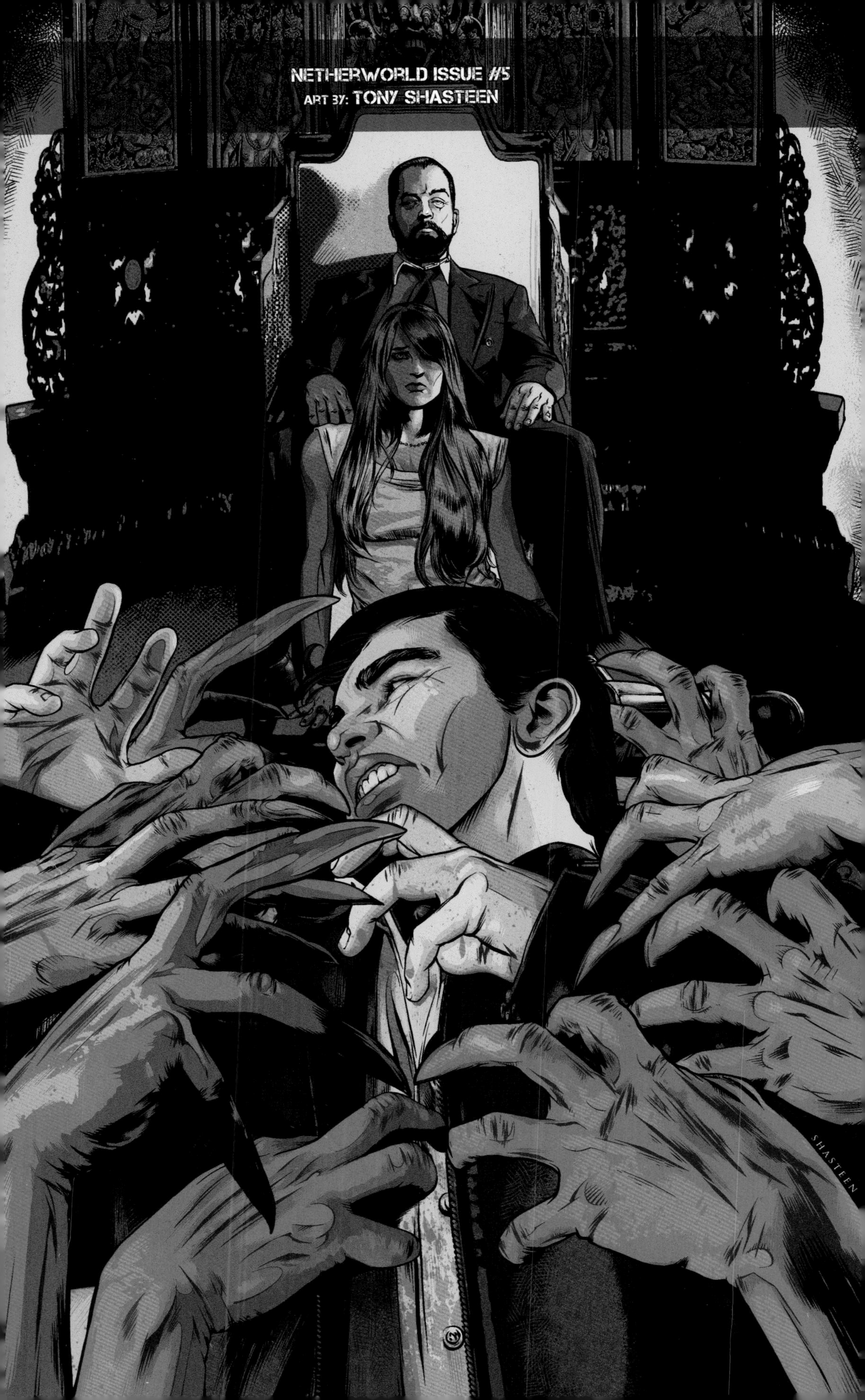
SHASTEEN

NETHERWORLD ISSUE #5
ART BY: TONY SHASTEEN

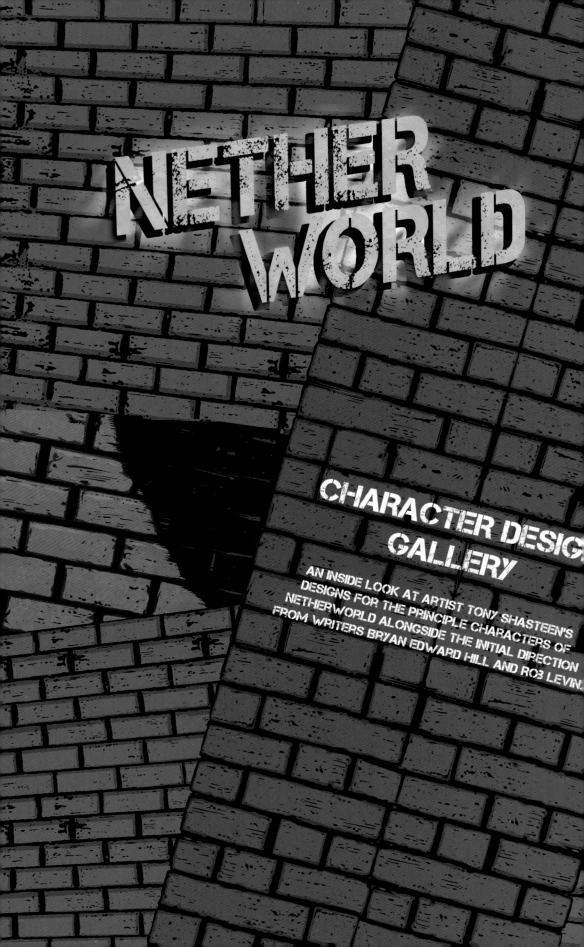

NETHER WORLD

CHARACTER DESIGN GALLERY

AN INSIDE LOOK AT ARTIST TONY SHASTEEN'S DESIGNS FOR THE PRINCIPLE CHARACTERS OF NETHERWORLD ALONGSIDE THE INITIAL DIRECTION FROM WRITERS BRYAN EDWARD HILL AND ROB LEVIN.

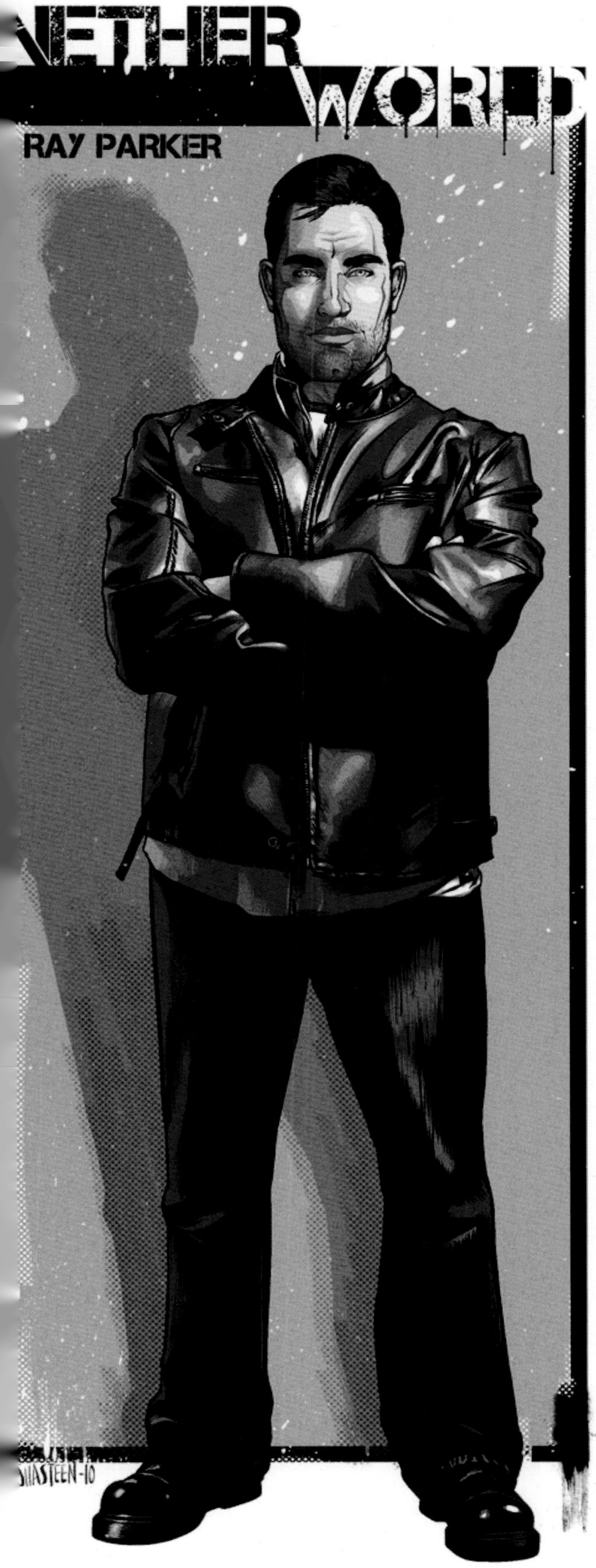
NETHER WORLD
RAY PARKER
SHASTEEN-10

OUR HERO, a man who always raises the level of violence in a situation. Rough. Hard. 30s. Think of him as a hammer rather than a scalpel. He's not a man of style or discerning taste. He should be able to take - and dish out - a serious ass kicking. We're thinking Gerard Butler or "Gladiator"-era Russel Crowe. His hands should be those of a working man or a brawler, large and worn, cracked knuckles and callouses. He'll be given a pocket watch during the story by the MiW.

NETHER WORLD

MADELINE

EIGHTEEN, toeing the line betwe[en]
innocent and sexy, but is lean[ing]
more toward the latter. She is the o[nly]
character in the city with BLONDE HA[IR.]
Think blonde, black eye liner, a bit tar[ted]
up. If you washed away the make[up,]
she'd look like a scared 18 year-[old]
girl, but that's a side of her we'll rar[ely,]
if ever, see. Think Blake Lively.

SHASTEEN-10

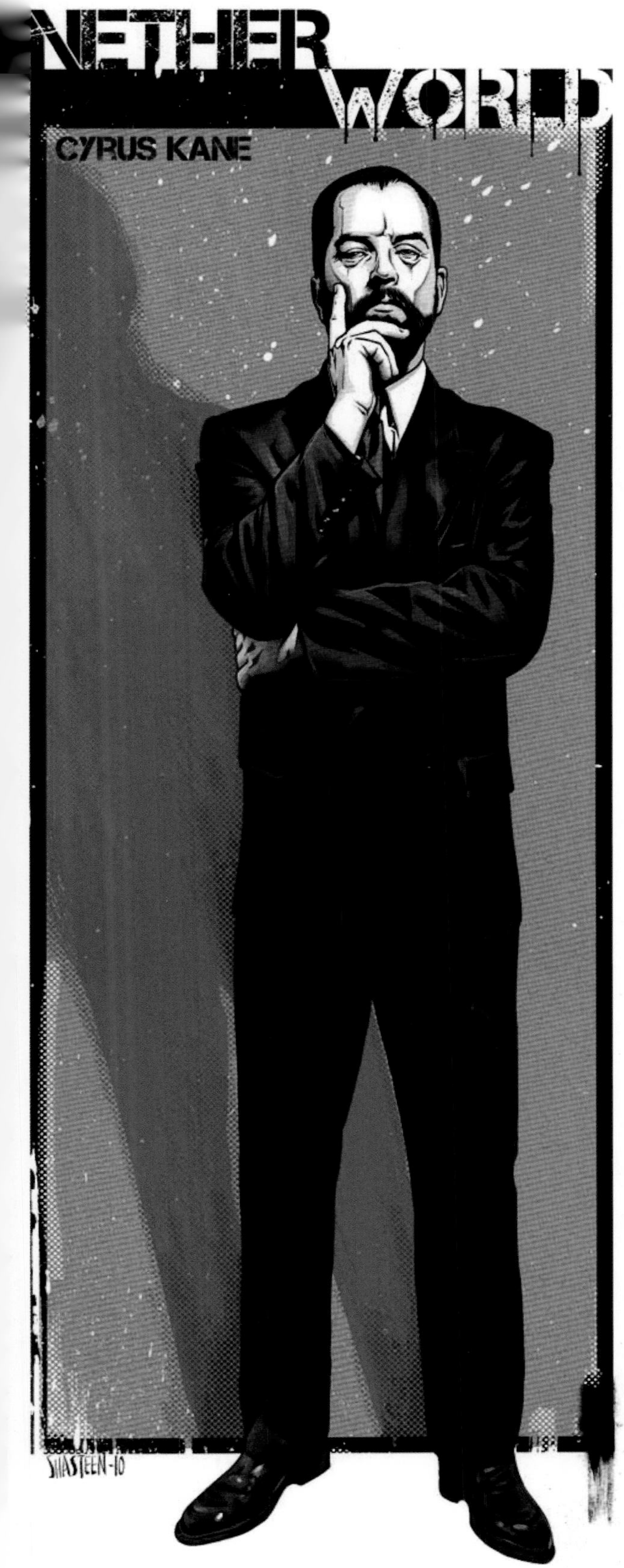
NETHER WORLD
CYRUS KANE
SHASTEEN-10

THE MOST POWERFUL BEING in this space. When hidden in the shadows, as he will be most of the story, he's modeled after Louis Cyphre (from "Angel Heart"). When he confronts Ray in the story, he will look like Ray, a dark mirror version of himself. He has a true form, but he is rarely seen in it. He is the evil in every man's soul, and his appearance reflects that in a very literal sense.

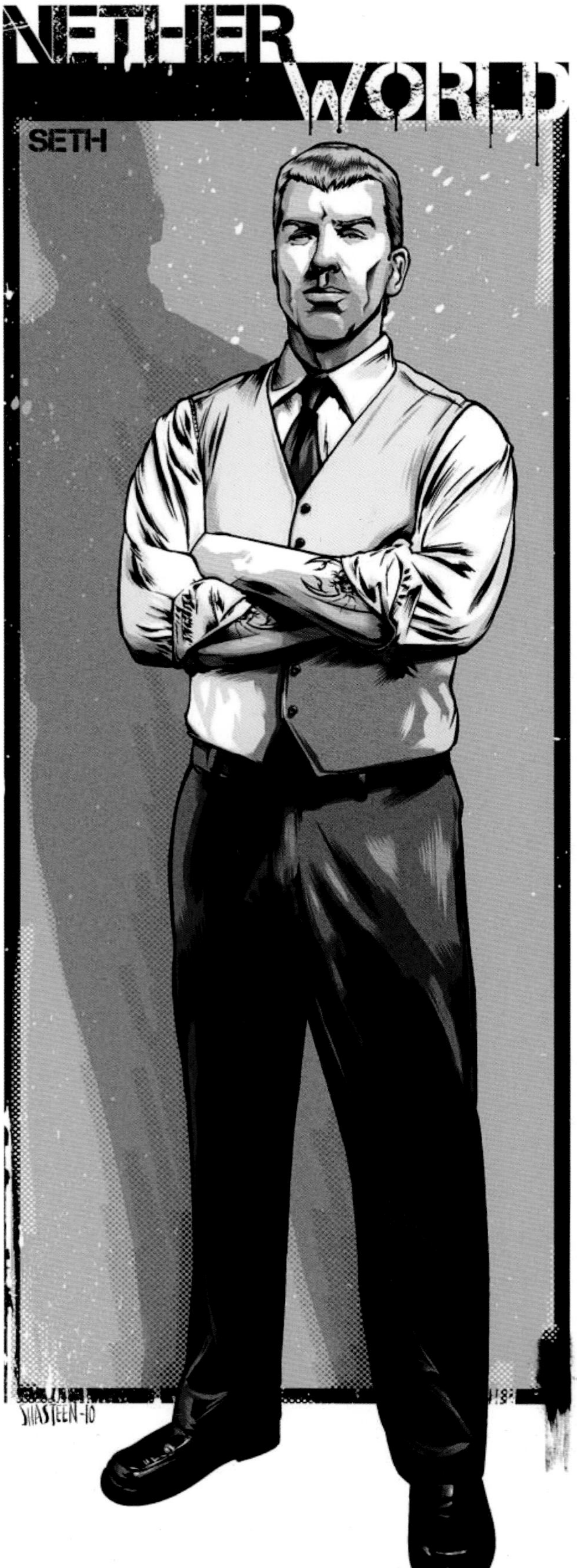
NETHER
WORLD
SETH
SHASTEEN-10

KANE'S #2, the Boba Fett of this wor He and Ray are both creatures violence, but Seth is the scalpel. He's man of style and taste, well groom and well-dressed. We shouldn't see h fully suited, but a 3-piece suit minus t jacket could be the move. He's taller a leaner, relying on skills and cunni to best his opponents as compared Ray's brute strength. Maybe a Jas Patric type.

NETHER WORLD

BEHIND THE SCENES: DESIGNING THE LOGO

DESIGNER PHIL SMITH SUBMITTED A NUMBER OF POTENTIAL LOGO DESIGNS FOR NETHERWORLD BEFORE FINALLY ARRIVING AT A VERSION, WHICH TOOK ITS CUE FROM THE FONT ARTIST TONY SHASTEEN HAD CHOSEN FOR THE "WE ARE ALL LOST" GRAFFITI TAG FOUND THE BACKGROUND OF THE CITY.

THE FIRST LOGO DESIGN EVOKED THE HORROR AND THRILLER ASPECT, BUT FELT SOMEWHAT DATED.

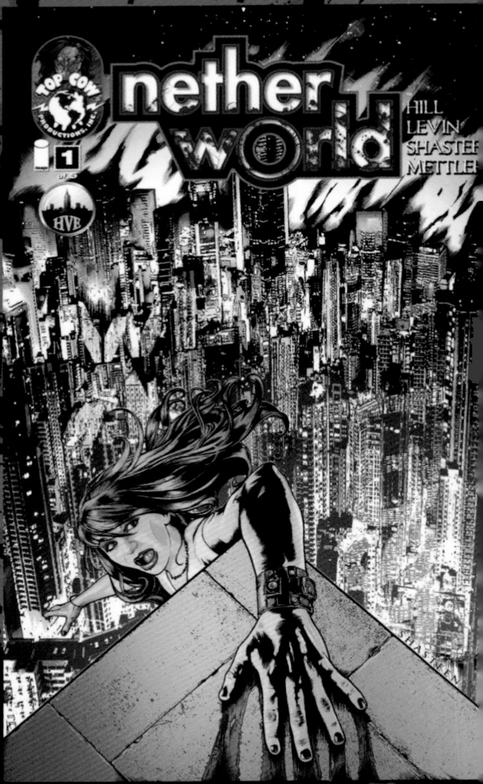
nether world
HILL
LEVIN
SHASTEE
METTLE

THE SECOND LOGO DESIGN WAS MEANT TO HINT AT THE NATURE OF THE CITY AS PURGATORY, BUT AGAIN DID NOT QUITE STRIKE THE VISUAL CORD EVERYONE WAS LOOKING FOR.

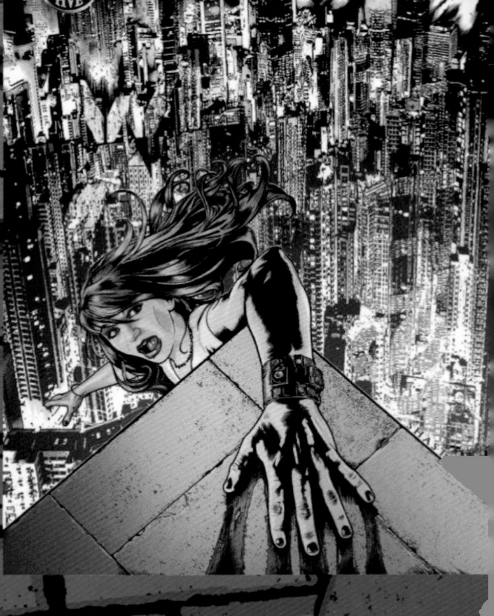
HILL • LEVIN • SHASTEEN • METTLER
NETHER WORLD

THIRD LOGO DESIGN FELT MORE MODERN AND
KED THE FEELING OF A NEVER ENDING NIGHT IN
CITY.

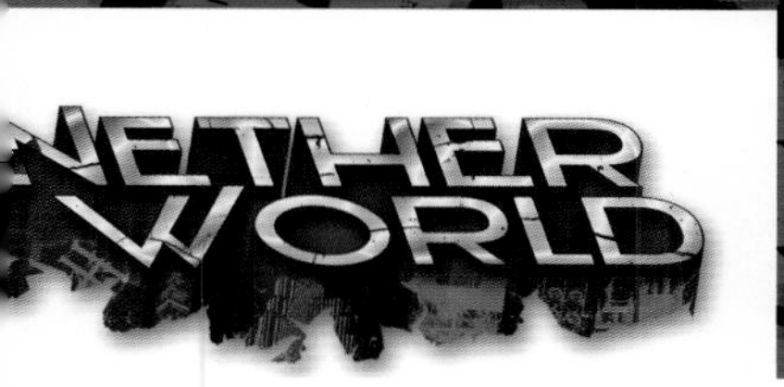
NETHER
WORLD

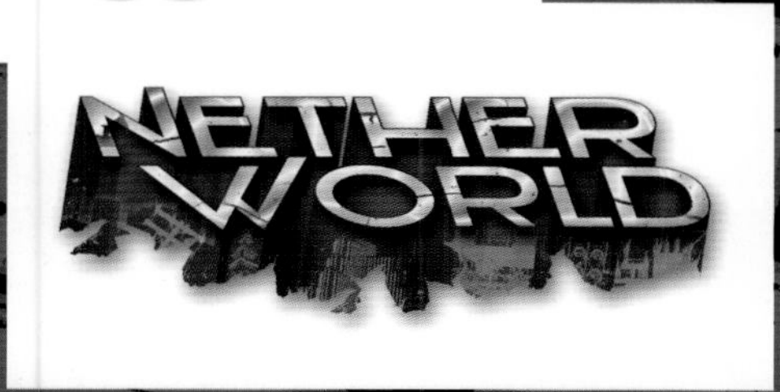
NETHER
WORLD

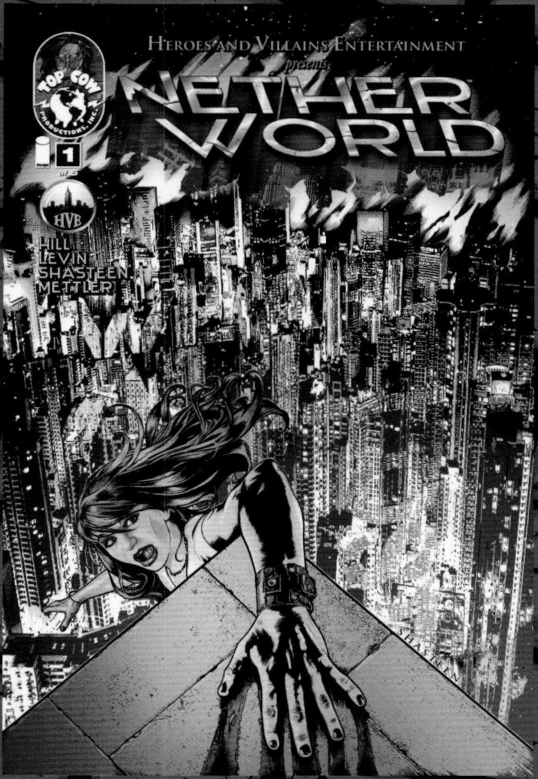
HEROES AND VILLAINS ENTERTAINMENT
presents
NETHER
WORLD
1
HVE
HILL
LEVIN
SHASTEEN
METTLER

FOURTH AND FINAL LOGO DESIGN UTILIZED
GRAFFITI TREATMENT, WHICH HAD ALREADY
HEAVILY USED IN THE "WE ARE ALL LOST"
L MARKETING CAMPAIGN. THE TILTED ANGLE
DROP SHADOW HELPED CREATE AN ETHEREAL
CT THAT HINTS AT THE CITY'S TRUE NATURE.

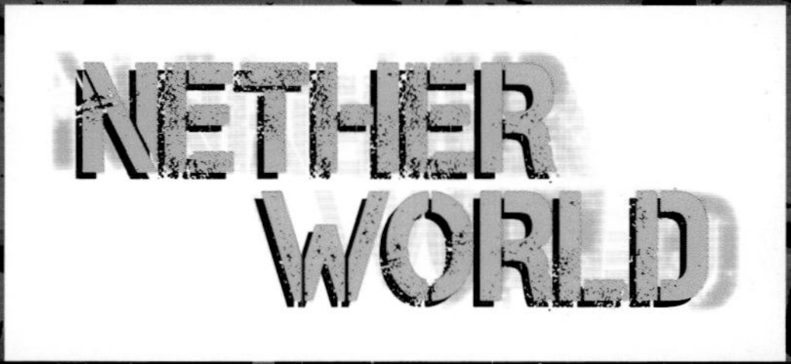
NETHER
WORLD

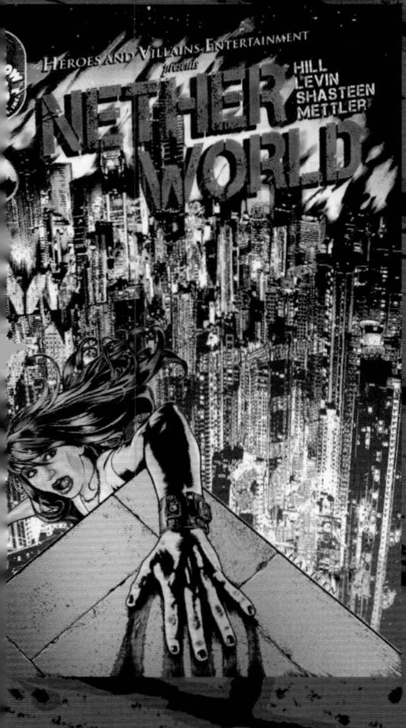
HEROES AND VILLAINS ENTERTAINMENT
presents
HILL
LEVIN
SHASTEEN
METTLER
NETHER
WORLD

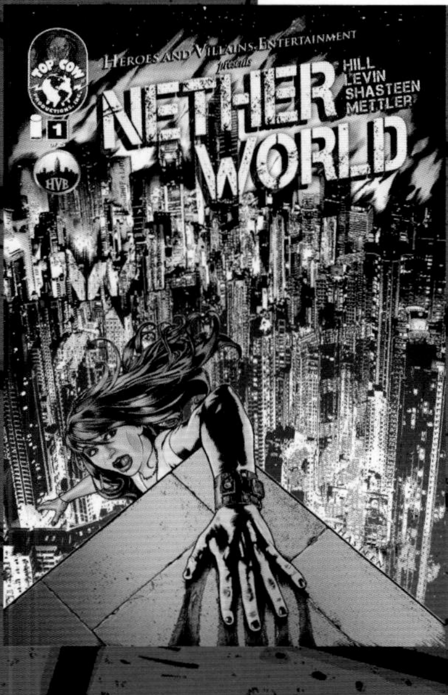
HEROES AND VILLAINS ENTERTAINMENT
presents
HILL
LEVIN
SHASTEEN
METTLER
NETHER
WORLD
1
HVE

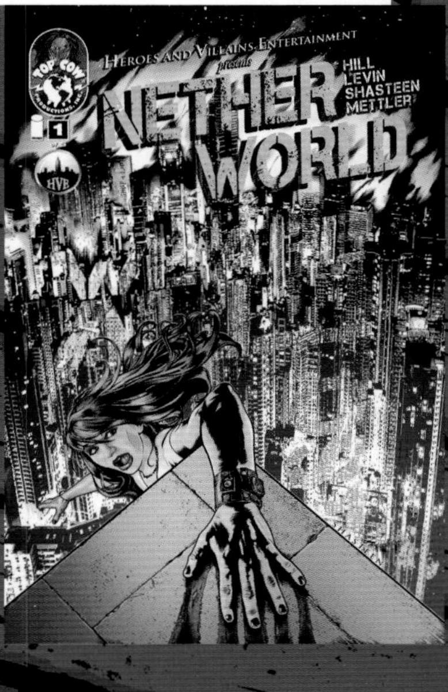
HEROES AND VILLAINS ENTERTAINMENT
presents
HILL
LEVIN
SHASTEEN
METTLER
NETHER
WORLD
1
HVE

NETHER WORLD

"WE ARE ALL LOST" COVER CONTEST

In anticipation of the launch of Netherworld, Heroes and Villains Entertainm and Top Cow Productions gave fans the opportunity to submit their art ir competition to have their work published as the Retailer Incentive variant cov edition of Netherworld #1.

With slim-to-zilch in editorial interference, fans were simply asked to utilize o take inspiration the "We Are All Lost" motif of the series within an urban sett and run wild with their imaginations. Completed entries were upload to T Cow's community site "The Barn" (topcow.com/barn) where everyone could the entries. Many entered, only three entries were selected as winners of contest:

RUNNER-UP
2ND PLACE WINNER:
GARY BLAUVELT (Connecticut)

WE ARE ALL LOST
GIRLS XXX
STOP
LUXE
STOP

RUNNER-UP
3RD PLACE WINNER:
MARK LAUTHIER (Western Austr

WE ARE ALL

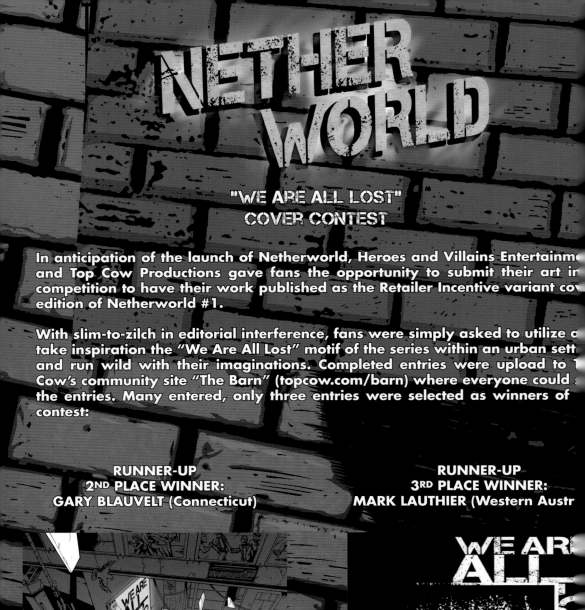

GRAND PRIZE WINNER:
BOZHIDAR SAVOV (Bulgaria)

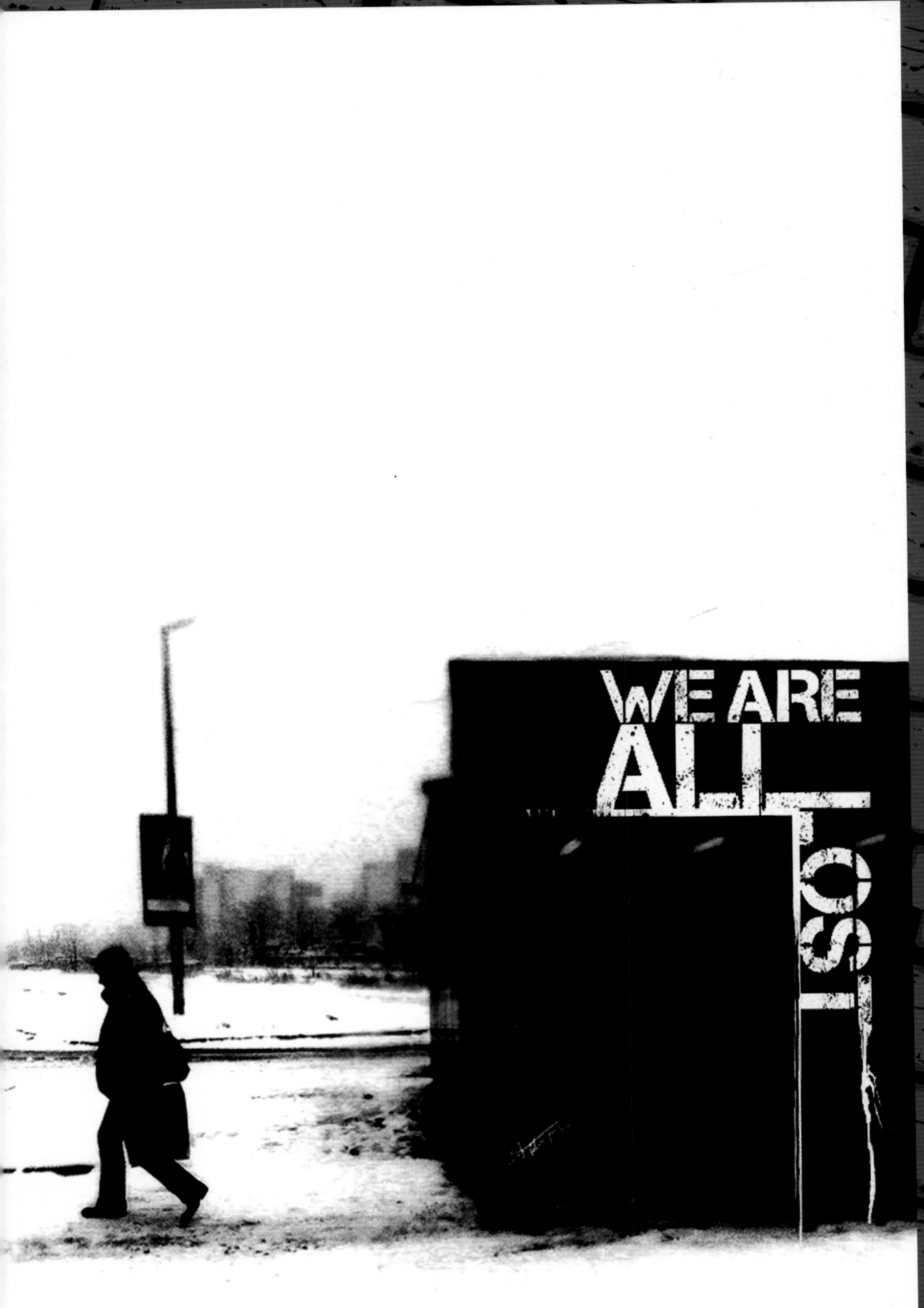
WE ARE
ALL
LOST

NETHER WORLD

BEHIND THE SCENES
ISSUE 1 SCRIPTBOOK

MASSAGE

PAGE 1
Hey Tony, can't wait to see you bring this world and the story to life. Speaking of the world, we really want it to feel like a character in the story. Any time the characters are outside, feel free to throw in interesting background elements or characters to really populate it and make it unique. We'll make mention of this on occasion, but we'd rather you fit it in where it works then us giving you 12 things to fit in a panel. And keep in mind, except at the very end of this story, it's always night...

In terms of overall visual style and flow, where we can we want this to be a book of pretty (if gritty) pictures. Graphic violence. Strong imagery. Where things can be combined to get that across, you have free reign to do so.

2 Panels

PANEL 1: Wide across the top of the page. A cityscape like the bottom jaw of a mechanical beast, gleaming with multicolored electronic light.

1 Homeless cap: "This place...
2 Homeless cap: "...it swallows us all."

PANEL 2: Basically a splash, takes up 70-80% of the real estate. We're in closer, focusing on a mains street from on high. The city TEEMS with life - pushers, hookers, bouncers in front of clubs, MASSES of life in search of sin. This should be crowded, like an ant colony, the citizens of this city always in motion.

If you see a place for it, scrawl the "We Are All Lost" tag on the side of a building. Nothing we need to notice, but a nice detail for observant readers.

[Tony, if you want to break this up into panels focusing on different things that's cool, we just want to really ground this thing in a place before we get off and, literally, running]

3 Homeless cap: "It doesn't judge. Doesn't discriminate.
4 Homeless cap: "It just TAKES."

PAGE 2
6 Panels

PANEL 1: On this page we're going to get to know some of the people in the city. Their designs are up to you, this is about flav not character. SKEEVY DUDE with a "Step into my office" grin, arm full of WATCHES and a hand full of CRACK VIALS.

1 Homeless cap: "It preys on the innocent.

PANEL 2: A WHORE, sexy in all the right places except for tha hollow, vacant stare.

2 Homeless cap: "It preys on the guilty.

PANEL 3: TWO STICK UP KIDS (anywhere from 12-15) rob an ACCOUNTANT-looking dude at knife point. One keeps the poir on the accountant's gut while the other rifles through his pockets

3 Homeless cap: "Writing's on the walls, friend."

PANEL 4: HOMELESS, an Asian bag lady wearing a clear ponc over her clothes, talks the ear off of BLANKET, a larger guy with a blanket pulled tight over him. All we can see are his eyes, focused at something across the street, the rest is all blanket anc shadows. It's RAY, but we'll find that out soon enough. They're o a set of stairs in front of an apartment and Homeless has her leg propped up, lecturing to Blanket/Ray. Where her leg is proppe up, the pants ride up just a bit, showing the MEN IN WHITE ICO tattooed on her ankle. (Men in White will be MiW from here on for brevity.)

4 Homeless: We are ALL lost. Know what I mean?
(break)
5 Homeless: You got any cash, blanket?

PANEL 5: A MASSIVE DUDE exits a STEEL SECURITY DOOR, the kind with the metal slats to see who's knocking.

6 Ray cap: "Sorry, lady. Working."

PANEL 6 (inset): Smash zoom to Massive's EYES. We read PANI

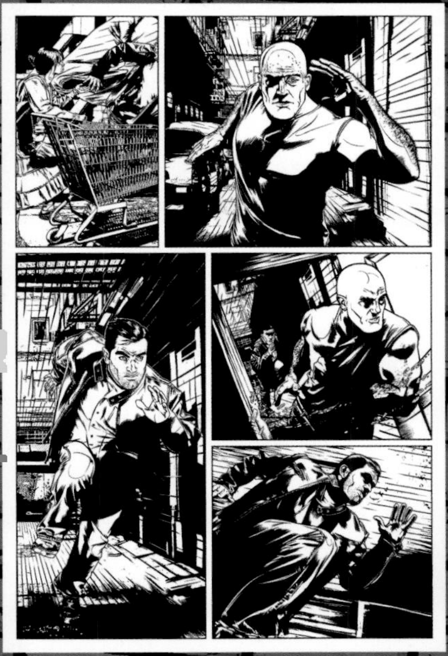

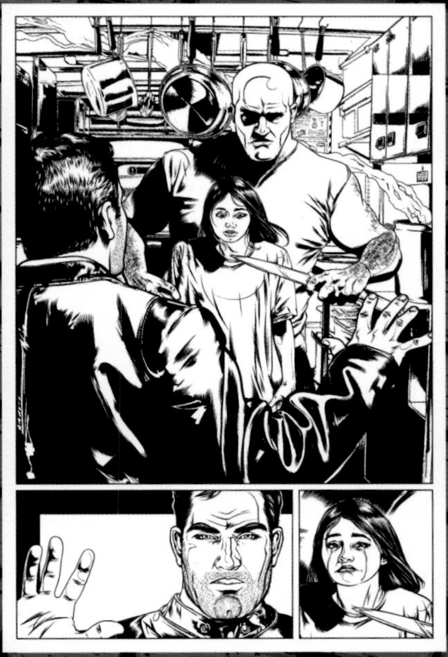

3
ls

1: Similar framing to Panel 4 on the previous page, but ET/RAY has sprung to life, tossing the blanket off and GING down the stairs after Massive. We catch just a glimpse egs in this panel.

eless: We'll be here when you're ready.

2: Massive runs down an alleyway – frantic – cold sweat across his face – clothes ruffled. His eyes are wild, a DEER g from the lion that is–

3: Big reveal of RAY PARKER JR., our hero. Ray's FEET D through puddles – gaining on Massive – a hunter's focus in ression.

4: Massive BURSTS through a door, Ray in pursuit behind ll gaining.

5: Ray moving swiftly down an empty hallway, cracked tile e jaundiced green of cheap flo lights. If this were a movie, ould FLICKER.

age (off): Aaaaahhhhh!

PAGE 4
3 Panels

PANEL 1: Big panel. From behind Ray, we're looking at MASSIVE, wild eyes, clearly capable of harm, holding a YOUNG KOREAN GIRL – BUTCHER KNIFE to her throat. She's CRYING, dressed in thin cotton. Clearly some kitchen worker that couldn't run fast enough. Next year, she'll be fifteen.

In the foreground by rain, STEAM billows around him from a LONG IRON STOVE boiling all kinds of FOUL SHIT.

1 Massive Dude: I'll slice to her spine, Parker.

PANEL 2: On Ray's eyes, NARROWED, a hint of recognition.

2 Ray: Easy does it.

PANEL 3: Push in tight on the girl, the TEAR from one eye GLISTENS and we read the fear in her eyes.

PAGE 5
4 Panels

Tony, we're going to be using flashbacks in the book to reveal Ray's backstory, how he died, and his connection to Madeline. Let's talk about how to make these sequences and panels really distinctive. They should be about FEELINGS, not DETAILS. Maybe we do it all in color with no inks, maybe we try a rougher style like your Gears of War piece, or maybe more photo-real like some of your commercial work.

PANEL 1: FLASHBACK. We're inside a BANK. It's large and open, the kind you'd imagine serving as a setpiece for an action film, not your local Bank of America. Good thing too, as we're looking at MASKED ROBBERS holding Colt Model 733 automatic weapons (http://www.imfdb.org/index.php/Image:Colt_Model_733.jpg). Each robber (4 in all) wears a DIFFERENT ANIMAL MASK.
The leader, PIGGY, is grabbing a GIRL (Madeline, but we can't see her clearly). TEDDY BEAR (aka RAY) holds his gun at the ready but not pointed at anything, he's watching Piggy. The other two robbers (your call on the masks, have fun) are keeping any hostages/would-be-heroes at bay.

Piggy: Down on the fucking ground, peons! This is a robbery!

PANEL 2: FLASHBACK. Piggy holds Madeline and presses a gun to her temple. (If it's easier, he can be holding a handgun - http://www.imfdb.org/index.php/Image:HK-USP.jpg - on Madeline and have the M733 strapped to him). We can't make out her face, but other than that this shot echoes 4/1.

Piggy: Heroes get bitches shot, you dig?

PANEL 3: FLASHBACK. On Teddy Bear, we can see his eyes through the mask, not liking this.

PANEL 4: FLASHBACK. Close on a TEAR falling from Madeline's face. We still can't quite make her out fully, but this is the best we see her. She's not wearing her dark eye makeup here. She looks innocent, the gun at her temple is MENACING. This shot echoes 4/3.

PAGE 6
5 Panels

PANEL 1: Angle on Ray, same stare as Teddy Bear, but we're bo[ck] in the present.

1 Massive (off): I'll kill her.
2 Ray: Then kill her.

PANEL 2: On Massive and the girl. He's slightly unsettled Ray's response, she's still crying.

3 Massive: I'm... I'm serious.
4 Ray (off): So am I. Kill her.
5 Massive: I–

PANEL 3: Ray stands there, arms crossed, looking like he couldn[t] give a shit about Massive harming this girl.

6 Ray: See, if you kill her I don't have to bring you in alive. I ca[n] do what I want with you, Lenny.
7 Ray: Right now you're just armed robbery. Escalate that to murder.
(break)
8 Ray: Make my life easier. Kill her.
9 Ray: Then I'll kill you before she goes cold. That's a promise.

[Troy, please separate each set of balloons on either side of Ray here.]

PANEL 4: Two-shot, Massive (and the girl, but she's not a focus) [on] the left, Ray on the right. Massive is thinking about all of this. He believes Ray, starts to take the mania out of his eyes.

10 Massive: I let her go, what happens then?
11 Ray: I have to bring you in alive and some other asshole gets all the fun.
12 Massive: I'm... I'm gonna let her go now.

PANEL 5: On Ray, something in his face. It looks almost like disappointment.

13 Ray: Don't talk about it. Be about it, Lenny.

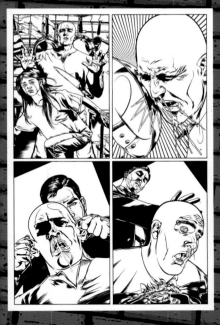

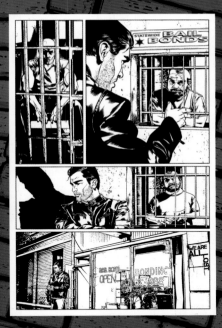

STATEWIDE BAIL BONDS
WE ARE ALL LOST
OPEN
BONDING

ls

1: Massive lets the girl go, she BOLTS immediately. His
sion says he knows he's done for.

ive: I can't go back, Ray...
ive: Tell 'em I–

2: A SKILLET collides with Massive's face, BREAKING HIS

SKERNCH

3: Worm's eye, Ray's moved behind Massive and has
ed him by the hair. Massive's in pain, and it's clear Ray's
ng this. Violence is the only thing that gives him peace.

You put a knife to that poor girl's throat. You see how scared
s?
ive: Ray, don't–

4: Ray has one of Massive's arms pinned behind his back,
's lower Massive's face close to a PILOT LIGHT. Massive's
rn into HARD BOILED EGGS - pure terror - the flame reflected
of them, praying to taste his flesh.

She was real scared, Lenny.
sive: Please, don't burn me!
Okay...

PAGE 8
4 Panels

PANEL 1: Cut to a HOLDING CELL. Massive sits in it, dried blood caked on his broken nose, but no sign of burns on his face. Feel free to go high contrast/noir with the lighting and have the bars fall across him, just make sure we can see he's not burned.

1 Ray Cap: "...you're scared too."

PANEL 2: Elsewhere in the same facility, Ray argues with a VERY FAT BAIL BONDSMAN at a counter. Above the fat man is a NEON SIGN reading: "Bail Bonds."

2 Ray: Deal was for five grand, not two.
3 Fat Man: Five clean. He's damaged.
4 Ray: The nose? Shit, you want me to catch them with pillows?
5 Fat Man: Two grand if they're injured. Take it, or I'll let him go and someone else will.

PANEL 3: Ray turns away from the counter, looking both tired and pissed as he leans against the wall. We can see the Fat Man behind him smiling and starting to count out cash from a small stack in his hand.

6 Ray: Cash.
7 Fat Man: Of course, Ray.

PANEL 4: Outside of the bail bonds office (nothing special, typical skeevy place), Ray counts his payment. Maybe this is another good opportunity for a "We Are All Lost" tag somewhere on the building or the sidewalk.

8 Alexis (off): Mr. Parker.

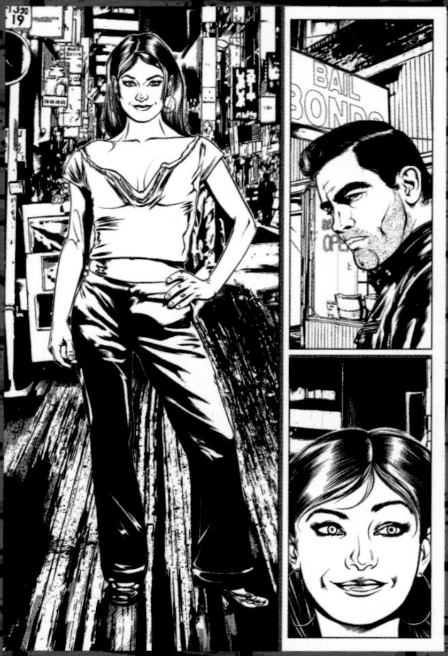
BAIL

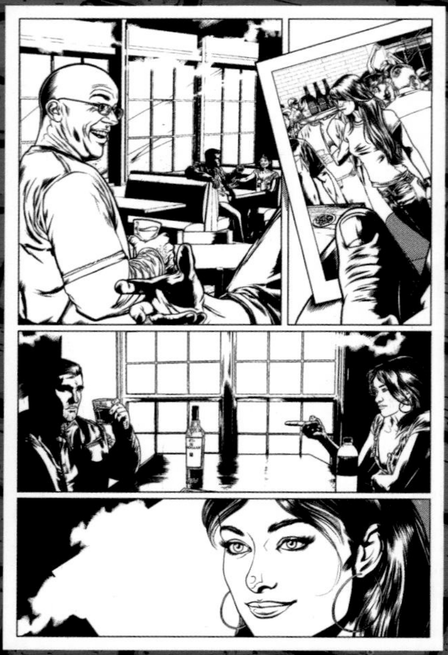

PAGE 9
3 Panels

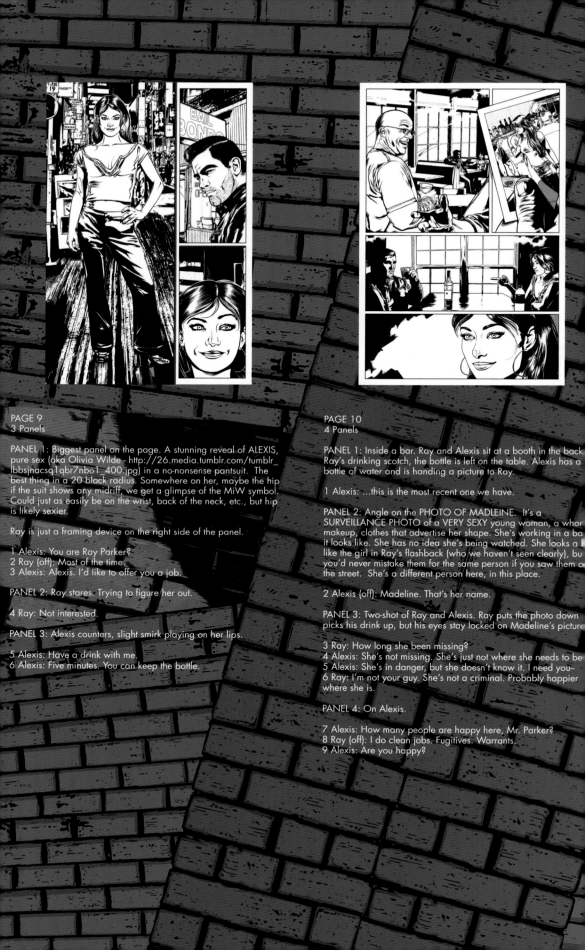

PANEL 1: Biggest panel on the page. A stunning reveal of ALEXIS, pure sex (aka Olivia Wilde - http://26.media.tumblr.com/tumblr_lbbsjnacsq1qbr7nbo1_400.jpg) in a no-nonsense pantsuit. The best thing in a 20 block radius. Somewhere on her, maybe the hip if the suit shows any midriff, we get a glimpse of the MiW symbol. Could just as easily be on the wrist, back of the neck, etc., but hip is likely sexier.

Ray is just a framing device on the right side of the panel.

1 Alexis: You are Ray Parker?
2 Ray (off): Most of the time.
3 Alexis: Alexis. I'd like to offer you a job.

PANEL 2: Ray stares. Trying to figure her out.

4 Ray: Not interested.

PANEL 3: Alexis counters, slight smirk playing on her lips.

5 Alexis: Have a drink with me.
6 Alexis: Five minutes. You can keep the bottle.

PAGE 10
4 Panels

PANEL 1: Inside a bar. Ray and Alexis sit at a booth in the back. Ray's drinking scotch, the bottle is left on the table. Alexis has a bottle of water and is handing a picture to Ray.

1 Alexis: ...this is the most recent one we have.

PANEL 2: Angle on the PHOTO OF MADLEINE. It's a SURVEILLANCE PHOTO of a VERY SEXY young woman, a whor makeup, clothes that advertise her shape. She's working in a ba it looks like. She has no idea she's being watched. She looks a like the girl in Ray's flashback (who we haven't seen clearly), bu you'd never mistake them for the same person if you saw them o the street. She's a different person here, in this place.

2 Alexis (off): Madeline. That's her name.

PANEL 3: Two-shot of Ray and Alexis. Ray puts the photo down picks his drink up, but his eyes stay locked on Madeline's picture

3 Ray: How long she been missing?
4 Alexis: She's not missing. She's just not where she needs to be
5 Alexis: She's in danger, but she doesn't know it. I need you–
6 Ray: I'm not your guy. She's not a criminal. Probably happier where she is.

PANEL 4: On Alexis.

7 Alexis: How many people are happy here, Mr. Parker?
8 Ray (off): I do clean jobs. Fugitives. Warrants.
9 Alexis: Are you happy?

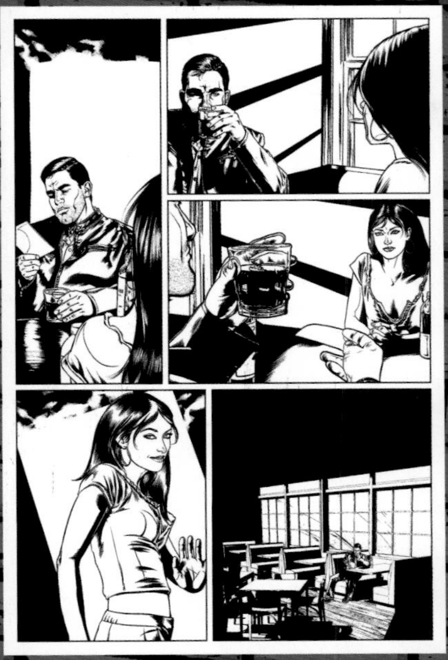

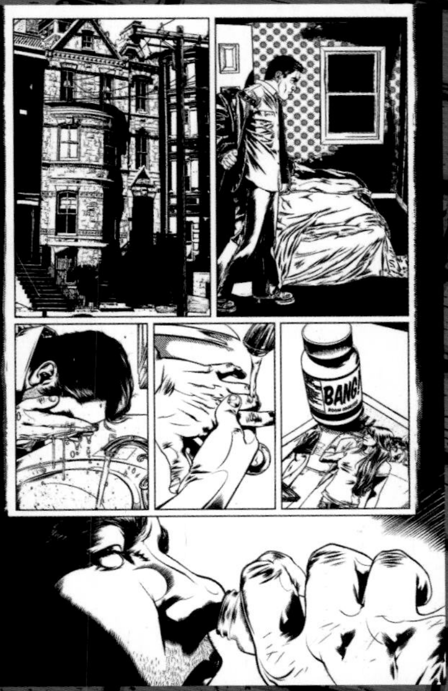
BANG!

11
ls

1: Ray picks up the photo again, staring into it like he's
g for something more.

This sounds personal.
is: It is.
Then I'm not interested. You don't need me for this.

2: Two-shot of Alexis and Ray, he's admiring his drink,
y with the conversation. She's cool as the other side of the
batting back everything he throws at her.

is: We're not the only ones looking for her. Most men who
at you do can be bought.
I'm no different.
is: You're lying, but you're no liar. Some part of you cares.
n't do this to catch criminals. You want to protect people,
at girl earlier.

3: Another two-shot. Alexis makes a last ditch effort. Ray's
ng but refuses to change his mind.

xis: My people are being watched. We need you to get
ine out of harm's way.
Lady, you choose to live here, you're already in harm's way.
xis: Keep the photograph, Mr. Parker. There are two
sses on the back.

4: Alexis accepts it and stands up.

exis: Madeline's at the first one. Bring her to the second.
exis: You're supposed to do this. You'll see that soon enough.
y(off): I'm–
exis: Keep it. People change their minds.

5: Pull back for a long shot from the other side of the bar.
lone, drinks his scotch and looks at the photo.

panel

PAGE 12
6 Panels

1 and 2 on a tier, 3-5 on an equilateral tier, 6 wide across the bottom.

PANEL 1: Small establishing shot of Ray's apartment building. It's an older 5-story brick walk-up that could exist in any major metropolis. Ditto for the DEALER on the front steps hocking his wares.

Location Cap: Ray's Apartment

PANEL 2: Inside Ray's apartment. It's more notable for what's not in it than what is. No photos. No furniture outside of the bed. No entertainment. It's sparse. Spartan. A place where Ray sleeps, not where he lives. Ray enters through the front door.

Silent panel

PANEL 3: Ray SPLASHING water on his face in the bathroom.

Silent panel

PANEL 4: Washing BLOOD off his cracked knuckles. He has the hands of an aging boxer.

Silent panel

PANEL 5: A POPPER (http://static.bbc.co.uk/surgery/img/hero/bart_poppers.jpg), with Madeline's photo next to it on the sink counter.

Silent panel

PANEL 6: Ray INHALES deeply. Fighting is his drug, but poppers are his vice.

Seth (off): You ever get tired of the cliché?

PAGE 13
6 Panels

PANEL 1: SETH stands in Ray's sparse living room. This is his glory shot/reveal. He stands with a cane (if he has one, might be cool) completely in control. If we see Ray, he's just a framing device to either side.

1 Seth: The red meat muscle for hire with the drug problem.

PANEL 2: A two-shot. Ray on the left, keeping a safe distance from Seth, but not so far that he's out of striking distance.

2 Ray: I don't know how you got in here–
3 Seth: I walked through the front door.
4 Seth: Spare me the posturing. This was the easiest place to find you.
5 Ray: Why find me at all?

PANEL 3: Close on Seth, using his words as skillfully as he would a weapon.

6 Seth: Cyrus Kane.

PANEL 4: Close on Ray. Serious.
[JD - Maybe do some kind of accent color behind Ray for added impact]

7 Seth (off): You know the name.

PANEL 5: Medium shot of Ray, getting his edge back and hardening.

8 Ray: I've heard the story of the gangster no one sees, keeps the whole city in his pocket.
9 Ray: I tend not to believe in things I can't see.

PANEL 6: Seth smiles, but there's no warmth in it. We get the feeling that when he smiles, it's only a moment before someone gets hurt. Leave some room for dialogue.

10 Seth: You can see me, Ray. I speak for Mr. Kane, and he's offering you an opportunity.
11 Seth: He doesn't want to change what you are. He doesn't want to change what you do.
12 Seth: He just wants you to do it for him.

PAGE 14
6 Panels

PANEL 1: Another two-shot. Ray relaxes a bit, perhaps willing to see how this plays out.

1 Ray: What does he think I do?
2 Seth: You're a finder. You locate people who don't want to be found.
3 Seth: From what Mr. Kane understands, you're no stranger to violence.

PANEL 2: Seth pulls a PHOTO from his jacket.

4 Seth: This is a skill Mr. Kane admires.

PANEL 3: On the photo in Ray's hands. It's a PHOTO OF MADELINE. Young. Happy. Innocent. Alive. [Note: We don't yet know it's the same girl from Ray's flashback. She looks familiar, but it's not definitive. She looks more like the flashback than the surveillance photo Alexis had, but there's a throughline in all of them.]

5 Seth (off): Madeline. Find her. Contact me.
6 Ray: Not interested.

PANEL 4: Seth smiles again. This could go bad in a hurry.

7 Seth: Of course you are. Don't let pride get in the way of your potential, Ray.

PANEL 5: Ray crowds Seth's personal space. Seth is still smiling.

8 Ray: Time's up, friend. Get out.
9 Seth: Madeline. Find her. Make your life better.

PANEL 6: Pull back for a longer shot from Ray's front door looking in. Seth is gone and Ray stands alone in the apartment, one hand holding the photo, the other CLENCHED in a fist. This echoes 11/4.

Silent panel

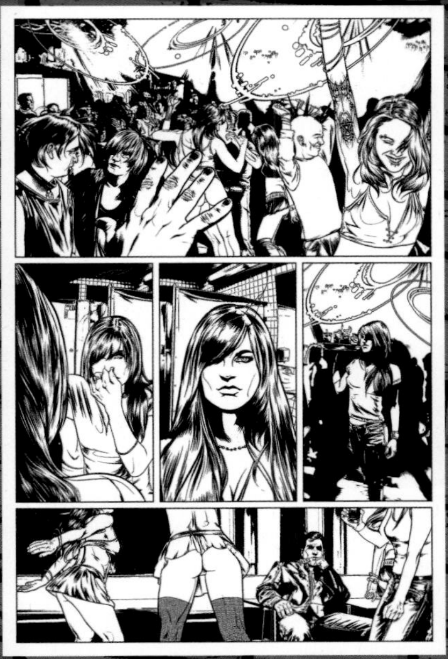

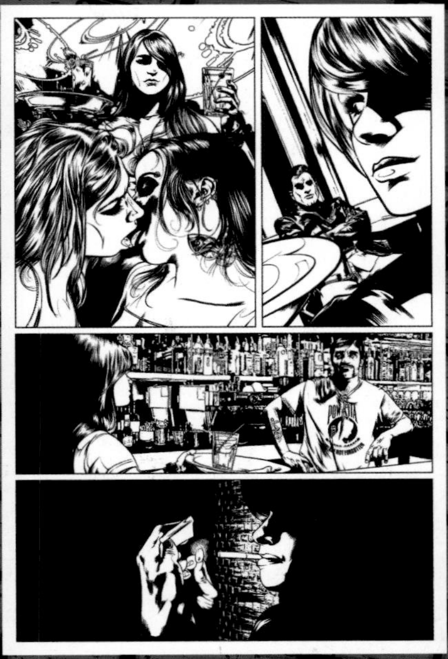

5
s

1: Inside a club. Colored light, hardbodies and vice on sale.
uld be an underground club anywhere but Amsterdam, but
andard for the city.

ı cap: The Pit Nightclub

2: On MADELINE in the club's bathroom, pinching her nose,
ritual after a cocaine bump. She looks more like the girl in
hoto than the one from Alexis.

anel
it works better, give her a small sniffle]

3: Madeline stares at herself in the mirror. No expression.
ı to read.
n either panel 2 or 3, we should have the "We Are All Lost"
ıewhere on the walls/stalls/mirror/etc.]

anel

4: Back inside the main area of the club, Madeline carries
of drinks.

anel

5: A DANCER gyrates on a small stage, in a cone of
light. Behind her, hit by another light, we see RAY, seated
ble by himself, looking at something other than the dancer.
earing his usual, which stands in contrast to the stylish
ıs of the club.

anel

PAGE 16
4 Panels

PANEL 1: TWO WOMEN furiously making out at a table as Madeline sets their drinks down. They pay no attention to her.

Silent panel

PANEL 2: Madeline makes eye contact with Ray. She doesn't like the look of him.

Madeline (small/whisper): Always with the fucking stalkers in this place...

PANEL 3: Madeline sets down her tray at the bar, speaks to the BARTENDER, a black dude with glasses and earlobe stretching earrings that are actually made from bullet casings.

1 Madeline: Taking my five. Need some air.
2 Bartender: Smoke one for me, kiddo.

PANEL 4: In the alleyway behind the club, Madeline lights her cigarette. It's dark out here, the flame providing most if not all of the light.

Silent panel

PAGE 17
4 Panels

PANEL 1: Madeline leans against the brick wall, taking a long drag from the cigarette. Needing it. Nerves. Through the CLOUD OF HER SMOKE, we can just barely see something moving toward her.

Silent panel

PANEL 2: THREE THUGS in prep school clothes (think your stereotypical date rapist from a good family) emerge, encroaching on Madeline.

1 Thug #1: You look familiar.

PANEL 3: Madeline looks at her cigarette, ignoring them and playing tough.

2 Madeline: A lot of bitches look like me.

3 Thug #1: But you're special.

PANEL 4: THUG #2 has taken Madeline's cigarette.

PANEL 5: and taken a puff. There's something perverse and unsettling about this. Thug #1 is close to Madeline, already acting out the nasty things he's going to do to her in his mind.

PANEL 6: Thug #1 has his hand on Madeline's waist, and we get the impression he's about to let it migrate north.

4 Thug #1: I can tell what kind of–
5 Ray (off): So this is why my scotch is late...

PAGE 18
4 Panels

PANEL 1: The thugs turn to see RAY. His body language is calm and open, but something suggests he's just waiting for an excuse to plant someone's teeth in the pavement. He's pointing a finger the off-panel Madeline. A thug or two can be in frame (maybe since he hasn't really been in the scene much).

1 Ray: See, that's my waitress.
2 Ray: Longer she's out here with you, the longer I have to wait my scotch.

PANEL 2: Thug one looks at Ray like he's crazy, but he's not lett Madeline go. Maybe he's bolstered on either side by one of his pals.

4 Thug #1: Fuck off, asshole!

PANEL 3: On Ray, smiling, he knows where this is heading and exactly what he wants.

5 Ray: I don't like to wait. Puts me in a foul mood.
6 Ray: Time for her to go back to work.

PANEL 4: The thug trio, pissed and ready to go.

7 Thug #1: Fellas... End him.

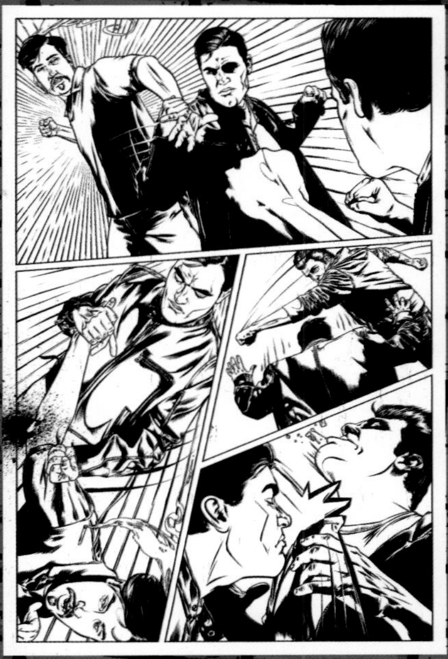

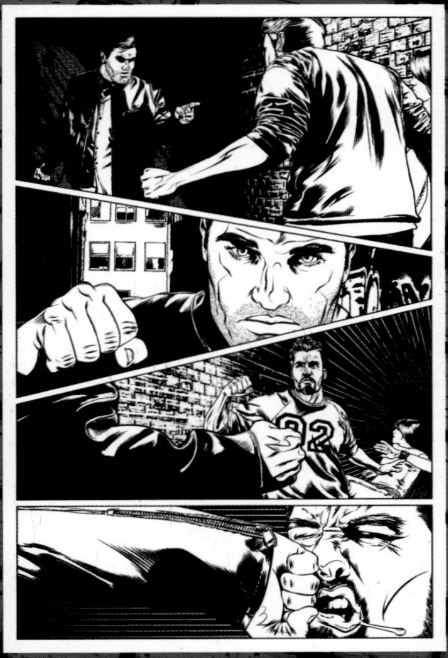

19
ɛls

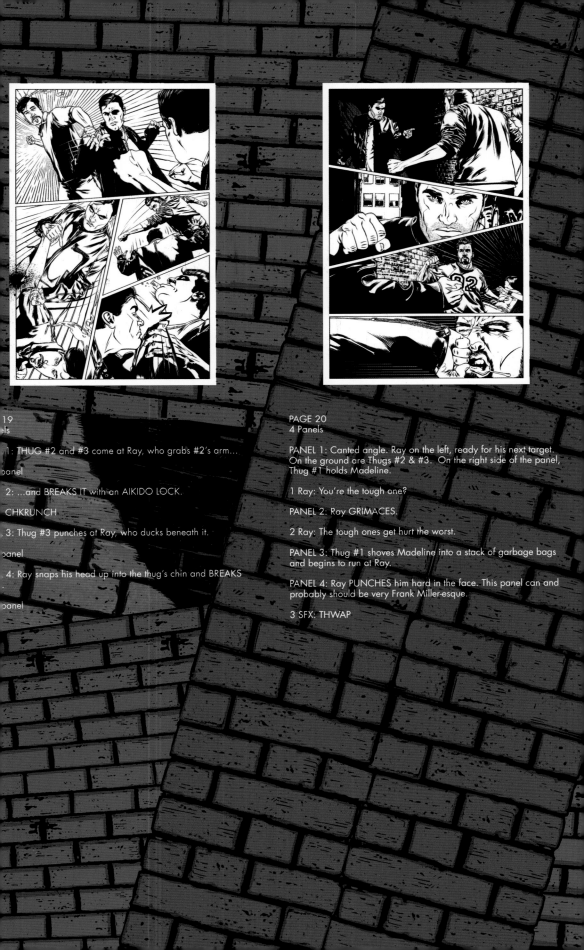

1: THUG #2 and #3 come at Ray, who grabs #2's arm...

ɔanel

2: ...and BREAKS IT with an AIKIDO LOCK.

CHKRUNCH

3: Thug #3 punches at Ray, who ducks beneath it.

ɔanel

4: Ray snaps his head up into the thug's chin and BREAKS
.

ɔanel

PAGE 20
4 Panels

PANEL 1: Canted angle. Ray on the left, ready for his next target. On the ground are Thugs #2 & #3. On the right side of the panel, Thug #1 holds Madeline.

1 Ray: You're the tough one?

PANEL 2: Ray GRIMACES.

2 Ray: The tough ones get hurt the worst.

PANEL 3: Thug #1 shoves Madeline into a stack of garbage bags and begins to run at Ray.

PANEL 4: Ray PUNCHES him hard in the face. This panel can and probably should be very Frank Miller-esque.

3 SFX: THWAP

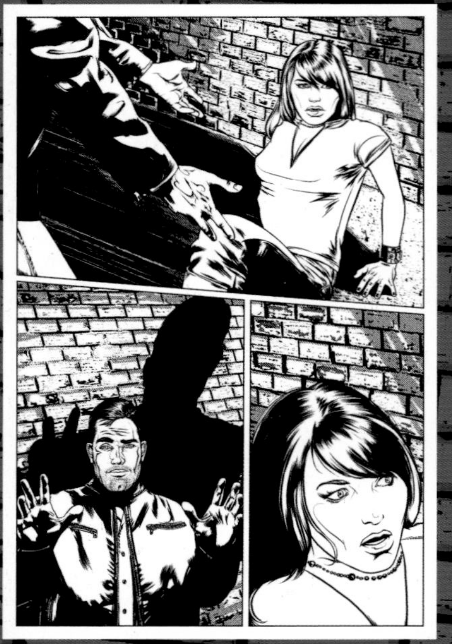

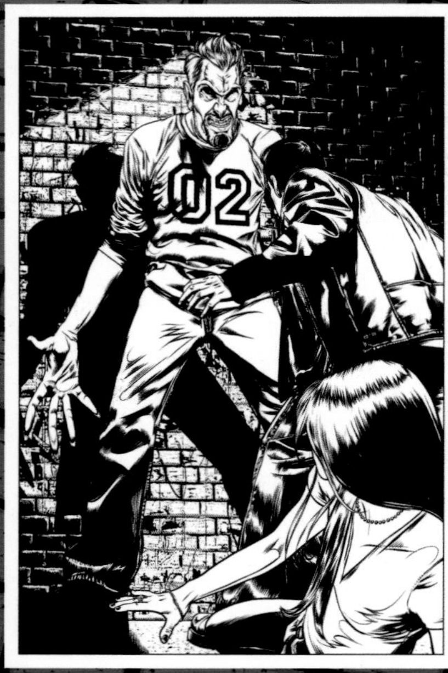
02

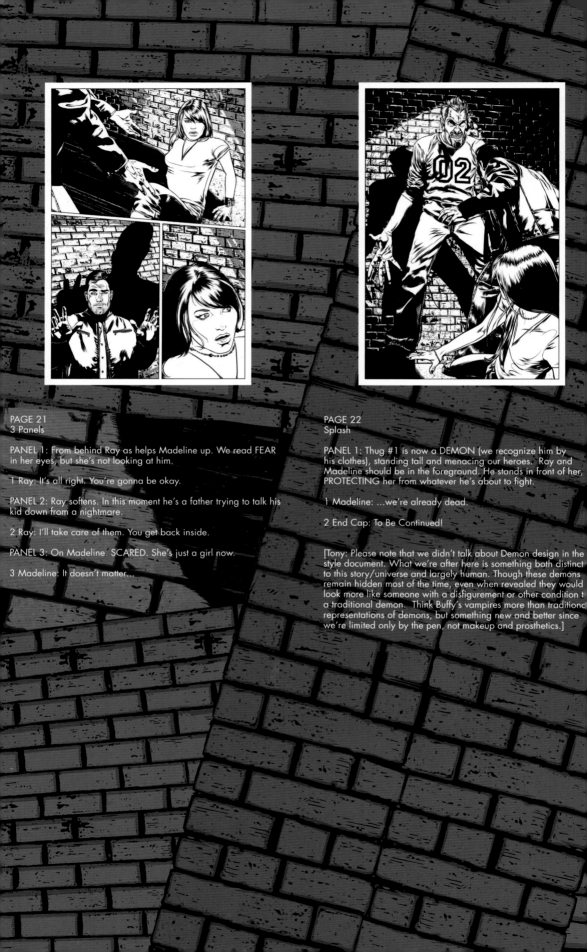

PAGE 21
3 Panels

PANEL 1: From behind Ray as helps Madeline up. We read FEAR in her eyes, but she's not looking at him.

1 Ray: It's all right. You're gonna be okay.

PANEL 2: Ray softens. In this moment he's a father trying to talk his kid down from a nightmare.

2 Ray: I'll take care of them. You get back inside.

PANEL 3: On Madeline. SCARED. She's just a girl now.

3 Madeline: It doesn't matter...

PAGE 22
Splash

PANEL 1: Thug #1 is now a DEMON (we recognize him by his clothes), standing tall and menacing our heroes. Ray and Madeline should be in the foreground. He stands in front of her, PROTECTING her from whatever he's about to fight.

1 Madeline: ...we're already dead.

2 End Cap: To Be Continued!

[Tony: Please note that we didn't talk about Demon design in the style document. What we're after here is something both distinct to this story/universe and largely human. Though these demons remain hidden most of the time, even when revealed they would look more like someone with a disfigurement or other condition t a traditional demon. Think Buffy's vampires more than traditionc representations of demons, but something new and better since we're limited only by the pen, not makeup and prosthetics.]

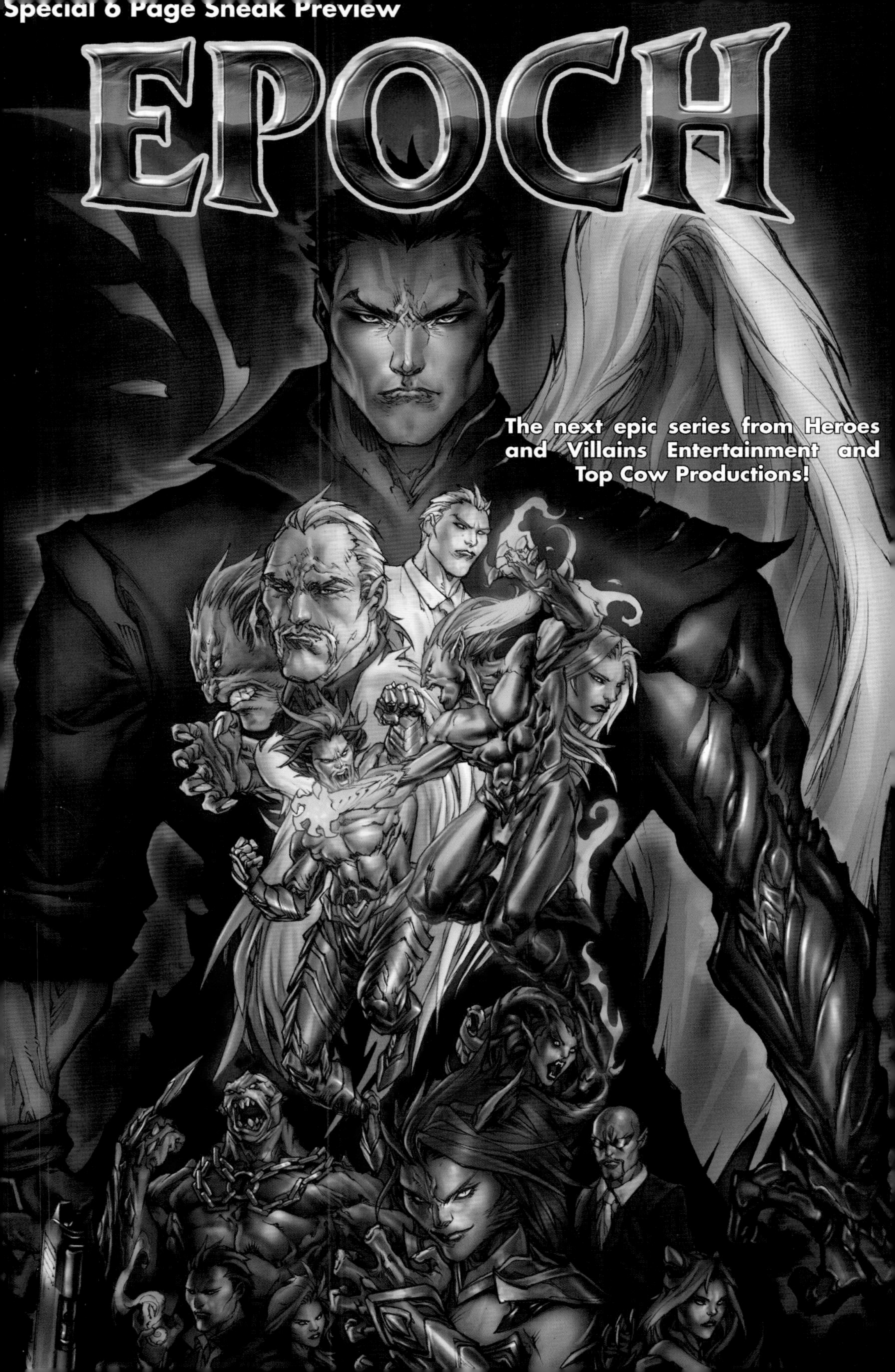
Special 6 Page Sneak Preview
EPOCH
The next epic series from Heroes and Villains Entertainment and Top Cow Productions!

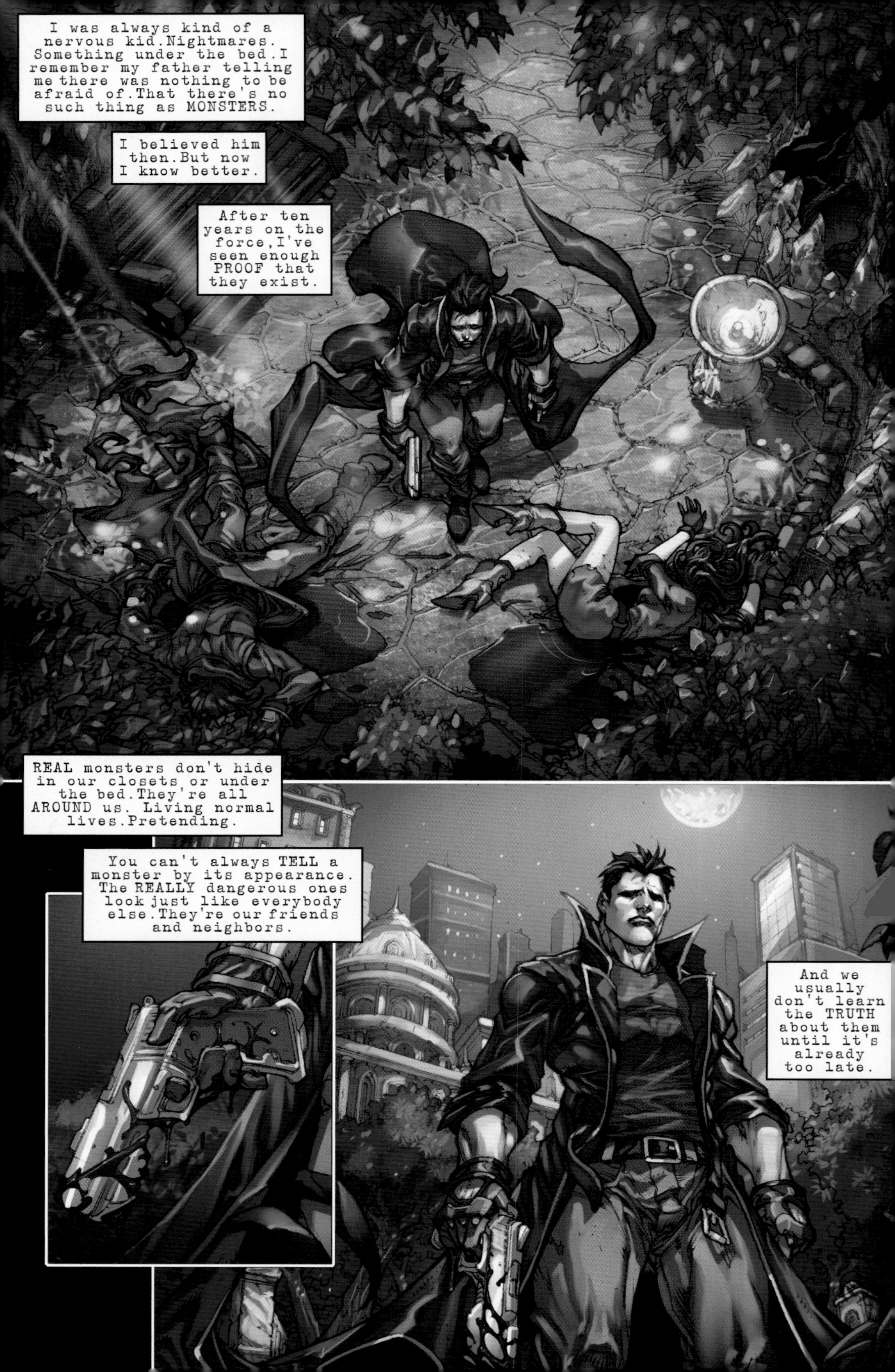
I was always kind of a nervous kid. Nightmares. Something under the bed. I remember my father telling me there was nothing to be afraid of. That there's no such thing as MONSTERS.
I believed him then. But now I know better.
After ten years on the force, I've seen enough PROOF that they exist.
REAL monsters don't hide in our closets or under the bed. They're all AROUND us. Living normal lives. Pretending.
You can't always TELL a monster by its appearance. The REALLY dangerous ones look just like everybody else. They're our friends and neighbors.
And we usually don't learn the TRUTH about them until it's already too late.

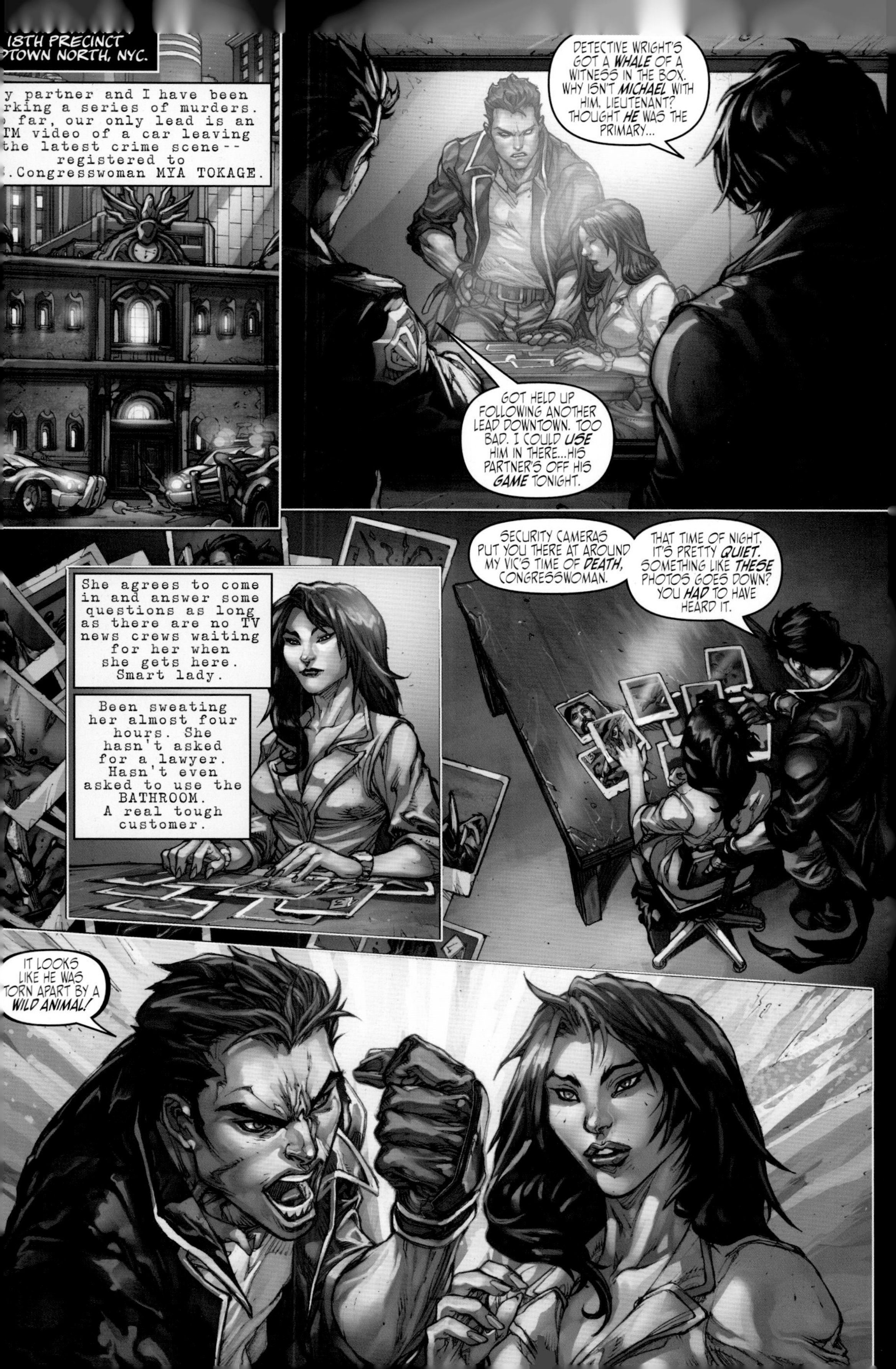
18TH PRECINCT
TOWN NORTH, NYC.
y partner and I have been rking a series of murders. far, our only lead is an TM video of a car leaving the latest crime scene-- registered to .Congresswoman MYA TOKAGE.
DETECTIVE WRIGHT'S GOT A WHALE OF A WITNESS IN THE BOX. WHY ISN'T MICHAEL WITH HIM, LIEUTENANT? THOUGHT HE WAS THE PRIMARY...
GOT HELD UP FOLLOWING ANOTHER LEAD DOWNTOWN. TOO BAD. I COULD USE HIM IN THERE...HIS PARTNER'S OFF HIS GAME TONIGHT.
She agrees to come in and answer some questions as long as there are no TV news crews waiting for her when she gets here. Smart lady.
Been sweating her almost four hours. She hasn't asked for a lawyer. Hasn't even asked to use the BATHROOM. A real tough customer.
SECURITY CAMERAS PUT YOU THERE AT AROUND MY VIC'S TIME OF DEATH, CONGRESSWOMAN.
THAT TIME OF NIGHT, IT'S PRETTY QUIET. SOMETHING LIKE THESE PHOTOS GOES DOWN? YOU HAD TO HAVE HEARD IT.
IT LOOKS LIKE HE WAS TORN APART BY A WILD ANIMAL!

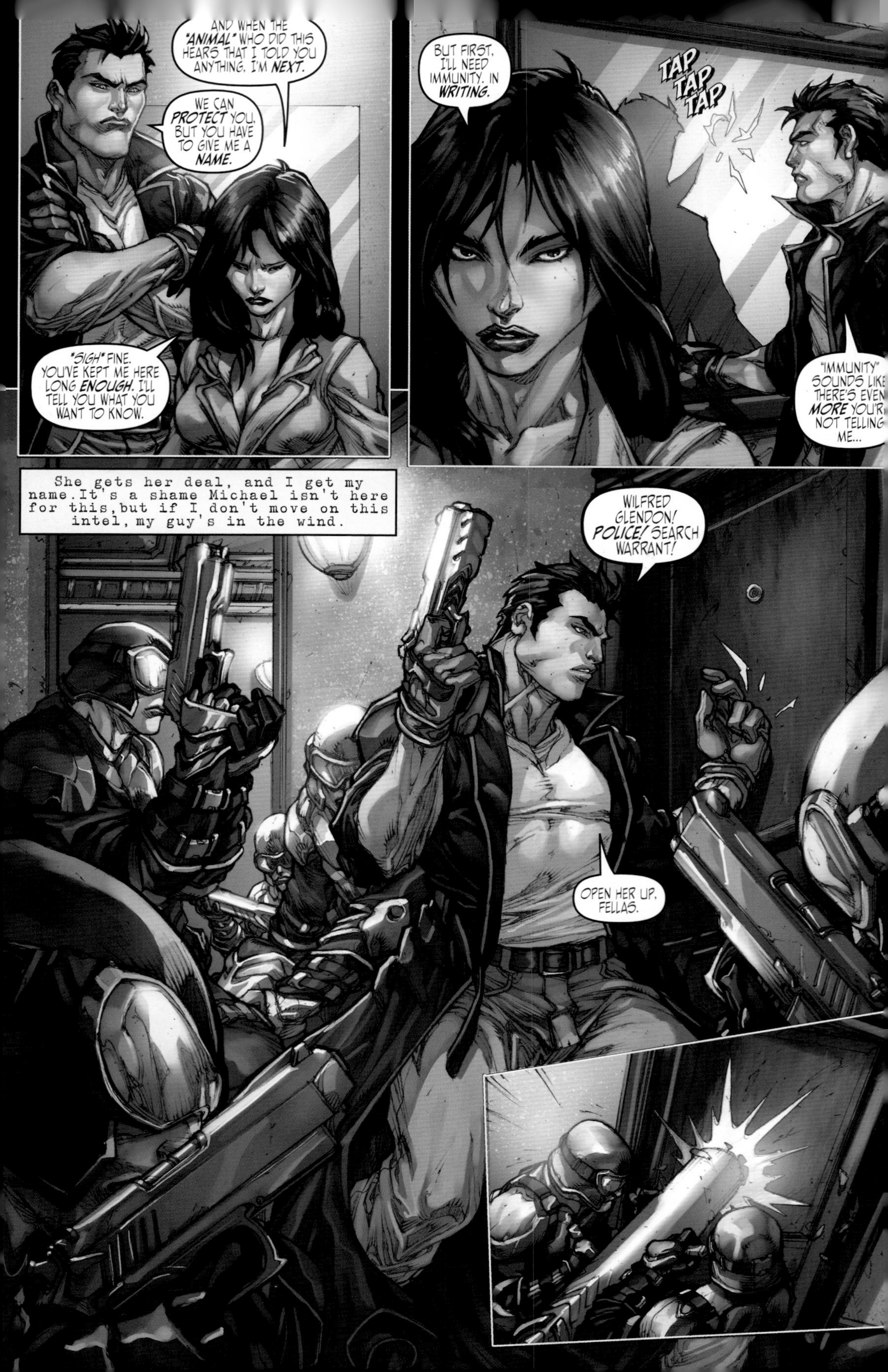
AND WHEN THE "ANIMAL" WHO DID THIS HEARS THAT I TOLD YOU ANYTHING, I'M NEXT.
WE CAN PROTECT YOU, BUT YOU HAVE TO GIVE ME A NAME.
SIGH FINE. YOU'VE KEPT ME HERE LONG ENOUGH. I'LL TELL YOU WHAT YOU WANT TO KNOW.
BUT FIRST, I'LL NEED IMMUNITY. IN WRITING.
TAP TAP TAP
"IMMUNITY" SOUNDS LIKE THERE'S EVEN MORE YOU'R NOT TELLING ME...
She gets her deal, and I get my name. It's a shame Michael isn't here for this, but if I don't move on this intel, my guy's in the wind.
WILFRED GLENDON! POLICE! SEARCH WARRANT!
OPEN HER UP, FELLAS.

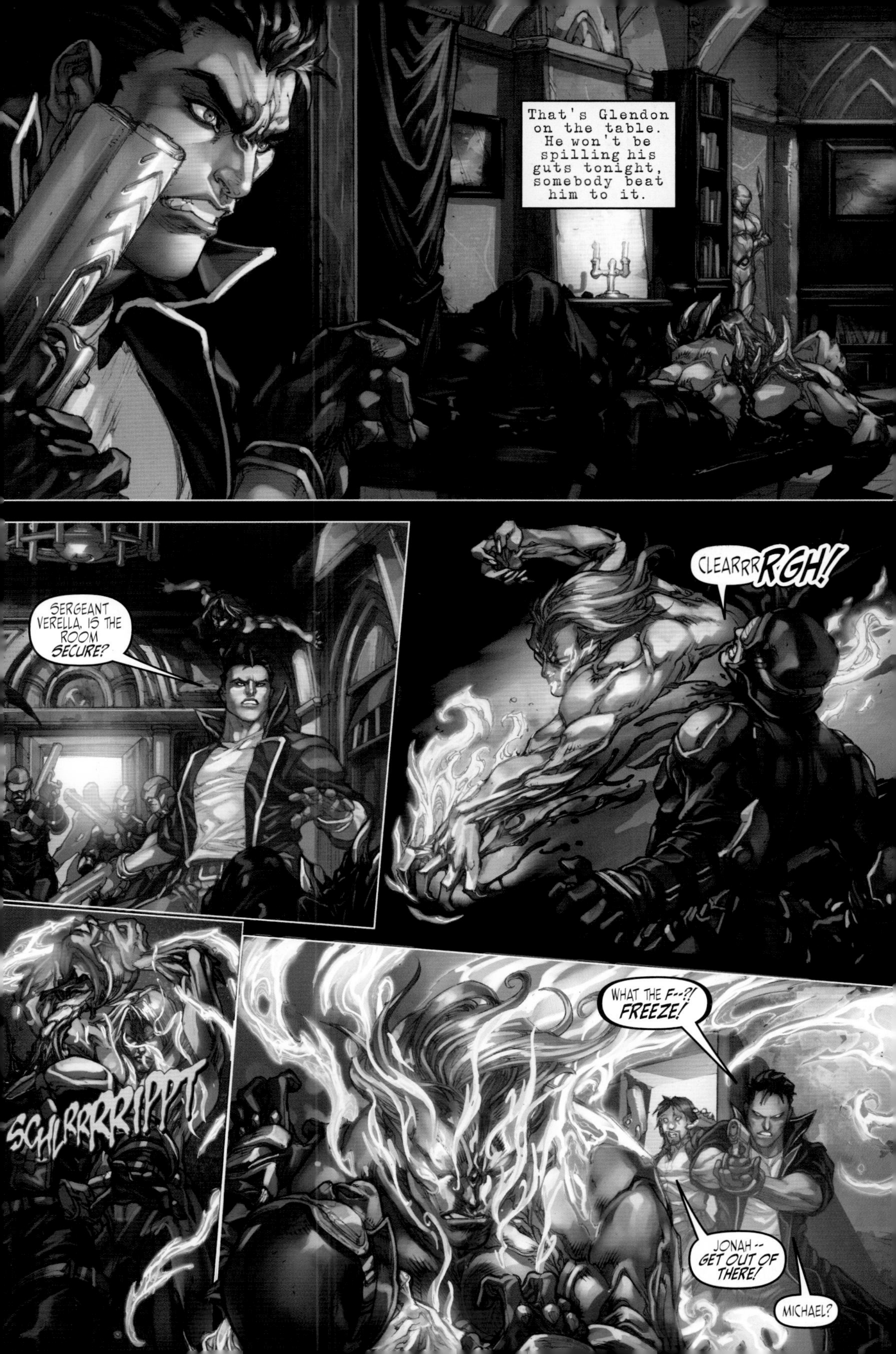
That's Glendon on the table. He won't be spilling his guts tonight, somebody beat him to it.
SERGEANT VERELLA. IS THE ROOM SECURE?
CLEARRRRGH!
SCHLRRRRIPPT!
WHAT THE F--?! FREEZE!
JONAH -- GET OUT OF THERE!
MICHAEL?

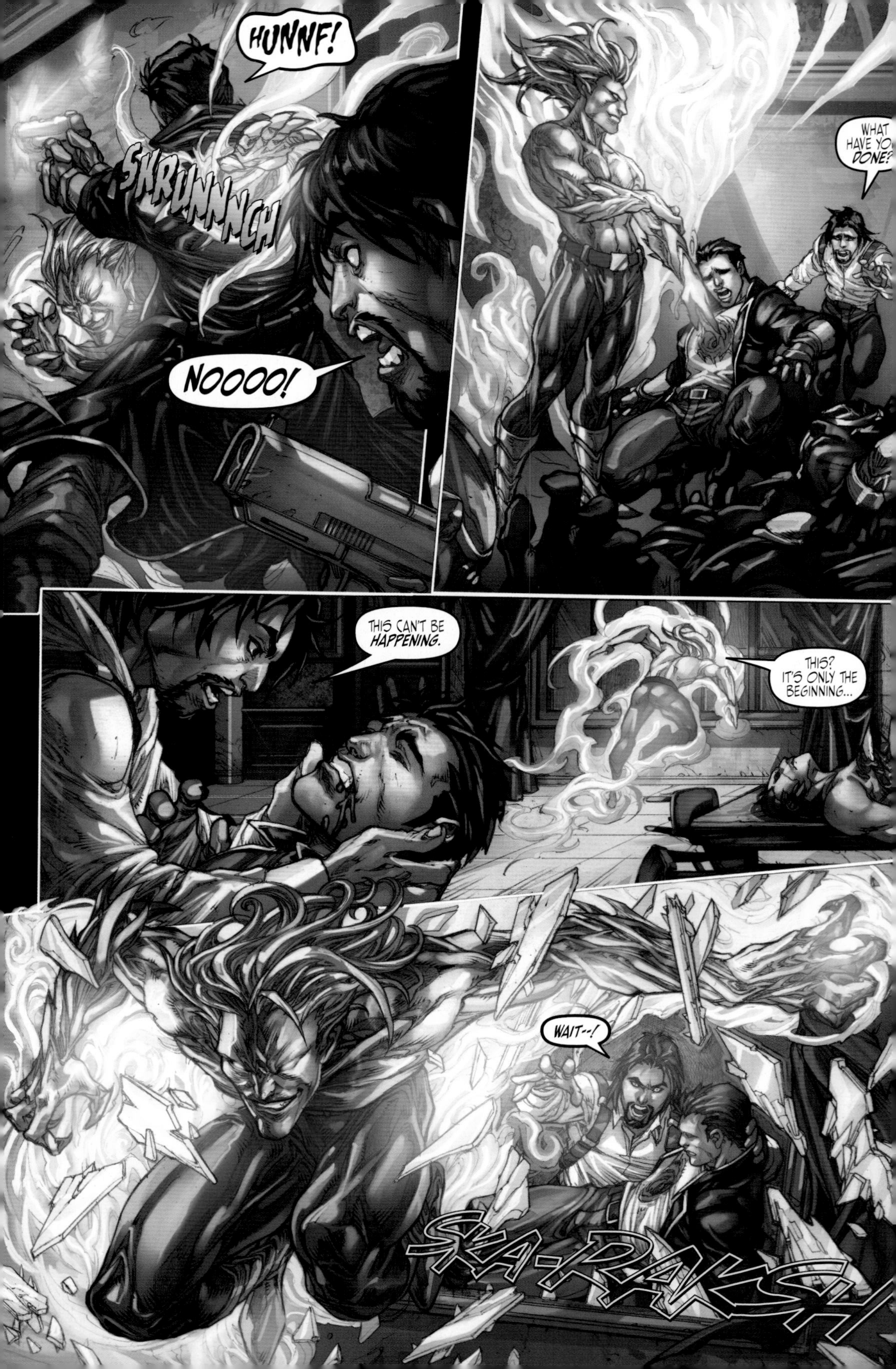
HUNNF!
SKRUNNNCH
NOOOO!
WHAT HAVE YOU DONE?
THIS CAN'T BE HAPPENING.
THIS? IT'S ONLY THE BEGINNING...
WAIT--!
SKA-RAKSH

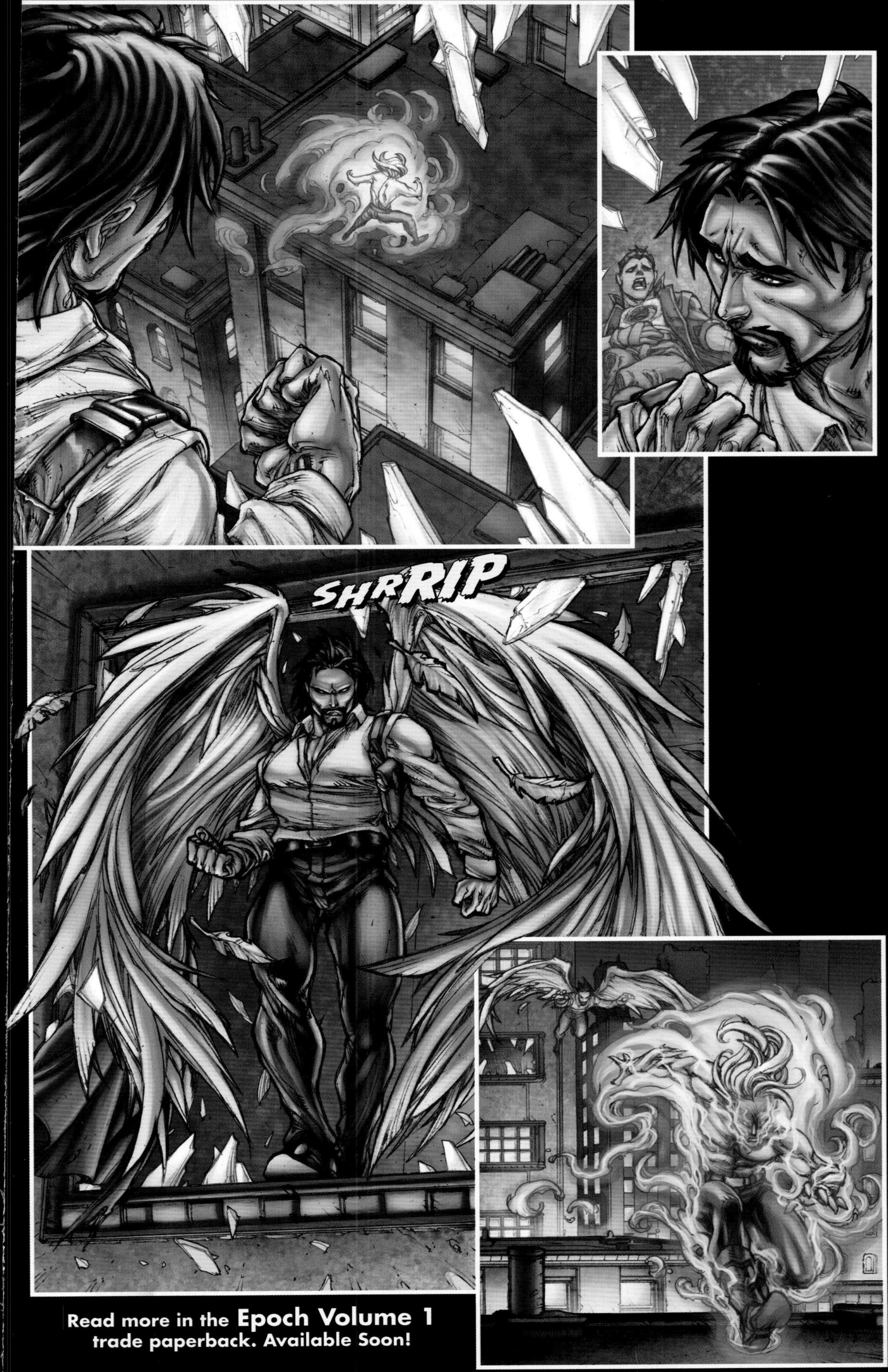
SHRRIP

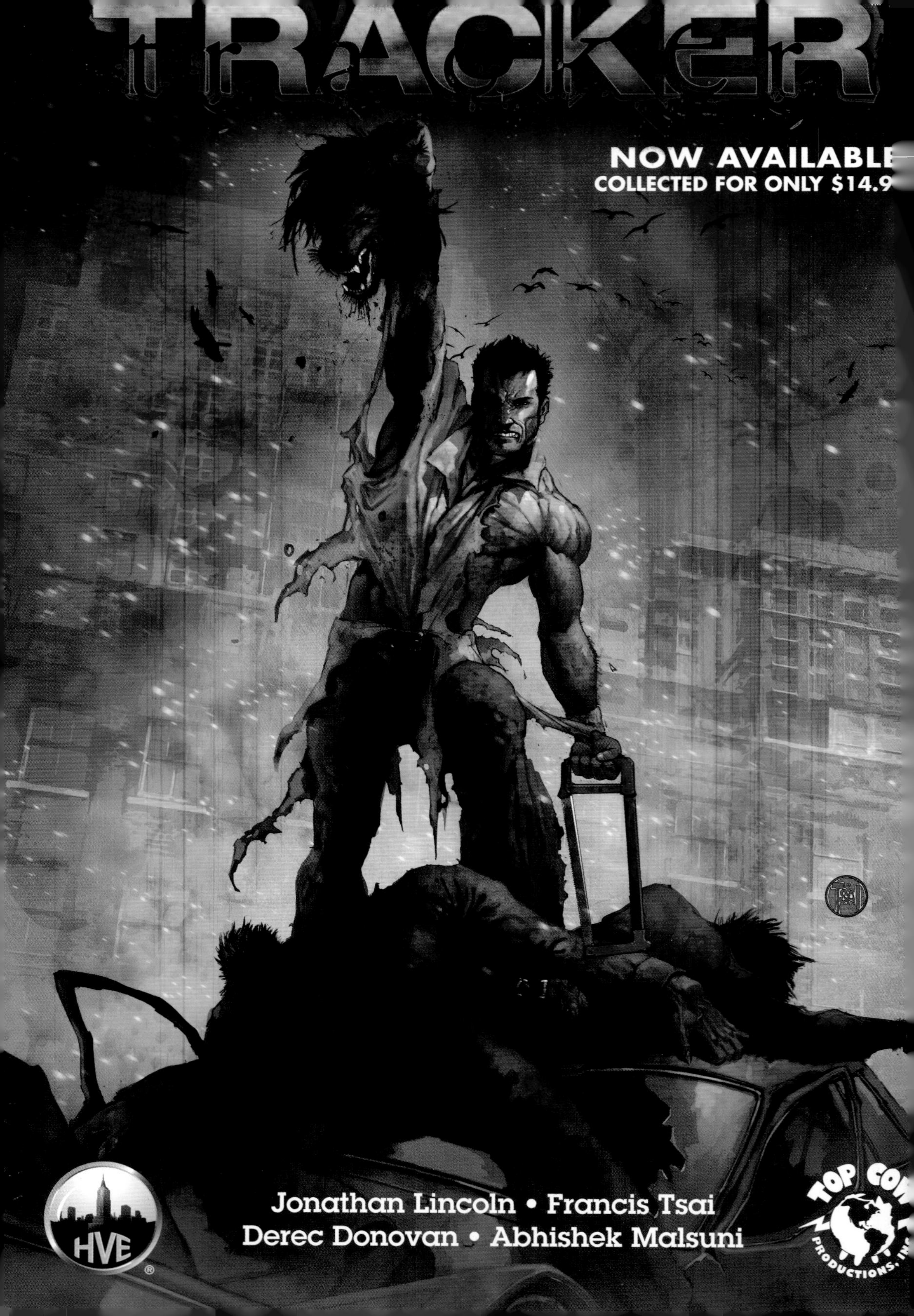
TRACKER
NOW AVAILABLE
COLLECTED FOR ONLY $14.9
Jonathan Lincoln • Francis Tsai
Derec Donovan • Abhishek Malsuni
HVE
TOP COW PRODUCTIONS, INC.

Join the Top Cow Universe with The Darkness!

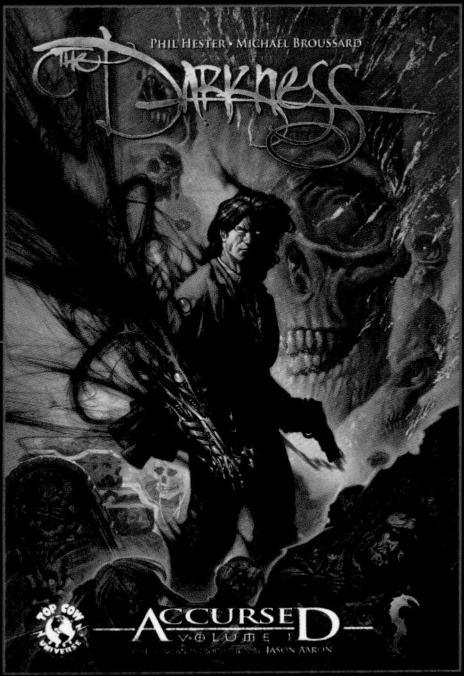
PHIL HESTER • MICHAEL BROUSSARD
ACCURSED
VOLUME 1

The Darkness
Accursed vol. 1

written by:
Phil Hester

pencils by:
Michael Broussard

Mafia hitman Jackie Estacado was both blessed and cursed on his 21st birthday when he became the bearer of The Darkness, an elemental force that allows those who wield it access to an otherwordly dimension and control over the demons who dwell there. Forces for good in the world rise up to face Jackie and the evil his gift represents, but there is one small problem. In this story... they are the bad guys.

Now's your chance to read "Empire," the first storyline by the new creative team of Phil Hester (Firebreather, Green Arrow) and Michael Broussard (Unholy Union) that marked the shocking return of The Darkness to the Top Cow Universe!

Book Market Edtion
ISBN 13: 978-1-58240-958-0
$9.99

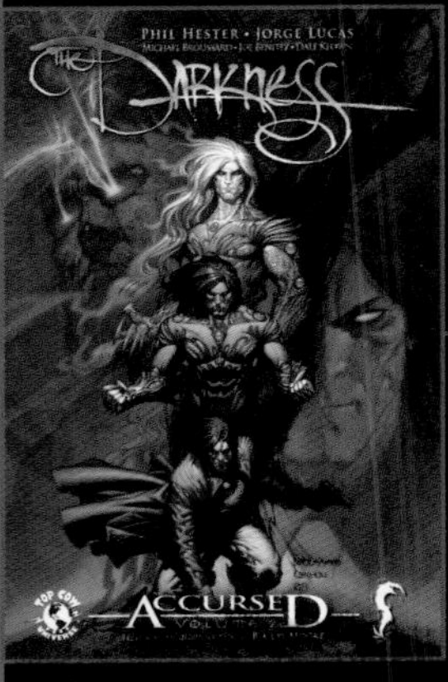
PHIL HESTER • JORGE LUCAS
ACCURSED

The Darkness
Accursed vol.2
978-1-60706-0-444
$9.99

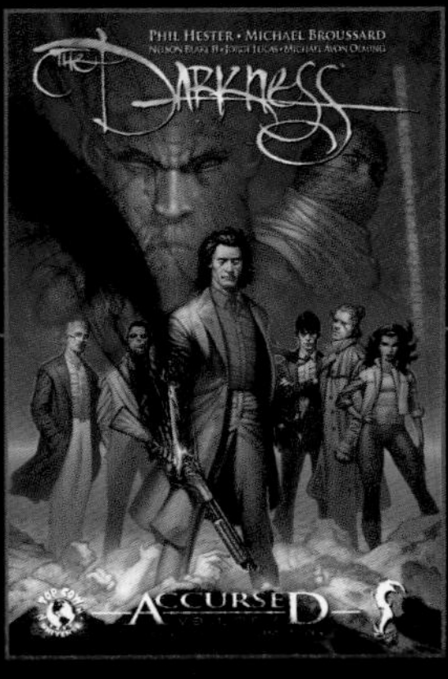
PHIL HESTER • MICHAEL BROUSSARD
ACCURSED

The Darkness
Accursed vol.3
978-1-60706-1-007
$12.99

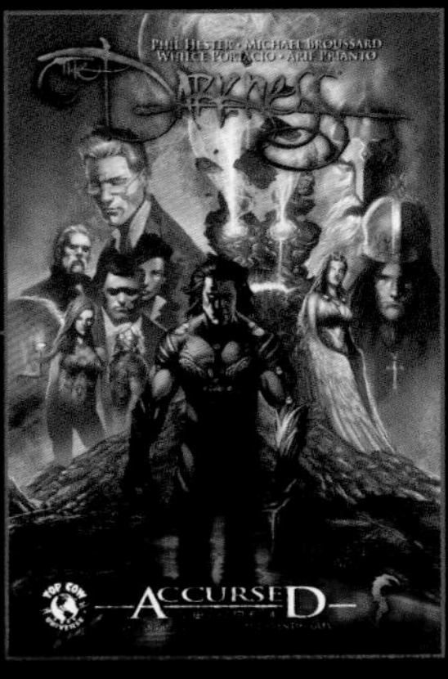
ACCURSED

The Darkness
Accursed vol.4
978-1-60706-1-946
$14.99

Ready for more? Jump into the Top Cow Universe with *Witchblade*!

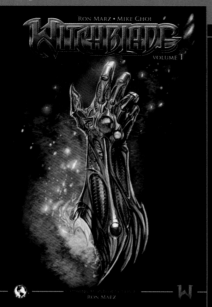

RON MARZ • MIKE CHOI
WITCHBLADE
VOLUME 1
RON MARZ

Witchblade

volume 1 - volume 8

written by:

Ron Marz

art by:

Mike Choi, Stephen Sadowski, Keu Cha, Chris Bachalo, Stjepan Sejic and more!

Get in on the ground floor of Top Cow's flagship title with these affordable trade paperback collections from Ron Marz's series-redefining run on Witchblade! Each volume collects a key story arc in the continuing adventures of Sara Pezzini and the Witchblade, culminating in the epic 'War of the Witchblades' storyline!

Book Market Edtion, volume 1
collects issues #80-#85
(ISBN: 978-1-58240-906-1) $9.99

RON MARZ • MIKE CHOI • CHRIS BACHALO • KEU CHA
WITCHBLADE
VOLUME 2
FEATURING AN INTRODUCTION BY PHIL HESTER

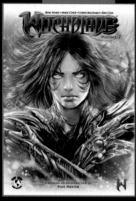

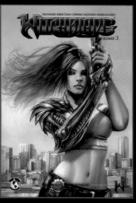

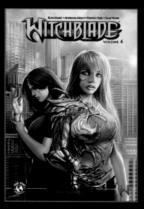

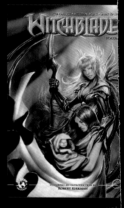

volume 2
collects issues #86-#92
(ISBN: 978-1-58240-886-6)
U.S.D. $14.99

WITCHBLADE
VOLUME 3

volume 3
collects issues #93-#100
(ISBN: 978-1-58240-887-3)
U.S.D. $14.99

WITCHBLADE
VOLUME 4

volume 4
collects issues #101-109
(ISBN: 978-1-58240-898-9)
U.S.D. $17.99

WITCHBLADE
FEATURING AN INTRODUCTION BY ROBERT KIRKMAN

volu
collects issues #110
First Born issues
(ISBN: 978-1-58240-8
U.S.D. $1

WITCHBLADE

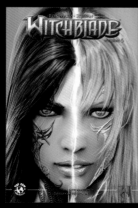

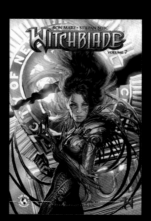

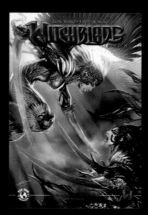

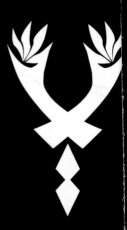

volume 6
collects issues #116-#120
(ISBN: 978-1-60706-041-3)
U.S.D. $14.99

RON MARZ • STJEPAN SEJIC
WITCHBLADE
VOLUME 7

volume 7
collects issues #121-#124 &
Witchblade Annual #1
(ISBN: 978-1-60706-058-1)
U.S.D. $14.99

WITCHBLADE

volume 8
collects issues #125-#130
(ISBN: 978-1-60706-102-1)
U.S.D. $14.99

Explore more of the Top Cow Universe!

Ron Marz • Michael Broussard
ARTIFACTS
volume 1
FEATURING AN INTRODUCTION BY
MARC SILVESTRI

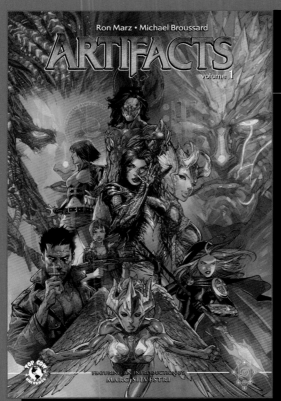

Artifacts

Volume 1

written by:
Ron Marz
pencils by:
Michael Broussard &
Stjepan Sejic

When a mysterious antagonist kidnaps Hope, the daughter of Sara Pezzini and Jackie Estacado, Armageddon is set in motion. Featuring virtually every character in the Top Cow Universe, Artifacts is an epic story for longtime fans and new readers alike.

Collects issues #0-4

(ISBN 978-1-60706-201-1)

From the pages of Witchblade
RON MARZ • STJEPAN SEJIC
ANGELUS
volume 1
FEATURING AN INTRODUCTION BY
ANGELA ROBINSON

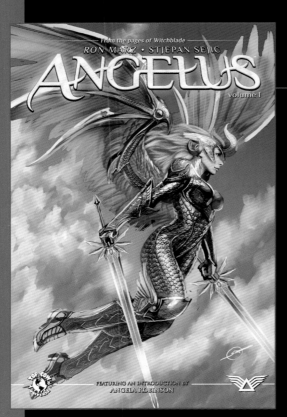

Angelus

Volume 1

written by:
Ron Marz
art by:
Stjepan Sejic

Like so many other twenty-somethings, Danielle Baptiste is trying to find her place in the world. But for Dani, that also means bearing up under the burden of acting as host for one of the Universe's primal forces - The Angelus! Returning to her hometown of New Orleans with her friend and romantic interest Finch, Dani must face an attack from her ancient enemy, the Darkness, as well as betrayal by the very warriors who pledged to serve her.

Collects issues #1-6

(ISBN 978-1-60706-198-4)

The Top Cow essentials checklist:

Artifacts Volume 1
(ISBN: 978-1-60706-201-1)

Art of Top Cow Softcover
(ISBN: 978-1-60706-099-4)

Broken Trinity Volume 1
(ISBN: 978-1-60706-051-2)

The Darkness: Accursed Volume 1
(ISBN: 978-1-58240-958-0)

The Darkness: Origins Volume 1
(ISBN: 978-1-60706-097-0)

First Born
(ISBN: 978-1-58240-854-5)

Freshmen Volume 1
(ISBN: 978-1-58240-593-3)

Magdalena Volume 1
(ISBN: 978-1-60706-206-6)

Rising Stars Volume 1
(ISBN: 978-1-58240-172-0)

Wanted
(ISBN: 978-1-58240-497-4)

Witchblade: Origins Volume 1
(ISBN: 978-1-58240-901-6)

Witchblade: Redemption Volume 1
(ISBN: 978-1-60706-193-9)

For more info, ISBN and ordering information on our latest collections go to:
www.topcow.com
Ask your retailer about our catalogue of our collected editions, digests and hard covers or check the listings at:
Barnes and Noble,
Amazon.com
and other fine retailers.
To find your nearest comic shop go to:
www.comicshoplocator.com

dedication

For my husband, Matt, my partner in the grandest adventure of all.

acknowledgments

Patty Murphy, I'm glad we could travel this road together! It has been a crazy, fun whirlwind, made better by sharing with you.

Sarah Phillips, thanks for putting up with another round of crazy. You're always there for me.

Many thanks to Andover Fabrics, Dear Stella Designs, FreeSpirit Fabric/Rowan Fabric, and Michael Miller Fabrics for providing fabrics used in this book.

A giant thank-you to Donnie Brandon for too many things to name.

Thanks to the Stash Books/C&T team, but most especially Liz Aneloski and Alison Schmidt. Y'all make me look good!

36

40

46

contents

68

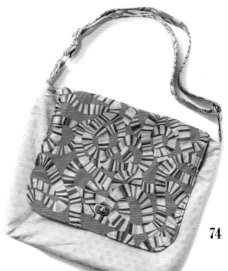

74

50

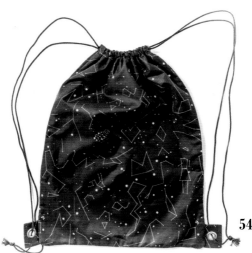

54

60

projects

80

88

94

introduction

This is not just a book of sewing projects. Sure, you can jump straight to the projects and make them, exactly as written, but that's just a small part of what this book is about.

I started using the Basic Tote Bag pattern in my learn-to-sew class because it met several criteria: It used basic sewing concepts, it didn't require a lot of supplies, it could be easily made in a short amount of time, and it was functional.

Through the years, I've watched hundreds of people sew this simple bag, their faces lighting up as they finish the last steps and see the results of their work. What's just as fun is watching my students compare their totes and realize how different they look just because they use different fabric.

One of my favorite aspects of the class is when I tell my students how easy it is to

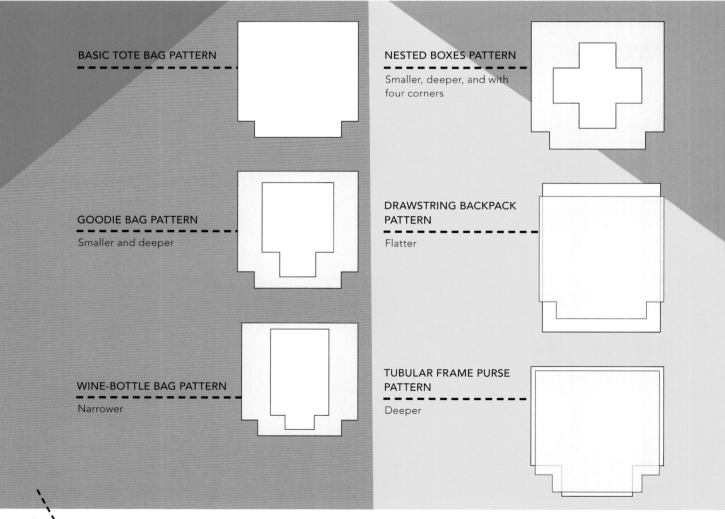

BASIC TOTE BAG PATTERN

GOODIE BAG PATTERN

Smaller and deeper

WINE-BOTTLE BAG PATTERN

Narrower

NESTED BOXES PATTERN

Smaller, deeper, and with four corners

DRAWSTRING BACKPACK PATTERN

Flatter

TUBULAR FRAME PURSE PATTERN

Deeper

transform this simple pattern. I love hacking patterns, and this one is primed for it. Add pockets. Make it larger. Make it smaller. Dress it up with ruffles, appliqué, monograms. The only limits to the options, really, are your imagination and willingness to try!

This book guides you through the process behind the hacks and then gives you the Basic Tote Bag pattern and ten pattern hacks to get you started. The illustrations below show you how the pattern hack (white) compares to the Basic Tote Bag pattern (gray). I truly hope that this book will be a starting point for you, now that you can see how easy it is to modify and make something that suits your style.

Happy hacking!

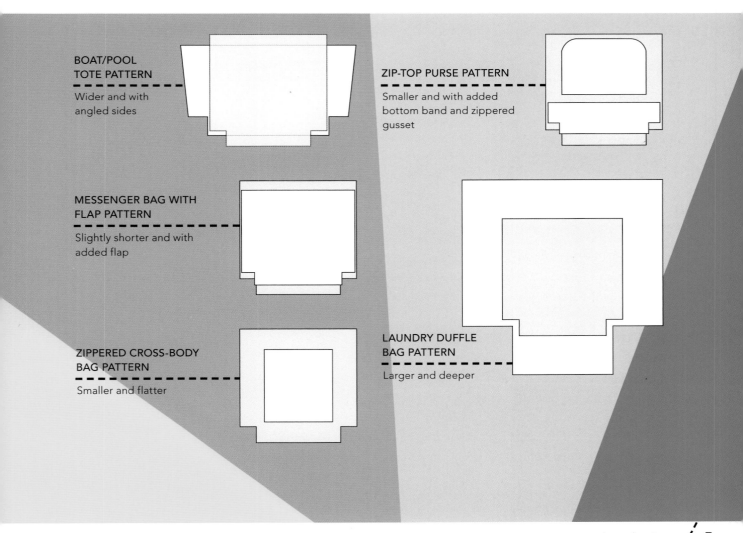

BOAT/POOL TOTE PATTERN

Wider and with angled sides

MESSENGER BAG WITH FLAP PATTERN

Slightly shorter and with added flap

ZIPPERED CROSS-BODY BAG PATTERN

Smaller and flatter

ZIP-TOP PURSE PATTERN

Smaller and with added bottom band and zippered gusset

LAUNDRY DUFFLE BAG PATTERN

Larger and deeper

anatomy *of the* tote bag pattern

Parts of the Tote Bag Pattern

Body

The body of the bag is oh so simple—a square—but easily manipulated to suit your needs. The height and width, in conjunction with the corners, determine the finished height, width, and depth of your bag.

Corners

The square notches cut from the bottom corners of the body pieces dictate the shape of the finished project. I always cut a square (or as close to it as possible) so the sides and bottom of the bag meet properly. The corners determine the depth and width of the bag.

Handles/Strap

The handles or strap on the bag do all the heavy work—literally—once your bag is finished. Placement is determined by the bag style as well as the corners of the bag. Imagine a line running vertically from the bottom of the bag to the top edge, through the seam allowance for the corners. Handles that connect to the widest part of the bag body need to be within this seam allowance. A single, long strap usually is centered over the side seams.

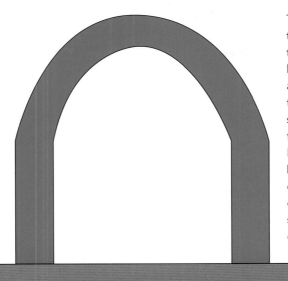

The distance from the apex of the handles to the top edge of the bag is called the drop. The length of the handles, as well as their placement, determine the drop. A bag carried on the shoulder needs a greater drop than one carried in the hand. Place handles on the side of the bag body at least ¼″ inside the corner notches. For a longer, cross-body strap, place the strap on the sides of the bag, centering it over the side seams.

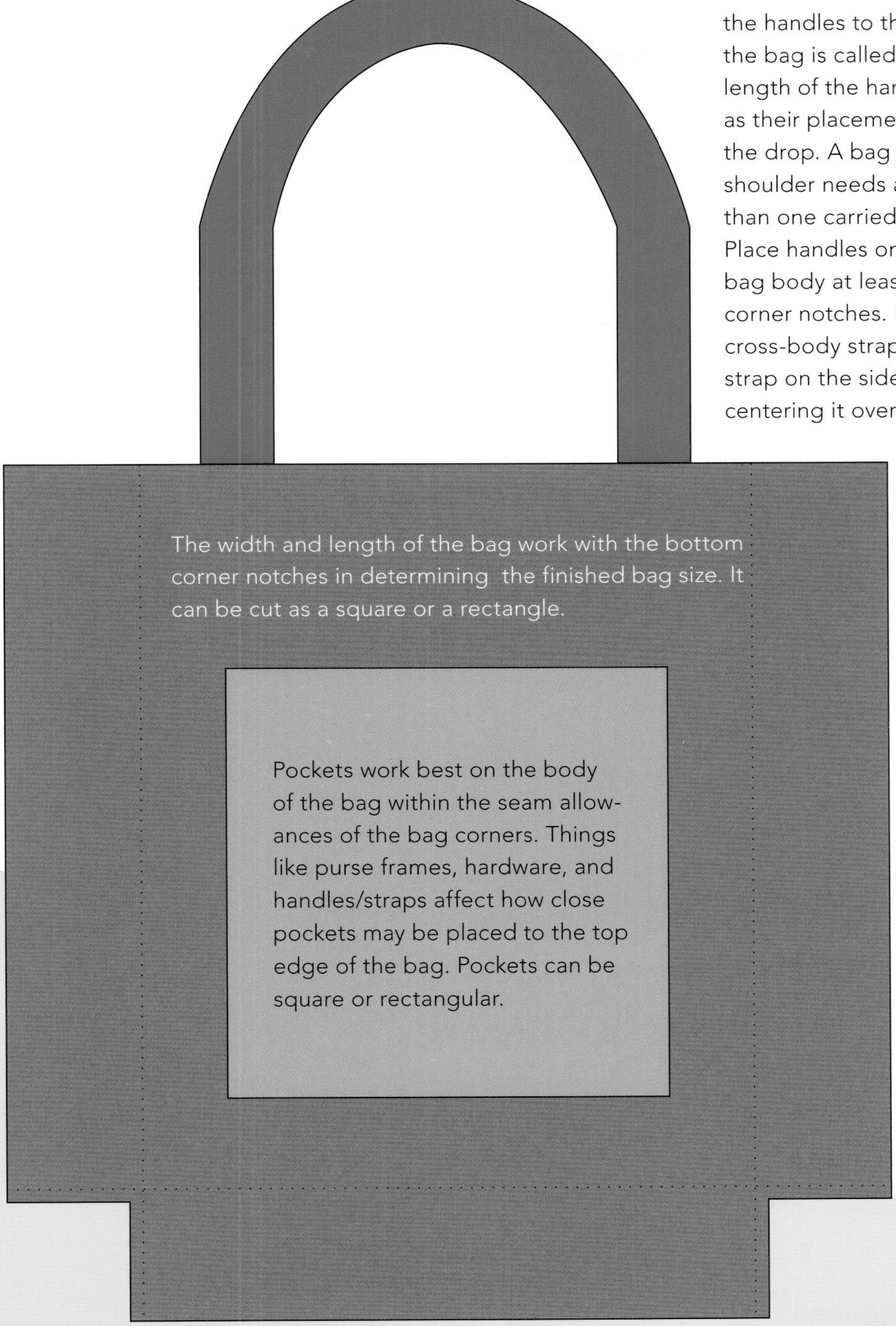

The width and length of the bag work with the bottom corner notches in determining the finished bag size. It can be cut as a square or a rectangle.

Pockets work best on the body of the bag within the seam allowances of the bag corners. Things like purse frames, hardware, and handles/straps affect how close pockets may be placed to the top edge of the bag. Pockets can be square or rectangular.

The bag corners are formed from square notches cut out of the bottom corners of the bag body. The size of the notches determine the depth of the finished bag.

overview *of* hacking the pattern

Changing Dimensions

I love how easy it is to enlarge or shrink—or skew—the proportions of the Basic Tote Bag! A calculator makes quick work of scaling up or down. Just multiply the length, width, and corner measurements by the percentage in decimals that you want to increase or decrease by. For a bag that's 75% smaller than the original, multiply 18″ and 2½″ by 0.75 to yield 13½″ and 1⅞″. To make the Basic Tote Bag 50% larger, multiply the same numbers by 1.5 to get 27″ and 3¾″.

Increase or decrease the height or width for a bag that's taller or wider. Just keep in mind that bag depth is dictated by the square notches cut for the corners.

The Boat/Pool Tote (page 68) takes the dimensional modification one step further by tapering in the sides slightly. This does make it a challenge to get completely square corner notches, however.

The projects in this book are a great starting point, but don't feel limited to using only the numbers I've given you. If you're not entirely comfortable with altering the dimensions, start by simply cutting the Basic Tote Bag into multiple rectangles for a pieced bag. This multi-fabric version (page 12) shows off a large novelty print, framed with contrasting fabric at the top and bottom.

To accomplish the change, I divided the height of the Basic Tote Bag (18″) by 2 (9″) and added the seam allowance twice for the center panel (18″ × 9½″). I divided the remaining half by 2 (4½″) and add the seam allowance to each (18″ × 4¾″). The corners are cut only from the bottom panel. Once the bag is pieced, the dimensions match those of the Basic Tote Bag.

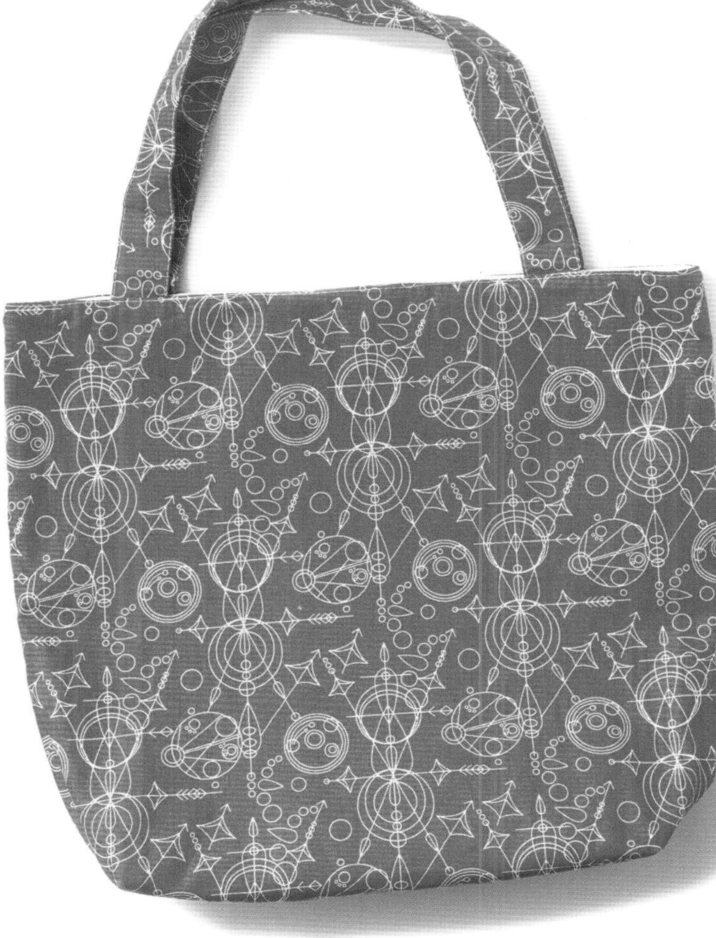

Modifying the dimensions of the Basic Tote Bag is easy.

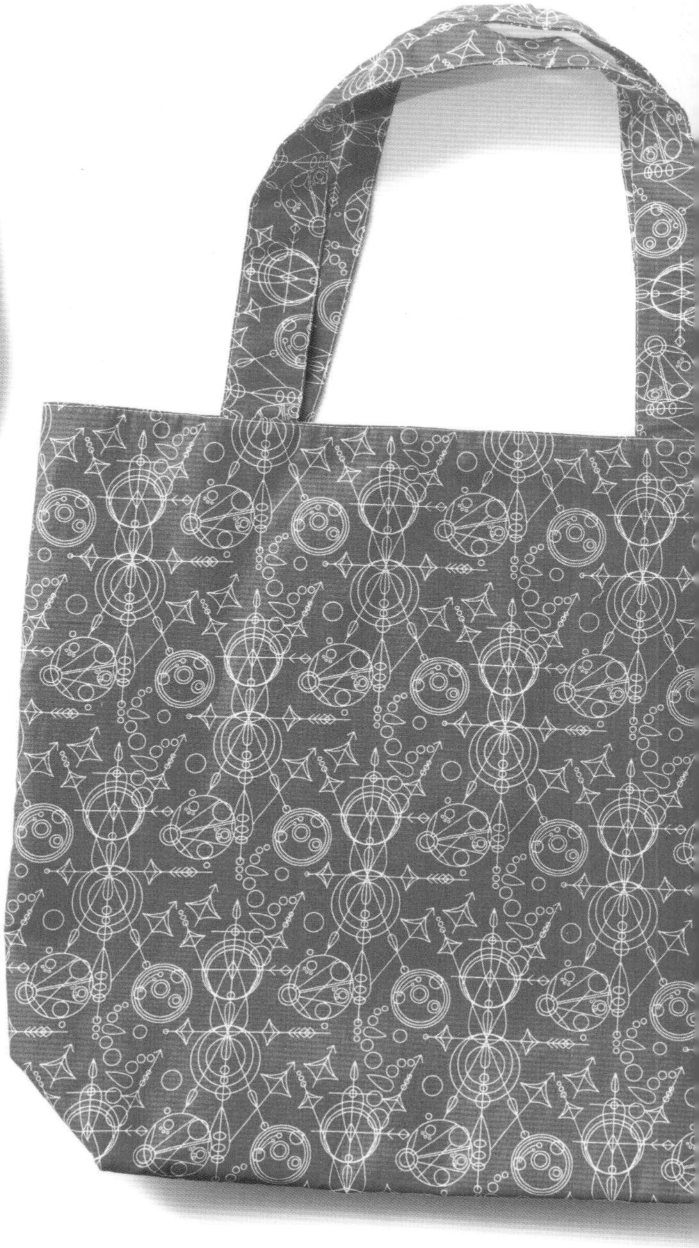

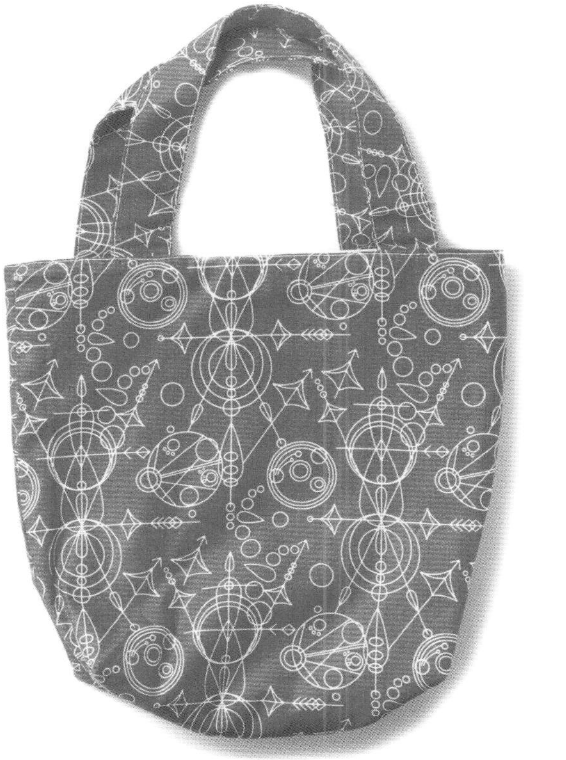

Dividing the Basic Tote Bag to use multiple fabrics is a quick way to change its look.

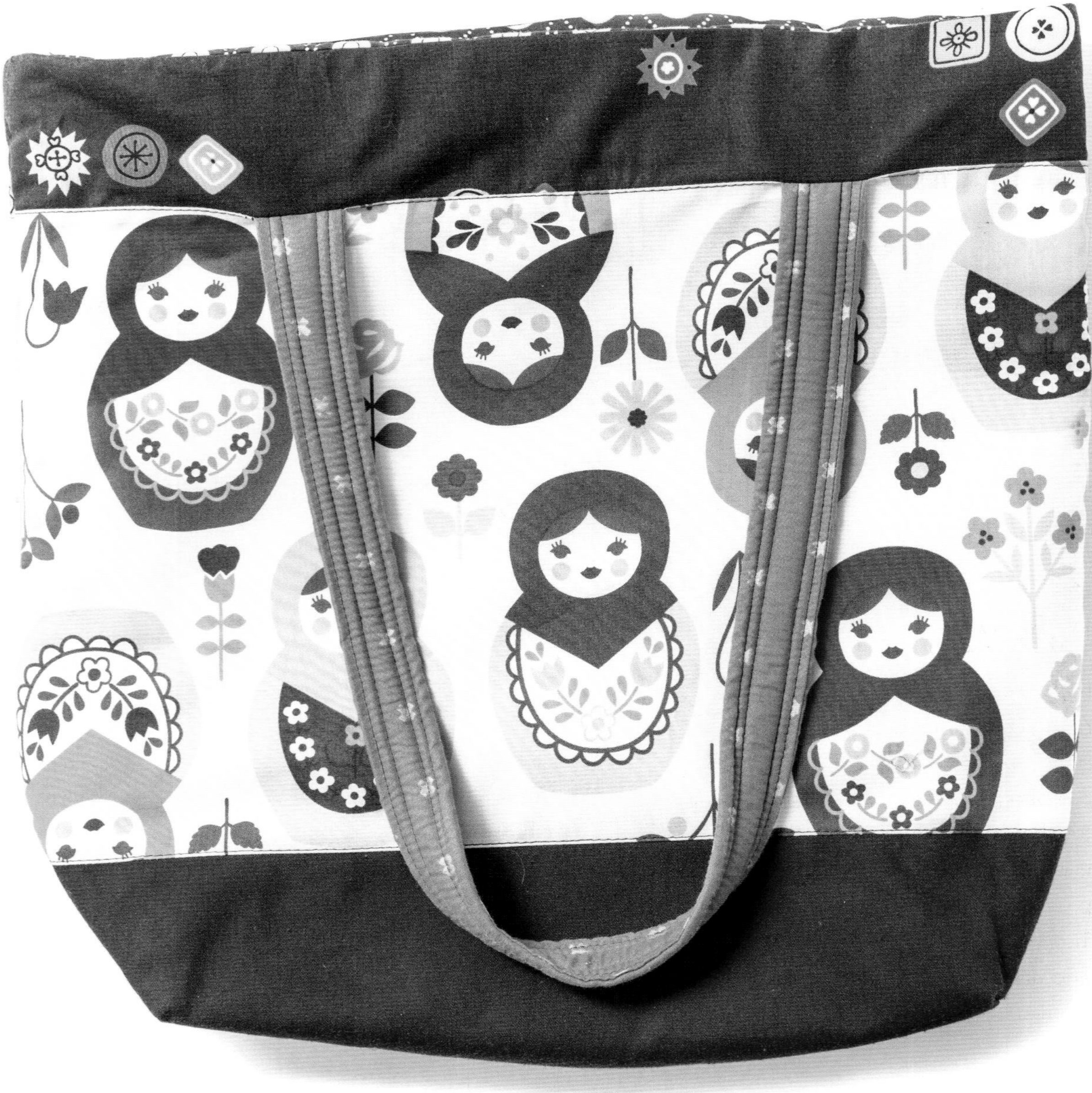

Corners

Other than making sure to always cut a square—or as close to square as possible—there really are no limits to the options for creating the corners. Smaller squares yield shallower bags. The bigger the corner, the more squared off your finished project will be if you start with squares for the bag body. Cut corners from the top edge to make a box (Nested Boxes, page 50). Make sure to take into account the corner and its seam allowances when plotting the finished dimensions of your bag. I find that deeper bags often need firm interfacings and/or bag bottom inserts (removable or otherwise) if a more structured finished shape is desired.

Handles/Strap

Because the handles or straps are vital to the function of the bag, I really prefer making them to last. Many of the projects in this book use rectangles cut at four times the finished width of the handles or straps, with half of the fabric folded inside the strap, in addition to some type of interfacing. When using any type of hardware in conjunction with the handles or straps, I let the hardware dimensions dictate the cutting width of the fabric. You may wish to adjust the strap length depending on how you intend to carry a bag and your height. For more options and ideas for handles and straps, see Elements (page 26).

Pockets

I love mixing and matching pockets to suit my needs. They can be placed inside or outside the bags. In all the projects in this book, the pockets are attached after interfacing and before the bag pieces are sewn together. It's important to think ahead to what bag hardware you will be using, as well as where and how you will be attaching the handles or straps, when planning pockets. For instance, the interior and exterior pockets on the Tubular Frame Purse (page 60) take into account the purse frame and handles.

fabrics

Fabric choices alter the look of any project as much as—if not more than—any of the pattern hacks. I see it every time I teach, when my students finish their Basic Tote Bags and show them off. In all my years, I've never had two students choose the same fabric!

I always tell folks that fabric is a personal choice. Selecting a fabric for a bag is not that much different from picking out a new top or jacket or even a ready-made bag. It's reflective of your style and tastes—and that's a great thing! One of my favorite bags I carry is the first Tubular Frame Purse (page 60) that I made, featuring a bright cartoon fabric with images of Wonder Woman, Supergirl, and Batgirl. It's an attention-getter, and I'm constantly stopped by people who love it and want to know where I bought it.

Through the years, I've come to realize that I do have a few preferences when it comes to choosing fabrics for bags. I nearly always select light-colored fabrics for bag linings. If you've ever struggled to find something in the bottomless pit of a dark bag, you'll understand my preference.

I also tend to choose darker fabrics for bag exteriors. Even though I usually work with machine-washable fabric, the finished product may not be washing-machine friendly. Darker fabrics help hide many of my "oops!" moments, like that time I spilled an entire iced coffee all over the right half of my body and my purse. (The purse survived. My white shirt, not so much.)

It's fun to fussy cut fabrics for bag projects, although it often requires purchasing additional yardage and takes a bit more time. A see-through ruler, template plastic, or a pattern piece made with a tracing material such as Create-a-Pattern or Pattern Ease can help. Simply put your ruler or pattern on top of the right side of the fabric and move it around until the fabric design works within your chosen area. If your goal is to match a pattern—like a stripe—across a seam, cut the first piece as desired and then use it to align the print at the edges (be sure to take into account the seam allowance on more complicated prints).

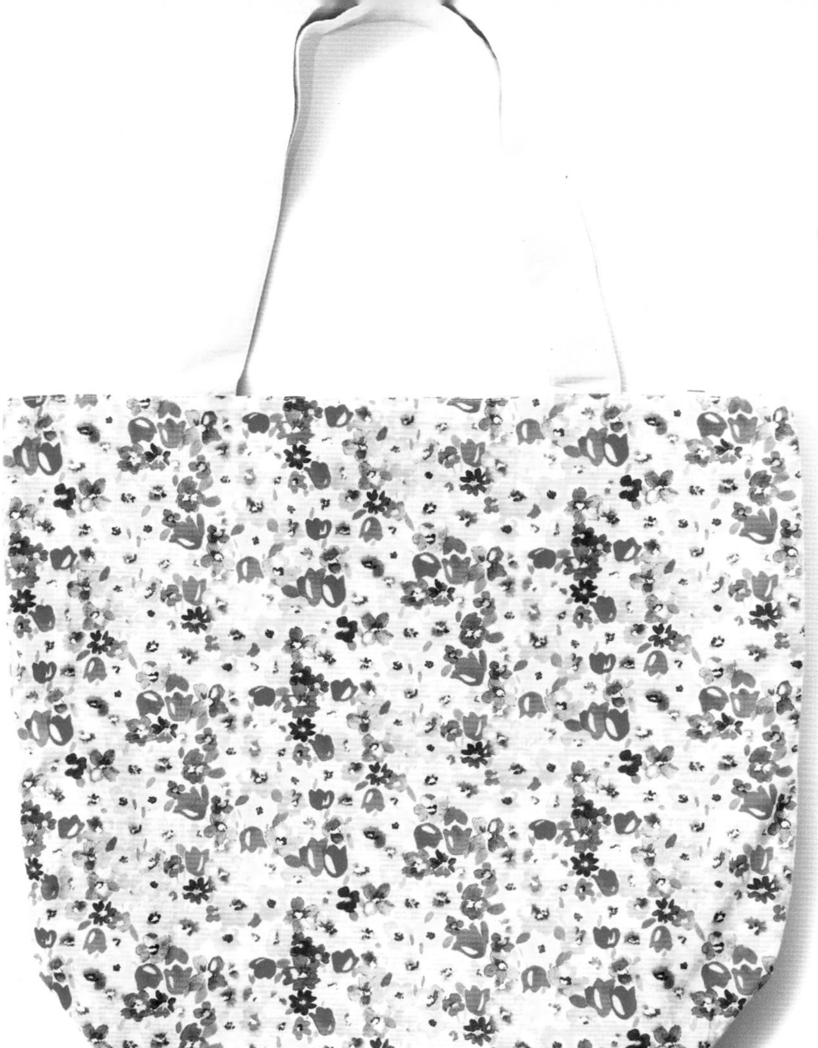

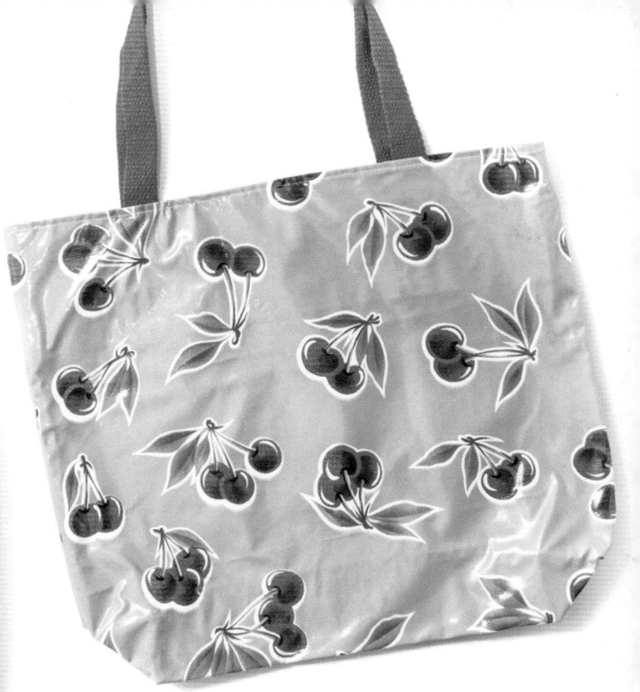

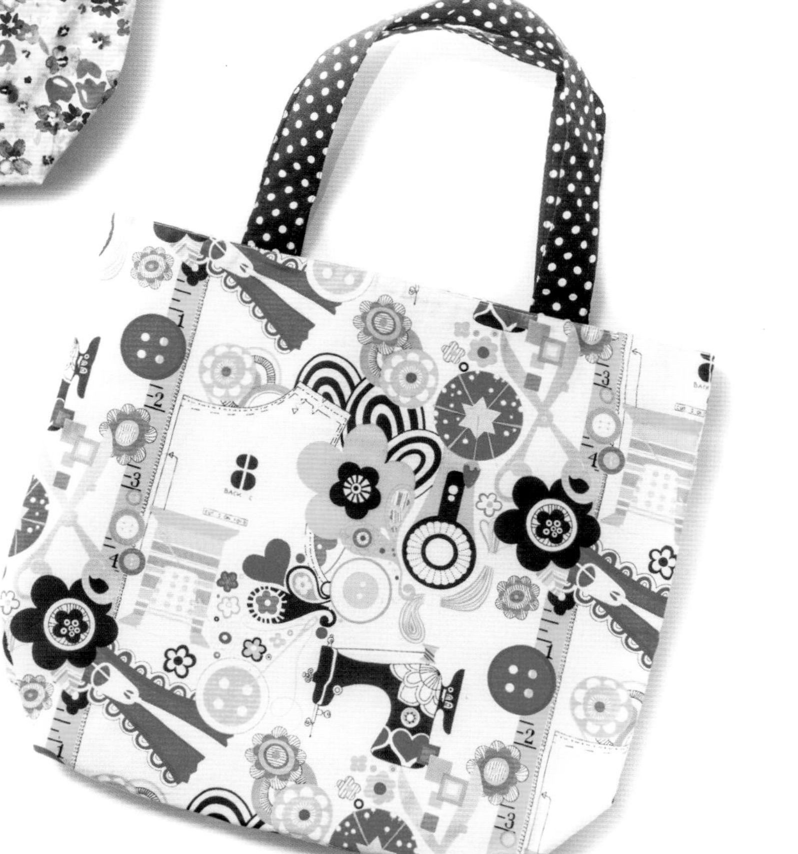

Fabric choices really change the look of the Basic Tote Bag.

Quilting Cotton

THE BROOKLYN DOG
SUPER
HOT DOG
RAD

I love using quilting-weight cottons for making pretty much all the projects in this book. They're widely available and affordable, and they're offered in a dizzying array of colors and prints. When I see a fabric I just adore but can't figure out what I'll make with it, I pick up a half-yard and use it to make a bag of some kind.

The downside of quilting cotton is that it's relatively lightweight, which means it may not hold up to long-term use. I've actually had fabric develop holes in places where it's repeatedly rubbed against something over time.

Heavier-Weight Fabrics

There's a whole world of options beyond quilting cottons, and some of them are as close as your local quilt shop. Here are a few you might consider:

Cotton/Linen Blends

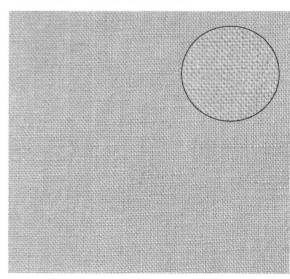

I first encountered cotton/linen blend fabric at a store specializing in imported Japanese fabrics. Since then, several U.S. fabric manufacturers have added this cloth to their offerings. The cotton/linen fabrics I've encountered are usually 85% cotton and 15% linen and are thicker than quilting cotton. The fabric has a slightly textured feel. It may be the same width as quilting cotton or as wide as 54″. It is machine washable, presses nicely, and is easy to sew. The cut edges may fray more than quilting cotton. Cotton/linen blends are available in solids and prints, although the range is limited compared to quilting cotton.

Home Decor

Canvas

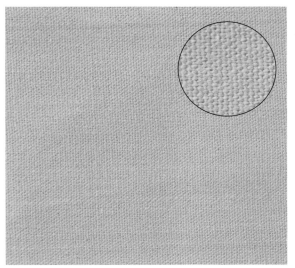

Several quilting fabric manufacturers market a cotton sateen fabric suitable for home decor projects, such as slipcovers, pillows, and curtains. It's also a great option for bags. Much of the home decor fabric I've come across is similar in weight to cotton/linen blends but has a smoother finish. Most is machine washable and available in 54˝-wide fabric. The scale of the prints tends to be larger than those on quilting cotton, which may make it unsuitable for smaller projects. Solids, geometrics, and florals are common, but the range is again not as wide as that of quilting cotton.

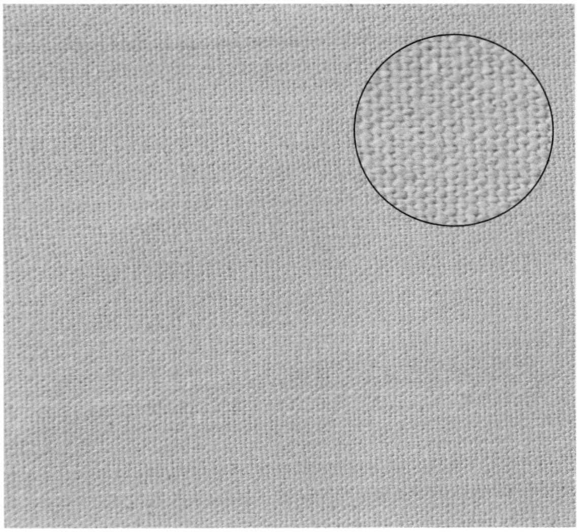

Most people think of canvas as a cotton fabric, but it might be a cotton blend or even a fully synthetic fabric, such as nylon or polyester. It's often marked with a weight—7 ounce, 9 ounce, 12 ounce—which indicates the thickness of the fabric. The higher the number, the heavier the fabric. The lower-weight canvas is similar in weight to cotton/linen blends, while 24-ounce canvas is commonly used to make heavy-duty boat bags. I like using midweight canvas for durable, unlined bags, such as the Laundry Duffle Bag (page 94), or using it as an interlining. If you think you will be washing your finished bag, be sure to measure, wash, and dry the cotton canvas—possibly multiple times—so any shrinking occurs before sewing. Solid colors of canvas are the most common. When using heavier canvas fabrics, you'll also want to use the appropriate sewing machine needle.

Denim

Vinyl

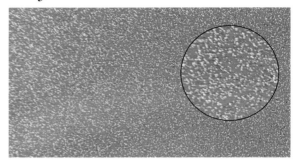

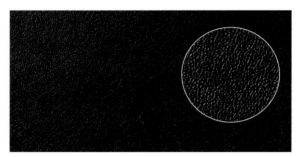

Much like canvas, denim is often marked with a weight. As more adventurous home sewists have started to explore using denim in their garment making, it's become easier to find stretch denims containing spandex or Lycra. While these fabrics are great for jeans and jackets, they are less suitable for bags. Denim is typically wider than quilting cotton (54″ or more) but more limited in color: mostly variations of blue, with some white, black, and primary colors. Although it may be possible to find printed denims, they often are made with stretch for use in apparel. When sewing with denim, you will want to choose the appropriate sewing machine needle.

Vinyl fabric is a 100% synthetic fabric that may have a nylon or polyester backing. It's often water resistant or waterproof. Vinyl is available in solids or finishes such as faux leather, metallic, and glitter. Because of its weight, vinyl may need little or no interfacing to help it maintain its shape. It is durable but requires a heavy-duty sewing machine needle and either a nonstick presser foot or rolling foot. Avoid ironing vinyl. Over time, vinyl may crack or fade. I like mixing vinyl with cotton or cotton-blend fabrics, using the vinyl in areas of the bag that typically get the most wear, such as the bottom and handles. Use clips instead of pins with vinyl, as holes made in vinyl are permanent.

Leather

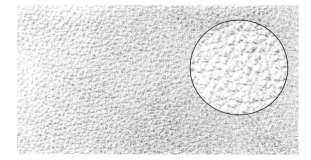

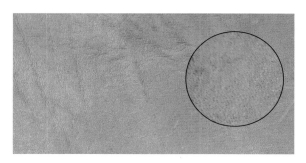

Laminated Cotton / Oilcloth

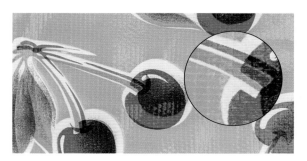

Leather, like canvas and denim, is categorized by weight in ounces. Rather than being sold by the yard, leather is sold by the square foot. Leather, like fabric, has a grain. Unlike fabric, leather may vary in thickness across the piece and often has imperfections and blemishes that you'll need to work around. It may be natural or dyed or have a metallic or pearlescent finish. Leather can be expensive, but it's more durable than fabric and thus well suited for use as handles or in high-wear areas like bag bottoms. If you don't want to make a huge financial investment, scour second-hand shops for leather garments to repurpose. Leather may crack or fade over time, and it may be damaged by water. Commercially available waterproofing sprays and leather conditioners can help with these issues. Use a leather sewing machine needle and avoiding pinning, as holes made in leather are permanent. Another option is kraft•tex (by C&T Publishing). It is durable and feels like leather, but acts like heavy fabric when you cut and sew it.

Oilcloth is a cotton fabric treated on one side with a waterproof coating that manufacturers claim is less likely to crack or fade over time. Laminated cotton has a similar look but has a vinyl coating applied to one side, which may crack or fade. Both oilcloth and laminated cotton are available in wider widths than quilting cotton (54″ or wider). While it's possible to iron both oilcloth and laminated cotton from the wrong side of the fabric, it's best to do so sparingly and with low heat. As with vinyl, avoid pinning oilcloth and laminated cottons, as holes are permanent. Use a nonstick presser foot or rolling foot when working with these fabrics, as they may stick or drag when sewn with a regular presser foot.

interfacings *and* stabilizers

Interfacing helps give your project shape and allows the piece to maintain that shape as it's used. Many of the commercially available patterns I've come across will use an interfacing for the exterior of the project but not the lining. My preference is to interface both in some fashion. This helps stabilize all parts of the bag or project and enables the piece to maintain its look and shape over time.

Interfacing may be fusible—either on one side or both sides—or nonfusible (also called "sew-in"). Fusible interfacings have a heat-activated adhesive that is ironed to the wrong side of the fabric. You may want to use a pressing cloth to protect your iron and ironing board from adhesive residue. Sew-in

interfacings, in contrast, are machine sewn within the seam allowance against the wrong side of the fabric. Fusible interfacings save time—it's usually faster to iron on the product rather than sewing a nonfusible interfacing—but may give a "citrus peel" look to your fabric over time. Fusible interfacings may also pull away from the fabric over time. Make sure the interfacing is always caught in the seam allowance so it doesn't end up shifting and bunching between the layers of your bag. It's easier to grade seam allowances to reduce bulk if you're using nonfusible products—simply trim away half the seam allowance or peel and cut away the interfacing/stabilizer within the seam allowance.

Interfacings help a bag maintain its shape.

These bags use (*from left to right*) no interfacing*, fusible woven and heavyweight fusible nonwoven interfacing, and foam interfacing with woven fusible interfacing.

* This first bag with no interfacing is actually more floppy than it looks (interior was stuffed for photography only).

Interfacings/Stabilizers and Their Uses

I used the following types of interfacings for the bags in this book.

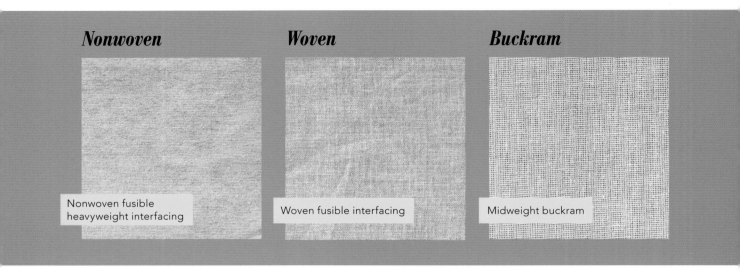

Nonwoven

Nonwoven fusible heavyweight interfacing

Woven

Woven fusible interfacing

Buckram

Midweight buckram

Nonwoven interfacing is typically made of 100% polyester or other synthetic materials. It does not have a grain, it can be flexible or crisp, and it comes in a range of thickness from featherweight to medium to heavyweight. Nonwoven interfacings are widely available and inexpensive. Some manufacturers package nonwoven products in small quantities—1 yard, for example—but the product is also sold on bolts. Widths vary from 18″ to 45″ or more. Nonwoven interfacing may be either white or black. I typically use Pellon Décor-Bond. A comparable product is Dura-Fuse.

Woven interfacing is often a cotton or cotton/polyester blend. There are far fewer woven interfacings available compared to the nonwoven options. Most woven interfacings are light- to midweight. They feel more like fabric because they are fabric. Woven interfacing has a grain and may be sold in widths as narrow as 18″–20″ or as wide as quilting cottons. Woven interfacing is usually white. I use Woven Fusible by Sewing Staple Aids most often in my projects. Pellon's Shape-Flex is also an option.

Buckram is a coarse fabric—sometimes linen—that's been stiffened with a glue product. It varies in weight and is often used in millinery (hat making). It may be sold on a roll instead of a bolt to reduce creasing and is often around 20″ wide. It is significantly thinner than craft stabilizers (page 24) but similarly firm, which makes it ideal for many of the projects in this book. Midweight buckram works best, while the heaviest weight of buckram—often sold as crown buckram—is meant for hand-sewn millinery projects. Buckram is usually off-white or natural in color.

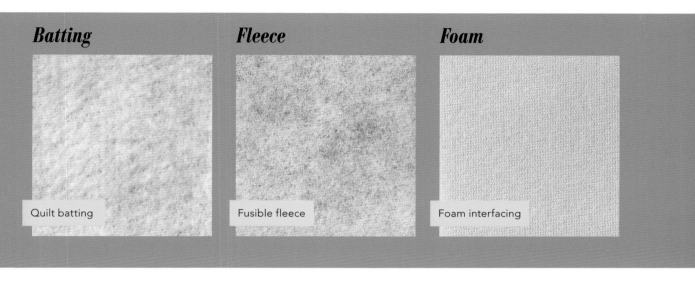

Batting

Quilt batting

Fleece

Fusible fleece

Foam

Foam interfacing

Quilt batting is soft but helps add body to a project. Unless you want a really "squishy" bag, it's best to use batting in conjunction with other, firmer interfacings and stabilizers. Batting may have a scrim to help it maintain its shape. It's available in 100% cotton, cotton/polyester blends, polyester, bamboo, silk, and wool. Thicknesses vary. I like using the leftover cotton batting from quilt tops in my smaller projects, such as the Goodie Bag (page 40), or inside straps for many of my bag projects. Batting is sold in packages, by the roll, or occasionally by the yard. Batting may be bleached white, natural, or black.

Fleece is a synthetic product often made from polyester that may feel similar to quilt batting when used in a project. It varies in thickness and density. Insulating fleece features a layer of heat-reflective material in addition to the fleece. It's often sold by the yard in widths comparable to quilting cotton. It may be white or black. My go-to products are Bosal's #325 Fusible Batting and Pellon's 973F Heavyweight Fusible Fleece.

Foam interfacings are relatively new but are growing in popularity and availability. A layer of foam is sandwiched between two layers of fabric. Although it feels substantial, foam interfacing compresses nicely and has great recovery, which makes it ideal for use in more structured bags, especially in conjunction with firmer products, such as buckram. Foam interfacing can be pinned, but it may be easier to use clips when dealing with multiple layers. Foam is available in both natural and black. My hands-down favorite is ByAnnie's Soft and Stable.

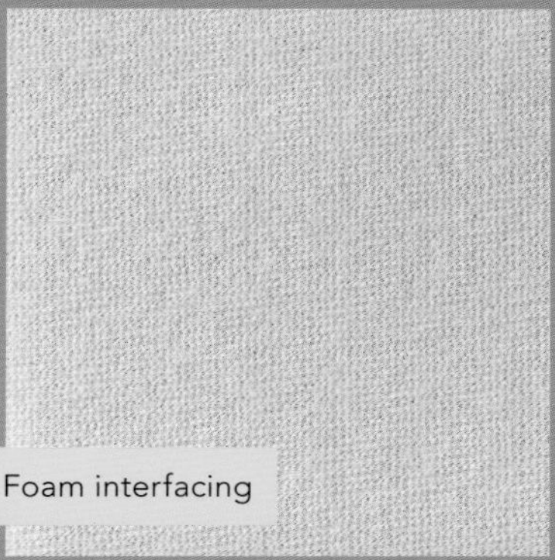

Craft Stabilizers

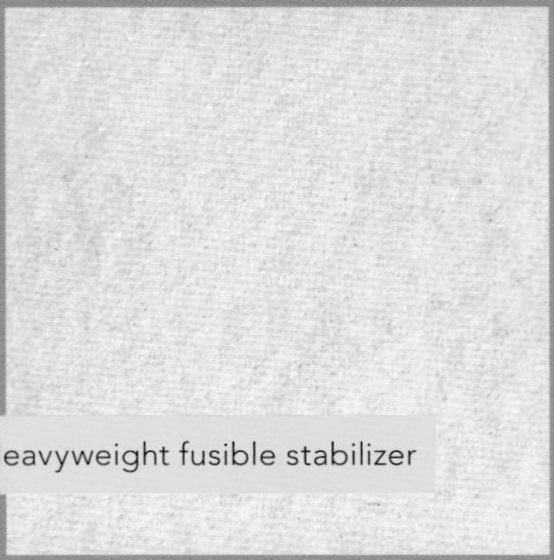

Heavyweight fusible stabilizer

Beyond the heaviest of interfacings lies a category of products called craft stabilizers. They're often sold near the interfacings and, at first glance, may look like them. But get your hands on one and you'll immediately realize the difference. Craft stabilizers—sold as fast2fuse, Peltex, and Timtex, among other brands—are stiffer and feel less like fabric or nonwoven interfacings than foamy cardboard. They may be sew-in, fusible on one side, or fusible on both sides. Craft stabilizers are best for projects that need long-term stability and shape and are constructed in a way that facilitates their use. Don't even try pinning projects with craft stabilizer. Clips are your best option, and you'll also need heavy-duty sewing machine needles. Because heavy craft stabilizers are so stiff, they can be a challenge to sew.

Fabric as Interfacing

Using fabric as interfacing isn't that different from using woven interfacing. While it will require machine basting within the seam allowance, fabric—particularly natural fibers—will not change the feel of the exterior fabric. Canvas, denim, home decor fabric, and even flannel can add body and shape to your project without too much bulk. They often are best used in conjunction with other interfacings such as buckram, foam, or craft stabilizers.

Considerations of Interfacings/Stabilizers

Not all interfacings and stabilizers are suitable for every project. A heavy stabilizer, such as Timtex, would not work well in a project like the Zippered Cross-Body Bag (page 80). Given the size of that particular bag, it may not be suited for a foam interfacing, either. On the flip side, a lightweight nonwoven interfacing would not provide enough structure for the Tubular Frame Purse (page 60). Foam works well in that project, but if it were to be scaled down for a smaller tubular frame, the foam might be too bulky.

When deciding on interfacings and stabilizers, it's also necessary to consider the fabrics you are using. Glitter vinyl, used as an accent on the Zip-Top Purse (page 88), is firm enough on its own, so just the fabric portion of the bag exterior is interfaced.

Quilting the exterior bag fabric is a great option for many projects. If you do this, be sure to cut all the pieces involved larger than the size you need and then trim to size after quilting. Depending on the style of quilting and the products you use, you may experience a little shrinkage in the quilting process. I prefer layering either foam, batting, or fleece with my exterior fabric and using another layer (canvas, flannel, or quilting cotton, depending on the project) on the back.

You may find that certain interfacings and stabilizers make for bulky seams that can be challenging to work with. The best way to deal with this is by grading the seam allowance: Use a small pair of scissors to carefully separate the layers of the seam allowance and trim away the excess interfacing. Be sure to look at the right side of your project before you begin to make sure you don't need to fix anything! Work slowly and carefully as you trim, and only trim one layer at a time.

Detail of Zippered
Cross-Body Bag

elements

Change up the parts of your projects to reflect your style.
Be sure to refer to Overview of Hacking the Pattern (page 10)
for important considerations about size and placement.

Handles

Double Handles

The Basic Tote Bag uses a pair of handles that extend from the top seam of the bag between the exterior and lining. This helps distribute the weight of the bag contents, and the handles fit comfortably on the shoulder. As the proportions of the bag shrink, you may prefer to make shorter handles for a handbag carried in one hand or hooked in the crook of your arm. Double handles are often the best option for deeper bags.

"Hugging" Handles

The Boat/Pool Tote (page 68) has double handles that "hug" the body of the bag, starting at the bottom seam. It's a functional touch that helps support the weight of the contents, but it's also a great way to change the look of the bag. You can easily add a pocket between the straps. Depending on the dimensions of the bag, you may need to sew lengths of fabric together to make a long enough strap. For this reason, I often will use canvas or nylon webbing.

Single Strap

A narrow bag, such as the Messenger Bag with Flap (page 74), is a great choice for a single strap connected to the side seams. The strap can be sewn into the top edge, between the bag exterior and lining, or with tabs and rings. For maximum flexibility, use with an adjustable buckle to allow the bag to be carried either across the body or over one shoulder. Make the strap detachable with latched swivel hooks!

Tabbed Handles/Straps

Nearly any of the handles and straps you might use can be attached to the bag with tabs— strips of fabric cut and interfaced and then sewn to rings. The size of the hardware dictates the finished width of the fabric tabs used with it.

Ready-Made Handles/Straps

It's getting increasingly easy to find ready-made handles and straps to use with bags, from acrylic to vinyl to leather and beyond. Some types of handles will need to attach to the bag with tabs, while others will have to be sewn by hand.